MILNER

MILNER

LAST OF THE EMPIRE-BUILDERS

Richard Steyn

JONATHAN BALL PUBLISHERS
JOHANNESBURG · CAPE TOWN · LONDON

Originally published in South Africa in 2022 by
JONATHAN BALL PUBLISHERS
A division of Media24 (Pty) Ltd
PO Box 33977
Jeppestown
2043

This edition published in 2022 by
JONATHAN BALL PUBLISHERS
An imprint of Icon Books Ltd,
Omnibus Business Centre,
39-41 North Road,
London N7 9DP
Email: info@iconbooks.com
For details of all international distributors,
visit iconbooks.com/trade

ISBN 978-1-77619-214-4
ebook ISBN 978-1-77619-179-6

Printed and bound in Great Britain
by Clays Ltd, Elcograf S.p.A.

CONTENTS

To my brother, Christopher, for his unstinting support

And in memory of Gordon Forbes and Jonathan Ball

Most of the world since civilisation began has lived under empires.

Deepak Lal, Indian economist

The most illuminating history is often written to show how people acted in the expectation of a future that never happened.

Roy Foster, Irish historian

Imperialism was more than a set of economic, political and military phenomena. It was a habit of mind, a dominant idea in the era of European world supremacy which had widespread intellectual, cultural and technical expressions.

John M MacKenzie, British historian

Thousands of people will immediately stream into the Transvaal and the balance of political power which even now is clearly ours in the whole of South Africa under a system of equal rights will turn quickly and decisively against the Boers for all time.

Sir Alfred Milner, 1899

I was born 84 years ago into a world that was a universe away from where we are today ... We were passionately committed to the resurrection of the Afrikaner nation. The memories of the Anglo-Boer War were still raw and painful. During that war our people were the victims of a crime against humanity in the course of which we lost almost ten per cent of our population – most of whom were women and children who died in British concentration camps. We remembered with bitterness Lord Milner's attempts to deprive us of our language and culture.

FW de Klerk, former State President of South Africa, 2021

Preface

It is hardly possible for any homegrown South African to write a dispassionate account of the life of Alfred, Lord Milner. As the principal instigator of the Anglo-Boer (or South African) War of 1899–1902, Milner provoked a conflict whose consequences are still felt a century and more later. The British journalist Leo Amery, general editor of a seven-volume history of the war for *The Times* of London, admitted that 'absolute impartiality' in dealing with its origins was probably unachievable. His own account, he confessed, had been written 'frankly from the point of view of one who is convinced that the essential right and justice of the controversy have been with his own country'.[1] I admit equally frankly to believing the justice of the argument to lie on the other side, though my aim in this book is neither to vilify nor justify Milner but rather to explain what I believe motivated this enigmatic and driven individual, whose actions have so influenced the lives of every South African.

As the incomparable historian CW de Kiewiet reminds us, those who write about this seminal time in South Africa's history often pay insufficient heed to the complexity of events and the motivations of the participants. 'The picture of the capitalists as men with gold in their hands, brass in their tongues, contempt in their faces, and treachery in their hearts', he noted, 'is as untrue as the picture of an Empire robbing a petty state of its independence out of envy for its wealth, or the picture of an ignorant and perverse old man leading his state into destruction rather than yield to a modern age.'[2] I have tried to bear this admonition in mind.

Milner, of course, was not solely responsible for bringing about a conflict that several others helped foment. Britain's Colonial Secretary, the duplicitous Joseph Chamberlain, ran him a close second, and there were firebrands in Kruger's ranks as well who were spoiling for a fight. Yet Milner wanted a war more than anyone else, and, as was the case with many men of superior intellect, he acted from what he believed were the highest motives. Like Chamberlain, he convinced himself that it was not only Anglo-Saxons who would profit from the Empire but the backward peoples of the world also – as the beneficiaries of being ruled by the greatest of all the governing races.[3] The governed, it should be added, were generally less enthusiastic.

Like his predecessor, Sir Bartle Frere, almost two decades earlier, Milner knew virtually nothing about South Africa before coming here, soon after the Jameson Raid. Although he learnt the rudiments of the Dutch language, he made no sustained effort to understand the feelings of Boer-Afrikaners, pursued results far too quickly and was prepared to use the necessary force to achieve them.[4] As the historian of Empire, Piers Brendon, notes caustically, it was Milner's learning of Dutch (the written language of the Boers at that time) that enabled him to misunderstand the Afrikaner position so comprehensively.[5] Perhaps that was to be expected of a man who confessed, before leaving England, that he was incapable of understanding the arguments of anyone who questioned 'the desirability or possibility of Imperial unity'.[6]

Yet, as one of Britain's three great proconsuls of the late Victorian era (Cromer in Egypt and Curzon in India being the others), Milner's reputation cannot be circumscribed by his association with South Africa alone. His other significant achievements during a career at the highest echelons of British society and politics make a full account of his life a worthy subject for any biographer.

Born with a 'copper spoon' in his mouth, the young Alfred Milner was an exceptionally clever, self-made man of modest means and strong moral convictions, who decided early in life on a career in the service of others. By his forties, his administrative abilities and experience were sufficient to have elevated him to the highest ranks of the Colonial

Service. In 1897, his deployment to South Africa – the most daunting and challenging appointment in the British Empire – was enthusiastically welcomed by Liberal and Conservative politicians alike. In the age of social Darwinism (often described using the phrase 'the survival of the fittest'), Milner, a believer in the theory subscribed to by intellectuals across the political spectrum – including such firmly left-wing figures as Beatrice Webb, HG Wells and even Karl Marx[7] – thought that mankind was organised hierarchically by race, with the Anglo-Saxons at or near the top of the pile.

For Milner – who proudly proclaimed himself a British 'race patriot' until his dying day – and his fellow imperialists, the English were a chosen people, driven by 'an insatiable need to exert their colonising genius for the benefit of less fortunate others'.[8] Besides promoting the material progress of mankind through free trade, the mission of the Victorian Empire was to spread enlightenment and good governance around the world, and by so doing to uplift people on the lowest rungs of civilisation – described by Kipling, the bard of Empire, as 'lesser breeds without the law'. The once radical Joseph Chamberlain justified imperial rule by emphasising the happiness, peace and prosperity it would bring to far-off peoples: 'In carrying out this work of civilisation, we are fulfilling what I believe to be our national mission, and we are finding scope for the exercise of those faculties and qualities which have made of us a great governing race.'[9]

What England 'must either do or perish', the social thinker and philosopher of British imperialism, John Ruskin, had declared in his celebrated inaugural lecture at Oxford University in 1870, is to 'found colonies as fast and as far as she is able, formed of her most energetic and worthiest men; seizing every piece of fruitful waste ground she can set her feet on, and there teaching those of her colonists that their chief virtue is to be fidelity to their country, and their first aim is to advance the power of England by land and sea.'[10]

Inspired by Ruskin and others, the youthful Milner recognised much earlier than his student contemporaries that if Britain were to maintain her paramount status in the world in the face of emerging powers such as Russia, the United States and Germany, the unification of the Empire was essential. But, unlike Ruskin, he believed that

Britain should develop the resources of the vast territories she already possessed rather than expand territorially simply for the sake of it. 'Our only strength', he claimed, 'lies in striving for [the Empire's] development rather than its extension.'[11]

Despite his declared interest in social reform, the dedicated, punctilious and financially astute Milner was never as committed to abstract *ideals* as he was to *systems*.[12] After a brief excursion into party politics, he soon grew impatient with the inefficiencies and compromises of the British parliamentary system and became a public servant of a special kind. In the words of James Morris, he was 'a genuine imperial technocrat ... from a class of statesmen of which history had time to produce, fortunately for the allure of Empire, only one or two'.[13]

His private secretary in South Africa for a time, John Buchan, the future historian, author and Governor General of Canada, observed Milner at close quarters, and 25 years later wrote perceptively of him: 'All his interests were centred on the service of the state ... He had the instincts of a radical reformer joined to a close-textured intellect which reformers rarely possess ... So at the outset of his career, he dedicated himself to a cause, putting things like leisure, domestic happiness and money-making behind him ... He had a mind remarkable for its scope and its mastery over details – the most powerful administrative intelligence – I think – which Britain had produced in our day.'[14]

Yet Buchan also thought that Milner was the last man who should have been chosen for the task in South Africa: 'He was not very good at envisaging a world wholly different from his own, and his world and [Paul] Kruger's at no point intersected. There was a gnarled magnificence in the old Transvaal president, but [Milner] only saw a snuffy, mendacious savage.'[15] 'It was a fashion among his critics to believe', Buchan wrote in his memoirs, 'that a little geniality on Milner's part, something of the hail-fellow, masonic-lodge atmosphere, would have brought the Bloemfontein conference [in 1899] to a successful conclusion.

'Such a view seems to me', continued Buchan, 'to do justice neither to Kruger, nor to Milner, men deeply in earnest who were striving for things wholly incompatible, an Old Testament patriarchal regime and a modern democracy ... [Milner] detested lies, and diplomacy demands something less than the plain truth. He was nothing of the countryman and could not understand the tortuosities of the peasant mind.'[16]

To Kruger and the Boers, even more suspicious of British motives after the Jameson Raid, Milner seemed as determined as Cecil Rhodes to secure British dominance throughout southern Africa. In their eyes, a rash adventurer had simply been replaced by a deadly diplomat.[17] Rhodes himself, when asked whether he had advised Milner to make war against the Boers, replied that although he sided with Milner's views, he did not advise him, 'for the very good reason that Sir Alfred Milner takes only one person's advice and that is the advice of Sir Alfred Milner'.[18]

In the measured judgement of South African-born historian Donald Denoon, Milner was 'a man of intense political vision, with a talent for analysing affairs in terms of a simple and static set of assumptions ... Above all, he was an egotist who not only relished his crucial role in Anglo-Saxon relations, but indeed exaggerated it.'[19]

For Milner, the war that devastated South Africa was only a prelude to the real task ahead: reconstructing and uniting the country and eventually bringing it under the British flag. After Vereeniging, the Boers were no longer seen to be an insurmountable obstacle to Britain's plan for a federation of southern Africa along Canadian lines, and Milner set about rebuilding the two former republics with the zeal of what Smuts described as a 'socialist autocrat'.[20] His ambitious programme, patiently nurtured during the years of a war in which he had to play second fiddle to army generals, envisaged a modern administration for the 'new colonies' of the Transvaal and Free State, based on a revitalised economy, land resettlement, an improved education system and a wide-ranging programme of anglicisation of the education system and civil service. Rebuilding the mining industry would not only provide the necessary 'overspill' of revenue for these purposes but would also serve as a magnet for skilled immigrants,[21] most of whom would speak English. In the fullness of time, these settlers would outnumber Afrikaners and enable South Africa's four colonies to be joined together under the British Crown.

Milner's failure to achieve most of his post-war goals in the short time left to him after the end of the war was not for want of trying. Despite some success in resettling burghers on their farms and giving them a living, introducing modern farming methods, building new schools, improving roads, railways and prisons, and reforming tax collection, he failed dismally in his aim of attracting enough immigrants 'to turn the balance in favour of the British'.[22] Unfortunately for him, he had overestimated the attraction of the land for new immigrants and completely misjudged the depth of Boer resentment and bitterness at the loss of their republics, as well as his anti-Dutch language policy.

Nonetheless, the so-called Kindergarten of brilliant young would-be colonial administrators he left behind in the Transvaal contributed significantly to the unification of South Africa, a process that moved into a higher gear not long after his departure. To his disgust, the new Union of South Africa was to fall quickly into the lap of the very Boer-Afrikaners he had fought so bitterly to subjugate. In the words of the eminent historian Eric Walker, Milner left for home realising that much of his work was endangered but hoping that at least some of it would stand. 'In a very real sense', Walker wrote, 'the greatest of the High Commissioners can claim to be one of the fathers (or was it stepfathers?) of the Union of South Africa.'[23]

As Basil Williams reflects in the British *Dictionary of National Biography*, Milner did not have the qualities of a great political leader, because he stood aside from party politics and could never have mobilised sufficient popular support to achieve his many ambitious aims. As he was to demonstrate anew upon returning home after eight years in South Africa, the inelasticity of his temperament made it impossible for him to yield a point or give way to what he regarded as an unsatisfactory compromise.

Yet Milner was undoubtedly one of Britain's greatest public servants of his time, helping to reconstruct the economy of Egypt (and

Alfred Milner, photographed in 1902. (*Wikimedia Commons/Duffus Brothers*)

writing a primer on imperial administration), serving at the right hand of successive Chancellors of the Exchequer, introducing income tax reforms that are still in operation today, and steering the activities of the Rhodes Trust and the Round Table. He played a significant role behind the scenes in the movement for tariff reform and in opposition to Home Rule for Ireland, was an active businessman and social reformer, and returned to public prominence to help bring Lloyd George to power during the First World War, before becoming his most effective cabinet member as War Secretary and Colonial Secretary.[24] In the latter role, he was instrumental in drafting the Balfour Declaration, which pledged to create a national homeland for the Jewish people.

Self-effacing and anti-jingo, Milner wanted no official biography written about him and declined to publish any account of his time in South Africa, which has not deterred several biographers, and a few hagiographers, from doing so. Some of the better assessments of his life have been made by American historians, able to view British imperialism and its excesses in hindsight with bemused detachment. They include AM Gollin and, in particular, J Lee Thompson, whose interest in Milner has resulted in two excellent books, one a full biography and the other a penetrating analysis of his imperial outlook. I am indebted to both these academic historians, and to John Marlowe and Terence O'Brien among other biographers.

In his posthumously published book *Rekonstruksie*, the revered Afrikaner historian Karel Schoeman writes that Milner has been so demonised in Afrikaans-language schools and by historiographers for his anglicisation policy that – difficult as it may be to do so – it is high time that his personal qualities and record were reassessed in the light of his adherence to the imperial ideals he believed in.[25] That is exactly what prompted me to write a book that anyone with an interest in South African history will agree is long overdue.

At the age of 67, only four years before he died, Milner married his devoted friend and ally of long standing, Violet (formerly Lady Edward) Cecil, a dyed-in-the-wool imperialist herself and long-standing admirer of his colonial endeavours. As the custodian of her late husband's voluminous papers, Lady Milner made it her mission to defend his controversial South African record by employing the journalist Cecil Headlam to compile two volumes of his correspondence and diary notes, with an accompanying text.

Headlam's obvious partisanship has not diminished the value to historians of his detailed record of Milner's years in this country. In my account of Milner's life and times, I devote more attention to his involvement in South African affairs than British and American biographers, while bypassing – in the interests of readability – historiographical arguments between nationalists, liberals, capitalists and Marxists over the causes and effects of the 'Boer War' that persist to the present day. Perhaps I should add another word of caution: this book is not aimed at an academic audience and is another of my attempts, as a journalist, to make South Africa's history accessible to a general readership. The portrait of Milner I seek to present is that of an exceptionally able, ego-driven and single-minded 'race-patriot', much liked and admired by the people who knew him well, but intensely disliked by the many who did not, or who failed to share his enthusiasm for British imperialism. He was, in truth, one of a kind – unusually tenacious in his purposes, disdainful of anyone who disagreed with him, and never shrinking from any action he thought necessary to further the causes he so unwaveringly believed in.

Johannesburg 2022

Editor's note: In his diaries and letters, Milner often made use of italics to indicate emphasis or underscore a particular point he wished to make. In the chapters that follow, unless otherwise indicated by the author, the emphasis is that of Milner.

Prologue

On the night of 23 March 1918, Britain's Secretary of State for War, Alfred Milner, crossed the English Channel to northern France, where the German army was threatening to overrun the vital railway junction at Amiens, the linchpin in the Allied defensive line on the Western Front. In a last despairing thrust, General Erich Ludendorff's forces had driven a wedge between the British and French armies, taking hundreds of guns and thousands of prisoners. The Germans' aim was to sever the link between the Allied forces before American troops could be rushed up to bolster the Anglo-French defences. If Amiens were to fall, the British would be driven westwards to the Channel ports and the French southwards in the direction of Paris. There would no longer be direct contact between the Allies' two biggest armies.

Milner's destination was Doullens, a hamlet near the Somme River, in the Picardy region. Here, a crucial meeting took place that settled the outcome of the First World War. A plaque on the iron gates of the town's *mairie*, in French and English, commemorates the occasion. The inscription reads: 'In this Town Hall, on the 26th March 1918, the Allies entrusted General Foch with the Supreme Command on the Western Front. This decision saved France and the liberty of the world.'[1]

Dispatched post-haste to the battlefront by Britain's Prime Minister, David Lloyd George, Milner was to play a crucial role in the decision to combine the British and French high commands under General Ferdinand Foch in a final, do-or-die attempt to keep the German army at bay. His decisiveness at that critical time helped to confirm the post-war verdict in Britain that Secretary Milner, next to Lloyd George himself, had been the most effective member of the War Cabinet.[2]

Up to then, Milner's public reputation had rested – for good or ill – largely upon his controversial role in the Anglo-Boer War (1899–1902) and subsequent reconstruction of South Africa. Such was his disaffection for British party politics after returning home that he had refused to involve himself on either side of the most important issues dividing Britain's political establishment in the run-up to the Great War, save for two – tariff reform and Home Rule for Ireland. Come the war, his sense of duty and belief that he could contribute positively to Britain's policy-making made him set aside his reservations and accept a position in Lloyd George's War Cabinet.

As Lloyd George recounted later in his self-serving memoirs: 'I decided that either Milner or myself must go over [to France] at once to see why and where the arrangement for mutual help had failed … and whether things could not be set right before possible disaster supervened … We both felt there was only one effective thing to do … put Foch in charge of both armies.'[3] It was agreed that Lloyd George would mind the store in London, but Milner should leave at once for the front, where relations between Philippe Pétain, the French commander-in-chief, and his British counterpart, Douglas Haig, were deteriorating rapidly. As the historian AM Gollin records, 'The situation at the front seemed desperate. A strong man was needed to restore it.'[4]

Milner arrived in France in the early hours of Sunday 25 March, and was immediately summoned to Paris for a tête-à-tête with the French prime minister, Georges Clemenceau. 'It was necessary at all costs', the Frenchman declared, 'to maintain the connection between the French and British armies, and that both Haig and Pétain must at once throw in their reserves to stop the breach.'[5] Still lacking, however, was a single directing mind to decide how these reinforcements should be deployed.[6]

Later that day, Milner attended a meeting in Pétain's headquarters at Compiègne, with President Poincaré in the chair, at which Clemenceau, Foch and Pétain were also present. Milner thought that Pétain was far too pessimistic in outlook, but formed a favourable opinion of Foch, who seemed much more alert to the danger posed by the German forces.

The next day, 26 March, Milner set off for Doullens, 32 km north of Amiens, accompanied by Sir Henry Wilson, about to become Chief of the Imperial General Staff. On their way to a conference attended by Poincaré, Clemenceau, Foch and Pétain on the French side and also by Haig and his three army commanders on the British side, Milner and Wilson agreed that the supreme command of Allied forces should be placed in the hands of Foch. In a detailed memorandum of the meeting, generally accepted as the most accurate account of the proceedings, Milner recorded: 'I was convinced that whatever might be his other merits or demerits as a soldier, General Foch possessed in a quite exceptional degree the promptitude, energy and resource necessary to get the most done in the time available, the whole question being evidently a race for time.'[7]

What happened next has been recounted, with minor variations, by a host of war historians. At the conference, Haig and Foch blamed each other for the shortcomings of their respective armies, and Foch made an attack on Pétain for not fighting with more determination.[8] At which point Milner decided to intervene, asking for a one-on-one meeting with Clemenceau, with whom he had always been on good terms:

> I told him quite frankly of [my] conviction ... that Foch appeared to me to be the man who had the greatest grasp of the situation and was most likely to deal with it with the intensest energy ... Clemenceau, whose own mind, I am sure, had been steadily moving in the same direction ... asked for a few minutes to speak to Pétain. While he took Pétain aside, I did the same with Haig ... [who] seemed not only quite willing but really pleased. Meanwhile, Clemenceau had spoken to Pétain and immediately wrote and handed me the following form of words [in French] to embody what he and I had just agreed to.[9]

The declaration read: 'General Foch is charged by the British and French Governments to co-ordinate the action of the Allied Armies on the Western Front. He will work to this end with the Generals in Chief, who are asked to furnish him with all the necessary information.'[10]

As Milner's admiring biographer Sir Evelyn Wrench records, 'At this grave moment, Milner, who had no specific authority entitling him to bind the British government, took responsibility "for a measure which would bring doom or victory to half the world" – and therein lay the greatness of his action. A smaller man would have felt obliged to refer to Whitehall for his instructions.'[11]

Another praise-singer, W Basil Worsfold – briefly editor of *The Star* in Johannesburg after the Anglo-Boer War – wrote of Milner that at Doullens 'he took upon himself a burden of responsibility than which none heavier was borne by any in the World War'.[12] Milner's biographer, TH O'Brien, concludes that Milner's decisiveness, initiative and readiness to commit his own government had contributed most to the outcome.[13] The historian Walter Reid notes that acknowledgement of Milner's role is evident from the naming of two streets in Doullens after military men, Foch and Haig, and a third after a civilian – the Boulevard Lord Milner.

Not wishing to take the credit away from Lloyd George or Haig (who both subsequently claimed a hand in Foch's appointment), Milner took a typically prosaic view of his role in the proceedings. In a letter to a journalist friend, he played down his own actions, regretting that accounts of the meeting at Doullens had come out in 'fragmentary revelations. I never said anything about it myself because I hate the scramble for credit which is going on, and in which I must say some of the soldiers are the worst offenders.' His own detailed memo of the meeting, Milner said, was 'minutely accurate. I wrote it all down the very next day, when every detail was fresh in my memory, though with no intention of making public use of it.'[14]

On arriving back in London on the night of 26 March, Milner immediately went round to 10 Downing Street to see Lloyd George, who approved his decision and promised to have it endorsed by the War Cabinet next morning. Eight days later, at Beauvais town hall in France, representatives of the British, American and French governments met and formally invested General Foch with the supreme command of the Allied armies.

❖

Within weeks of the Doullens conference, Foch had shifted 45 French infantry and six cavalry divisions into place to counter the Germans, whose numbers had been boosted by reinforcements from the Eastern Front following Russia's hasty withdrawal from the war. Walter Reid comments that in more than just a physical sense, Britain and France were now closer than they had ever been at any point during the war. '[They] shared reserves and co-ordinated their activities properly for the first time. Foch had the power to move armies and tell them where to fight ... He had ... a concerted strategic vision to which even the Americans submitted.'[15] By early November 1918, the Germans had sued for peace and the Great War was over at last.

In an enthusiastic appraisal of Milner's career, the English journalist Edward Crankshaw singled out as the most striking example of Milner's steadfastness and good decision-making his elevation of Foch to the supreme command of the Anglo-French army 'as it were between lunch and tea' on that fateful day in Doullens. 'In the eyewitness accounts of this episode', wrote Crankshaw, 'what is chiefly remarkable is the total absence of argumentation, of fuss, of face-saving reservations. Milner knew very well he could carry Lloyd George with him ... But in those terrible hours after the collapse of the Fifth Army, alone, a British politician among soldiers, he behaved as few subordinates have ever behaved in matters of great weight, never for one moment raising a doubt in the minds of the soldiers, never hesitating to do the logical thing ... and fully prepared to take on himself the responsibility for failure. There was no failure. Had there been, the responsibility would have been his and his alone. But the credit for success could not be his.'[16]

Instead, the acclaim went to Lloyd George, Britain's Prime Minister.

CHAPTER 1

Youth
1854–1879

Mary Milner tried as hard as she could to ensure that her German-born son, Alfred, grew up to be an Englishman. The young widow of an Anglo-Irish army officer shot dead by republican rebels, Mary had moved to Germany in an attempt to educate her two young sons on a tiny income – to the little university town of Giessen, 48 km north of Frankfurt, in today's federal state of Hesse. There, she engaged the services of an attractive young medical student, Charles Milner, to tutor her boys. Mary and Charles fell in love, and in due course were married at the British consulate in Bonn. She was 41 and he only 22 years old.

Charles was the son of a wine merchant, James Richardson Milner, sent from England in 1805 to open a branch of the family business in the Rhineland. His mother was Sophia von Rappard, daughter of a German civil servant and his part-Dutch wife, who bore her husband six children. Except for the eldest, Charles, all the Milner siblings and their offspring were German subjects.

On 23 March 1854, Mary and Charles's son, Alfred, was born at Giessen. He was to be their only child. As was customary then, his parents affirmed their newborn son's nationality by having him baptised by the British chaplain in Bonn. When Alfred was one and a half, the family moved to Tübingen, a university town in Württemberg, where Charles qualified as a doctor in 1856.

Besides being a cheaper town to live in, Tübingen offered Charles plenty of the riding, hunting and other outdoor activities he found much more enjoyable than working. Lively and well read, he was variously described as 'straightforward, jolly, and sensible' by one friend[1] and by another as 'an impossible man, gifted, wayward, and incapable of looking after anyone'.[2] Basil Williams, a journalist with *The Times* of

London, called Dr Milner 'a man of brilliant parts, but with interests too varied to make him a success in his chosen profession'.[3]

Early schooling

It fell to the reserved and deeply devout Mary, an Englishwoman of sweet disposition, to hold the family together and oversee little Alfred's upbringing.[4] When Charles was unable to find employment in Tübingen, at her insistence the family moved to London, to be closer to her relatives and benefit from their financial assistance. Always short of money, the Milners had to take modest lodgings in the Old Kent Road in southeast London, before moving into the home of Mary's cousin, John Malcolm, in more upmarket Pimlico.

Although never in the best of health, Charles Milner MD opened a practice in Chelsea in 1861, and for the next six years he and Mary settled into their new milieu as a middle-class Victorian couple.[5] The comfort of his family's new circumstances made a lasting impression on young Alfred, whose father was always more interested in shooting and walking with family and friends, choosing 'rabbits and pheasants over patients and fees'.[6] As his practice foundered, Dr Milner had to fall back on his skills as a tutor to make ends meet. He began teaching Latin at home to his son, who was already displaying a keen interest in natural history.

Alfred's early formal education began as a day scholar at St Peter's Church School in Eaton Square, Belgravia, where he soon showed exceptional promise. Despite being something of a 'loner', by the age of 12 he was popular enough to be chosen as head boy. Sadly for him, though, his parents decided it was time to move back to Germany, where the ever-restless Charles had secured a readership in English literature at Tübingen University.

At Tübingen, the Milners had to share their family home with a succession of English schoolboys sent over to Germany to be tutored by Dr Milner, who needed their fees to supplement his meagre academic salary. Still in his formative years, Alfred intensely disliked the strict discipline of his new *Gymnasium*, but after three years of 'frightful sweat' he remastered the German language and came top of his class.[7] In later life, this German upbringing during his most formative years was held against him by chauvinistic English critics, who claimed he was a foreigner and therefore not really to be trusted. (Though Milner eventually lost his German accent, he was never able to pronounce 'th' in English properly.)

In 1869, when only 15, Alfred's life changed radically, and for the worse, when his beloved mother died after a protracted battle with cancer. Mary's death at the age of 58 brought about the break-up of the Milner family. Her teenage son was inconsolable: his mother was not only his ideal woman but represented his whole world.[8] As Headlam records, Mary's influence was to remain with her son always: 'So great was the impression she made upon him that he may be said to have lived all his life by the light of the torch she lit.'[9] HWJ Picard observes that when Milner's mother died, something broke within him that was never altogether mended.[10] From then on, he grew up with little experience of close human warmth or family support.[11]

King's College

Mary Milner had been determined that Alfred should be brought up 'English', and before she died she made arrangements with her brother, Colonel Charles Ready, that her youngest son would be taken under his wing. Her two elder sons, now grown up, were away in India and China, respectively. Colonel Ready immediately brought Alfred back to London and arranged for his accommodation with John Malcolm, a barrister and widower with a 26-year-old daughter, Marianne.

Alfred was enrolled as a dayboy at King's College, London, housed in the basement of Somerset House, in the Strand. Mary had been able to leave a small legacy for her son, which was entrusted to Malcolm, who managed to lose most of it by the time of his own death a year later. Marianne Malcolm, 11 years older than Alfred, became his surrogate sister and for the next few years his closest companion.

Given their severely limited means, Marianne's and Alfred's lives in London were far from easy. A classmate of his at King's remembers Alfred as a 'grave, serious and thoughtful boy', top of the class in classics, French and German, who always carried off all the prizes;[12] another described him as 'tall, dignified, aloof and old beyond his years'.[13] But he also had a less serious, more boyish side, attractive enough to gain him several close friendships that would endure into old age.

After two and a half years, Alfred left King's with many academic honours but very little money. Taking the advice of his respected classics teacher, he applied for a scholarship to Balliol College at Oxford, under the renowned mastership of Benjamin Jowett. Dr Charles Milner, still teaching in Germany, advised his son to apply for admission to the Indian Civil Service, but after much argument reluctantly pledged £50 towards Alfred's education at Oxford, provided he did not have to fund any future shortfall in fees.

The long summer holidays gave Alfred a welcome opportunity to leave Marianne in London and spend time in the German outdoors with his father. On one memorable visit, in 1870, he arrived in Tübingen to find the country up in arms as a result of France's reckless declaration of war on the German confederation, led by Prussia. Walking through the Black Forest together, Charles and Alfred watched the bombardment of Strasbourg from afar and were struck by the military efficiency of the Prussian army. According to Headlam, the experience made a profound impression on the young man, who never forgot the impact of warfare on a people under duress. He saw at first-hand how a highly organised and conscripted German army turned the tables upon a French nation ill-prepared for war, and drew from it the lifelong lesson that it was 'madness' for any rich and peacefully minded nation to be unable to defend itself properly.[14]

Balliol

Alfred had no relatives or friends of influence and financial means who could be called upon to ease his way into Oxford, so he spent the summer holidays of 1872 being coached to write the five-day open scholarship examination for Balliol. The college was then at the height of its fame, renowned for being the pre-eminent centre in Britain for the training of future public servants for duty at home and abroad. Its fabled Master, Jowett, asserted that success in life should depend on merit and hard work, not aristocratic connections and wealth: the role that men should play in the world was to give disinterested service to the welfare of their fellow human beings. Jowett was a close friend of and mentor to Florence Nightingale, once writing to her to say that he 'should like to govern the world through [his] pupils'.[15] Among his students would be a future British prime minister, Herbert Henry (HH) Asquith, and three successive viceroys of India, Lords Lansdowne, Elgin and Curzon, all of them devoted alumni of Jowett's Balliol.

Throughout his student career, Milner suffered from a fear that he had performed badly in every scholarship exam he wrote. For the 'Balliol', he thought he had done well in the first three papers but 'gone to the dogs' in the last two. Yet the excellence of his essay on the Franco-Prussian War had put him far ahead of his fellows, and he duly pipped a dismayed set of 'Varsity men' from other colleges and other public schoolboys to the main scholarship prize. As Headlam recounts, when the winner was announced to the expectant candidates thronging Balliol Hall as 'Mr Milner, King's College', 'there was dead silence. No one had ever heard of him.'[16]

A stipend of £80 from Balliol helped to ease Alfred's financial circumstances, though Marianne's father's mismanagement of their finances and her frequently poor health meant they both had to budget carefully, with Alfred obliged to regard his own income and Marianne's as one.[17] Out of necessity, he formed a lifelong habit of keeping a careful account of his expenditure. Knowing of Milner's financial circumstances, Jowett, who had taken an immediate liking to his brilliant new acquisition, found him pupils to tutor in order to supplement his income.[18]

Three aspects of Milner's character set him apart from the other 180 Balliol undergraduates: his part-schooling in Germany, which made him fluent in a foreign language, his intellectual ability and unusually thoughtful demeanour, and his meagre income. He had continually to seek other scholarships to keep himself at Balliol, and became a self-described 'scholarship-hunter'.[19] While at Oxford, he won no fewer than four significant scholarships, failing only to win the most coveted of all, the 'Ireland', because he tore up his final paper (on Greek verse) and walked out of the exam in frustration. Jowett told him afterwards that if he had not done that, he was so far ahead of the other candidates he would have walked away with the prize.

Milner found life at Oxford exhilarating. Besides working harder than anyone, he threw himself into campus activities and took regular exercise on the River Isis, once rowing 60 km to Reading in the company of friends. He also helped to found the Balliol Shakespeare Club and joined the Oxford Union, the famous nursery for future politicians of which he became treasurer and president. As is usual in student bodies, Balliol consisted of a number of cliques – intellectual and athletic – but Milner took great care not to identify too closely with any one of them. His modest and unaffected disposition won him many friends, who respected his intellect as well as his strength of character.

Like many of his Balliol contemporaries, Milner was deeply influenced by the Master's views on politics, religion and the merits of public service. Jowett was a theologian and distinguished classicist, whose religious views were anathema to the ruling Anglican establishment at Oxford as they progressed from orthodox to radical to heretical. Though he had to preach in public, Jowett privately became more and more critical of his pious academic colleagues – and of narrow-minded, party-bound politicians. An ambitious man, he would say, 'though always willing to act with a party', should 'keep his mind above party feelings and motives'.[20] His beliefs struck a chord with Milner, who became a lifelong disciple.

There were other influences on the minds of Balliol's young idealists. Four years before Milner's arrival, a prominent Liberal MP, Charles Dilke, had written an influential book, *Greater Britain*, which predicted that the Anglo-Saxon race was destined to rule the world by its unique ability to govern through a constitutional system that combined 'liberty, justice and efficiency'.[21] This, Dilke suggested, was no accident but in furtherance of a Higher Purpose – the progress towards freedom for all mankind.[22]

A decade later, a Cambridge don, JR Seeley, published a runaway bestseller, *The Expansion of England*, in which he predicted that within half a century the United States and Russia would dwarf European countries such as France and Germany. And Britain would go the same way, Seeley warned, unless it abandoned its absent-minded and haphazard approach to imperialism and failed to take advantage of two significant developments: more Englishmen and -women were now living in the colonies than at home, and the new technologies of the telegraph and steamship were making it possible to unite the scattered

Empire as never before. Only by putting together a 'Greater Britain' could such a relatively small country hope to remain among the superpowers of the future.[23] It was a message that mainstream British politicians began to take seriously.

Seeley's exhortation was also grist to the mill of a new generation of imperialists, eager to substitute single-mindedness for absent-mindedness and to take advantage of the 'Scramble for Africa' that took place after the Berlin Conference of 1884–1885, when Britain, France, Germany and other colonial powers began to compete seriously with one another for territorial acquisitions across Africa. Among this new generation was a fellow undergraduate at Oriel College at Oxford, one Cecil John Rhodes, only nine months older than Milner. Both young men thrilled to the prospect of emulating imperial Rome and establishing new, well-run and prosperous colonies under the British flag.

In Milner's view, however, public life meant public service, and any expansion of the Empire abroad had to be accompanied by social reforms at home, in order to undo some of the damage caused by uncontrolled industrialisation in England. He described himself in those days as being 'from head to foot one glowing mass of conviction',[24] whose role in life and new secular religion would be to promote Britain's imperial destiny in the role of 'civilian soldier of the Empire'.[25]

Among Milner's new friends at Balliol was Herbert Asquith, a future Liberal prime minister of Britain. The pair formed a close bond during their three years together as students, and their friendship continued when both took up legal careers after graduating. Another close friend was a much older postgraduate student, George Parkin, a fervent advocate of an imperial federation between Britain and his native Canada. However, the person who most inspired the young idealists in Milner's circle was Arnold Toynbee (uncle of the famous historian Arnold J Toynbee), a remarkable young tutor and social reformer, only 18 months older than Milner, who helped prepare Balliol undergraduates for careers in the civil service.

Physically striking, eloquent in conversation and an inspiring thinker, Toynbee', with his progressive views on social service to the weak in society, became, in J Lee Thompson's words, the 'centre, the idol, the model' of Milner's world at Oxford.[26] As a tutor in political economy, Toynbee pricked the social conscience of his students, underlining their duty, as members of the elite, towards the lower classes. Away from the lecture hall, Toynbee could be found in the midst of every student campaign to improve the lot of people in slums, their lives blighted by the Industrial Revolution. Of all his Balliol friends, Milner was to say that Toynbee, at the age of 30, had exercised the most decisive influence upon him, not merely because of his intellectual gifts but for 'the nature of the man – his truthfulness, his unrivalled loftiness of soul'.[27]

Conflicting beliefs

Milner's four years at Oxford endowed him with an unusual political philosophy that combined two seemingly conflicting ideals: imperial advancement abroad coupled with social reform at home. Although his party-political inclinations were Liberal, he was actually closer to Benjamin Disraeli's brand of Conservatism, with its enthusiasm for Empire, extension of the franchise to the masses and concern for social upliftment. His coterie of friends were 'earnest, socially conscious, dutiful and exceedingly clever, and … lastingly influenced his view of public life and private duty'.[28] As Milner's biographer John Marlowe records, he had a kind of 'genius for friendship', even though 'deficient in *bonhomie* towards casual acquaintances' and lacking 'the common touch'.[29] Keith Breckenridge observes that Milner was 'a generous listener and a charming conversationalist', and that throughout his life, 'he collected powerful personal friends like precious works of art, and they became his most effective political agents'.[30]

Shortly before leaving Balliol, Milner underwent one more five-day scholarship examination – for a postgraduate fellowship at New College, which offered an annual stipend as well as board and lodging for as long as the recipient remained unmarried. Once again, Milner walked away with the scholarship, which provided him with the domestic and financial security he had never known before. His new fellowship gave him more time to ruminate about politics and society and give thought to the contribution he might make himself to the fortunes of his country[31] – and in time to the wider Empire.

CHAPTER 2

Early Career
1881–1889

For a young man such as Milner, with a first-class academic record and political ambitions, reading for the Bar was the most obvious career path. Although tempted by the offer of a tutorship at New College, he had decided – thanks to Jowett – that his future lay eventually in public service and he began 'eating dinners' at London's Inner Temple. Two years later, in 1881, he was called to the Midland Circuit of the Bar, but his practice failed to take off and at the age of 28 he gave up the law and sought more satisfying work elsewhere. Confiding to his diary, Milner wrote: 'Resolution fixed. Bar thrown overboard. Off I go upon the wide ocean … as long as I keep my health … I have nothing to fear in a life, the first condition of which is celibacy. One cannot have everything. I am a poor man and must choose between public usefulness and private happiness. I choose the former, or rather I choose to strive for it.'[1]

While at the Bar, Milner had suffered a bout of deep depression. He had moved back into lodgings with Marianne, who, at the age of nearly 40 – unmarried and lonely – had turned to the bottle and become mentally unstable. It was only his sense of obligation to the Malcolm family that persuaded him to stay on with her, but her frequent illnesses and mood swings made their life together anything but pleasant.

As a diversion from the law's drudgery, Milner had taken to writing regular articles for the *Pall Mall Gazette*, a journal of influence in political circles. In 1883, its respected editor, John Morley, a future Liberal statesman (and opponent of imperialism and the first Anglo-Boer War) retired, to be succeeded by William T Stead, a social reformer, ardent imperialist and pioneer of a new brand of populist journalism.

Milner accepted an invitation to become Stead's assistant editor, viewing the post as a form of apprenticeship for politics.[2] Despite having similar ideals, he and Stead could hardly have been more different in temperament – the editor impassioned and mercurial, his deputy requiring 'a great deal to arouse him'.[3] Milner described Stead as a cross between PT Barnum (the circus impresario) and Don Quixote,[4] and wrote approvingly that 'he loved to develop his ideas dialectically, in discussion with someone personally congenial to him, but whose habit of mind was as dissimilar as possible to his own'.[5]

Stead observed that his assistant felt the strain of his work and was easily exhausted: 'His physical energy was deficient. He often suffered from sleeplessness, and he needed to take care of himself'.[6] John Buchan also observed of Milner that 'early in life he became aware that he had a limited stock of vitality, bodily and mental'.[7] Throughout his career, overwork would give rise to health problems.

In 1882, Milner received news of his ailing father's death in Tübingen, at the age of only 52. He rushed to Germany just in time for the funeral and was touched by the number of university officers and townsfolk present at the graveside. Dr Charles was buried alongside Mary. After visiting his relatives, sunk in gloom and not wishing to return to the turmoil of life in London, Milner spent several weeks with friends in Normandy, where congenial company, plenty of swimming and his first experience of life in a carefree peasant community – in whose dances he joined on Sunday evenings – restored his flagging spirits. He remained despondent about his work and prospects, however, noting in his diary that 'my life is passing and I have done no work of value'.[8]

Returning to London, he decided it was time to make a break from Marianne after 14 years together. (She was by now an alcoholic and fated to die less than two years later.) Moving into rooms within five minutes' walk of the offices of the *Gazette*, he often found himself in the editor's chair during Stead's frequent absence on some or other crusade. On matters imperial, the *Gazette* had been critical of Prime Minister William Ewart Gladstone's 'capitulation' to the Boers of the Transvaal after the Battle of Majuba Hill in February 1881, opting for peace and granting recognition to Paul Kruger's South African Republic (SAR), also known as the Transvaal. Stead was paying close attention to the negotiations in progress in London between Lord Derby, the Colonial Secretary, and Kruger, ranting in the *Gazette* that the burghers of the SAR should 'shoot them down if necessary' to end their defiance of the British.[9]

A devastating blow for Milner in early 1883 was the death of his mentor, Arnold Toynbee, who had been in ill health for some time. Stead recalled years later that during his years at the *Pall Mall Gazette*, Milner was exceptionally kind to everyone, 'but he loved Arnold Toynbee in a way in which I have never known him care for mortal man'.[10] As a tribute to Toynbee, Milner and his friends founded a charitable organisation in his name to alleviate poverty in the East End of London. Toynbee Hall survives to this day, and Milner became an active supporter for the rest of his life, serving for many years as chairman of its council.[11]

Goschen

Milner's interest in politics and social activism brought him to the attention of George J Goschen, a prominent Liberal politician who had declined to continue serving in Gladstone's cabinet because of the latter's lukewarm enthusiasm for imperialism, and insistence on further extending the electoral franchise. The 52-year-old ex-minister and the much younger Milner had much in common: German connections (Goschen's family had emigrated to Britain from Leipzig), a passion for social reform and a determination – rare in politics – to put principle above party attachment.[12] While at the *Gazette*, Milner began to 'devil' in his spare hours for Goschen and in 1884 became his part-time private secretary, besides fulfilling his editorial duties. The close relationship – professional and private – that grew up between the two men was instrumental in developing Milner's political thinking, and in shaping his career path.[13] Goschen had a particular interest in Egypt, where he had negotiated on behalf of British bondholders invested in the Suez Canal project, and was critical of Gladstone's apparent intention to withdraw from the Middle East.

Milner's dual responsibility to his two masters, Stead and Goschen, worked well for a time, until he began eventually to tire of the *Gazette*'s crusading zeal and was embarrassed by some of Stead's sensationalist campaigns.[14] By the end of his first year with Goschen, Milner had become more of a colleague and adviser rather than secretary to the older man, writing two notable speeches for him that won Goschen a seat in Edinburgh, as 'a detached moderate',[15] in the 1885 general election. In the meantime, Milner's journalistic career and job as Goschen's secretary came to an abrupt end when he was persuaded to stand himself as the Liberal candidate for Harrow in the closely fought national poll, which resulted almost in a dead heat between the two main parties – and a hung Parliament.

During his campaign, the youthful Milner made more than 90 speeches, in one of which he touched on relations with the Transvaal in the 1880s. 'It was proved', he asserted, 'that the Boers never desired to come under our government, and we had done an act of injustice in forcing that government upon them.' Acknowledging that 'the weaker enemy had proved himself to be in the right', he endorsed Gladstone's decision not to escalate the conflict, declaring 'on that view of British honour I take my stand'.[16] How different would be his attitude during his meeting with Paul Kruger in Bloemfontein some 20 years later.[17]

According to Marlowe, as a campaigner Milner had none of that 'extrovert boisterousness' so useful to the successful democratic politician.[18] Despite his firm beliefs, he was not a staunch party man and seemed to be deficient in political passion. Much better at arguing on paper than from a public platform, Milner, with his 'squeaky' voice, could seldom arouse an audience. Critics said of him that 'he could not speak with real effect until he was hit in the eye'.[19] Although he put up a brave fight in Harrow, he lost the contest to a Conservative candidate by a thousand votes. It was his first and last attempt to enter the House of Commons and convinced him to forego a career in politics. 'I am afraid I should never make a good party man, but I hope to make a fairly decent Englishman,'[20] he wrote afterwards.

In one noteworthy campaign speech on 'Liberalism and Foreign Policy', Milner gave a foretaste of the issues he would pursue with enthusiasm over the next few decades – enlightened patriotism, imperial unity, compulsory military training and preparedness for war. To these ends, he asserted, Britain needed a dominant Royal Navy, one that would carry on ruling the waves – in cooperation with her far-flung colonies – and produce 'a common nationality between Englishmen at home and Englishmen beyond the sea'.[21]

The Liberal Unionists

Gladstone's resignation in 1885 over a budget issue precipitated another indecisive election that brought Lord Salisbury's Conservatives temporarily into office for a few months before the veteran Liberal leader, supported this time by Irish nationalist MPs, went to the country again in early 1886 with a proposal to grant Home Rule to the troublesome Irish. In response, 93 Liberal MPs, led by the former Radical, Joseph Chamberlain, who were strongly in favour of retaining British rule over Ireland, walked out on Gladstone and formed the Liberal-Unionist Association. Prominent among them was Goschen, supported by Milner, whose own reasons for leaving the Liberal Party for the Unionists were tactical (and pro-imperialist) rather than born of true conviction.

Working once again for Goschen, Milner threw himself 'heart and soul'[22] into running the Liberal-Unionist Association's anti-Home Rule campaign, making many speeches on the new group's behalf. His efforts during the election campaign, in which Gladstone's Home Rule Bill was defeated by only 30 votes, were described by the association's head committee as 'impossible to overestimate'.[23] The election, which cost Goschen his Edinburgh seat, put Lord Salisbury's Conservatives into power for the next six years in an unofficial alliance with the Liberal-Unionists, who declined to enter into a formal coalition with the Tories for fear of being absorbed by their larger partner.

Milner celebrated the Unionists' electoral success by taking off on a six-week tour of Ireland. He wrote to Goschen afterwards to express thanks for having been influenced by him against Gladstone on the 'Irish question' – the new dividing line in British politics. 'All my natural leanings were to Home Rule', Milner wrote, 'and in the far future, I still think it may be the best, or the only constitution for Ireland, but, under present circumstances, I am sure it would have meant a most fearful disaster [for the Empire] … I have no hesitation in saying that I am, for all practical purposes, a Tory. I don't mean however to question for a moment, the wisdom, nay the absolute necessity, of keeping up the Liberal-Unionist Party, for the time being at least, as a separate organization.'[24]

The Treasury

Not long after Milner's return from Ireland, the Salisbury administration was confronted by an internal upheaval that threatened its survival in government. In a fit of pique, the mercurial Lord Randolph Churchill, the Chancellor of the Exchequer (and father of Winston), had tendered his resignation after his proposed budget cuts in military expenditure were rejected by his colleagues. Assuming he was irreplaceable, Churchill was surprised – and dismayed – when his offer of resignation was accepted. Needing to keep leading Liberal-Unionists on his side, Salisbury quickly offered the chancellorship to the sure-footed and financially experienced George Goschen.

Though initially hesitant to serve in a Conservative-led government, Goschen was persuaded by Milner, among others, that he should put country before party and accept appointment. As Chancellor, one of his first acts was to make Milner his principal private secretary – and right-hand man at the Treasury. It proved an inspired choice, for in his secretary Goschen had found someone with a hitherto unrevealed aptitude for figures. As Milner was to say of himself, 'when I have once read a balance sheet or a budget, the figures seem to be written on the wall in front of my eyes'.[25] Years later, his wife would say of him, 'he could not forget figures – once seen'.[26] Milner's wide grasp of financial issues helped Goschen to reduce Britain's national debt in a ground-breaking budget in 1888.

Milner served Goschen at the Treasury for the next three years, his work at the heart of government in complete contrast to his time spent working for Stead or behind a desk in the Liberal-Unionists' cramped headquarters. At the age of 33, a comfortable bachelor with rooms in St James's and Oxford, as well as membership of several London clubs, Milner was utterly absorbed by a job that he found both worthwhile and challenging. In his leisure hours, he enjoyed an active social life, with a circle of friends drawn by his exceptional intellect as well as a genuine interest in what others were doing or saying, which made him attractive to younger people – and especially small children.[27]

He also seems to have had premonitions about his future career direction. Since his Oxford days, he had been especially interested in two countries with a substantial English-speaking presence – Egypt and South Africa – whose internal dynamics posed a threat to the unity of the British Empire. In Goschen, he had found a like-minded imperialist whose experience of Egypt as a banker had whetted Milner's interest in the Middle East, and who had become perturbed by Gladstone's hands-off approach to the two strategically important territories at opposite ends of the African continent. Milner's interest in South Africa had been further kindled by an ardent Liberal-Unionist friend and colleague, AL Bruce, married to the daughter of David Livingstone and chairman of the African Lakes Company, who had extensive experience of sub-Saharan Africa and wished to put an end to the slave trade in Central Africa and promote 'Christianity and civilisation' in the South.[28]

A sign of Milner's growing reputation at the Treasury was an invitation from the new Viceroy-designate of India, Lord Lansdowne, a fellow Balliol man and Liberal Unionist, to accompany him to Delhi as his private secretary. Rather surprisingly, Milner turned down this plum position – which carried considerable status and a high salary – because he feared he was not physically strong enough for the rigours of what was bound to be an exhausting assignment.

Milner proposed, instead, to undertake a tour of southern Africa in the second half of 1889, but called it off when he learnt, probably via Goschen, that the post of director general of accounts in the Egyptian government might become vacant. In due course, an offer arrived from Sir Evelyn Baring, the British Agent and Consul General in Cairo. Milner took his time before replying and consulted Goschen, who thought his aide would like Cairo because he had 'a touch of the adventurous' and would enjoy the 'independence and individuality of a foreign position.'[29]

Fed up with the intrigues of the constant party politicking that were making even his successful tenure at the Treasury uncertain, Milner decided to chance his luck in Egypt in the hope that it might open a door for him in the imperial civil service. The post on offer would provide him with an excellent opportunity to exercise his humanitarian skills while furthering the cause of Empire.[30] As he explained to Goschen, 'Egypt is an important place, and it is important, from the Imperial point of view, that Englishmen holding any sort of responsible position there should be English-minded. And I think I may say I am that.'[31]

As for the future, 'between the service of England abroad ... and civil service at home, there is a great deal to be said for the former. The individual counts for more. It is more exciting. You have a larger scope. Of course, it is not so safe or comfortable, but then I am a single man, with innumerable ties of affection certainly, but nothing of duty, to England.'[32]

Since Napoleon's invasion of Egypt in 1798, France had been a major investor in Egypt, whose foreign business was usually conducted in French. In typically thorough fashion, Milner immediately took himself off to Normandy to sharpen up his skills in the language. Though wishing his assistant well, Goschen lamented his loss to the Treasury, saying it was as though he 'had lost his right hand'.[33] Milner recorded his gratitude to Goschen for having been a great chief, 'who was at the same time an excellent friend'.[34]

CHAPTER 3

Egypt
1889–1892

Milner took up his appointment as Director General of Accounts in the Egyptian finance ministry at a timely moment in Anglo-Egyptian relations. Though still part of the Ottoman Empire, the nominally independent Egypt was run as a private fiefdom by successive Khedives, who had vastly overspent on infrastructural development and were no longer able to repay the interest on their foreign loans. For most of the 1800s, French rather than British investors had taken the lead in developing the economies of Asia Minor and Egypt, and especially in financing the Suez Canal, the strategically important waterway to the Far East that opened to shipping in 1869. The Suez Canal had reduced the voyage to and from India, Britain's most precious colonial possession, by several weeks and many thousands of sea miles.

Always hovering on the brink of insolvency (and civil implosion), Egypt had been forced to allow the two foreign governments to whom it was most indebted – Britain and France – to take over the running of its treasury in return for Egypt's relinquishing control over the Suez Canal. By the 1880s, Suez had become a vital conduit for British trade: 21 per cent of Britain's exports and 16 per cent of its imports went through the Canal[1] and four out of five steamships passing through it were British.[2]

Successive British governments under Gladstone and Disraeli, both of whom had privately bought shares in the company operating the Canal, had taken unilateral action to ensure that British interests in Egypt were protected. In 1882, they upstaged the French by sending troops to put down an anti-European uprising in Alexandria – by then there were some 37 000 Europeans resident in Egypt – and leaving the army behind, 'temporarily', to safeguard the lifeline to India. Every year for the next 40, Britain vowed to leave her 'veiled protectorate' once a stable, solvent and properly run government had been established there, but never actually did so.[3]

With two-fifths of cultivated land along the Nile under cotton, most of it exported to Britain, Rudyard Kipling memorably described Egypt as 'not a country, but a longish strip of market-garden, nominally in the charge of a government which is not a government but the disconnected satrapy of a half-dead empire, controlled Pecksniffingly by a Power which is not a Power but an Agency.'[4] But what made this 'market-garden' of such strategic significance to European powers was, of course, the Canal, the conduit to Asia. The protectorate was also the northern gateway to the territories along the White Nile down to its source near the equator. For some obscure reason, the Foreign Office was of the view that control of the headwaters of the Nile was essential for the prosperity of Egypt and the region.[5]

By the time of Milner's arrival in Cairo in November 1889, Britain had become the predominant influence in Egypt, having established a protectorate run from London without ever formally colonising the country. Its de facto ruler was Britain's Agent and Consul General, Sir Evelyn Baring, known by his detractors as 'Sir Over-Baring', and as 'El Lord' by the awed Egyptians. In J Lee Thompson's vivid description, the imperious Baring – about to become Lord Cromer – was 'physically imposing, supremely self-confident, cold, reserved, well-read, a good diplomat and extremely well-organised – a perfect imperial administrator.'[6] Over the years, he had put in place a system in which the Khedive remained the nominal ruler, but behind him was a network of British advisers and officials who ran the government, the economy, the police and the army.[7] For more menial services to the *fellahin* (peasantry), Baring employed a coterie of local administrators and tax collectors, whom he regarded with barely concealed contempt.

The Sudan

As British Agent, Baring was also the effective ruler of the neighbouring Sudan, a long-standing Egyptian dependency. When El Lord took up his post in Cairo in 1883, a religious revival was under way in the Sudan, inspired by Ahmed Mohammed, a former Egyptian slave trader, now a charismatic Muslim preacher known as the 'Mahdi' (one who offers divine guidance in the right way).[8] Sweeping across the Sudan, the Mahdi's 'Dervishes' crushed a 10 000-strong, well-armed Egyptian force led by a British officer, Colonel William Hicks, in November 1883 and laid siege to the capital, Khartoum. With the disastrous Indian Mutiny of 1857–1859 in mind – when nationalists had forged an alliance with militant Islam – a fearful British government decided to abandon the Sudan altogether and rather take measures to prevent Mahdism from spreading into Egypt or across the Red Sea.

In early 1884, fearing losses that might threaten Britain's hold on Egypt and egged on by a press campaign led by an indignant WT Stead, a reluctant Gladstone sent the devout and 'slightly mad' General Charles Gordon, a decorated Crimean War veteran, to the Sudan with orders to relieve British garrisons and then let go of the territory. Gordon set out for Khartoum and on reaching the military base outside the city decided to ignore his instructions. Believing he had a prior duty to God, he decided to stay put in the hope of arousing a public outcry at home that would force the government to reverse its policy and agree 'in the name of civilisation' not to withdraw from the Sudan but to free the territory from the evils of the Mahdi.

His unorthodox tactics worked: Gladstone reluctantly agreed to send a relief force up the Nile, and in January 1885 Khartoum was liberated after three days of fierce fighting in which Gordon himself died bravely. Gladstone was held to be publicly responsible for the death of a heroic Christian bravely upholding his faith in the face of barbarism, and Baring was blamed too, even though he had opposed the mission to free Khartoum from the outset. It was to take 13 years before Gordon's death would be avenged by General Kitchener's invading Anglo-Egyptian army.[9]

Reconstruction in Egypt

Within a few years of arriving in Egypt in 1883, Baring and his financial guru, Sir Edgar Vincent, had managed to accomplish the seemingly impossible task of putting the protectorate's finances in reasonable order.[10] Under their stewardship, Egypt emerged from bankruptcy and even produced a budget surplus. In addition, irrigation projects were launched, the judicial system overhauled, forced labour abolished, the railways rebuilt and discipline instilled in the army.[11] Yet, it was the *fellahin* rather than the British taxpayer who bore most of the cost of Baring's endeavours.

Despite the material improvements that British officialdom had wrought, like colonialists everywhere they were not popular among the people they ruled. To Baring's admirers at home, he was a brilliant administrator who had saved Egypt from financial ruin and rescued the *fellahin* from the worst aspects of colonialist exploitation. Yet in the eyes of Egyptians – and Liberal anti-imperialists in Britain – the Agent and Consul General epitomised 'the worst aspects of colonial domination and condescension ... and instituted a form of one-man rule with distinct shades of megalomania'. On his daily travels through Cairo, Baring is said to have ordered a servant to run ahead of his carriage, shouting out his name and telling people to get out of its way.[12]

It did not take Milner long to master the intricacies of Egypt's finances and demonstrate his talents as an administrator.[13] Settling into a furnished apartment in Cairo, along with an Arab manservant, he began immediately to acquaint himself with the country's politics and learn Arabic, which he came to regard as 'an appalling language'[14] and was never able to master. He found the Egyptian capital 'unbelievably unsanitary in all its arrangements', and among its curses, the 'fleas, flies, mesquitoes [*sic*] and dust'.[15] Yet these inconveniences were not sufficient to deter 'half the civilized world' from invading Cairo for the fashionable winter social season.[16] Following the example of Baring, who not only regarded Egyptians as beneath him but also kept away from the Turkish ruling classes and visiting Europeans, Milner avoided the frivolities of the season 'as much as politeness allowed'.[17] 'With foreigners', he admitted, 'one practically does not mix.'[18]

Egypt's financial problems were exceedingly complex, and Milner revelled in dealing with the finances of a country in which 'the connection of economics with politics and morality' was so apparent.[19] He developed a high regard for Baring, whose 'unostentatious supremacy' he described as 'a masterpiece of political management'.[20] Baring was equally impressed with Milner, regarding him as 'one of the most able Englishmen who have served the Egyptian government', and as one of three men in the Empire capable of being his successor.[21]

Milner's administrative experiences in Egypt served to confirm his belief in the racial superiority of Englishmen, and to strengthen his conviction about Britain's ability to govern other races more fairly and efficiently than they could rule themselves.[22] In his book *England in Egypt,* he wrote patronisingly of the Egyptians: 'Such a race will not of itself develop great men or new ideas, or take a leading part in the progress of mankind. But under proper guidance, it is capable of enjoying much simple content.'[23] These views would be taken with him to South Africa.

New acquaintances

During his service in Egypt, Milner encountered for the first time two fellow Englishmen destined to play significant roles in his future career: the ambitious, thrusting Liberal-Unionist MP Joseph Chamberlain and the upwardly mobile military officer Horatio Herbert Kitchener.

The flamboyant Chamberlain, a fastidious dresser who wore a monocle in one eye and an orchid in his lapel and had a gift for attracting attention to himself, was a wealthy screw manufacturer and former mayor of Birmingham who had gone to work at the age of 16 and made enough money by the age of 34 to retire from business and go into politics.[24] Cutting his teeth as a radical, anti-imperialist Liberal, he rose swiftly through the ranks to become President of the Board of Trade in Gladstone's second ministry (1880–1885), but subsequently fell out with his elderly leader over the proposal to grant Home Rule to Ireland.

A late convert to the benefits of imperial trade and protective tariffs, which he now believed were essential to provide jobs for Britain's industrial workforce, Chamberlain was to become the driving force behind a split in Liberal ranks and a breakaway of pro-imperial party members from Gladstone. Had Chamberlain not broken with Gladstone over Ireland, he would almost certainly have become the next Liberal leader, and in time Britain's prime minister. Distrusted by MPs in both major political parties, at the time of his visit to Egypt 'Pushful' or 'Jingo' Joe had been languishing unhappily on the parliamentary backbenches for almost a decade.

Joseph Chamberlain, Britain's Colonial Secretary, who sent Milner to South Africa.
(*Wikimedia Commons/Elliot & Fry*)

In Cairo, Milner was able to have a lengthy conversation with Chamberlain, whose recent trip to the United States and Canada had served to strengthen his imperialist instincts. The MP for Birmingham had been keeping a close eye on developments in Egypt and concluded that it was imperative for Britain to retain control over the region. In Milner, he found a man of similar convictions.

When a new Tory-Liberal imperialist coalition under Lord Salisbury won the general election of 1895, Chamberlain was offered any post in the cabinet except that of Foreign Secretary. Seizing his opportunity, he shrewdly chose the Colonial Office over the Chancellorship, thereby becoming responsible for administering the affairs of almost one-fifth of the land surface of the world and some 50 million people,[25] and making him the standard bearer of the 'New Imperialism' in British politics. Looked down upon by the aristocrats around Salisbury because of his middle-class origins, Pushful Joe became famous as Britain's 'Minister for Empire', having 'an irresistible appeal for the masses of the 1890s – who loved flash'.[26] A non-admirer described him as 'the grandest specimen of the courageous, unscrupulous schemer our politics have ever seen'.[27]

The Inspector General of Police during most of Milner's time in Egypt was Colonel Herbert Kitchener, recently promoted for his courageous service against the Mahdi in the Sudan. A self-contained, rather remote individual of delicate tastes and a trademark moustache that would one day become famous on a First World War recruiting poster, Kitchener aroused jealousy among his fellow officers for his vaulting ambition. He had also incurred the hostility of the expatriate community in Cairo by his ill-concealed contempt for their society.[28]

Milner was able to observe at close quarters Kitchener's efforts to reform Egypt's interior ministry, which was responsible for the Egyptian police force. 'Of [Kitchener's] energy and industry, there can be no doubt', he recorded in his journal. 'The question is whether he is on the right lines. He is certainly ruthless in his treatment of other interests ... and he is not easy to keep in check. A strong self-willed man, not absolutely straight, he might very easily cause trouble, not only with the natives, but among the English themselves.'[29]

Promotion

Less than a year after arriving in Egypt, Milner was promoted, on Baring's recommendation, to the post of Under-Secretary of Finance, the second-most senior official in the ministry. He continued to keep in regular touch with Goschen, confiding to his mentor that one of the things that made Egypt work was 'the extremely good relations existing between all the leading Englishmen here. They all row in the same boat, and are really a *wonderfully strong crew*. It is a pleasure to have to deal with so many able, straight and thoroughly English-minded men on terms of perfect good fellowship.'[30]

To Goschen, Milner expressed his admiration of the 'immensity of the service which Baring *constantly* renders to this country. Despite all his great superficial faults – his brusquerie, his conceit, his long-windedness ... he is a statesman of a very big order, and above all, a perfectly extraordinary instance of the right man in the right place.'[31]

A salary increase enabled Milner to move out of Cairo to Helwan, a spa in the nearby desert overlooking the Nile. He revelled in the clean country air and 'above all the nights most fresh and beautiful'.[32] Two Arabian horses of his own enabled him to keep fit by riding every day. From visitors, and his voluminous correspondence with Goschen and others, he was kept well-informed about political developments 'at home'.

After 15 months in Egypt, Milner went back to England on leave and lost no time in renewing old friendships. He spent an entertaining evening at Wimbledon with WT Stead, who talked 'with his wonted brilliancy' about all and sundry, but particularly about Cecil John Rhodes and the prospect of maintaining the political unity of the English race.[33] Stead, who had fallen for Rhodes's enthusiasm two years earlier when 'the Colossus' – as Rhodes was nicknamed – was in London to rally support for the granting of a royal charter for his British South Africa Company (BSAC), remarked presciently that if Rhodes lived for another ten years, 'he will make or mar the Empire'.[34]

Although Rhodes had been Milner's contemporary at Oxford the two had never met, and it was Stead who made the introduction. Milner was far more sceptical than Stead of Rhodes's 'commercial' brand of imperialism. According to historian Robert Rotberg, Stead thought Rhodes personally unprepossessing but full of ideas: 'He believes more in wealth and endowments than I do. He is not religious in the ordinary sense, but has a deeply religious conception of his duty to the world and thinks he can best serve it by working for England.' With financial backing from Rhodes, Stead went on to found another well-regarded political journal, *The Review of Reviews*.[35]

Margot

Milner's sojourn in England also brought him the first serious romance of his life. Over a meal at Balliol, Benjamin Jowett had deliberately seated him next to the vivacious social butterfly Margot Tennant, ten years younger and aptly described as 'the electric charge' of every gathering she attended.[36] The strength of Margot Tennant's voltage stunned Milner, who had never met anyone as flamboyant and flirtatious. Although having several other suitors in tow at the time, Margot was fascinated by Milner's 'quick mind and lightning wit'. In her journal, she described him as having 'dark skin, melancholy, [with] highly expressive eyes and a humorous mouth'. Jowett had told her that 'although Milner did not smoke, hunt or play golf, he was not a prig, but the most enjoyable company in the world.'[37]

Milner and Margot ran into one another again at a succession of house parties, and he became so enamoured of her that before going back to Egypt, with marriage in mind, he went all the way to Scotland to call on Margot's parents at their family castle and invite them to visit Egypt with her at the end of the summer. The night before he left for Cairo, Milner wrote to Margot professing his love and assuring her that she had encountered 'something genuine' this time.[38]

In late November 1891, the Tennant family arrived in Cairo and embarked on a three-week cruise along the Nile. Milner was too busy to accompany them but kept up a lively correspondence with Margot. After their return to the city, the visitors stayed on for another three months, during which Milner and Margot saw each other frequently. Shortly after Christmas, the two rode out to the Pyramids, where he asked her to marry him.

Not keen to exchange her busy social life in England for life in Egypt, Margot declined. She was also being courted at this time by Milner's old friend from Oxford, the womanising HH Asquith, whose wife had died only three months earlier, leaving him to bring up five children. Margot was indiscreet enough to tell Asquith of Milner's interest in her. He wrote in reply, confessing that although Milner had been his friend for 20 years, he could not 'help noticing a certain commonplaceness, a slight and indefinable want of depth and delicacy, a lack as it were of flavour and fragrance both in sentiment and in the expression of what he writes. Am I wrong?' he asked. 'I would not say it to anyone but you, for I know him to be a true and loyal friend.'[39] A political observer who knew both men well described the patrician and snobbish Asquith as Milner's 'lifelong, devoted enemy'.[40]

HWJ Picard speculates that, along with the loss of his mother, Milner's failure to persuade Margot Tennant to become his wife may have been one more reason for his personal reticence, and for the absence of social warmth noted by people as diverse as John Buchan and Olive Schreiner. For most of his career, Milner struck outsiders who did not know him better as a rather lonely and reserved bachelor, whose life was devoted mostly to work.[41]

Paddling his own canoe

In the spring of 1892, the chairman of Britain's Inland Revenue Board, Sir Algernon West, wrote to Milner inviting him to become his successor in one of the highest posts in the civil service. West, who had been quietly canvassing support for Milner for four years, wrote to him to say, 'As long as I live, I shall never forget the wrong Goschen did in letting you go [to Egypt]. The sin far outweighs any good deed he has done.'[42]

Torn between remaining abroad and returning home, Milner decided that the offer from West was too great a compliment to turn down.[43] As Britain's chief tax gatherer, he would be his own man in a job 'in which self-effacement (although I am good at it) is not the only cardinal virtue'.[44] Goschen wrote to congratulate his protégé on the public approval of his appointment, notwithstanding his 'comparatively young age'. As Lord Salisbury's Chancellor, the older man doubted that he would have long to work with Milner: a general election was imminent and Goschen thought it might be good for the country if the

Liberals came back into power with a small majority over the Unionist coalition.[45]

Milner confided to Goschen that he would be leaving Egypt with mixed feelings. The work there was 'vastly more interesting and varied than anything I shall find at Somerset House. And the climate has been the making of me', but it would be 'a satisfaction … to paddle for once one's own canoe.'[46] He resolved that before becoming too absorbed in his new position, he would write a book about Egypt and the benefits that British rule had brought to that country.

CHAPTER 4

Tax Gatherer

1892–1897

Milner's new office at Somerset House, in the Strand, was located next to his former prep school, King's College, in the west wing of one of the grandest buildings in London. As Chairman of the Inland Revenue Board, he reported directly to the Chancellor of the Exchequer, his mentor and friend George Goschen. Still preoccupied with the affairs of Egypt, his immediate aim was to finish the writing of his book before turning to the many tax matters in his in-tray.

England in Egypt, published in late 1892, made a concise, well-reasoned case for the benefits – to both countries – of Britain's occupation of the Land of the Pharaohs. Milner dealt crisply with a range of issues covering Egyptian politics and economics since the start of British occupation, and put forward suggestions about Britain's future policy in the region. His aim was to justify Britain's reasons for keeping Egypt under her thumb and to defend what he hoped would be a temporary occupation. Marlowe describes the book as 'a splendid piece of propaganda' that not only helped to 'make British rule in Egypt a source of pride to an important section of British public opinion, but also to justify the … beneficence and … profitability … of the … New Imperialism.'[1]

'It is not only, or principally, upon what Englishmen do for Egypt that the case for England rests', Milner explained. 'It is upon what England is helping the Egyptians do for themselves. British influence is not exercised to impose an uncongenial foreign system upon a reluctant people. It is a force making for the triumph of the simplest ideas of honesty, humanity and justice, to the value of which Egyptians are as much alive as anybody else.'[2] Yet the real truth was that British political leaders of all persuasions regarded the retention of

Egypt as strategically vital for the passage to India. It was never about uplifting the Egyptian people.

Winston Churchill, by now one of Britain's most prominent journalists, described Milner's opus as 'more than a book ... The story-teller had a wit and style that might have brightened the dullest theme. The words ran like a trumpet-call which rallies the soldiers after the parapets are stalled, and summons them to complete the victory.'[3] *England in Egypt* ran to 13 editions over the next three decades and its success transformed Milner from obscure civil servant to an up-and-coming imperial figure.[4]

Cecil Rhodes read the book while travelling down the Nile and wrote to the author: 'It just gives one, without being tiring, correct information on all the questions which occur to a man's mind when he travels in a new country ... I should say there is more chance of trouble coming if we retire [from Egypt] than if we remain.'[5] Rhodes, at the time, was energetically promoting his own plan to run a telegraph line, followed by a rail link, from the Cape all the way up Africa to Cairo.

Lord Cromer (as Baring was now) also gave Milner's book high praise, saying it was excellent in form and substance and covered all the essential aspects of the situation in a most readable style. He was waiting, however, to see what 'the locals made of it, but it is as well that they should occasionally hear the truth'.[6] Most Egyptians did not appreciate the book's underlying message, bridling at the prospect of the British remaining in their country indefinitely.[7]

Shortly before *England in Egypt* appeared, Britain underwent another change of government in the election of 1892. This time, Irish nationalist MPs switched their support back to the pro-Home-Rule Liberals, who won 40 more seats than the alliance of Tories and Liberal anti-Home Rulers, putting Gladstone in power for a fourth term. For Milner, the new administration's two most significant appointees were Sir William Harcourt, who succeeded Goschen as Chancellor, and his influential Liberal-imperialist friend, Lord Rosebery, as Foreign Secretary.[8] Like Milner, Rosebery and his supporters 'believed in combining social reform and strong defence at home with the vigorous advancement of Empire worldwide'.

New brooms

As a prominent civil servant, Milner had to appear neutral on the divisive issue of Irish Home Rule, but his political instincts were firmly with Rosebery. His new master, Harcourt, a former Cambridge law professor and member of three past Gladstone cabinets, was a man of elephantine build, hence his nickname 'Jumbo'. Able and quick-tempered, Harcourt was the most ardent Home Ruler among leading Liberals and regarded as the likely successor to Gladstone.

The main item on Milner's agenda was to devise a way of balancing the tiny surplus that Goschen had left his successor against a steady rise in government expenditure. His formula was to raise the small estate tax that Goschen had introduced into more substantial 'death duties', to be levied on the rich. Too sensitive a measure to be imposed on wealthy landowners ahead of a contentious Home Rule Bill, Milner's proposal was deferred to a later budget.

Now nearing 40, with a good income, an apartment in fashionable St James's and several club memberships, Milner had enough free time to enjoy a busy social life, spending most weekends in the country houses of rich aristocrats in whose company he had come to feel at ease. He also kept up his close friendships, including some with people lower down the social ladder. Having sworn himself to celibacy as a young man, he now thought better of it and found himself a mistress, a little-known actress named Cecile Duval, born Priscilla Peckham on Jersey in the Channel Islands in 1860.[9] In the discreet Victorian upper-class manner, he set 'C' up in various lodgings and spent many nights with her until his departure for South Africa some years later. He was to keep in distant touch with 'C' for the rest of his life, and on his death left her a small annuity.[10]

Someone else whom Milner ran across in society circles was the woman he would marry some 30 years later. She was the attractive, vivacious Violet Maxse, the 24-year-old daughter of Admiral Frederick Maxse, a retired naval officer, radical Liberal and social activist. Milner makes no reference in his diaries to their first meeting, perhaps because Violet was at the time engaged to be married to a lieutenant in the Grenadier Guards, Lord Edward Cecil, the fourth son of Lord Salisbury.

He continued to correspond with Margot Tennant, who wrote to him in early 1894 to break the news, before it became public, that she had decided to marry HH Asquith. Expressing the hope that Milner would not go out of her life, she thanked him 'for the deep and beautiful love which you have honoured me with'.[11] Writing back to congratulate Margot, he assured her that his affection was too deep and her influence on his life too immense 'for you to ever pass out of the warmest sanctuary of my heart and thoughts'.[12] On the eve of the marriage, he sent her a poem he had written about their love affair. Unable to bring himself to attend the wedding ceremony – a highlight of the London season – he pleaded urgent budget business as an excuse to absent himself from the celebrations.[13]

Death duties

On 1 March 1894, the 85-year-old Gladstone resigned the premiership on an impulse because of his opposition to naval rearmament, saying 'things are best done by those who believe in them'.[14] A relieved Queen Victoria, who had never liked her long-serving prime minister, sent immediately for Rosebery and asked him to form a government. 'Jumbo' Harcourt was deeply slighted at being passed over but agreed to carry on under Rosebery as Chancellor.

Milner now embarked on his most challenging assignment and enduring achievement at Inland Revenue – helping Harcourt to draft the ground-breaking 'Death Duties Budget' of 1894, which introduced a form of taxation still in operation today. Aimed at the well-off propertied class, the budget merged property and sundry taxes into a duty on all estates valued at over £1 million. It also raised income tax and increased the duty on wines and spirits. There were anguished cries of 'creeping socialism' from the wealthy, but the income had to be found somewhere to fund the largest army and navy expansion in British history (driven by growing tension with Germany).[15] Harcourt's 1894 budget added markedly to the powers of the state and drove many voters away from the Liberals to their Conservative opponents, never to return. Yet the increased revenue proved so useful that successive governments in power could not afford to repeal the legislation.

After various readings, the furiously contested Death Duties Bill squeaked through the Commons by a mere 20 votes. Harcourt revelled in his triumph, but it was Milner who had navigated his way through the complexities of Britain's arcane tax system. The Chancellor wrote to Milner after the vote to thank him for 'the splendid and unwearied aid you have given me in the Budget ... without you the ship could not have floated for a day'.[16] That was true, for, according to Wrench, Milner had more than once whispered to a friend that Harcourt never really understood the details of the new tax and never would, 'however much he managed to impress the House of Commons'.[17] In time, Milner was to view with dismay the way in which his 'new system of plunder'[18] was used and abused by future Chancellors.

Among those impressed by Milner's performance at Inland Revenue was HH Asquith, now Secretary of State for Home Affairs, who wrote to Milner to offer him the permanent under-secretaryship of the Home Office, saying, 'There is no man in or out of the civil service whose qualifications for a place compare with your own, or whom on every ground, personal or public, I should so delight to see there.'[19] As Asquith suspected, however, Milner regarded drafting budget estimates as 'rather tame compared with empire-making'.[20] In deciding to stay on at Somerset House, he was hoping some more challenging assignment might open up elsewhere.

In early 1895, not knowing that his path would shortly cross with theirs, Milner dined at a London club with Albert Grey (4th Earl of Grey), Lord Lansdowne, Cecil Rhodes and Dr Leander Starr Jameson – ardent imperialists all. A topic under discussion would have been the decision by Lord Ripon, the Colonial Secretary, to send the superannuated Sir Hercules Robinson, later Lord Rosmead, back to South Africa for his second term as High Commissioner and Governor of the Cape. Milner also renewed links with a young friend from his *Gazette* days, Edmund Garrett, about to leave for the Cape to edit the pro-imperial *Cape Times* newspaper.[21]

To keep physically fit, Milner embraced with enthusiasm the newest craze – bicycling. The penny-farthing cycles of the late 1880s had recently given way to the two-wheel safety bicycle with pneumatic tyres. The new invention meant that for the first time, almost anyone could visit neighbouring towns or just get out into the countryside. Not surprisingly, men and women of all classes found the experience both eye-opening and exhilarating. Soon after preparing the 1895 budget for Harcourt, Milner and five friends (attended by four servants) took off to Normandy for a week's cycling. Characteristically, it was he who studied the guidebooks, kept the accounts and wrote up a daily journal, duly circulated to the others later.[22]

Soon after returning from France, Rosebery's Liberal government narrowly lost a vote of confidence in the House of Commons over the alleged failure of the War Secretary, Henry Campbell-Bannerman, to ensure that the army had sufficient supplies of cordite.[23] (Campbell-Bannerman, often known as 'C-B', had been born with the surname Campbell, but had been left an inheritance by a rich uncle on condition he added 'Bannerman' to his name.) Lord Salisbury then formed his third administration and in the ensuing general election won a sweeping majority of 152 seats, including those of 71 Liberal Home Rulers. Goschen and other Liberal imperialists now formally joined the governing Conservative Party, whose members collectively became known as 'Unionists'. Under Salisbury and then Arthur Balfour, the Unionists were to retain power in Britain for the next decade. 'Jumbo' Harcourt was replaced as Chancellor by a parsimonious Tory, Sir Michael Hicks Beach, while 'Pushful Joe' Chamberlain became the new Colonial Secretary.

At Harcourt's request, before leaving office Rosebery wrote to Milner offering him a knighthood. Accepting the honour, Milner received public confirmation of the award during a tryst with 'C' at Marlow, on the Thames, and was duly inundated with letters of congratulation, 'many of them from eligible female friends'.[24] On 2 August 1895, he was invested with the Order of the Bath on the Isle of Wight by Queen Victoria. Not long afterwards, the newly titled Sir Alfred took a nasty tumble on his bicycle and was laid low for a time, with his leg in plaster. Writing to his successor in Egypt, Clinton Dawkins, he said he expected to be at Inland Revenue for the next two years: 'Afterwards, I hope it may be a case of "tomorrow to fresh woods and pastures new".'[25]

Opportunity knocked sooner than he anticipated. Only five months later came the sensational news from South Africa that, 'in a spasm of madness', Rhodes's accomplice Dr Jameson and members of the BSAC had attempted to invade the Transvaal from Bechuanaland, and

Lord Salisbury, Prime Minister and leader of the Unionist coalition during most of Milner's time in South Africa. (*Wikimedia Commons*)

had been routed and captured by the Boers. The diplomatic disaster –
aptly described by historian Thomas Pakenham as a 'kick in the stomach straight from the South African veld'[26] – shocked the Salisbury government, delighted Britain's European rivals and was to have profound
consequences for the Empire. The Jameson Raid, as the episode was
dubbed, came at a time when Milner was helping Lord Cromer to write
his long-awaited two-volume book *Modern Egypt* (published in 1908).
Milner's mind was focused, however, on the northern end of Africa
rather than the travails of the imperial government at the southern tip
of the continent.

CHAPTER 5

A New Challenge
1896–1897

By the time of the Jameson Raid, Milner had been at Inland Revenue for four years and had become restless, writing, 'I always hope to
get out of my present place – hard, important, boring – some day or
other.'[1] Sales of his book were boosted by the latest news from
Egypt, where Kitchener had begun his advance up the Nile towards
Omdurman, intent on avenging General Gordon's death at the hands
of the Mahdi's army 13 years earlier. Milner believed that the Sudan
belonged rightfully to Egypt, the frontier between the two territories
being the division 'between civilisation and the most savage barbarism.'[2]

He speculated that if Lord Cromer were about to retire, he might
be the front-runner to succeed him, but on learning from Clinton
Dawkins, in Cairo, that Egypt's overlord was intent on soldiering on,
he lamented: 'I do think I should be the best man if Cromer went, but
firstly he is not going, and secondly it would be rather a bold stroke to
send me, and governments very rarely do bold things in this humdrum
epoch.'[3]

The only challenging imperial positions left, in Milner's view,
were in India and South Africa, so he stayed where he was, at Somerset House.[4] A few months later, his patience was rewarded when he
received a message saying Joseph Chamberlain would like to see him at
the Colonial Office.

Since becoming Colonial Secretary in 1895, Pushful Joe had
been in imperialist overdrive, pronouncing the English to be 'the
greatest governing race this world has ever seen ... so proud, tenacious, self-confident and determined ... infallibly the predominant
force of future history and universal civilisation.'[5] A lifelong Unitari-
an, he was determined to portray imperialism at home and abroad as

'a high-minded crusade for civilisation, and a beacon of light for millions in the undeveloped lands of Africa and the East'.[6] Yet behind the moralising braggadocio – so absurd to the modern ear – lay some shrewd strategic calculation.

Chamberlain was a new and unusual breed of imperialist. Unlike his predecessors, he had come to regard the Empire as not merely marginal but central to his economic philosophy.[7] At the back of his mind was the concern that at some point in the future, a war in Europe was possible if not probable, and outposts such as South Africa and India might be needed to help defend the Empire.[8]

Having once held radical views on imperialism similar to those of the self-righteous Gladstone, Chamberlain had undergone a conversion and, as Colonial Secretary, now had three political aims: to extend the power and reach of the Empire; to improve the economic viability of the colonies; and to bring about some form of imperial federation between the white, self-governing entities of Canada, Australia, New Zealand, the Cape and Natal, all of which he hoped to draw closer to the United Kingdom 'for the mutual advantages of trade and defence'.[9]

The astounding expansion of Empire that took place during the last decade of Queen Victoria's reign may be ascribed to a combination of Britain's financial strength, naval reach and military power. By the time of her Diamond Jubilee in 1897, Victoria ruled over a quarter of the world's land surface and a similar proportion of the global population.[10]

Chamberlain was one of several politicians aboard the imperial bandwagon trumpeting the importance of the Empire to the raising of living standards for the British people. The chorus of a popular music-hall song at the time contained the refrain: 'We don't want to fight, but by Jingo if we do; We've got the ships, we've got the men, we've got the money too.' 'Jingoism' (an exaggerated sense of patriotism) made the masses 'absurdly proud' of their country as the leading imperial and military power, causing them to react with fury if any government of the day lacked decisiveness or sufficient determination to uphold the status quo.[11]

Another significant spur to jingoism was the triumphalism of a rapidly expanding popular press. As the owners of newspapers aimed at working-class readers were quick to realise, expressions of imperial pride and stories of military heroism were lapped up by the hundreds of thousands of new readers. The avowedly populist *Daily Mail*, owned by Alfred Harmsworth (later Lord Northcliffe), proudly proclaimed itself 'the champion of the greatness, the superiority of the British Empire ... the embodiment and mouthpiece of the imperial idea ... If Rudyard Kipling can be called the voice of Empire in English literature, we may fairly claim to be the voice of Empire in London journalism.'[12] (The paper's successful sales formula has changed little since then.)

Founded in 1896, the *Daily Mail* sold at half the price of its competitors, and its imperialist fervour quickly made it the world's largest-selling newspaper. The Prime Minister, Lord Salisbury, described it as a paper for people 'who could read, but not think'.[13] And, as Roy Hattersley observed drily, espousing high imperial ideals has never been inconsistent with the pursuit of profit.[14] Even the passionate liberal WT Stead, editor of the upmarket *Gazette* and founder of *The Review of Reviews*, was an early enthusiast for Empire and supporter of Rhodes's plans in Africa, describing himself as 'an imperialist plus the ten commandments and common sense'.[15]

As the noted historian Niall Ferguson points out, whatever its economic advantages or disadvantages, jingoist imperialism excited the British public: people who had never left the country's shores or heard a shot fired in anger developed 'an insatiable appetite for tales of military derring-do' in far-off places. As a source of entertainment – and psychological gratification – the Empire's importance to British morale in late Victorian times could hardly be exaggerated.[16]

Sceptics

Not all politicians and opinion-makers were as convinced of the virtues of imperialism as Britain's new Colonial Secretary, however. Prime Minister Salisbury was far more sceptical of his countrymen's true motives. 'If our ancestors had cared for the rights of other people', he declared, 'the British Empire would not have been made.' Its purpose was not to spread sweetness and light, but to increase Britain's wealth and power.[17] As the archetypal High Tory, Salisbury had no patience with the 'superficial philanthropy' of altruistic Liberals who advocated expansion for the betterment of mankind, and he scorned the likes of Rhodes, whose jingoism he considered to be a cloak for greed. In his view, any new territory was only worth acquiring or defending if it strengthened Britain's position both economically and strategically.

Of all Britain's imperial possessions besides Egypt, only two were regarded as being of critical importance: India, for its trading links and supply of manpower, and South Africa, a geographic expression rather than a country in the 1890s. The harbour at the Cape of Good Hope was, even after the opening of Suez, an important port of call and refuelling stop for shipping on its way to India. What made South Africa so much more attractive had been the discovery in 1886 of the richest goldfields in the world, in Paul Kruger's Transvaal. In the eyes of British politicians, a united South Africa – like Canada and Australia – could be a source of financial strength to the Empire, instead of a constant expense.[18] And southern Africa provided another glorious 'opportunity for the British race to go forth and multiply'[19] – its wealth as much as its numbers.

In March 1896, Chamberlain and his deputy, Lord Selborne, presented the Unionist cabinet with a memorandum on South Africa. The key to the future of the country, the pair asserted, was the Transvaal, 'the richest spot on earth'.[20] However, Britain's long-held hopes of creating a federal South Africa along Canadian and Australian lines was now under threat from leading European powers, and by internal (white) rivalries. To avoid the disastrous prospect of South Africa, like the United States, being lost to the Empire, firm action was needed to establish British supremacy in the region. The longer Kruger's SAR retained its stubborn independence, the greater the risk that the Crown colonies of the Cape and Natal could be attracted away from the Empire.[21] This would be a boost to rival European powers, vainly hoping that Britain's imperial possessions might dissolve into independent nation-states, thereby undermining her position as a world power.[22]

Although there was general agreement in the corridors of Whitehall on the imperial aim in South Africa, there was no consensus on strategy and timing. In essence, Britain had two options: either to extend Rhodes's policy of encircling Kruger's republic by gaining control of Delagoa Bay in Portuguese East Africa and cutting off the Transvaal's supply of weapons from Europe, or to increase the pressure on Kruger to enfranchise the numerous Uitlanders (foreigners), the potential 'Trojan horse in the kraal'.[23] The second alternative seemed more easily achievable than the first.

Speaking in the House of Commons in May 1896, Chamberlain tempered his own inclinations and urged a policy of restraint with these prescient words: 'A war in South Africa would be one of the most serious wars that could possibly be waged. It would be in the nature of a civil war. It would be a long war, a bitter war and a costly war ... it would leave behind it the embers of a strife which I believe generations would hardly be long enough to extinguish ... To go to war with President Kruger, to force upon him reforms in the internal affairs of his state, with which [we] have repudiated all right of interference – that would have been a course of action as immoral as it would have been unwise.'[24]

The right man

At the age of 43 – not much younger than Chamberlain himself – Sir Alfred Milner was just the sort of dedicated, disinterested administrator the Colonial Secretary was looking for. The two men were not close friends, but Chamberlain was appreciative of Milner's work in Egypt. He knew enough about him to realise that they had much in common – middle-class backgrounds, radical views on social reform and a passionate belief in expanding the Empire.[25]

When they met, Chamberlain first held out the position of under-secretary at the Colonial Office, but Milner – with designs on a posting abroad – declined. A few weeks later, on 18 January 1897, he was summoned again and tempted by an offer he could scarcely refuse – that of Governor of the Cape Colony and High Commissioner for Southern Africa, in succession to the ailing Lord Rosmead.[26] Milner had no hesitation this time. 'I'll do it', he replied.[27]

Since Rosmead, in Cape Town, was unaware of these machinations, Chamberlain insisted on strict secrecy until the approval of Lord Salisbury and his senior colleagues had been given. Unexpected opposition came from Harcourt's 'sour-visaged' (Milner's words) successor as Chancellor, Sir Michael Hicks Beach, who was aggrieved at not being

consulted and initially withheld his consent.[28] Milner's exasperation –
and eagerness for change – was evident from the letter he wrote to
Hicks Beach, saying he would rather quit the Crown's service than
spend the best years of his life in a London office: 'I may be wanted, but
to speak quite frankly, I cannot be kept – for any great length of time.'[29]
Hicks Beach took the point and conceded gracefully.

On 15 February 1897, Milner's appointment was officially announced, and three days later he was summoned to Windsor to kiss the
hands of Queen Victoria. His elevation to high imperial rank was greeted with approval on both sides of the political divide. In the *Gazette*,
Stead commented: 'A man with a better judgement, a leveller head, or a
kinder heart you will not find easily in a long day's march.'[30]

Milner was showered with 'a hailstorm' of celebratory lunches and
dinners, most notable among them a banquet attended by no fewer than 16 former presidents of the Oxford Union – 11 of them from
Balliol. Asquith led the acclamation, saying of Milner, 'No appointment of our time has been received with a larger measure both of the
approbation of experienced men and of the applause of the public[31] ...
We know that he takes with him as clear an intellect, and as sympathetic
an imagination, and if the need should arise, a power of resolution as
tenacious and as inflexible as belong to any man of our acquaintance.'[32]

Also present at the dinner was Chamberlain, who, during what Milner described as a 'rather bellicose' speech clearly aimed at Pretoria,
declared that it was up to the Transvaal to extend the hand of friendship, as the British had done to the Dutch in the Cape and Natal, as well
as 'to the large number of foreigners who had contributed so largely to
the success and prosperity of the state'. While Britain had no intention
or desire to interfere with the independence of the Boer republics, she
was determined to maintain her rights as 'the paramount power' in
South Africa.[33]

In a more conciliatory reply to Chamberlain's toast, Milner said
that 'being cursed with a cross-bench [non-partisan] mind', he understood the arguments of those who questioned the possibility or
desirability of greater imperial unity, yet it was the one issue 'upon
which I have never been able to see the other side[34] ... We should
maintain religiously the ties which exist, seize every opportunity of

developing new ones, spare no effort to remove misunderstanding and mistrust … It is a great privilege to be allowed to call oneself "a civilian-soldier" of the Empire.'[35]

Despite his cross-bench inclinations, and perhaps as a result of his upbringing, Britain's new envoy also had a self-confessed loathing of compromise.

That Milner was aware of the magnitude of the challenge facing him was evident from his letter to an old friend, the Rev MG Glazebrook: 'I shall know so much better what the chances are when I have been out there for six months. It is an *awful* job, though I never hesitated when asked to undertake it, and without the favour of the High Gods it cannot be successfully dealt with. Shall I have that?' he wondered rhetorically.[36]

Making preparations

Milner still had one important task to perform before his departure from Inland Revenue – preparing Hicks Beach's first budget, which was duly presented in the House of Commons in March 1897 without arousing much opposition. As Chamberlain's new appointee, he also had to familiarise himself with the workings of the Colonial Office, meet a wide cross-section of influential politicians, investors and journalists interested in South Africa and select the key members of his staff. As his military secretary, he chose Major John Hanbury-Williams, mentioned in dispatches for his role in the Anglo-Egyptian hostilities in 1892, and as private secretary Osmund (Ozzy) Walrond, who was to serve him loyally for the next seven years. Since Milner had no spouse, Mrs Hanbury-Williams was deputed to act as his official hostess.

Milner also took great care to define his relationship with an important official in Pretoria, Conyngham Greene, an Oxford-educated career diplomat of similar age who had served at The Hague and spoke fluent Dutch.[37] The no-nonsense Greene's appointment to the key post of British Agent in Pretoria in late 1896 was an indication of Chamberlain's hardening approach to Kruger. Milner saw to it that the Agent would send all confidential reports to the Colonial Secretary in London 'under flying seal to the High Commissioner', who could append his own comments if necessary. He was insistent on having the authority to summon Greene and instruct him to communicate – by interview or letter – with the President of the SAR.[38]

Conscious of his need for support from London's leading news-papers – the public's only semi-reliable source of foreign news – Milner made sure that he burnished his links with journalism. At the Conser-vative-supporting *The Times*, the most influential of the dailies, he had good friends in Moberly Bell, the manager, and George Buckle, the editor. Among his former colleagues at the *Gazette* had been Edmund Garrett, now editor of the pro-Rhodes *Cape Times*, and ET Cook, editor of the influential Liberal organ, the *Daily News*. Another friend, EB Iwan-Muller, was a leader writer on *The Daily Telegraph*, while JA Spender was editor of the Liberal-inclined *Westminster Gazette*. In the middle market, Milner could count on the strident backing of Harmsworth's *Daily Mail*, as well as the support of the Imperial South African Association – destined to become a crucial voice in anti-Boer propaganda campaigns.[39]

During his regular visits to the Colonial Office, Milner found of-ficials there in 'a great fluster' over the South African question. A day after his appointment was announced, the postponed parliamentary committee of inquiry (or 'Committee of No Inquiry', as it was dubbed) into the Jameson Raid held its opening public session. Hoping to dis-tract attention from the proceedings, the wily Chamberlain had sent Kruger a stiff message of protest over the Transvaal's alleged infringe-ments of the suzerainty clause in the London Convention of 1884 – entered into three years after the first Anglo-Boer War – which had imposed an ill-defined curb on the Boer republic's freedom of action in its international relationships.

After the Jameson Raid, Kruger had alarmed Chamberlain by forg-ing, without consultation, a defensive alliance with the Orange Free State, and by using gold revenues to steadily build up the republic's stock of armaments.[40] Clause IV of the London Convention clearly stated, however, that the SAR 'will conclude no treaty or engagement with any other state or nation *other than the Orange Free State*' (author's emphasis; see Chapter 6). To further heighten Britain's concern, the wily Transvaal President had also been making friendly overtures to the Germans, already active in South West Africa and East Africa.[41] Despite Hicks Beach's reluctance to spend money unnecessarily, the War Office quietly took the precaution of increasing British troop numbers in South Africa to some 8 000.

Besides Chamberlain, the central figure at the parliamentary inquiry was the instigator of the Jameson Raid, Cecil Rhodes, now one of the richest businessmen in the world, who had succeeded in adding African territories the size of Western Europe to the British Empire. The fallout from the Jameson Raid had forced Rhodes to resign as premier of the Cape Colony and chairman of the BSAC. For most of 1896, he had tried to talk Chamberlain out of launching a parliamentary investigation from which both men had much to lose. When the Colonial Secretary pointed out that he was obliged to hold an inquiry, Rhodes resorted to blackmail, threatening to reveal the existence of incriminating, hitherto undisclosed telegrams in the hands of his solicitor, Bourchier Hawksley. But Chamberlain, for his part, had an even stronger hand – the power to strip Rhodes's BSAC of its royal charter. Each man, therefore, had sound reason to cover his tracks and go easy on the other.

Chamberlain's means of keeping his nose clean was to lumber the parliamentary select committee with an ineffectual chairman and to carefully choose its members, the majority being leading pro-imperial MPs from the two main parties, including Harcourt, War Secretary Henry Campbell-Bannerman, Hicks Beach and the Rhodes-supporting Tory MP George Wyndham. The tenth member of the panel – to keep an eye on the witnesses – was none other than Chamberlain himself.[42]

This loaded panel allowed most of the leading participants, especially Rhodes, to evade any awkward questions about the involvement of the Colonial Office, and no member requested sight of the critical cable traffic that would have established Chamberlain's complicity in the pre-Raid build-up. Rhodes, incredibly, was allowed to plead at the inquiry that he could not incriminate third parties.[43] As Rotberg records, an 'inability to remember, refusals to talk about the doings of others, clever but uninformative ripostes, gibes, parryings, and partial replies were the accomplishment of nearly six months of testimony'.[44]

Little wonder the inquiry was called by its critics the 'Lying in State at Westminster'.

Chamberlain had also taken advantage of the public's indignation, fuelled by the popular press, over Kaiser Wilhelm II's mischievous and provocative telegram of congratulation to Kruger, sent on behalf of 'friendly powers', for having thwarted the Raid.[45] (Robert Massie gives a gripping account of the effect of the Kaiser's telegram on relations between Britain and Germany, concluding that the Jameson Raid and the telegram led directly to the naval rivalry and arms race that culminated in the Great War.[46]) The young and impulsive Kaiser's message had been calculated to annoy Lord Salisbury and his government, as well as Wilhelm's elderly grandmother, Queen Victoria. When the telegram was published in *The Times* of 4 January 1896, it aroused a wave of resentment in Britain that overshadowed Jameson's folly. The incorrigible Colonial Secretary, sensing an opportunity to shift the public mood in his favour, urged Salisbury to make some bold gesture that would 'soothe the wounded vanity of the nation'. 'It does not much matter which of our numerous foes we defy', Chamberlain declared, 'but we ought to defy someone.'[47]

Scrambling to settle his affairs before leaving London, Milner watched the select committee's proceedings with apprehension. 'What is the use', he asked his old boss, Harcourt, plaintively, 'of sending me out with a penny squirt [a few extra troops] to try to extinguish the raging fire in South Africa, if the great and wise at home are going to pour gallons of oil upon it all the time?'[48] Among those with whom Milner held last-minute discussions were Chamberlain and Selborne, several of the star witnesses at the inquiry (including a long session with Rhodes), Lord Loch, a former High Commissioner for Southern Africa, prominent British and South African 'gold bugs' and his younger friend Edmund Garrett, on a visit to London from the Cape for health reasons.[49]

To avoid any fanfare – and lurking reporters – early on the morning of 17 April 1897, Milner slipped away from Waterloo station to Southampton, where he boarded the SS *Norham Castle* bound for Cape Town. Besides numerous official papers, his reading material included a new biography of Jowett, Olive Schreiner's *The Story of an African*

Farm, Todd's ('heavy as lead') *Parliamentary Government in the British Colonies,* Sir CP Lucas's *History of South Africa* ('I think very good'[50]) and, intriguingly, a copy of Machiavelli's *The Prince,* the celebrated primer on the art of political expediency.[51]

CHAPTER 6

Playing Himself In
1897–1898

Milner was a poor sailor and spent most of a storm-tossed, 17-day voyage to the Cape immersed in his books and papers and taking lessons in Dutch. From Madeira, he sent a long missive to Selborne, urging him to hold the War Office to its decision to send three artillery batteries and an infantry regiment to South Africa to be deployed at key points such as the Laing's Nek pass in Natal. A Boer incursion into the Cape Colony could be risked, Milner reckoned, but what ought never to be chanced was being turned out of Natal: 'Just think of the effect of that, not only in South Africa, but throughout the Empire.'[1] To his imperialist friend George Parkin, now a private school headmaster in Canada, Milner wrote, 'My life has been greatly influenced by your ideas, and in my new post I shall feel more than ever the need of your enthusiasm and broad view of the Imperial future ... South Africa is just now the weakest link in the Imperial chain, and I am conscious of the tremendous responsibility which rests upon the man who is called upon to prevent it from snapping.'[2]

The *Norham Castle* reached the Cape on 5 May 1897. Milner's diary records: 'After a very rough night the sea was calmer as we approached Cape Town and the view of Table Bay and Mountain was very beautiful. Whales, porpoises and all sorts of birds in abundance as we approached the shore. We anchored about 2 [pm] and Sir Gordon Sprigg [Prime Minister of the Cape Colony] and several others came on board. Landed at 3 and travelled to Government House to take the Oath. Address presented on the way. I had a magnificent reception.'[3]

Sir James Rose Innes, a future Chief Justice of the Union of South Africa, recorded his first impression of Milner as having 'a friendly smile and a pleasant manner, in appearance a scholar rather than a man of

action, but with an air of grave assurance which indicated fixity of purpose, a man more apt to give than to take advice. Certainly a Governor
of a different type and in a different class from either of his predecessors.'[4] As they walked down Parliament Street after the ceremony, his
colleague John X Merriman remarked percipiently: 'Mark my words,
we shall have to have a rough and tumble with that fellow.'[5]

Milner's first few weeks were taken up with a round of official
functions, receptions, dinners and attendances at race meetings and
cricket matches, at which he was introduced to the leading citizens of
'the Colony'. His outwardly gentle and charming manner, and his ac-
cessibility, concealed a deep dislike for these social activities. Writing
privately to one of his pen friends, as he did regularly and at length,
he let off steam: 'Socially it is the most detestable sort of life you can
imagine, and I should not stay 6 months so utterly do I hate it – if I did
not think it a public duty.'[6]

His new posting had other consolations, nonetheless: daily horse
or bicycle rides in the early morning, which gave him the physical
exercise he needed to offset the long hours spent at his desk. A keen
swimmer, rower and cyclist who, despite his fragile health, believed that
regular exercise was essential to his well-being, he would often walk
along the slopes of Table Mountain in the company of his colleagues
Ozzy Walrond and Lionel Curtis or visiting friends.[7] And the Hanbury-
Williams couple had proved to be an inspired choice. Milner recorded:
'I have a thoroughly good Military Secretary ... and his wife is a perfect
trump. She is more popular than any Governor's wife has been, and fills
her most difficult post to my constant admiration.'[8]

Cape politics

The Cape Colony at this time lay at the heart of Britain's imperial project in South Africa, so Milner's most immediate task was to get to grips
with its politics. From 1872, the Cape had been a self-governing colony,
with an elected assembly similar to those in the Australian states and
Canadian provinces.[9] As Governor, Milner was the Queen's representative only, and obliged to act on the advice of Cape ministers, whereas
as High Commissioner for Southern Africa he had to implement the
policies of the British government.[10]

Cecil John Rhodes. *(Wikimedia Commons/Alexander Bassano)*

Since the Jameson Raid, political opinion in the Cape had become sharply polarised between the more numerous 'Dutch' (or Afrikaners) and the pro-British colonists. In Parliament, the Progressive Party – led by the uninspiring Sir Gordon Sprigg but still financed by Rhodes despite his resignation as premier – held a narrow majority over an opposition consisting mainly of supporters of the Afrikaner Bond.[11]

Before the Raid, Rhodes had achieved political power in the Colony by assiduously wooing the Bond, the largest party in the Cape Parliament, headed from outside the legislature by the father-figure of local Afrikanerdom, Jan Hendrik Hofmeyr, known to all as 'Onze Jan' (Our Jan). The Rhodes-Bond coalition had given the Cape six years of strong and stable government,[12] but Jameson's foolhardiness had brought Rhodes's term as prime minister to a sudden and ignominious end. Although no longer formally in office, the Bond remained the effective 'arbiter of power' in the Colony and its loyalty was thus a matter of crucial importance to the new Governor.[13]

Founded in 1880 at Hopetown and at two other towns in the Cape as a kind of guild or pressure group, the Afrikaner Bond held its first congress at Graaff-Reinet in 1882. The Bond's early aim was bring about a united South Africa under the Dutch-Afrikaner flag. Yet Rhodes had skilfully drawn the movement onto his side by backing Hofmeyr's efforts to contain the black franchise in the Cape, restrict certain competitive imports from Britain, and recognise the equality of the Dutch and English languages. Persuaded of Rhodes's good intentions, Onze Jan undertook to work with the Englishman towards the eventual unification of the country under the British flag, on condition that the Cape Colony retained its dominant position in South Africa.[14] Though broadly sympathetic to their fellow-Afrikaners in the Boer republics, Hofmeyr and the Bond were fed up with Paul Kruger for imposing heavy rail tariffs on Cape goods and for his refusal to form a customs union after the discovery of gold on the Witwatersrand.[15]

Back in 1889, Rhodes had founded the BSAC, which in due course was given a royal charter by Chamberlain to develop 'Zambezia' (Mashonaland and Bechuanaland) as a key step in the Colossus's strategy of advancing Britain's interests in southern Africa and surrounding Kruger's republic in the west and north. While premier of the Cape,

Rhodes's undeclared aim had always been the eventual overthrow of
Kruger, but in the interim he had a tacit understanding with the Bond
that he would not act on matters of concern to Afrikaners without first
consulting Hofmeyr.

Among other Cape Afrikaners seduced by Rhodes was an ambitious young lawyer, Jan Smuts, recently returned from a brilliant
academic career at Cambridge. 'The Dutch set aside all considerations
of blood and nationality', Smuts wrote, 'and loved and trusted [Rhodes]
and served him because they believed he was the man to carry out the
great idea of an internally sovereign and united South Africa, in which
the white race would be supreme … the cry of our forefathers as it is
our cry today … With the exception of a very small minority the whole
Dutch people in the Cape Colony shared this faith in and admiration
for Mr Rhodes.'[16]

The Jameson Raid brought home to Cape Afrikaners how misplaced their faith in the devious Rhodes had been. Making matters
worse was Rhodes's flat refusal to apologise for the Raid. Hofmeyr felt
personally betrayed by an Englishman he had always trusted, while
Smuts, who had supported Rhodes from public platforms, was so disillusioned that he abandoned the Cape for the Transvaal to join Kruger's
ranks, thereby forfeiting his British citizenship. As premier, Rhodes
was succeeded by the aforementioned Sprigg, a pro-imperialist farmer
from the eastern Cape, whose tenure in office depended on the
'lukewarm and reluctant' support of the Bond, now led by the former
Attorney General, WP Schreiner.[17]

The Boer republics

To the north, beyond Britain's – and Governor Milner's – jurisdiction,
lay the Boer republics of the Transvaal and Orange Free State. Less
than two decades earlier, Britain and Kruger's SAR had fought a short
war over Boer independence. British policy was aimed at creating a
federation along Canadian lines, and the Colonial Secretary, Lord
Carnarvon, had coerced a weak, near bankrupt Transvaal into accepting British paramountcy by sending Sir Theophilus Shepstone up
from Natal in January 1877 to annex the Boer republic to the British
Crown.

Shepstone's intervention met with little resistance. As the visiting English novelist Anthony Trollope recorded, 'I visited the Transvaal in 1877. The Boers had not congregated even for defence. No taxes had been paid for many months. The mail service was all but discontinued. Property had become worthless. Education had fallen lower and lower. My conviction is that had the English not interfered, European supremacy throughout a large portion of South Africa would have been endangered. I think the annexation was an imperative duty.'[18]

To save face, President Thomas Burgers recorded his formal protest at the annexation, but even Paul Kruger reluctantly accepted office under Shepstone and became a paid member of his Executive Council. The error the British made, however, was not to act on Shepstone's advice to convene the Volksraad (legislature) immediately and have the annexation formally ratified.[19]

It did not take long for the Boers to resent the high-handed attitude of the British High Commissioner, Sir Bartle Frere, and become impatient with imperial rule. Urged on by Burgers' successor, the much tougher-minded Kruger, Boer self-confidence began to reassert itself after British redcoats had put down the threat from the Zulu in the aftermath of their humiliation at Isandlwana in January 1879. Kruger eventually led two deputations to London to complain about the annexation, though without success, after which the Boers began to realise that passive resistance was useless.

In the early 1880s, the Transvalers took up arms against the British in a series of skirmishes, mainly along the Drakensberg escarpment. The conflict never developed into a full-scale war because Gladstone's new Liberal government, preoccupied by its problems in Egypt, Sudan and Ireland, was reluctant to commit more troops to a distant military campaign that promised to be costly, protracted and of little material benefit.

After a British force under General Sir George Colley had been shot to pieces by Boer marksmen during a clash at Majuba Hill in Natal in February 1881, a truce was declared, and after three months the short war for Transvaal independence was officially over. However, because it left a scar on Britain's national honour, Majuba acquired great symbolic importance: 'Remember Majuba' became the rallying cry for

British troops when they went into the field against the Boers in 1899.[20]

Under the Pretoria Convention of August 1881, Britain agreed to reinstate the independence of the Transvaal, subject to certain conditions: the Boers had to accept the Queen's nominal rule and concede control over external relations and 'the conduct of native affairs'. In 1884, the Pretoria Convention was superseded by the London Convention, which restored full self-government to the Boers, who insisted that suzerainty – a vague concept derived from the British occupation of India which gave the Crown control over the Transvaal's international dealings – was no longer applicable. In 1899, Chamberlain was to assert, however, that despite 15 years of official silence, the suzerainty clause was still enforceable.

In 1886, the discovery of gold on the Witwatersrand propelled the struggle for supremacy between Britain and the Boers into a new phase. As Lawrence James writes, it was the Transvaal's sudden transformation into the richest independent state in Africa that turned Boer nationalism from being a tiresome irritant to the British into a political and military force that had seriously to be reckoned with.[21]

While gold had been found before in distant parts of the Boer republic, the scale of the Witwatersrand deposits set off an economic revolution that altered the balance of power in southern Africa. Within 12 years, the revenues of the once almost insolvent Transvaal had multiplied 25 times, making it the world's leading gold producer and the economic focus of the subcontinent.[22] Gold also ended the paramountcy of the Cape as the region's leading domestic economy.

Massive new investment from the City of London enabled Kruger's republic to stock up on armaments and to build a railway from Pretoria to the port of Lourenço Marques (today Maputo) on Delagoa Bay, where a new harbour was soon under construction. Having direct access to the outside world at last, the Transvaal no longer needed to export its goods through British-controlled railways and seaports in the Cape and Natal.[23] And foreign fortune seekers, mostly from Britain, who became known as Uitlanders, poured into the SAR in their thousands.

As the historian Iain Smith observes, the Uitlanders were no monolithic body but a 'motley collection' of individuals of diverse nationalities, divided by class and disunited, many of them 'birds of passage' drawn to the Transvaal for a short time to make money on the mines before returning home.[24] Within a year after the discovery of gold in Johannesburg, the original mining camp of some 3 000 diggers had grown into a city of 100 000 inhabitants.[25] Not many of the new immigrants showed willingness to relinquish their foreign passports in order to become citizens of the SAR.

No one viewed the suddenly growing strength of the Transvaal republic with greater apprehension than the premier of the Cape, the arch-imperialist Rhodes, then at the peak of his power and influence. Kruger and his ruling Boer oligarchy in Pretoria were now a major impediment to the Colossus's dream of a British-ruled federation in southern Africa. After persuading the Afrikaners of the Cape that he was on their side, Rhodes began plotting secretly to overthrow their Transvaal compatriots by staging a coup d'état. A force assembled by the Rhodes's right-hand man, Dr Jameson, across the border in Bechuanaland would link up with pro-British elements in Johannesburg to overthrow Kruger and bring his republic under British control. What Rhodes, Jameson and company failed to comprehend, however, was that men rarely risk their lives or stage coups in the midst of a financial boom. Most Uitlanders, as well as their supporters in the mining industry, wanted the reform of Kruger's republic, not its violent overthrow.[26]

The misconceived Jameson Raid merely reinforced the Boers' belief that Britain was intent on using force to bring an end to their independence once again. Within two years, the Transvaal's military budget had increased fourfold and, without informing the British, Kruger had entered into a defensive alliance with President Marthinus Steyn of the neighbouring Orange Free State, as he was entitled to do in terms of the London Convention.[27]

Standing firm

The bitter recriminations from the Jameson Raid ensured that when Milner arrived at the Cape in 1897, relations between Britain and the Transvaal were almost at breaking point again. In late 1896, the Kruger government had begun implementing two contentious pieces of legislation, the Aliens Act and the Alien Expulsion Act, intended to check the influx of 'undesirable foreigners' into the SAR and secure the registration of those Uitlanders already there. Joseph Chamberlain chose to regard the 'Aliens legislation' as a deliberate breach of the London Convention and sent a strongly worded cable to Pretoria demanding its repeal. He also dispatched a British warship to patrol the waters off Delagoa Bay. Playing for time, Kruger had second thoughts and rescinded the legislation, thereby reinforcing Chamberlain's (and Milner's) belief that being tough on the Boers paid dividends.

Despite the Colonial Secretary's insistence on a strict adherence to the London Convention, his instructions to Milner – whether as Governor or High Commissioner – were to avoid giving unnecessary offence to the Transvaal republic.[28] While emphasising Britain's rights under the London Convention, Chamberlain wanted to avoid putting pressure on the Transvaal over 'less important grievances'. He was particularly concerned that the furious indignation of Cape Afrikaners at Rhodes's betrayal might drive them into the arms of Kruger. In any war, said Chamberlain, 'the Transvaal must be the aggressor, so that the Imperial government would have the support of the Dutch in the Colony'.[29] His other great fear was that another imperial war, in the year of Queen Victoria's jubilee, 'unless upon the utmost and clearest provocation', would be highly unpopular in political circles in Britain, besides requiring a large troop deployment that would cost the Exchequer millions.[30]

In June, Milner told his friend Albert Grey, a director of Rhodes's BSAC, that 'the Boers, as usual, give way a bit when they see we are in grim earnest, and will not defy us'.[31] To Chamberlain he reported that the Colonial Secretary's uncompromising stance had averted a war in South Africa, for 'within a fortnight of my arrival the Government of the SAR had made a distinct retreat'. Chamberlain reminded Milner that while they had agreed a year earlier that the elderly Kruger's rule could not go on indefinitely, 'patience' and a 'waiting game' were still the best way forward.[32]

As we shall see, the Colonial Secretary's instructions would be honoured more in the breach than in the observance.

CHAPTER 7

Widening Horizons
1897–1898

On 22 June 1897, mere weeks after Milner's arrival in South Africa, hundreds of thousands of Queen Victoria's loyal subjects lined the streets of London to celebrate the 60th anniversary of her accession to the throne. At the Spithead Review in the Solent, 164 warships of the Royal Navy were drawn up in four lines each five miles long, in the greatest display of sea power the world had ever seen. The Empire was at its zenith, and the publicity-canny Joseph Chamberlain had seized the opportunity to twin the Diamond Jubilee with a spectacular 'Festival of Britain' in order to celebrate the true crown jewels of Empire – the colonies and territories around the globe under the monarch's dominion. In one of history's strange quirks, at a state banquet before the celebrations began, Victoria was seated alongside the Austrian Archduke, Franz Ferdinand, whose assassination in 1914 was to lead to the First World War and hasten the end of several European empires, and in due course Britain's.

Shortly before leaving London for South Africa, Milner had met, over a lunch at a London club, with Rhodes and others present, a man who was to become among his greatest admirers and closest friends, the staunchly pro-imperial poet, novelist and journalist Rudyard Kipling.[1] After the Jubilee was over, *The Times* of 17 July carried, alongside Victoria's message of thanks to her people for their display of loyalty and affection, a poem by Kipling expressing his unease at the triumphalist tone of the revelries. The sombre-toned 'Recessional', one of his two celebrated poems of that year, the other being 'The White Man's Burden', was a cry from the heart for a more meek and penitent approach to Britain's imperial responsibilities. Its most famous and often-quoted stanza reads:

The tumult and the shouting dies;
The captains and the kings depart:
Still stands Thine ancient sacrifice,
An humble and a contrite heart.
Lord God of Hosts, be with us yet,
Lest we forget – lest we forget!

No one was more astounded by the poem's instant popularity than the poet himself, now acclaimed far and wide in imperial circles. Ten years later, on receiving an honorary doctorate at Cambridge University, Milner's like-minded friend was hailed in Latin as 'the poet laureate of our Navy, our soldiers, and the whole British Empire'.[2]

In far-off Cape Town, despite the Afrikaner Bond's anger over Rhodes's perfidy, Parliament gave enthusiastic support to festivities marking the Jubilee. Interrupting his efforts to get to know the Cape's leading politicians, the new Governor presided over several days of celebration, which included a service in St George's Cathedral, a massed children's choir on the lawns of Government House, a colourful multiracial procession down Adderley Street, entertainment for the naval contingent aboard three warships in Table Bay and a Royal Salute to the Queen by the guns of the Land Battery. Writing to Goschen afterwards, Milner reported that the Jubilee was 'an immense success here, but it nearly killed us all'.[3]

From London, Milner's correspondent Canon Glazebrook wrote to say that the only coverage of the Cape celebrations in British newspapers had been of Mrs Hanbury-Williams' kissing the cheeks of a little white girl and a little black girl, who had presented her with posies. In reply, Milner agreed rather cynically that the incident was the most important thing to have happened since his arrival – 'at least it has excited the greatest amount of general public interest and curiosity. I think she was right. Most white people think she was wrong. There you have the great S. African problem posed at once. It is the Native Question. The Anglo-Dutch friction is bad enough. But it is child's play compared with the antagonism of white and black.'[4]

Merriman

Of the Cape politicians whose measure Milner needed quickly to take, the most experienced and talented was the maverick, British-born immigrant John X Merriman, Rhodes's former ally and treasurer-general. After resigning from the government because of his distaste for the premier's business dealings, Merriman had also become a harsh critic of Jan Hofmeyr, whom he dubbed 'the Mole' for dictating the affairs of the Bond from outside Parliament. His relationship with Rhodes now irreparable after Jameson's escapade, Merriman had headed the Cape Parliament's inquiry into the Raid, from whose proceedings Rhodes had absented himself with the excuse of having to deal with an insurrection in Matabeleland.

In its findings, Merriman's panel was harshly critical of Rhodes for 'engaging in a conspiracy at odds with his position of prime minister', but could not prove the latter's direct responsibility for the Raid, so its report to Parliament had minimal impact. The pro-imperial *Cape Times* recorded derisively in its 'classifieds' section that the Select Committee on the Jameson Raid had given birth – 'to a mouse'.[5]

According to his biographer, Phyllis Lewsen, on meeting Milner for the first time Merriman detected a certain 'fanaticism' about the new Governor. This feeling became stronger during another 'long talk' between the two men a few weeks later, which left the veteran Cape politician with the impression of 'a very clever intellectual man, with a charming manner, but an official of officials, who profoundly distrusts and despises Parliament'. 'I gathered also that he is a strong Rhodes and anti-Transvaal man. He may yet end like Bartle [Frere] did ... a supreme pity, for a man of his mental acquirements ... might do so much.'[6]

At their meeting, Milner indicated his intention of putting unremitting pressure on the Transvaal to implement internal reforms. Merriman replied bluntly that such a policy would lead to war and the creation of 'another Ireland in South Africa'. To this prescient warning Milner paid no heed, writing Merriman off as 'a crank'.[7]

Merriman voiced his early misgivings about Milner to another of Rhodes's erstwhile political colleagues, WP Schreiner, brother of Olive, describing their early encounters as friendly and uncontroversial but nonetheless filling him with 'profound apprehension and uneasiness':

'Milner seems to me to be in absolute ignorance of the South African question and to be dominated by a steady and persistent hostility to the Transvaal ... He reverted more than once to the notion that a crisis must come in the Transvaal – that Kruger had done nothing to meet them ... I feel there is a sinister undercurrent. What do we know about Gt Britain's attitude to the Transvaal? Nothing! Yet Rhodes knows everything – and I feel that this is not the right position for a responsible government.'[8]

Going north

With Britain's responsibilities in the Transvaal still resting in the hands of Chamberlain, Milner requested the Colonial Secretary's permission to embark on an extensive programme of travel to familiarise himself with the interior of the Cape Colony, and visit distant British outposts at Kimberley, Gaberones, Bulawayo and Salisbury. Unlike a predecessor, Lord Loch, he promised not to take with him a large entourage, thus avoiding unnecessary expenditure.[9]

Writing privately to Dawkins, Milner said it would be 'idle to suppose that for years and years to come, if ever, we shall have any hold on [this] place beyond that which a strong garrison, a considerable squadron, and the clear intimation that we don't mean to stand more than a certain amount of insolence, will give us ... Half the white people in this Colony ... while owing a formal allegiance to Great Britain, are at heart fellow-citizens with the Free Staters and Transvaalers. As long as there is no friction between Great Britain and the Republics, they don't mind being British subjects. But the moment Great Britain and either of the Republics are at loggerheads, they side openly and vehemently with the latter.'[10]

In August, Milner set off on a month-long tour of Cape country districts by train, ox-cart, horseback and horse-drawn 'spider'.[11] The itinerary took him via the Karoo ('the air is brilliant and most bracing'), through areas 'with a sizeable Dutch population' to the 'English' centres of East London, King William's Town, Grahamstown and Port Elizabeth. At frequent stops along the way, and in every *dorp*, the Governor was presented with an address of welcome and had to make a short speech in reply. It was not a role he enjoyed playing.

Reporting to Lord Selborne on his trip, Milner said he had travelled through one of the most neglected parts of the colony, the extreme south, to which none of his predecessors had been for 40 years, if ever. He had gained a good idea of what the rural population was like and his reception had been extremely cordial. 'The impression I derived was that the country people are generally well affected – the English absolutely so, the Dutch quite disposed to be so if they were let alone. A great effort is, however, being made to work up Afrikander feeling ahead of the election next year. As the Dutch farmers are very ignorant, and only read papers which systematically mislead them, it is difficult to avoid false impressions ... I intend to be more movable than my predecessors.'[12]

Rhodesia

On 22 October 1897, the British High Commissioner boarded the first train to run from the Cape, via Kimberley and Mafeking, to Bulawayo. A subsidiary of the BSAC had extended the rail link from Mafeking and it was now possible for Milner to examine at first hand Rhodes's achievements in Rhodesia. In Kimberley, he visited the De Beers mine and was entertained by the board, though Rhodes himself was absent due to illness. 'De Beers people', Milner noted in his diary, 'were violent Rhodes-ites to a man – not his followers but his servants ... The company was magnificently organised ... a huge and unscrupulous monopoly, but giving munificent funds to public purposes,' with good native compounds and paying liberal wages. Prospects for profits were good for a long time to come.[13]

Reaching Bulawayo on 2 November, Milner presided over the formal opening of the new segment of the railway, and met for the first time the Governor of Natal, Sir Walter Hely-Hutchinson, present along with many other visitors from Britain, South Africa and other parts of the world. In his speech, Milner paid tribute to Rhodes as the prime mover in the construction of the Bechuanaland railway and the founding of Rhodesia. Although he did not defend all of Rhodes's methods – some of which had attracted strong criticism in Britain – 'now that authority had been firmly established, it would be a disgrace to the white man if the land were not [now] a better land to live in, even for the native races, than it was under their old savage rulers.' Already, the railway had saved thousands of people from starvation in drought-stricken districts, Milner said.[14]

The meandering route from Bulawayo to Salisbury by ox-cart and mule relays took Milner's party all of ten days. At Fort Victoria, a large indaba of 'quiet and well-behaved' but primitive tribesmen had gathered to greet the distinguished visitor.[15] At a public luncheon in Salisbury, he told his audience that he thought the development of Rhodesia might be 'the turning point of South Africa', but poured cold water on any expectations of 'immediate prosperity'.[16]

After a series of meetings with Sir William Milton, Rhodesia's acting administrator, Milner journeyed on to Umtali, where Dr Jameson called on him, and where he concluded discussions with Rhodes about a constitution for Rhodesia.[17] From Umtali, he headed east by train, through Portuguese territory to the seaport of Beira, from where he embarked on a 'very uncomfortable voyage' back to Cape Town.

In the course of a lengthy dispatch to Chamberlain, Milner set out his frank assessment of the situation in Rhodesia, where there was 'payable gold' – not in enormous quantities as in the Transvaal but sufficient 'to give the country a start in the next two to three years, if there is peace and decent government'.[18] The territory was going to be neither a fiasco nor a rapid success and was no El Dorado, but it ought gradually to be quite as rich as any in southern Africa, except for the Transvaal. 'And it did not have so much of the racial – Dutch-English – trouble as any of the others, less even than Natal.'[19]

His main concern was 'not to throw an impecunious undeveloped country bigger than France' onto the British Treasury, which would starve Rhodesia of funds. Additional money would be needed from the Chartered Company, and from Rhodes's private purse.[20] This, he predicted, might enable the British government to 'win the South African game all round' without having to pay the enormous cost of doing so.[21]

On the administrative question, Milner was severely critical of the BSAC, describing it as 'a bad story'.[22] On the one hand, land was alienated in the most reckless manner to companies and individuals, while on the other 'a lot of unfit people were allowed to exercise power … especially with regard to the natives, in a manner which cannot be defended'. He acknowledged, however, the great difficulty the company faced in finding enough capable people to run such a large and undeveloped territory and to exercise the necessarily 'wide powers' that were open to abuse.[23]

Corresponding with his former love interest, now Mrs Margot Asquith, Milner confessed that after his first few months in southern Africa, he was still far from having any decided views. 'I have great faith in the power we British have of worrying through almost any jungle, in a blundering way no doubt, by a kind of thick-witted tenacity & patience. So I dare say we shall come successfully through this S. African tangle which is the worst I have ever seen, much worse than people in England, who only think of the English-Dutch row & hardly at all of the much more difficult & complicated Native Question, have any idea of.'[24]

In London, WT Stead continued to sing Milner's praises in the *Gazette*. Since the new envoy had arrived in the Cape, 'everyone has felt that there is a man once more at the helm'. Now that Milner had had the time to exert his authority, 'we may confidently expect that things will go well in South Africa'. The High Commissioner was 'in his prime and, as he had never failed to score yet when it was his innings, we may confidently anticipate that when he leaves Cape Town, it will be for some still higher post in the Imperial Service'.[25]

Contrary to Stead's assertion that Milner was winning 'golden opinions from everyone' in the Cape, things were not going so swimmingly for the insular and introspective new Governor, who 'exuded a dauntingly patrician air'.[26] As he had done in Egypt, Milner limited his social circle in the colony to like-minded, pro-British partisans such as the ever-loyal Edmund Garrett and others.[27] He made little attempt to engage with Hofmeyr and the Afrikaner Bond, or with other leading members of society, and it did not take long for his distaste for Capetonians to become widely known. Catherine Knox quotes Milner as saying that one of his job's disadvantages was 'living among uncongenial people' and after three months he expressed his true feelings to a friend: 'Apart from the work the life here bores me to death. It is a hundred thousand times less amusing than Egypt … my only personal interest is in my English friends and my only amusement hearing from them.'[28]

When he complained to Marie Koopmans-De Wet, from a lead-ing Afrikaner family, that he had 'met no interesting or clever people out here', he was met with the retort that there were many interesting people among all nationalities in the Cape, if only he would make the effort to 'come in touch with them'.[29]

CHAPTER 8

Choosing Sides
1898

Paul Kruger's decisive victory in the Transvaal presidential election of February 1898 should not have come as a surprise to the British, but it did. The Jameson Raid had given Boer-Afrikaners ample cause to rally round their 72-year-old paterfamilias – for the fourth consecutive time. The fallout from the Raid had cut the ground from under the feet of Kruger's two opponents, Vice-President Piet Joubert, who had almost beaten him in the1893 poll, and the up-and-coming Progressive, Schalk Burger, chairman of an official commission that had recommended the abolition of the state dynamite monopoly on the grounds that both mine owners and the state would benefit thereby.[1] The poor timing of Chamberlain's dispatch, on the eve of the election, demanding that Britain's ill-defined suzerainty under the London Convention be upheld had merely added impetus to the Krugerites' cry of 'Beware of Rhodes and keep your powder dry'.[2]

The British had shared the hopes of Progressive Boers in the Transvaal and most of the mining industry that Joubert or Burger might triumph this time, but the scale of Kruger's victory – by more than the combined votes of his two opponents – helped to convince Milner, if not the Colonial Secretary, that time was no longer on Britain's side. By now, Milner had made up his mind that the independence of the SAR was incompatible with the interests of Britain, because the republic was the wellspring of Afrikaner nationalism in South Africa. And Afrikaner nationalism was Britain's real enemy.[3]

A triumphant Kruger had responded to his re-election by rejecting outright the reforms proposed by Burger's Industrial Commission and then dismissing his arch-foe, the reform-minded Chief Justice, John Kotze, a critic of the President who had political aspirations of his own. To Milner, these acts merely strengthened his conviction that the Transvaal government was incapable of, or had no intention of, reforming from within.

In a dispatch to Chamberlain for the public record, Milner set out a litany of complaints against the Kruger administration, chief among them the peremptory dismissal of Kotze and the extension of the dynamite monopoly. In a lengthier private letter, he expressed his true feelings: 'I am afraid that after a few months' respite, we are once more on the verge of serious trouble with the Boers ... There is no way out of the political troubles of S. Africa except reform in the Transvaal or war. And at present the chances of reform in the Transvaal are worse than ever ... Schalk Burger has proven a broken reed. Kruger has returned to power, more autocratic and more reactionary than ever ... He has immense sources of money and any amount of ammunitions of war, to which he is constantly adding. Politically, he has strengthened his hold on the Free State, and the Colonial Afrikanders continue to do obeisance before him.

'*Looking at the question from a purely S African point of view*, I should be inclined to work up to a crisis, not indeed by looking about for causes of complaint, or making a fuss about trifles, but by steadily and inflexibly pressing for the redress of substantial wrongs and injustices. It would not be difficult to work up an extremely strong *cumulative* case. It means that we shall have to fight, and to fight *more or less* at a moment chosen by the other side.'[4]

The more cautious Chamberlain remained unpersuaded, however. In replying to Milner, he reminded him that 'the principal object of HM Government in S. Africa at present is peace. Nothing but the most flagrant offence would justify the use of force.'[5] A letter to Milner from Under-Secretary Selborne followed shortly after, setting out 'in the clearest manner' the limits beyond which he should not go. 'Peace is undoubtedly the first interest to South Africa ... Our object is the future combination of South Africa under the Union Jack ... We all feel that, if by the evolution of events this combination can be achieved without a rupture or war of any sort between the two white races in South Africa, it will have a more durable and valuable result than it would have if the same result were achieved by war.'[6]

Chamberlain also wrote confidentially to Milner to say that he

Paul Kruger, President of the South African Republic. (*War Museum of the Boer Republics, Bloemfontein*)

saw no reason to alter the 'no-war' policy upon which they had jointly agreed before the latter left England. The same considerations still applied: 'We must endure a great deal rather than provoke a conflict.' A war would be greatly resented by British subjects in the Cape Colony and in Britain itself.[7] Among additional reasons the Colonial Secretary advanced in support of a policy of 'reserve and delay' were Britain's 'serious difficulties' with France, Russia and Germany, and other imperial operations requiring more troops in the Sudan and on the northwest frontier of India.[8]

Thus rebuffed, Milner had no choice but to obey orders. He wrote back to Chamberlain: 'You may rely on me not to do anything to render the situation more acute ... When we are once more in quieter waters, it will be for Her Majesty's Government to consider whether we ought to acquiesce permanently in the situation of having a strong and bitter enemy for ever on our flank, only waiting for the occasion of our being definitely involved elsewhere in order to fly at our throats. For the present time there is no more to be said on that subject. I know where I am and shall act accordingly.'[9]

If the headstrong High Commissioner felt constrained by the order not to deliberately stir up trouble in the Transvaal, he was not going to be similarly inhibited in his role as Governor of the Cape. Intolerant even of the opinions of moderate Afrikaners such as Hofmeyr and the Chief Justice, Henry de Villiers, Milner pressed ahead on the assumption that those not obviously for him must be against him.[10]

Sheep and goats

Milner's state of mind as early as February 1898 may be gleaned from two revealing letters he wrote at the time. To the Governor of Natal, Hely-Hutchinson, he expressed strong disapproval of the Natal premier Sir Henry Binns's routine message of congratulation (sent for diplomatic and commercial reasons) to Kruger on his re-election, stating bluntly that 'there has got to be a separation of the sheep from the goats in this sub-continent, by which I don't mean the English and the Dutch, but those who disapprove and are not afraid to show their disapproval of the present dishonest despotism at Pretoria, and those who either admire or truckle to it.'[11]

And to a female friend in London, after Kipling had renewed their acquaintance in Cape Town, Milner confided, 'I am very glad he saw through that utter imposture, the simple-minded Boer patriot, dear to the imagination of British Radicals. Not that I want to run down the Dutchman, still less join the vulgar outcry raised against him by the least estimable section of the English out here. The Boer has his strong points, but the *political Boer* is an awful humbug, for ever crying out that he is being oppressed and plotted against, where as a matter of fact he has got his foot well planted on the necks of his neighbours and means to trample them as long as he can.'[12]

A regular visitor to the Cape in summer despite his aversion to 'the Dutch', Kipling held similar views to those of Milner, whom he held in high esteem. Both staunch imperialists, disdainful of politics and politicians, he and Milner were birds of a feather whose lifelong friendship had its roots in colonial South Africa.

Graaff-Reinet

Milner's limited knowledge of conditions in Kruger's Boer republic was derived from his earlier briefings from the Colonial Office, the opinion he had formed of the Cape's Afrikaner population and regular reports from officials such as Conyngham Greene, the British Agent in Pretoria. Despite the anti-English sentiment engendered by the Jameson Raid, if Britain's new High Commissioner had really wished to take the Boers' temperature, he could easily have found a pretext to visit the Transvaal, and it was telling that he chose not to do so. Although professing to have similar pacific aims to Chamberlain, it was already apparent the two did not see eye to eye on tactics. Milner was in favour of bringing the dispute with the Transvaal to a head, while Chamberlain (and Selborne) wished to proceed more slowly.[13]

On 3 March 1898, Governor Milner took himself off by train to Graaff-Reinet, in the Karoo, to open a new branch of the Cape-to-Kimberley railway line, and to make his first deliberately controversial speech since arriving in South Africa. He was the first dignitary to travel along the new 150 km track from Middelburg to Graaff-Reinet, a journey that still took several hours.[14] On arrival in Graaff-Reinet, he was taken aback when presented with an address by the local chapter of the

Afrikaner Bond, whose members wished to affirm their loyalty to the Empire and reject the doubts cast on the Bond by the recently formed, pro-imperialist South African League. Some last-minute alterations had to be made to his carefully worded, 35-minute address, delivered in the town's Market Hall that evening.

Many Cape Afrikaners had been deeply affronted by the insinuation that they were disloyal to the British Crown. The Bond, they pointed out, had always shown its respect for the monarch and expressed appreciation for the protection of the Cape coast by the Royal Navy. Out of courtesy, Cape members had sent a telegram of congratulation to Kruger on his re-election, as Binns had done in English-speaking Natal, but that message had helped to convince Milner that the Bond's sympathies were Afrikaner-republican and were to be regarded with suspicion and mistrust.[15]

Replying directly to the Bond's address after dinner, Milner told his predominantly Afrikaner audience that he was pleased to be assured of their loyalty to the Crown but would have preferred to take that for granted: 'Why should I not? What reason could there be for disloyalty? You have thriven wonderfully well … The progress in material wealth is enormous, and the prospects of future progress are greater still; and you have other blessings which by no means always accompany material wealth … a free system of government, an independent judiciary and court system and – between the white races … perfect equality of citizenship.

'Well, gentlemen, of course you are loyal. It would be monstrous if you were not.'[16]

While he believed the great majority in the Cape Colony – English and Dutch – were loyal, the Governor continued, some assumed that Britain has 'some occult design on the independence of the Transvaal … and is seeking causes of quarrel in order to take that independence away'.[17] That assumption was the 'exact opposite of the truth'. It was not the aggressiveness of the British government, but the 'unprogressiveness, I will not say the retrogressiveness, of the government of the Transvaal' which kept up the 'spirit of unrest in South Africa'.[18] Some in the Cape seemed to think that if they could only impress upon the British government that in a war with the Transvaal, Britain might find a great number of her own subjects on the side of Kruger, this would prevent such a calamity.[19] Milner went on:

> Now I wish to be perfectly fair. Therefore, let me say that this suspicion [of the British government], though groundless, is not, after all that has happened, altogether unnatural. But those who wish to preserve the South African Republic and promote good relations between it and the British colonies and Government should use all their influence ... not to encourage the Transvaal in its obstinate resistance to all reform, but to induce it to bring 'the temper and spirit of its administration' into line with the other free communities of South Africa, such as this colony or the Orange Free State. That is the direction in which a peaceful way out of these inveterate troubles, which have now plagued this country for more than 30 years, is to be found.[20]

In the judgement of Iain Smith, writing in 1996, Milner's address in Graaff-Reinet that evening was a clear and premeditated warning to Cape Afrikaners sympathetic to Kruger, and his words 'exuded menace'. For the first time, a representative of the British government had come down off the fence and hinted publicly, even if obliquely, at the possibility of war between Britain and the Transvaal. The speech was interpreted as the Governor's personal manifesto and its impact was electrifying: every colonist had in effect been asked to choose sides 'in a forthcoming struggle between Britain and the Boers for supremacy'.[21] In Pretoria, Kruger told his executive that Milner reminded him of Sir Bartle Frere, who had precipitated the war in 1880–1881.[22]

Reflecting afterwards, in a letter to his friend Bertha Synge, that his speech had made 'an immense sensation locally – and rather deserved to – as it was an awful show-up of greasy humbugs',[23] Milner forwarded a copy to the Colonial Office, admitting that one of its purposes had been to give the British community 'something to cheer them up, while at the same time dividing the extremists from the moderates in the Afrikaner Bond'.[24]

Three weeks after returning from Graaff-Reinet, Milner wrote again to Synge: 'I am 44 today – more's the pity – I keep perversely

well. Why I should do so, with such incessant, disgusting work, and no
fun at all, it is hard to explain … I am off to Basutoland [Lesotho] next
week which everybody says is both beautiful and bracing. And it will be
rather amusing to study the wild and wily Basuto on his native mountains. We are going to *ride* – no more Cape carts or mule-drawn coaches
for me … thank you.'[25]

Milner spent most of April in Basutoland, whose relations with
the neighbouring Orange Free State were the cause of frequent dispute. Letting his hair down in a private letter to a friend, he described
the Crown protectorate as 'a real Native Reserve, where the European
hardly comes except in the harmless shape of a High Commissioner or
other official, and Nature is still boundless, and the aborigines still pic-
turesque. Needless to say, colonial civilisers are anxious to make an end
of it … It is all very amusing, and, thanks largely to the mountain air
and the novelty of everything, very exhilarating, and for the last week
I have enjoyed myself for the first time in this beastly year that I have
spent in South Africa.'[26]

On his way to Maseru, Milner had stopped off in Bloemfontein,
where he was cordially welcomed by President Steyn, with whom he
had a long talk, and by 'perhaps the most influential man in the State',
Abraham Fischer, a long-standing member of the executive.[27] At a
banquet that night, Milner referred to his efforts to acquire a working knowledge of the 'Taal' and said it was of vital importance that
every resident in the country should know both Dutch and English.
Steyn wrote afterwards to say that 'Sir Alfred's visit had done a great
deal of good', but he wished his travels could have been extended to
the Transvaal, which would enable him 'to understand the peculiar
difficulties under which President Kruger labours'.[28]

Go-between

Before leaving for Graaff-Reinet, Milner had formed his first significant association with a born-and-bred South African. He was Percy
FitzPatrick, the son of an Irish judge of the Cape Supreme Court, who
had been at a prep school in England and matriculated in Grahamstown. After a chequered career as a bank clerk, transport rider, gold
digger and journalist, FitzPatrick had become head of intelligence

at the mining house Wernher, Beit/H Eckstein & Co in Johannes-burg. His pro-imperialist beliefs and Uitlander sympathies had led to his appointment as secretary of the pro-Uitlander Johannesburg Reform Committee at the time of the Jameson Raid – and his subse-quent disbarment from any political activity for the following three years. (FitzPatrick would later become famous as the author of *The Transvaal from Within* and *Jock of the Bushveld*, both of which received international acclaim.)

On holiday at Muizenberg in February 1898, but worried about the deteriorating political climate in the Transvaal, FitzPatrick – a keen cyclist – mounted his bicycle one evening and rode over to Milner's residence at Newlands House in the hope of meeting the High Com-missioner. He arrived shortly before dinner. Not having come across many Transvalers before, Milner greeted his visitor with unusual warmth, and the two men struck up an instant rapport. Before leav-ing to attend a formal dinner, the Governor plied FitzPatrick with questions, insisting that he should return around 10 pm so that their conversation could continue. After Milner left, FitzPatrick amused himself by riding towards Constantia in a fruitless search for something to eat. When Milner returned, the two men talked 'under the oaks' until the early hours of the morning, when a famished Fitzpatrick re-mounted his bicycle and rode the almost 20 km back to Muizenberg as the dawn was breaking.[29]

Exhilarated by the meeting, FitzPatrick made an extensive note of their conversation: 'Milner wanted to know *everything* and was very frank in return.'[30] Both men were critical of Chamberlain's policy in respect of the Transvaal. FitzPatrick told Milner that he did not see the point of the British government giving the Transvaal a prod every now and then, because this merely irritated the Boers, who took it out on the Uitlanders. Unless the British government was determined to see 'the whole thing' settled, it was better not to meddle. Milner agreed that Britain should build up a 'cumulative case' against Kruger's government, to be presented when a suitable opportunity arose.[31]

When FitzPatrick expressed the fear of many Uitlanders that hav-ing worked up to a situation in which a settlement in the Transvaal might be imposed by the British government, they might once again be left in the lurch, Milner said firmly he would not let that happen. And when FitzPatrick voiced his doubts that the Transvaal government would yield to pressure, Milner responded by saying, 'There is only one possible settlement – war. It has got to come.'[32]

For FitzPatrick, ten years younger than Milner, the meeting was a life-changing experience; it was not only the beginning of a long and close friendship but also gave the excited FitzPatrick the sense that the future of southern Africa 'hinged upon the exchange of views that had taken place at their meeting'.[33] The relationship that resulted was never one of equals but was valued by two men who both had an interest in politics, despite being critical of politicians, and who shared the same assumptions regarding the solution to southern Africa's difficulties.[34] For the rest of his life, a star-struck FitzPatrick regarded Milner as his role model and political mentor.[35]

The wider significance of the Milner-FitzPatrick encounter, however, was the important link it established between the High Commission, the Uitlanders and the mining industry. Over the next 18 months, FitzPatrick was to throw his weight behind Milner's strategy of encouraging and exploiting Uitlander agitation to hasten the British government's intervention in the internal affairs of the Transvaal – in order to accelerate the outbreak of the Anglo-Boer War.

CHAPTER 9

The Rhodes Factor
1898–1899

Only two years after resigning the premiership of the Cape in ignominy, Rhodes was back in the thick of the colony's politics, as unapologetic as ever and determined to reassert his authority over the Cape Parliament. Actively encouraged by the editor of the *Cape Times*, Edmund Garrett, he poured money into the coffers of the Progressive Party, headed nominally by the 'eternal stopgap', Sprigg,[1] who had forfeited the support of the Bond because of his antipathy to Kruger, and clung to office only because of Rhodes's backing.

The Progressive movement in the Cape had originated a few years earlier as an informal association of liberals grouped around Merriman, Rose Innes and Schreiner, after the trio had resigned in disgust from Rhodes's cabinet. Its purpose was to oppose 'racism' (ie between the two white language groups), but once Rhodes returned to politics, most of the group banded together in the South African Party (SAP), under the centrist leadership of Schreiner, to thwart the designs of the Colossus.

The anti-Bond, pro-imperialist 'jingoes' who remained formed themselves into the Progressive Party and found enthusiastic support from the vocal South African League.[2] The League had been founded by pro-imperialists in the eastern Cape soon after the Jameson Raid. It grew rapidly among English pro-British loyalists, urban free traders and progressive sheep-farmers in the Cape, Natal and the Transvaal, and even opened a branch in Britain. Anti-Dutch, anti-Afrikaner Bond and anti-Kruger, the League's undisguised aim was to enhance British interests in South Africa.

Having been let off the hook by Chamberlain in London after the Raid, Rhodes was now an even more ardent advocate of the Colonial

Secretary's imperialist policies. With elections due shortly, the new dividing line in Cape politics was the colony's relationship with Kruger's Transvaal. Should the Cape give its backing to Rhodes (and Milner) in their efforts to compel the SAR to capitulate to Uitlander demands, even if it meant war, or not? Confident of Progressive support, Rhodes set about his own objectives 'with a fervour that was as usual as his politics were heretical'.[3] He vilified his former supporters in the Afrikaner Bond, now in the SAP, who remained firmly opposed to 'jingoism' and 'Kruger-baiting'.

In March 1898, in the first electoral contest between the two parties for seats in Parliament's upper house, the Legislative Council (or Senate), the Progressives beat the SAP-Bond coalition by 14 seats to 9. Attention then turned to the mid-year House of Assembly elections. Whatever Milner's (and Chamberlain's) private reservations about Rhodes, they had no option but to settle for him as their local champion. Writing to Selborne, Milner said he regarded Rhodes as the only man in South Africa big enough to carry out a policy of federation under British rule, but considered him to be 'too self-willed, too violent, too sanguine and in too great a hurry'. Rhodes, he said, was 'undaunted and unbroken by his former failure, but also untaught by it' and was 'much too strong a man to be merely used'.[4]

Bitter election

The election of June 1898 was the most acrimonious, bitterly contested and corrosive in the colony's history. In his desperate desire to regain power, Rhodes and the mining mogul Alfred Beit 'spared no effort and no expense' to secure votes for the Progressives, paying candidates to stand against the Bond[5] and even purchasing farms at inflated prices in Afrikaner strongholds in order to settle pro-British families on them.[6] As Rotberg records, 'the vitriol and calumnies of the partisan press (much of it beholden to Rhodes) were matched only by the discreditable rumours spread by both sides, and the personal invective that laced the campaign speeches of many candidates'.[7]

On the hustings, the newly Progressive Rhodes urged his followers to reject any candidates supported by the Afrikaner Bond. By backing the Bond, he asserted, the unification of South Africa would be postponed, Krugerism would triumph and the English-speaking population of the Transvaal – not to mention that of the Cape – would find itself utterly isolated. The Colossus also revealed a hitherto well-concealed concern for non-white voters, coming up with the new slogan of 'equal rights for all civilised men'. This was a revised version of his earlier slogan of 'equal rights for all *white* men south of the Zambezi'.[8] When pressed for a definition of a 'civilised man' at a public meeting, Rhodes responded, 'Well ... he is a man, white or black, who has sufficient education to write his own name, who has some property, or works ... in fact, is not a loafer.'[9]

Rose Innes recorded in his memoirs that Milner now 'began to show himself that constitutionally anomalous phenomenon, a Governor with a policy, a High Commissioner who held, with all the fervour of conviction, that the paramountcy of England was in danger and it was his duty to save it'. Rhodes's return to politics caused the 'tide of sentiment' that swept through the English community to be met with a 'wave of sympathy for the Transvaal which surged over Dutch-speaking South Africa ... Apart from the years of actual war, I remember no period when racial feeling ran higher than it did during 1896–99.'[10]

The threatening situation in the Transvaal was not the dominant issue in the Cape election, however. It was Rhodes and his manipulative methods that really divided the parties.[11] While the Progressives claimed to be fighting the Bond in order to resist Krugerism, the SAP, led by Schreiner and backed by the Bond, stood on a platform that was neither pro-republican nor pro-Kruger but called for good relations with all neighbouring states, including the SAR. Even Milner, who was hoping for a Progressive victory, acknowledged in a letter to Chamberlain that a Schreiner-led government would be one of 'compromise and conciliation': 'It was unlikely to be hostile to British interests, or to the Imperial Government, but only to 'the personal domination of Mr Rhodes, to the Chartered clique, their corrupt methods of government, [and] the influence of Mammon in politics.'[12]

Despite Rhodes's munificence, when the ballots were tallied in August, the Progressives had won a narrow majority of votes cast but only 39 seats against the 40 of the SAP-Bond alliance. Winning a no-confidence motion in Parliament, Schreiner formed a moderate

William P Schreiner, who led the SAP-Bond opposition to Rhodes, Sprigg and the Progressives in the Cape Parliament. *(Wikimedia Commons/Elliot & Fry)*

administration, his cabinet of six containing only two Bond members. Rhodes took over from Sprigg as party leader and Milner reported to Chamberlain that the size of the official opposition would make the tenure of the new SAP government extremely tenuous – and preclude the possibility of any extremism.

Like a modern-day Donald Trump, Rhodes (and Sprigg) at first refused to relinquish parliamentary power, attempting without success to persuade three Bondsmen to cross the floor and thwart Schreiner's election victory. Their efforts ran into the opposition of a principled Milner, who had hoped Sprigg might avoid defeat but 'disbelieved absolutely' in Rhodes's dubious tactics. He accused Rhodes of failing to see that 'there was a moral side to such matters or even that *straightforwardness* may have a tactical value'.[13] By doing all he could to keep Sprigg in office, Milner wrote, Rhodes showed that he did not care 'two pins how ridiculous he made himself look in the process'. His scheme for keeping the Progressives in office 'was just the Raid all over again'.[14]

Sensing a lack of enthusiasm in the Colonial Office for his unbending stance towards Afrikanerdom, Milner wrote to Selborne at great length in May to set out his views on 'our relations with the Transvaal as a whole', in case the two of them were not 'quite in accord'.[15] After dealing with the Judge Kotze case in some detail, Milner continued: 'While I still by personal temperament sympathise with ... a policy of patience, and while such being my orders, I shall faithfully carry them out, I am less hopeful than I was of an ultimate solution on these lines. Two wholly antagonistic systems – a mediaeval race oligarchy and a modern industrial state, recognising no difference of status between various white races – cannot live side by side in what is after all *one country*. The race-oligarchy has got to go, and I see no sign of its removing itself ... There are no two sides to this question in the opinion of all the friends of British influence in S. Africa.'[16]

Selborne replied on 28 June that if Great Britain were to intervene in the Transvaal, the general case against the SAR had to be 'glaring, patent and actual ... Where I think you are pessimistic, and where I venture with great deference to differ from you, is my estimate of the influence of Time. I think Time is on our side ... Kruger's death must eventually make a difference.'[17]

Smuts

One important government official in the Transvaal who accurately divined Britain's ultimate intentions was Kruger's new State Attorney, the 28-year-old Jan Smuts, recently arrived in Johannesburg from the Cape. With an academic record at Cambridge to rival Milner's at Oxford, Smuts's antennae had alerted him a year earlier to a perceptible change in Britain's attitude towards the Transvaal. In an unpublished 30-page paper, he pointed to a 'far deeper and more momentous issue which ought to overshadow every other ...: the parting of the ways in the South African policy of Great Britain'. He posed the rhetorical question of whether England was going to 'revert from the traditions of her greatest colonial statesmen' and try to introduce 'that element of material force which has gradually been receding from her colonial empire'.[18]

> When I saw how Mr Chamberlain ... continually referred to the maintenance of England's rights in South Africa *even by force*, I thought of the same phrase as it was bandied about the floor of the Houses of Parliament in the years preceding the War with the American colonies.[19]

According to Smith, Smuts warned that the British Empire could not be kept together 'by force and armaments'; any 'vigorous policy' towards the SAR would have repercussions on Britain's position throughout the length and breadth of South Africa, and affect the Empire as a whole. Republicanism was a grand cause all over the world and 'nowhere in the world has it such a chance as in South Africa'. Afrikaner loyalty to Britain, he stressed, was fragile and owed nothing 'to a blood-relationship ... nor to an overwhelming feeling of gratitude': 'It rested upon the by no means unshakeable conviction that British rule was fair and just ... and this sentiment of loyalty will soon vanish into thin air ... War policies, vigorous policies and "jingoistic movements" are only likely to stiffen resistance.[20]

'To my mind the die is already cast in the Colony; the Dutch are absolutely committed to the support of the [Transvaal] Republic and should an ambitious Colonial Minister choose to bring his "vigorous" policy into operation, the entire South Africa will be speedily involved in a final conflagration.'[21]

That the Uitlanders on the Rand had grievances could be admitted, Smuts continued, even if these grievances were exaggerated, but no redress could be expected while 'Chamberlain was flaunting war in the face of Republican South Africa'. As for the Uitlanders' political grievances, they were 'too absurd and dishonestly put forward to merit the least consideration'. Quoting the opinion of mining magnate Lionel Phillips that 'the English Uitlanders don't care a fig for the franchise', Smuts estimated that if the vote were offered tomorrow, only ten per cent of Uitlanders would accept it.[22] And regarding Britain's claim to be the 'paramount power' in South Africa, international law did not recognise 'paramountcy', which had been superseded anyway by the London Convention.[23]

Notwithstanding the conclusions of his paper, and his unrelenting opposition to the policies of Chamberlain and Milner, State Attorney Smuts was to become the leading voice for reform in the Kruger government. Unlike Milner, he would go to great lengths to avert war. As Iain Smith observes, for the rest of his life Smuts believed that Britain's actions in South Africa were a betrayal of her liberal traditions. Looking back after the Anglo-Boer War, Smuts would maintain that in the greatest of all British colonial wars of the 19th century, South Africa had played a vital part in the extinction of 'assertive imperialism'.[24]

Delagoa Bay

In July 1898, Milner wrote to Chamberlain to say that he regarded possession of Delagoa Bay as 'the best chance we have of winning the great game between ourselves and the Transvaal for mastery in South Africa without a war'.[25] There was no better way to bring pressure on the Transvaal, Milner asserted, than to command its trade routes. But if Delagoa Bay were to fall into unfriendly hands, it could 'do infinite damage to all the Cape ports as well as to the Cape railway'.[26]

For most of the 1890s, the Colonial Office had been engaged in sporadic discussions with Portugal over the future of the port and its facilities. Though not directly involved himself, Milner had kept a watchful eye on developments. The Portuguese, desperate to secure a foreign loan from either Britain or Germany to ease the dire state of their economy, were nonetheless reluctant to use either of their colonial possessions in southern Africa – Angola and Portuguese East Africa – as collateral for their debts. However, with a resurgent Germany now posing a threat to Britain's 'complacent supremacy'[27] in southern Africa, the Colonial Office was eager not only to keep the Kaiser away from the riches of the Transvaal but also to establish a pre-emptive claim over Portuguese East Africa should Portugal decide to relinquish the territory. By so doing, Whitehall reckoned, Britain would not only gain control over the nearest harbour to the Transvaal but further isolate the SAR by taking charge of the rail link between Kruger's republic and the sea.[28]

Germany, at this time, was actively trying to extend its influence over South West Africa and part of East Africa, and watching with interest British attempts to checkmate Kruger's SAR. The German government intervened in the Anglo-Portuguese negotiations to insist that its interests had to be taken into account in any agreement the two parties might reach. In the meantime, an alarmed Portuguese government thought better of mortgaging its colonial possessions and resolved to seek the required loan elsewhere.[29]

Though irritated by Germany's 'preposterous' claim to have any right of interference in southeast Africa, Chamberlain perceived correctly that the Germans' real purpose was colonial expansion elsewhere on the continent. In a secret protocol to an agreement between the two countries over the Kaiser's territorial claims elsewhere in Africa, Britain secured an undertaking that Germany would have no say in the future of Delagoa Bay, and an acknowledgment that it had no interest in becoming an ally of the Transvaal – notwithstanding the Kaiser's overtures to Kruger after the Jameson Raid. In 1899, a leading German diplomat assured Joseph Chamberlain that 'all the sensible politicians in Germany, as well as the capitalists, look upon absorption of the Transvaal by England as an historical and commercial necessity'.[30] Except for their Free State ally, Kruger and his republic were now internationally isolated. In any conflict with Britain, the SAR would be on its own.[31]

Home leave

For British loyalists in the Cape, the disappointment of the 1898 election outcome was leavened by the good news, in September of that year, that Kitchener had captured Omdurman – across the Nile from

Khartoum – from the Mahdi. Parliament passed a unanimous resolution of congratulations and Milner reported that there was much
public interest in the colony in Britain's looming conflict with the
French, who had never forgiven themselves for their decision in 1882
to leave Egypt in British hands and were now seeking to gain control of the White Nile basin by occupying the small mud fort on the
river at Fashoda.[32] As Robert Massie points out, the French already
held large territories in Africa along the Niger River and in the Congo
and Somaliland. France's axis on the continent was east–west, from the
Indian Ocean to the Atlantic, whereas the British axis was north–south,
from the Cape to Cairo. A clash seemed inevitable.[33] The British were
ready to go to war over Fashoda; the French were not, and eventually
backed down. An agreement was reached whereby Britain would not
move west of the waters of the Nile.

With the Cape Colony's new SAP government in place, Milner now
felt able to make a much-postponed return to England to enjoy his first
leave in well over a year. His chief objective was to persuade the Colonial Office, and particularly his friends in the newspaper world, of the
correctness of his policy, as Chamberlain's man on the spot, towards
the 'Dutch' in South Africa.

Before his departure, his friend George Wyndham, at the War
Office, had written to say how thankful the British government was to
have Milner 'out there', and that the High Commissioner enjoyed the
confidence of the entire press, from the extreme right to the extreme
left. That was simply untrue. One leading journal to have changed its
view of imperialism was WT Stead's *Pall Mall Gazette*. The mercurial
editor had been outraged by the Jameson Raid, and even more by
the subsequent cover-up, and suspected that Milner, far from being
a brake on the Colonial Secretary in South Africa, was now actively
encouraging him. Stead's subsequent labelling of Milner, along with
Chamberlain, as a 'bogeyman of Empire' brought their once-close
friendship to an end.[34]

On the voyage to England, Milner's ship crossed another carrying
his temporary 'stand-in' as High Commissioner, Sir William Butler, to
Cape Town. Butler had been sent out by the War Office, without consultation with the Colonial Office, to become the commander-in-chief

of the British garrison in South Africa. A 61-year-old, anti-imperialist Irish Catholic of erratic temperament, Butler had served previously in South Africa and written a biography of General Colley, the British commander who lost his life at Majuba. His sympathies were known to be pro-Zulu, pro-Boer and anti-Uitlander, and, like many serving officers, he held the War Office in low regard. According to Butler's biographer, one could scarcely have found anyone on the British side whose views were less like Milner's.[35] The inappropriateness of his appointment as Britain's military chief in South Africa 'was one of those ironies of history which must wake the laughter of the gods'.[36]

CHAPTER 10

Tensions Rise
1898–1899

Arriving in England in mid-November 1898, Milner was unsurprised by the lack of interest in matters South African. He understood that people found it difficult to focus on more than one issue at a time and were captivated by the drama on the Nile, where Kitchener and the French were at odds over control of the Sudan. Writing to his political secretary, George Fiddes, Milner reported that as far as he could judge, a 'no war policy' in South Africa was still in place 'in the highest quarters', but he was lying as low as possible, as the issue had ceased to interest anybody.[1]

Lying low did not mean avoiding a hectic programme of social engagements, including a royal command from the Queen to stay at Windsor and flying visits to the Prince of Wales at Sandringham and to the Prime Minister, Salisbury, at his grand house, Hatfield. Milner was an honoured guest at weekend house parties and countless lunches and dinners – a highlight being the farewell banquet in London for his friend Lord Curzon, about to become Viceroy of India at the age of only 39.

He also took pains to brief a cross-section of influential Liberal and Conservative politicians and others about the state of play in South Africa. They included Arthur Balfour, Rosebery and Asquith, as well as the Lords Lansdowne and Loch, and old friends such as Goschen, Philip Gell and Albert Grey – chairman-designate of the BSAC. He saw military men such as Kitchener and Edward Cecil (and his wife, Lady Violet), the financier Baron Rothschild and leading mining magnates such as Alfred Beit, Julius Wernher and Cecil Rhodes. All these efforts 'to stamp on rose-coloured illusions about S. Africa', he confessed, 'were most exhausting ... but I hope to have sown some seeds.'[2]

During talks with Chamberlain, Milner insisted once again on 'an

89

active and resolute policy [towards the Transvaal], even at the risk of its leading to war'. But he found Chamberlain in no mood to precipitate a further crisis: 'Our policy is not *to bring* things to a head,' the Colonial Secretary told him firmly; 'let them *come* to a crisis. The Boers must put themselves in the wrong.'[3]

As a former journalist, Milner recognised the urgency of creating a climate of pro-Uitlander opinion in Britain, by ensuring the 'right information' about the Transvaal would be fed to the home audience. This would underpin his diplomacy and help produce a receptive environment for the policy he would be setting out in dispatches over the next few months.[4] In Wernher and Beit, both German-born mine owners with mansions in London and Johannesburg, he found 'a kind of new and astonishing millionaire: men with some higher conception than the piling up of money' who were prepared, via their South African holding company, Eckstein's, to support an English-language press in the Transvaal sympathetic to Britain's imperial cause. The pair were already financing the *Transvaal Leader*, a fervently pro-Uitlander, anti-Boer paper, set up in opposition to the hostile, Kruger-supporting *Standard and Diggers' News*.[5]

While in London, Milner was able to help Wernher and Beit find an editor for *The Star*, the biggest daily newspaper in the Transvaal, owned by the Argus Company but supported by mining interests such as Eckstein's. An Argus director had revealed candidly in a letter what the board expected of the new appointee: 'The proprietors of *The Star* will not interfere ... provided the Editor is honest and capable and holds the right views. He must have faith in the English-speaking race and be able to render substantial aid to Sir Alfred Milner in forwarding the Imperial Policy in South Africa ... His mission would be to educate and unite men on the Rand who read English and who are for the most part today an incoherent and factious crowd.'[6]

Drawing on his former press contacts, Milner recruited yet another Balliol alumnus, WF Monypenny of *The Times*, to fulfil the dual role of editor of *The Star* and correspondent for *The Times* in South Africa. With Garrett, editor of the *Cape Times*, South Africa's largest daily, already in his corner, he could now count on the support of two of 'English' South Africa's most powerful opinion-formers, enabling him to reach his target audience in the Cape, the Transvaal and the UK at a critical time.

Despite 'the tremendous pace' of his last weeks at home,[7] the hard-driving Milner made time for recreation, slipping away for regular liaisons with his mistress, Cecile – including a six-day midwinter cycling tour of Hampshire. It was the last occasion in their ultra-discreet, nine-year relationship that they would spend time together, as she subsequently married and emigrated to Canada. On 28 January 1899, Milner set sail for Cape Town, accompanied on the long voyage by Conyngham Greene and a new aide-de-camp, 22-year-old Second Lieutenant Hugh Grosvenor, the Lord Belgrave, known to his friends as 'Bendor', destined to become the Duke of Westminster and one of the wealthiest property-owners in England.

The Edgar case

While Milner had been away, a furious head of steam had built up in the Transvaal over the case of Robert Edgar, a drunken Uitlander shot dead by an armed 'Zarp', or Boer policeman. The latter had been charged with manslaughter and acquitted. The case having been seized upon as a political issue by the Transvaal chapter of the South African League and its supporting newspapers, the Uitlander community held a well-attended protest meeting and drew up a strongly worded petition to be sent to the Queen. The petitioners also listed a parade of grievances suffered by people of all colours on the Rand and claimed they had no voice in government, could not appeal to an independent judiciary and were not able to defend themselves against harassment by the Zarps.[8]

But Acting High Commissioner Butler refused to forward the petition to Whitehall. Unlike Milner, who was disinclined to probe the motives of British subjects, Butler was deeply suspicious of the Uitlanders in Johannesburg, a town he regarded as 'a Monte Carlo superimposed on Sodom and Gomorrah' anyway, whose citizens were 'probably the most corrupt, immoral and untruthful assemblage of beings in the world'.[9] In his view, the Uitlanders were simply out to make trouble, while the South African League was 'an agency of disquiet' and Rhodes a threat to the peace of the country. What

South Africa needed, Butler believed, was not 'a surgical operation' but 'compromise and conciliation'.[10] He was annoyed, too, at the incendiary role of the press, which had published the League's petition to the Queen before it was presented to him, and used that as a pretext for pigeon-holing an appeal that Chamberlain, for one, regarded as important because it gave Her Majesty's Government 'the right of remonstrance and action'.[11]

In London, Milner was furious when told that Butler had sat on the Uitlanders' petition, but he decided not to overreact. Feigning nonchalance,[12] he wrote to Selborne during his return voyage to Cape Town to say that 'amusement at Butler's idiotic proceedings overcomes annoyance ... Also, as I shall have to get on with our friend somehow, it is just as well that I should not land in a bad temper.'[13] As High Commissioner, he made sure nonetheless that Butler's days in South Africa would be numbered.

Milner reported to Selborne that his visit to London had not changed anything: *'my views are absolutely unaltered* [author's emphasis], but I have come to the conclusion that ... it is no use trying to force them on others at this stage. If I can advance matters by my own actions ... I believe that I shall have support when the time comes. And if I can't get things "forrarder" [moving forward] locally, I should not get support, whatever I said.'[14]

At the Colonial Office, Chamberlain's views had not altered either. Realising the situation in the Transvaal might yet become untenable, he still saw no reason for hastening a clash, believing – as did Rhodes – that if armed conflict really threatened, the Kruger government was more likely to capitulate than risk going to war.[15]

Dynamite

During Milner's sojourn in England, another clash had arisen between the Colonial Office and the Transvaal of far greater significance than the Edgar case. It turned on Britain's disputed right under the London Convention to exercise control over the external relations of the SAR. If upheld in international law, suzerainty would rule out international arbitration in matters of contention between the governments of Britain and the SAR, thus diminishing the republic's

sovereign independence.[16] In late 1898, the issue was Kruger's decision to extend the monopoly over the manufacture of dynamite for the
mines, awarded to a German immigrant, Edouard Lippert, for another
15 years, and to maintain a ban on the importation of dynamite. Instead
of making the dynamite locally, Lippert imported it from Germany
and sold it to the mines at a 200 per cent mark-up,[17] a scam that raised
the cost of gold production significantly and directly affected British
mining interests, which comprised 70 per cent of the industry.[18]

Reluctant at first to argue over what he regarded as 'a capitalist's
question pure and simple', Milner subsequently changed his mind
and wrote to the Colonial Office saying, 'I really cannot see how some
action on the part of HM's Government can *now* be avoided'.[19] The
dispute chimed conveniently with his plan to work steadily towards
confrontation.

Thus encouraged, Chamberlain sent another formal dispatch
to Kruger in January 1899, expressing displeasure at the Transvaal
government's refusal to adopt the recommendations of its own
Industrial Commission, and advising that the British government
would not recognise either the concession or the continuation of the
dynamite monopoly.

At its annual general meeting on 2 February 1899, the Chamber
of Mines in the Transvaal adopted a motion condemning both the
monopoly and its lengthy extension.[20] Instead, the Chamber offered to
raise a loan of £600 000 to buy out the dynamite concessionaire. Jan
Smuts warned Percy FitzPatrick, representing the mining houses, that
Kruger was unlikely to accept the offer as it appeared to be a further
attempt to interfere with 'the corner-stone of the country's independence'.[21] Predictably, the SAR government duly refused the loan and
Whitehall's protest over the dynamite monopoly was rejected.

Members of the Transvaal Volksraad were far from united over the
dynamite issue, however, initially voting down the proposal to extend
the monopoly by 15 votes to 13. Kruger had to use all his powers of
persuasion – and a probable resort to bribery – to force through the
necessary resolution. It took three years of war, and the overthrow
of his government, to finally bring an end to the hugely lucrative
dynamite-making franchise.[22]

By early 1899, an economic recovery had begun to take effect on the Rand, thanks to significant advances in deep-level mining brought about by the 'second industrial revolution' spreading across Europe.[23] As a result, pressure on the SAR government for reform mounted from within both the mining industry and the Chamber of Commerce, representing the wider business community, while the Uitlanders were busy garnering wider support for a second petition to demand an extension of the franchise. Worried too by the growing influence of the South African League, and anxious to defuse Uitlander dissatisfaction, the Kruger administration decided on a bold move – to ignore Chamberlain's strictures and approach the mining industry directly with a 'peace proposal' to settle the matters in dispute between them. Negotiations over a potential 'Great Deal' took place in Johannesburg during most of March 1899. FitzPatrick, deeply involved on behalf of the mining industry, kept Milner well informed of progress.

The main issues in dispute between the government and the mining and business communities were the outdated qualifications for the Uitlander franchise, the under-representation of Johannesburg in the Volksraad, the rights to land adjacent to the mines (the *bewaarplaatsen*) and the controversial dynamite concession. Although no deal was ultimately concluded, the negotiations were significant for revealing the Kruger administration's readiness to contemplate change, and for the mining industry's insistence on coupling its demands with those of the Uitlander population.

Briefed by FitzPatrick, Milner wrote to Chamberlain on 22 March predicting that without a substantial concession by the Transvaal government, the negotiations in Johannesburg were likely to break down over the franchise question.[24] Defending the activities of the South African League, he said its members were habitually misrepresented as being anti-capitalist and 'political mischief-makers' by the pro-Boer press, but the League aimed at nothing more than 'the reasonably fair treatment of the non-Boer resident population of the Transvaal'.[25] As Milner predicted, without any agreement on the franchise, the talks fizzled out on 27 March. Their failure marked a 'watershed' in the growing Boer-British conflict.[26]

Helots

While the 'Great Deal' negotiations were in progress, the Uitlanders had gathered over 21 000 signatures for their second petition to the British government, which closed as soon as the talks in Johannesburg came to an end. Claiming to constitute a majority of the people of the Transvaal who contributed most to the republic's 'intellect, wealth and energy', the petitioners requested Whitehall to intervene because of the 'well-nigh intolerable' conditions under which they laboured, including the absence of political rights or a voice in government, mal-administration, poor education and a police force that failed to protect the citizenry.[27] Taking no chances this time, the South African League kept in close touch with the British Agent in Pretoria and Milner in the Cape.

The delivery of the Uitlanders' second petition, at the end of March 1899, gave the British government the justification it sought to intervene in the affairs of the Transvaal.[28] Smith describes it as the 'crossing of the Rubicon' in the development of British policy towards Kruger's SAR.[29] It sparked off a month of intense lobbying in South Africa and London before the Colonial Office acknowledged receipt of the Uitlanders' representations in early May.

In Cape Town, Milner congratulated a visiting FitzPatrick on the 'consummate statesmanship' he had displayed in securing cohesion and unanimity between the mining industry and the Uitlander population. There had been much more progress than he (Milner) had expected. Now it all depended on how the petition was received by officialdom in London; it would require a sustained press campaign that FitzPatrick should organise because Milner could not do so himself.[30]

As soon as Chamberlain had persuaded the British cabinet to formally accept the petition, he asked Milner for a clarifying statement suitable for publication. Milner needed no encouraging and, on 4 May 1899, sent off the notorious dispatch in which he claimed that the case for intervention in the Transvaal was now 'overwhelming'. Parts of his lengthy telegram read: 'The spectacle of thousands of British subjects kept permanently in the position of *helots*, constantly chafing under undoubted grievances and calling vainly to Her Majesty's Government for redress, does steadily undermine the influence and reputation of Great Britain and the respect for the British government within its dominions.'[31]

Besides Milner, the classical scholar, not many Uitlanders would have known the meaning of 'helot', the term given to the serfs of ancient Sparta, mistreated for being neither slaves nor citizens. The description could hardly be ascribed to migrant workers temporarily in the Transvaal of their own volition to enrich themselves by digging for gold, but a new word had entered South Africa's political lexicon. As Salisbury was later to concede, 'universal suffrage, mainly exercised by a floating population of mining adventurers ... could not be an ideal form of government'.[32] And even Rhodes admitted publicly that if he had been Kruger, he might not have given the vote to the Uitlanders because it would have brought his power to an end.[33] (It is worth noting that the suffrage in Britain at that time was neither universal nor based on any right of citizenship.)

When Milner's 'helot' dispatch reached Chamberlain, he scribbled on it, 'This is tremendously stiff and if it is published, it will make either an ultimatum or Sir Alfred Milner's recall necessary.'[34] As the ever-sympathetic Headlam records, the High Commissioner 'was risking upon it his reputation and career'.[35] Yet Chamberlain was still wary of any ultimatum. In an earlier memorandum to the cabinet, he had warned that if the prayers of the petitioners were once again ignored, Britain's position in South Africa would be severely weakened. On the other hand, if an ultimatum were issued and Kruger made an 'offensive reply ... we shall then have to go to war or accept a humiliating check'.[36]

The terseness of Chamberlain's cabled reply to him, on 8 May, caused Milner some concern. He wrote to Hely-Hutchinson to say that while he had no doubt the British government was in earnest this time, he did not expect any ultimatum. He predicted that London would send a dispatch so strong that it would practically necessitate intervention if Kruger did not grant reforms: 'If he does, the uitlanders must take them and work them *bona fide* ... Perhaps it would be best if Kruger hardened his heart, and the smash came. But I don't think we ought to aim at that.'[37]

On 9 May, desperate to avoid the looming clash in the Transvaal, the Afrikaner Bond's leader, 'Onze Jan' Hofmeyr, proposed over dinner with Milner that the High Commissioner should meet face to face with Kruger in the Free State capital, Bloemfontein. A meeting of the two men had been mooted before, but Milner had felt the timing was not right. Urged on also by Cape premier WP Schreiner, but still without the official response from London to the 'helot' petition he was anxiously awaiting, Milner hesitated and then reluctantly agreed.

Writing to Conyngham Greene on 12 May, he reflected that 'the funk here on the part of the Afrikander party during the last week or so has been something terrific.' He regarded the formal invitation from Kruger's fellow republican leader, President Steyn of the Orange Free State, as a 'very clever move' that had already had the effect of 'mollifying the British press a bit, but also relaxing unfortunately, the screw upon the enemy'.[38]

In a letter to his friend Selborne on 17 May, Milner repeated his belief that the Boers and their sympathisers had 'never been in such a funk for many years. Therefore, my advice to you is, if I fail with Kruger, to assume at once the diplomatic offensive and to back it with a strong show of material force ...' If there were to be a fight, 'it would be better to fight now than five or ten years hence, when the Transvaal, unless the uitlanders can be taken in in considerable numbers, will be stronger and more hostile than ever'.[39]

A week later, Milner addressed another 'Very Secret' letter to Selborne, knowing it would be passed on to Chamberlain, in which he confided that he was not hopeful of progress in Bloemfontein, 'but would, of course, do my very utmost to get *any* settlement which has the possibility of improvement in it'.[40] 'One thing is quite certain: if we can't get reforms now by negotiation with so much in our favour, we shall never get them, and we must either be prepared to see Kruger carry out his policy of suppressing his English subjects or compel him to desist from it. The latter means a greatly increased force and *may* mean war.'[41]

CHAPTER 11

Bloemfontein and Beyond
1899

The Bloemfontein meeting between Milner and Kruger was the only time the two antagonists ever met. On the morning of Wednesday 31 May 1899, the pair were introduced to one another by President Steyn at a reception at his official residence in the Free State capital. Kruger had arrived 15 minutes early; Milner was 20 minutes late. Offering no apology, the High Commissioner observed diplomatic protocol by making straight for his hosts, the Steyn couple, to shake hands,[1] before turning to greet the elderly Transvaal president, who had risen slowly to his feet.

The first encounter was cordial, though stiffly formal.[2] To those present, the contrast in outward appearance could hardly have been more striking: Milner, spare of frame, clean-shaven and clad in a morning suit; the elderly Kruger, burly, bearded, swollen-eyed, and dressed in a tightly buttoned frock-coat. In a note to his wife, Smuts scribbled: 'Milner is as sweet as honey, but there is something in his very intelligent eyes that tells me that he is a very dangerous man – more dangerous than Rhodes ... a second Bartle Frere.'[3]

As the details of the proceedings in Bloemfontein have been recounted in every history of the Anglo-Boer War, it is not necessary to give more than a broad outline here. Suffice it to say that neither side expected to achieve much by going to the Free State capital. Milner regarded it as necessary to go through the motions for the sake of public opinion at home, and had not come to negotiate. Like Chamberlain, he actually cared little for the interests of fortune-seeking, working-class Uitlanders: his intention was to create a pretext for Britain to extend her supremacy in South Africa.[4]

At the Colonial Office, Sir Frederick Graham, head of the South

Africa desk, regarded the tone of Milner's messages as an indication that he had made up his mind that 'either he gets what he wants, or there must be war'. Graham himself thought the High Commissioner ought to be told firmly that 'at present, British public opinion would not support threats or forcible measures'.[5] Chamberlain, however, neglected to restrain Milner or give him any instructions as to how to conduct himself in Bloemfontein.[6]

According to Smuts, Kruger had little hope that the conference would serve a useful purpose either. Ever since the Jameson Raid, the SAR president had regarded another war with Britain as inevitable, 'not because there is a cause, but because the enemy is brazen enough not to wait for a cause'.[7] If the franchise were to be extended to temporary so-journers hoping to share in the Transvaal's mineral wealth, he believed, British numbers and capitalist interests would simply overwhelm the Boer people and put paid to their long struggle to rule themselves and be free from British domination.[8]

President Steyn had made plain to Kruger before the talks began that the Transvaal had to make some concessions on the franchise question: a 14-year residence qualification for foreigners was both undemocratic and unreasonable. The Free State leader said that if Kruger did so, he (Steyn) would support him fully. Kruger replied that he would try his best to resolve his difficulties with the British. 'I will do anything,' he said, 'but they must not touch my independence.'[9] As Picard observes, by showing willingness to negotiate, Kruger proved more prudent than rigid, and much less obstinate than history often makes out.[10]

Determined to confront the SAR president man to man, Milner had declined Chamberlain's advice to include WP Schreiner in his team, in case the settlement-seeking Cape premier might be a restraining influence. If true negotiations were ever seriously contemplated, Steyn as host was the obvious candidate to mediate between the two parties, but the Free Stater was not invited to participate and no agenda was agreed in advance of the meeting. At Milner's insistence, a full verbatim record of the conference had to be published, which meant that both leaders would be speaking for the public record rather than trying to find each other across the conference table.

For tactical reasons, Milner had decided to focus entirely on the franchise question, calculating that if Kruger continued to refuse reasonable demands for the vote, that alone was a *casus belli* (reason for going to war). He refused point-blank to discuss several other matters, including international arbitration, that the ageing Transvaal president in his slow rambling manner tried without success to put on the table. The root cause of the tension between Britain and the Transvaal, Milner maintained, was the republic's refusal to grant acceptable voting rights to foreigners. He proposed, therefore, that the vote be given to every immigrant who had been a resident of the Transvaal for the last five years, and that seven more seats be created for their representation in the Volksraad.[11] (Up to 1890, the Transvaal Volksraad had been unicameral. In that year, a Second Volksraad was created, with limited powers and easier residence qualifications, to give foreigners a vote. The discussions at Bloemfontein were about voting qualifications for elections to the First Volksraad, as well as the SAR presidency.)

Kruger replied that if he gave in to the demand for a five-year franchise, let alone seven more seats in the Volksraad, 60 000 foreigners would outnumber his 30 000 burghers, and the freedom of his republic would no longer exist – a fate even worse than annexation. Alleging that the second Uitlander petition had been instigated by 'capitalists', whose interests were detrimental to the entire population of the SAR, he produced a counter-petition signed by more than 23 000 burghers, as well as many Uitlanders, which indicated their satisfaction with the Transvaal government.[12] Milner was unimpressed.

For two days the talks meandered along, going nowhere, until the third day, when Kruger surprised Milner by pulling out the draft of a Reform Bill (devised by Smuts) to be put before the Volksraad immediately after the conference: it proposed a seven-year, retrospective franchise that would halve the current 14-year qualification and give the vote immediately to thousands of Johannesburg-based Uitlanders. But the president wanted to know what the Transvaal might expect in return. Next morning, Kruger went further, apologising for having forgotten to add that he would request the Volksraad to create four or five new electoral divisions in the republic as well.[13]

Although admitting privately that Kruger's proposals were a

significant step forward, Milner had no intention of accepting them: his aim was his opponent's capitulation. Crudely dismissing the proposed Reform Bill as 'a kaffir's bargain', whatever that meant, he insisted it would not give the Uitlanders the immediate recognition without preconditions that Britain demanded, and refused to negotiate further.[14] On Sunday 4 June, a day of rest, Kruger sent Milner a note saying he was not prepared to modify further the main parts of his Reform Bill.[15] Milner cabled Chamberlain to say that although he had been 'studiously conciliatory' throughout, the conference was likely to founder over the franchise question.

In reply, the Colonial Secretary counselled 'compromise and patience' with the Boers, who were used to 'a good deal of haggling'. He reminded Milner that it was of the utmost importance 'to put the President of the South African Republic clearly in the wrong'. Chamberlain also suggested – as a basis for discussion – that if Kruger would concede a five-year franchise, he should be offered a formal guarantee of Transvaal independence.[16] This was not what Milner had expected or had any intention of accepting.

We will never know whether Chamberlain's advice would have made any difference, because his cable only arrived in Bloemfontein on the Tuesday, by which time Milner had abruptly called off the conference. While Kruger was keen to continue the discussions, the High Commissioner had concluded that the President had gone as far as he could, and saw no point in prolonging the proceedings. On Monday morning (5 June), impatient with the interminable 'haggling', Milner declared the conference to be 'absolutely at an end, and there is no obligation on either side arising from it'. A stricken, humiliated Kruger kept repeating, 'It is our country you want,' his eyes watering behind his green-rimmed spectacles.[17]

From the written record of the conference, many historians have concluded that the dominating Briton had run rings around the supposedly slower-thinking Boer leader. Milner's biographer Marlowe is one who did not. The truth is, he wrote, Kruger 'gave nothing away: he made the Englishman lose his temper more than once; created the impression that it was Milner, and not he, who was being intransigent, and loaded Milner with the onus of breaking up the Conference … This was craft on the President's part. Unlike Milner, he had no interest in forcing matters to an issue.'[18]

Smuts was particularly incensed that a situation was being forced on the Boers from the outside 'in order by an armed conflict to forestall or defeat the work of time'. 'I have great hope', he wrote to Merriman, 'that within a few years all just causes of complaint will have disappeared altogether, and it fills me with a savage indignation to think that the work of those who are spending their ... lifeblood for South Africa is to be undone in a moment by academic nobodies who fancy themselves great Imperial statesmen.'[19]

Nine days, later, in a lengthy report to Chamberlain, Milner conceded that he had been wrong to end the conference so suddenly: he would not have done so had the Colonial Secretary's cable reached him in time. But he harboured no regrets: the discussions would have gone 'on and on' even though the other side's determination to 'not really admit the uitlanders' was all too evident, as was the readiness of Free State politicians 'to accept Kruger's nickel as silver'.[20] Chamberlain was less than impressed, suggesting to colleagues that his envoy might have been 'over-worked'. He cabled to say he would issue fresh instructions once Milner's fuller dispatches had been received and considered. He did make public, however, the contents of the 'helot' telegram and the cabinet's official reply to it, which heightened the tension in both Britain and South Africa.[21]

Taking stock

As Milner, though not Chamberlain, had hoped, the failure of the Bloemfontein negotiations brought the prospect of war much closer, while each side's prior suspicions of the other's intentions had been reinforced. Milner was convinced that Kruger was not truly serious about reform; Kruger was certain the British were intent on war. While frantic efforts to persuade both sides to settle their differences peacefully continued, the arguments became more and more heated.

Britain's politicians were sharply divided over the next step: an uneasy Prime Minister Salisbury wrote to Lansdowne at the War Office to complain that 'Milner and his jingo supporters' were forcing the government 'to make a considerable military effort – all for a people we despise, and for something that will bring no profit and no power to England.'[22] The Liberals were incensed by what they perceived as Chamberlain's and Milner's bellicosity, particularly the latter's insistence that 'the case for intervention is overwhelming.'[23] Liberal-supporting newspapers, led by WT Stead's *Gazette*, had become harshly critical of both men. But the influential mouthpiece of the Tory establishment, *The Times*, declared the breakdown at Bloemfontein to be entirely Kruger's fault, and endorsed Milner's decision to call off the conference.

At this juncture, both governments paused temporarily to take stock and reflect on their political and military options. From Europe, the 40-year-old Hollander Dr Willem Leyds, acting as the Transvaal's roving ambassador, advised Kruger to play for time in the hope that the Uitlanders might back down, or the Liberals might come to power in Britain, or the mine owners – fearful of the losses that a war would bring – might somehow intervene.[24] In Johannesburg, an Uitlander Council was formed, which endorsed Milner's franchise demands as an 'irreducible minimum'[25] and called for 'equal rights for all white men.'[26] In response, the *Standard and Diggers' News* declared that the British government's demands could not possibly be fully conceded without seriously compromising the country's independence. Chamberlain and Milner mulled over the advisability of issuing an ultimatum to the SAR, but Milner, rather surprisingly, was against it, on the grounds that Kruger, 'if sufficiently pushed',[27] might yet give way and adopt Britain's proposals.

Publicly, Salisbury's Unionists were anxious to avoid giving the impression they were being provocative or bullying towards two of the world's smallest states. The prime minister reported to the Queen that 'this country as well as the Cabinet, excepting perhaps Mr Chamberlain, were against a war.'[28] Ministers such as Hicks Beach thought Britain should not be 'too impatient', while Salisbury's second-in-command, Arthur Balfour, was of the view that if he were 'a Boer, brought up in Boer traditions, nothing but necessity would induce me to adopt a constitution that would turn my country into an English Republic or a system of education that would reduce my language to the patois of a small and helpless minority'. Balfour saw no reason not to exact concessions, but did not think international law would 'justify us in doing more'.[29]

Propaganda war

Milner on the one side and Smuts on the other were well aware of the value of propaganda in winning support for their respective causes. After learning by chance that FitzPatrick had written an account sympathetic to the Uitlander movement titled *The Transvaal from Within*, which he had withheld from publication for three years while in political purgatory after his support for the Jameson Raid, Milner asked to see the manuscript and was so impressed with it he urged the author to go to London immediately and have it published.[30]

FitzPatrick's book chronicled the struggle of the Uitlanders from before the Jameson Raid to the breakdown of the Bloemfontein Conference. Published in October 1899, with war talk in the air, the book's timing was fortuitous: it sold an astonishing 250 000 copies in English (and was translated into French and Dutch)[31] and was hugely influential in persuading public opinion in Britain that going to war with Kruger's republic would be justified.

In London, FitzPatrick suddenly found himself a celebrity, a man whom leading newspaper editors and society hostesses scrambled to meet and entertain. The scholarly Balfour, acting as prime minister with Salisbury indisposed, told the proud author that 'by means of a book, you have completely changed the opinion and feeling of a great nation in a moment of crisis, and I know of no other instance in history in which this has been done'.[32]

In the Transvaal, Smuts was equally aware of the need to put the republic's case before a wider audience. He was incensed at the publication in Britain of a 'Blue Book' (an official government document), in response to the 'helot' telegram, containing 243 pages of Uitlander grievances. In reply, Smuts drew up a savage indictment of British transgressions in southern Africa, which he called *A Century of Wrong*. In it, he wrote, 'If England should venture into the ring with Afrikanerdom without a formally good excuse, her cause in South Africa would be finished. And then the sooner the better, as we for our part are quite prepared to meet her ... Of the outcome I have no doubt. Either we shall be exterminated, or we shall fight our way out, and when I think of the great fighting qualities that our people possess, I cannot see why we should be exterminated.'[33]

Down in the Cape, however, Hofmeyr took issue with Smuts's assumption that the whole of Afrikanerdom would rally to the Transvaal cause. 'Cherish no illusions,' he warned, 'you must not expect that Colonial Afrikaners will rush *en masse* to arms if hostilities break out – especially as most of them know nothing about the bearing of arms.'[34]

A defiant Smuts wrote to Schreiner saying that the Transvaal and Free State together could put more than 50 000 fighting men into the field, and 'to cope with such a defensive force, composed of such stuff as Boers are made of when fighting for home and country, England will require an offensive force of at least 150 000 to 200 000 men. Is England going to embark lightly on such an undertaking? Would she not by so doing expose herself in other parts of the world?' he asked rhetorically.[35]

Another man who thought Britain would be foolish to attack the Boers on home turf was none other than General Sir William Butler, military commander at the Cape. He had little regard for the War Office's plans to deploy a mere 8 000 to 9 000 troops in South Africa by mid-1899. A war between the two sides would require at least 40 000 men, he believed, and would be 'the greatest calamity that ever occurred in South Africa'.[36]

Butler was determined not to provoke the Boers unnecessarily, and refused to support Milner's wish for troops to be stationed along the vulnerable Cape and Natal frontiers.[37] In dispatches to the Colonial Office, Milner complained repeatedly about his military chief, saying once to Chamberlain, 'The General ... is too awful. He has, I believe, made his military preparations all right, but beyond that I cannot get him to make the least move or take the slightest interest ... His sympathy is wholly with the other side.'[38]

On 21 June, Butler sent Lansdowne at the War Office a lengthy explanation of his view of the political impasse in South Africa. An angry Milner noted in his diary, 'things have become very critical now. Butler or I will have to go.'[39] From London, Chamberlain continued to counsel patience, saying that the general's recall would cause a 'great commotion' and be 'taken up by opponents of your policy and would embarrass me in my efforts to support you'.[40] Despite being instructed by the War Office to back Milner 'loyally', Butler remained impenitent. However, at the end of August, as war looked likely, he resigned his command in disgust and to Milner's relief departed the Cape for home.

Afrikaner unease

In Afrikaner circles, there was intense activity after the failure of the Bloemfontein Conference. Hofmeyr and Schreiner in the Cape and Steyn and Fischer in Bloemfontein may have disliked Milner's attitude towards the Transvaal, but they disliked the thought of war even more and brought their collective pressure to bear on the Kruger government.[41] The Free Staters also took the precaution of putting in a large order for arms and ammunition, just in case.

Schreiner found himself in a particularly awkward situation: he could not be too critical of Milner for fear of being dismissed and replaced by Sprigg. Unable to protest formally, he asked the Governor to convey to Chamberlain instead the Cape government's view that Kruger's franchise proposals were 'a practical, reasonable and a considerable step in the right direction ... and would not justify interference in what were the internal affairs of the Transvaal'.[42] Milner agreed to disagree, but forwarded the message to London nonetheless.

In July, Hofmeyr addressed the Transvaal Volksraad in secret session, again warning that if war broke out in the north, nothing but moral support could be expected from Cape Afrikaners. Together with Fischer and Smuts, Hofmeyr managed to persuade the Volksraad to pass, on 26 July, a new franchise law based on a seven-year residence qualification, but hedged with so many conditions that it required an accompanying explanation from Smuts.[43]

The Volksraad's new proposal produced momentary excitement in London, with Chamberlain congratulating Milner on his 'great victory' and declaring that no one would dream now of fighting over a two-year residence qualification. 'We ought to make the most of this and accept it as a basis of settlement', the Colonial Secretary telegraphed.[44] The Uitlander Council immediately cabled back urging Chamberlain not to depart from the five-year qualification demanded at Bloemfontein.[45] And Milner hastened to add that the new franchise measures were not genuine and were wide open to manipulation. The franchise would be 'a fiasco', he said, and represent a 'diplomatic defeat in the eyes of our supporters in South Africa'.[46]

On 28 July, during the last debate on South Africa before the House of Commons adjourned for its summer recess, Chamberlain back-tracked again, saying he hoped Kruger's latest proposal might form the basis of a settlement and inviting him to agree to a joint Anglo-Trans-vaal inquiry into the effect of the new franchise law. The greater issue, he said, was 'the predominance of Great Britain in South Africa', not a quibble about a seven- or a five-year franchise.[47] The nub of the matter was whether there would be 'immediate and substantial representa-tion' for all citizens. For the Liberals, Campbell-Bannerman claimed there was no case for intervention at all. It was the strangest notion, C-B declared, 'that we should go to war in order to hurry our own fellow-citizens into the citizenship of another country'.[48]

CHAPTER 12

Build-Up to War
1899

By now, Milner had realised the Kruger government would never concede changes to the franchise that might put its control of the Transvaal at risk. And if reforms were introduced, they could easily be reversed by a simple majority of the Volksraad. Even under Kruger's concessions at Bloemfontein, the Uitlanders were likely to remain an ineffective minority for a long time to come.[1] Rather than surrender, Kruger would go to war, which was not a prospect from which he (Milner) shrank. Like most Englishmen, he took for granted that the clash of arms would be short and sharp and result in the downfall of the SAR government and the reannexation of the Transvaal by the Crown. That, in his view, would settle the South African problem once and for all.

In London, Chamberlain and most of the cabinet still believed that Kruger would capitulate rather than fight a war he could never hope to win. Rhodes was another 'expert' who thought the wily old Transvaal president would go to the brink and back down at the last minute – as he had done in the past. 'The President is doing the usual thing; he is playing up to the Raad',[2] the colony's ex-prime minister declared: '[T]here is not the slightest chance of war.' In private talks with Milner, Rhodes predicted 'no bloodshed': 'I feel absolutely sure Kruger will concede everything that HMG demands.' Speaking in the Cape Parliament, Rhodes insisted that Kruger would 'climb down at the end', taking side bets with his associates the SAR would capitulate.[3]

It was evident from its lack of adequate preparation that the Salisbury government was not seriously contemplating having to fight. The War Office, under the weak authority of Lansdowne, was at daggers drawn with the Colonial Office and unable to persuade the politicians that a war was likely, or even that Britain should plan for one. Having to expend huge sums on 'forward campaigns' in the Sudan and India, MPs were opposed to incurring military expenditure that might, in the end, prove unnecessary.[4] Much easier to go along with the conventional wisdom that, if push came to shove, Kruger would yield reluctantly.

There was also a general consensus that any fighting would be over quickly, though old warhorses such as the Army chief, Lord Wolseley, were unconvinced. He feared – with good reason – that the politicians might land him in a situation for which no proper provision had been made. Only three days after the Bloemfontein Conference, Wolseley had called for the immediate mobilisation of at least 50 000 troops, to be assembled on Salisbury Plain under a general who would lead them in South Africa, if it proved necessary.[5] The cabinet, under the influence of the parsimonious Chancellor, Hicks Beach, turned Wolseley down flat.

Kruger's apparent flexibility on the franchise, and Chamberlain's proposal for a joint Anglo-Transvaal inquiry into issues in dispute, surely meant that decisions in London on troop deployments could be postponed even further. Viewing with concern the steady build-up of arms in the Transvaal and Free State, Milner regarded even Wolseley's Plan B – the immediate dispatch of 10 000 more men – as hopelessly insufficient.[6] Fortunately for him, his counterpart in India, Curzon, aware of divisions within the Salisbury cabinet, had taken the precaution of diverting 6 700 homeward-bound troops under Sir George White to Durban, in case Britain's inadequate defences in Natal needed reinforcement. The War Office also decided to send another 2 000 men to Natal, boosting British troop numbers in South Africa to around 12 000.

On 12 August, War Secretary Lansdowne presented a memorandum to the cabinet indicating that it would take *four months* to mobilise, equip and station 50 000 troops in South Africa. For an additional £1 million, it might be done in three. Still hoping to avert war – and save costs – Chamberlain and Salisbury decided not to spend money that could never be recovered – war or no war.[7]

Last offer

A day after Lansdowne's warning of the 'scandalous' state of Britain's military preparedness in South Africa, word reached London of some remarkable new proposals conveyed by Smuts, on Kruger's behalf, to Britain's representative in Pretoria, Conyngham Greene. This last-minute attempt to reach a political settlement was the result of strong pressure on Kruger from the Dutch and German governments, as well as advice from Leyds in Brussels, to accede to British demands and avert a war he could not possibly win.

Indicating to the British Agent – during three days of preliminary discussion – that the Transvaal could not accept Chamberlain's suggestion of a joint inquiry because it would infringe the republic's autonomy, Smuts made informal proposals that, at face value, seemed extraordinary:[8] a five-year residence qualification for foreigners and eight more seats for the Witwatersrand in the Volksraad. Further negotiation would be necessary on the issues of suzerainty, international arbitration and non-intervention in the Transvaal's internal affairs, but the franchise proposals could become law within a fortnight. Suspicious as ever, Milner was determined to resist the overture.[9]

Fuming at being upstaged by a subordinate, and distrusting the SAR's motives, Milner forwarded Conyngham Greene's messages to London, declaring that 'nothing but confusion could result from this irregular method of negotiations'. Chamberlain, who thought Milner was being 'unnecessarily suspicious and pedantic', was initially euphoric. 'This is a complete climb-down on Kruger's part', he told Salisbury. 'I really am sanguine that the crisis is over.'[10] In a message to Milner, the Colonial Secretary observed that if the proposals were genuine, they constituted 'an immense concession and even a considerable advance on your Bloemfontein proposals'.[11]

Milner was instructed to inform the Transvaal government that its proposals would be considered if formally submitted, which was done on 19 August. Two days later, State Secretary FW Reitz added an official rider stipulating that the proposals were *expressly conditional* upon the receipt of three guarantees from the British government: an undertaking not to interfere in the internal affairs of the SAR; not to insist on upholding suzerainty; and to agree to international arbitration. The Smuts proposals were not to be regarded as a one-sided concession on the franchise: the Kruger government had to be given something substantial in return.[12]

This belated 'manoeuvring' on the Transvaal's part annoyed the British government and tempered Chamberlain's enthusiasm that an agreement was in sight. Milner was able to persuade him that the proposals showed the Transvaal's 'absolute determination not to admit our claim to have a voice in their affairs ... They will collapse if we don't weaken, or rather if we go on steadily turning the screw.'[13] Salisbury was inclined to agree: he did not believe Kruger would back down but regarded South Africa as being 'too important strategically' to be allowed 'to go its own way'. As he told his son-in-law, Selborne, 'the real point to be made good to South Africa is that we, not the Dutch, are boss.'[14]

Addressing a political rally in his hometown of Birmingham on 26 August, a fired-up Chamberlain – always more belligerent in public than in private – complained that Kruger 'dribbles out reforms like water from a squeezed sponge and either accompanies his offers with conditions that he knows to be impossible or refuses to allow us to make a satisfactory investigation of the nature of those reforms ... The issue of war and peace are now in the hands of President Kruger ... The time has come to establish once and for all which is the paramount power in Southern Africa.'[15]

Lady visitors

Unable to get Lansdowne at the War Office, with whom he was scarcely on speaking terms,[16] to persuade the Salisbury cabinet to give him the number of troops he required, Wolseley had secretly sent ten Special Service Officers to Cape Town in the interim to organise the defence of the Colony's frontier if war were to break out. Among them were Colonel Robert Baden-Powell and his second-in-command, Major Edward Cecil, who was accompanied by his wife, Violet. Major Cecil was to help Baden-Powell recruit a corps of 'irregular' Uitlander volunteers to augment the British garrison at the remote outpost of Mafeking.

Pakenham describes Cecil, unkindly, as a 'tall, drooping, rather melancholy young officer, one of the prime minister's less successful younger sons'. Lady Violet, by contrast, 'was neither shy nor melancholy at all'.[17] As friends of Milner's in London society, the Cecils were invited to stay at Government House.[18] It says much about the political detachment of Britain's upper classes that the couple – members of Lord Salisbury's immediate family – had arrived in the Cape 'quite unaware of the urgency of the situation'.[19]

Another guest at Government House was the budding English activist Violet Markham, well-off and well-connected in Liberal circles, an ardent feminist who would become another of Milner's admirers and lifelong supporters. Before the Cecils left in mid-August for Mafeking, the two unshrinking Violets often discussed their mutual regard for Milner. Markham described him 'as a reserved, austere personality on whom the burden of great events rested heavily, with a mind narrowed down to one issue – the upholding of British rights in South Africa'.[20]

As Julia Bush writes, Violet Markham was no normal tourist: while in the Cape, she inquired extensively into local social and political affairs, which provided material for two books defending Britain's policies in South Africa and led to her self-appointment as a 'leading apostle of Milnerism'. It was Milner's writings on Egypt, Markham recalled in her autobiography, that 'shook me away from my liberal moorings and made me for a long time a convinced Imperialist'.[21] Shortly before the war broke out, she left for home, and her first book, *South Africa Past and Present*, appeared a year later. Before long, Violet Markham had become one of Britain's leading social reformers, and a champion of the pro-imperial, pro-Milner female pressure group, the Victoria League.

Lady Violet Cecil, who enjoyed walks in the garden and long rambles with the Governor – during which he unburdened himself to his lively young visitor – recorded that she had become attracted to Milner in a way she had never felt before. On the day of her departure for Mafeking, she noted in her diary, 'Seeing so much of Sir Alfred has been delightful. I am immensely impressed by him; he seems to me to have grown bigger, on very fine lines. He has kept his gentleness and charm and to them has added a firmness and a certainty of purpose which seem to me very unusual.'[22] Violet Markham was to recall, waspishly, that her friend Violet's 'wonderful fascination and cleverness' meant she always had 'a train of men about her'.[23]

Witwatersrand woes

Up in the Transvaal, the first six months of 1899 had produced record profits for the mining industry – the result of better yields from new deep-level mining and the closure of many unproductive operations. However, the stand-off at Bloemfontein had precipitated an immediate downturn in economic activity, which intensified as the political uncertainty grew.[24] With the rumour mill running wild, companies began transferring their banking accounts and securities to the coast, while rich and poor alike left the Rand in droves. By mid-year, trade in Johannesburg was almost at a standstill. Many Uitlanders were out of work and making for the safety of the Cape or Natal. In a reverse gold rush, an estimated 100 000 whites fled the Transvaal, as did an equal number of Africans thrown out of work after some 66 major mines closed as a result of shortages of coal, water and, above all, unskilled labour.[25]

The mine owners, as disunited in 1899 as they had been in 1895, viewed with dismay the mounting political stand-off, in which they were not central participants and for which they did not feel responsible. Intent as usual on furthering their own interests, they were secure in the knowledge that whoever ruled the Transvaal – Boers or British – would need to come to terms with the mining industry. It was the uncertainty that bothered them and led to a hardening of attitudes and a growing conviction that matters had to be brought to a head, even if it meant war.

Yet these 'capitalists', as their critics called them, were far from unanimous in their outlook – or in their advice to politicians. Even within the firm of Wernher, Beit/H Eckstein & Co, for example, there were differences of opinion: Eckstein, a partner who kept in close touch with Milner, thought that Kruger's government would give way only when Britain sent out more troops to South Africa. His general manager, Rouliot, by contrast, warned that if Britain *did* send out more troops, war was inevitable. Writing to Milner, Rhodes repeated his belief that Kruger would 'bluff up to the last moment'[26] then concede 'everything that HMG demanded', and predicted that another conference on the franchise was near at hand.[27] The Colossus was to be proved wrong once again.

Ultimatums

Realising that the British were unlikely to accept his latest proposals, Kruger withdrew the offer of a five-year retrospective franchise on 2 September and reverted to the earlier seven-year term qualification, sparking off a series of terse formal exchanges between the two governments. On 8 September, Selborne advised Milner by cable that the cabinet had decided to dispatch 10 000 more troops to South Africa. The deputy Colonial Secretary appended a 'pen-ultimatum' to be sent to Kruger, warning that unless the SAR agreed to a five-year franchise without preconditions, as well as to a joint inquiry, it could expect to receive an ultimatum from the British government.

On 22 September, Chamberlain confirmed, in a secret message to Milner, that the cabinet was now 'unanimous and resolves to see matter through': proposals for 'a final settlement of the issues' would be forthcoming within a week.[28] However, the formal notice would be sent by sea mail and take four weeks to arrive, which would give reinforcements time to disembark in South Africa.

As it happened, Britain's final demands were never formulated, because the Transvaal government decided to take matters into its own hands. On 26 September, Milner tipped Chamberlain off that 'everything points to likelihood that the Boers will anticipate [our] ultimatum by some action or declaration ... This being so, consideration of ultimatum becomes unnecessary.'[29]

Milner's tip-off proved correct. Far from frightening Kruger, the transfer of 10 000 more British troops to South Africa – with the threat of more to come – produced the opposite effect. As the Transvaal's forces and those of the Free State outnumbered the British by four to one, there was no time to lose. A prescient Smuts had already drawn up a battle plan for the Boers to take the offensive and invade Natal and the Cape before further British troop reinforcements could arrive. On 28 September, the Transvaal government began to call up its commandos. Kruger told President Steyn that Leyds had warned him that no help would be forthcoming from European countries and advised him to 'attack immediately before the English are ready'.[30] Still hoping for a diplomatic solution, Steyn took until 2 October before following suit. Next day, British troop reinforcements from India arrived in Durban and were rushed up to the border between Natal and the Transvaal.

At 5 pm on 9 October, State Secretary Reitz called on Conyngham Greene to deliver an ultimatum from the Kruger government. Its demands were uncompromising: arbitration on 'all points of difference'; the withdrawal of British troops near the Transvaal's borders; the return of all British troop reinforcements who had arrived since 1 June; and the diversion from South African ports of 'all British troops now on the high seas'. Unless the British government complied with these demands within 48 hours, the SAR would 'with great regret' be compelled to regard non-acceptance as 'a declaration of war'.[31]

In London, Chamberlain was busy finalising the wording of Britain's ultimatum, to be printed in a Blue Book and put before Parliament. When news of Kruger's demands reached him early on the morning of 10 October, the Colonial Secretary exulted: 'They have done it'.[32] His government had been presented with the perfect excuse for going to war, and was freed of the burden of making the case for war to Britain's politicians and the general public.

Lansdowne, at the War Office, echoed the Colonial Secretary's elation: 'Accept my felicitations', he wrote to Chamberlain, 'I don't think Kruger could have played our cards better than he has … My soldiers are in ecstasies'.[33] And a much-relieved Salisbury declared that 'a defiance so audacious … [had] liberated us from the necessity of explaining to the people of England why we are at war'.[34]

In Cape Town, Merriman viewed the Boer ultimatum as 'a calamitous misjudgement'.[35] To a friend, the Liberal academic and anti-imperialist Goldwin Smith, he wrote: 'In all human probability long before you get this, the first shot will have been fired in one of the most criminal and ill-judged enterprises that our country [England] has ever embarked on.'[36]

Early in the evening of 11 October, the Colonial Office delivered a curt reply to Pretoria, saying the peremptory demands of the Transvaal government were 'impossible to discuss'. Next day, Boer commandos began crossing the borders into the Cape and Natal.

A year after his return to England to persuade Chamberlain to reverse his policy of 'no war' in South Africa, Sir Alfred Milner had succeeded in bringing about the conflict he wanted. On the day war was declared, he cabled Selborne: 'We have a bad time before us and the Empire is about to support the biggest strain put upon it since the [Indian] Mutiny. Who can say what will befall us before that army corps arrives?'[37]

CHAPTER 13

Strategic Blunders
1899–1900

Cape Town, in the early months of the war, was 'perhaps the most interesting place in the world', according to Cecil Headlam. The docks – lit by electricity at night – presented 'an amazing spectacle', as thousands of khaki-clad troops disembarked from ships 'piled high' with supplies of food and hay.[1] Many of the Empire's most celebrated names – military figures such as Buller, Kitchener, Roberts, French and Haig, and literary men of the likes of Kipling, Churchill, Conan Doyle, Buchan and Amery – could be found at one time or another browsing and sluicing in the bars of the newly opened Mount Nelson Hotel.

Since August of that year, the threat of war in South Africa had cast a long shadow southward. The streets of Cape Town were thronged with English-speaking 'refugees' from Johannesburg – from wealthy mining magnates and their fashion-conscious wives and children to the less affluent families of blue-collar workers, shopkeepers and small traders, as well as many Cornish miners and Lancastrian artisans who jocularly called themselves 'white kaffirs'. In the last days of peace, an estimated 30 000 people crowded onto the open coal trucks of trains leaving the Transvaal for the Cape. It was, as Pakenham records, 'a Great Trek to freedom – British style'.[2]

On 12 October, the opening shots of the Anglo-Boer War rang out when an armoured train bound for Mafeking came under cross-border fire from an 800-strong Transvaal commando, led by Koos de la Rey. On the same day, a force of 14 000 Boer fighters, under their ponderous, 68-year-old Commandant-General, Piet Joubert, invaded Natal, to be joined by 6 000 Free Staters. Ranged against them were roughly 16 000 of the 27 000 British troops then in South Africa.

In strategy, tactics, operating methods and culture, the contrast between the two combatant armies could not have been more stark: the British Army professional, hierarchical, disciplined, slow-moving and led by class-conscious aristocrats; the Boers a mobile, mounted force of farmers and civilian conscripts, uncomfortable with uniforms and military rank, and averse to discipline.[3] Its officers had to be democratically elected. Neither side had much regard for the fighting capabilities of the other on the dry, dusty and hilly South African terrain.

The first few weeks of the war were notable for strategic blunders on both sides. In Natal, the British made the error of splitting their forces north of the Tugela River and sending 4 000 men under Major General Sir William Penn Symons up north to Dundee to draw a defensive line across the road and rail links with the Transvaal. The bulk of the army, under General Sir George White, stayed behind to guard the strategic railway junction at Ladysmith.

The war's first pitched battle took place at Talana, a hill overlooking Dundee, during which Penn Symons was mortally wounded, dying three days later. It was followed by a second engagement, at Elandslaagte next day, at which both forces sustained heavy casualties. On 30 October, the Boers took 1 200 'khakis' prisoner at the mountain pass at Nicholson's Nek and at Modderspruit, forcing White back into Ladysmith, where he and his men were besieged for the next four months.

Superior, in the early stages, in numbers, mobility and firepower, the Boers – under the direction of a group of Joubert's deeply cautious generals, who had little appetite for war – made the cardinal error of disregarding Smuts's plans for a dash to the coast before British reinforcements could arrive in numbers. Their strategy – such as it was – was to lay siege to the nearest enemy garrisons at Ladysmith, Kimberley and Mafeking, in the hope of bottling up the British forces, who would then sue for peace, as they had done after Majuba. By the time the three sieges were lifted many months later, British troop numbers would comfortably exceed those of the Boer commandos.

In the Cape

At Government House in the Cape Town Gardens, after hostilities had opened, Milner found himself run off his feet. He had not only to consult closely on military matters with Butler's replacement, General George Forestier-Walker, but also to hold receptions and lunch parties for visiting celebrities, receive deputations, inspect troops, organise refugee relief and take to the public platform to reassure the anxious colonists.[4] Convinced that all Afrikaners were at heart Kruger loyalists, he was in frequent disagreement with the Prime Minister, WP Schreiner, who was loath to do as the Governor wished and impose martial law throughout the colony, except for districts overrun by anti-British rebels.[5]

Dismayed by Milner's antipathy towards Afrikaners, Schreiner and Merriman – the Cape's two leading parliamentarians – did their best to calm excited, rebellious feelings.[6] The premier, a brother-in-law of Transvaal State Secretary FW Reitz and a moderate who enjoyed the support of the Afrikaner Bond, was one of many Capetonians with Afrikaner sympathies who nonetheless regarded themselves as 'loyal colonists' and subjects of Queen Victoria. Divided loyalty, however, was not a concept the single-minded Governor could understand. As Marlowe observes, Milner's mistrust of more than half of the white inhabitants of the Cape Colony was no different from Kruger's doubts about the Uitlanders, and provided tacit justification for the Transvaal's reluctance to give foreigners the franchise.[7]

The British-born Merriman, the colony's most experienced politician by far, had split loyalties of a different kind. On Christmas Day 1899, he wrote to his sister in England (whose husband and sons supported the war): 'I know so well what it is – justice and freedom on one side and one's country on the other, coupled with that invincible race feeling that makes it impossible for us to wish the Republics to win, and yet – they have right on their side.'[8] To the Liberal MP and historian James Bryce, Merriman confided despairingly, 'At any stage in the last six months, a little sympathetic diplomacy could have produced a settlement. But every concession was met with fresh demands and it was only too evident that no finality was wanted. As a result, the Free State, the Cape's best and firmest friends, were converted into stern and determined foes ... The disgrace to our country [Britain] of the past six months seems to me, who have lived in the midst of it, indelible.'[9]

Buller comes – and goes

On 31 October 1899, Britain's newly appointed commander in South Africa, Sir Redvers Buller, and his entourage arrived in Cape Town on the *Dunottar Castle*. Also aboard was *The Morning Post*'s already famous young war reporter, Winston Churchill, bearing a letter to Milner from Chamberlain, which introduced him as the son of Lord Randolph rather than as a journalist. 'Winston', wrote the Colonial Secretary 'is a clever young fellow ... with a reputation for being bumptious. Put him on the right lines.'[10] The day after his arrival, Churchill was given a detailed briefing by the media-savvy Milner, enabling him to send home an admiring write-up to his London newspaper.

Buller had arrived a few weeks ahead of the bulk of his Army Corps, filled with foreboding. Having served in South Africa before, he had a healthy respect for the Boers' fighting abilities and did not share the ignorance (or wishful thinking) of people in Britain that the war would be over 'by teatime'. After a ceremonial ride in an open landau from the dockside to Government House, a grim-faced Governor handed the new commander-in-chief a sheaf of cables from White containing details of another disaster in Natal.[11]

There was more bad news for Buller from Mafeking, where Baden-Powell had been talked out of a silly plan to invade the Transvaal from Rhodesia.[12] The little town had come under siege by 5 600 burghers (subsequently reduced to just over 3 000). Kimberley, to which Rhodes had repaired to look after his diamond interests, was also under siege. In the first of many tactical errors, Buller endorsed White's decision to lock up his troops in Ladysmith until Army Corps reinforcements could arrive to relieve the garrison.[13]

The grim tidings from Natal caused Buller to revise the plans he had hatched with the War Office for a concerted advance on Pretoria by way of the Orange Free State. In despair, he split the forces at his disposal into three unequal units: the largest to be sent to Ladysmith, the second largest to Kimberley and the remainder to the Cape border to try to prevent the Boers from infiltrating the colony via the Free State.[14]

Leaving General Lord Methuen to relieve Kimberley, and Generals Gatacre and French to protect the Cape's northeastern frontier, Buller secretly departed Cape Town in late November, without informing the Governor, to take personal command of operations in Natal. When Milner, who had done his best to dissuade Buller from leaving his military headquarters, was given the news, he refused at first to believe it. Writing later to Chamberlain, he said that Buller's going to Natal was 'a great mistake'. 'The military situation there is no doubt difficult and bad. But it is comparatively simple. Here it is immensely complicated. He [Buller] cannot judge the position here from Natal ... We are therefore just drifting here militarily without initiative, without foresight.'[15]

Buller's abrupt departure left the already overstretched Governor carrying an undue share of the military burden.[16] Besides having to oversee shipping and railway movements and the regular arrival of Army Corps units throughout the last two months of 1899, Milner had to take measures to prevent a threatened rebellion by Afrikaners in the outer reaches of the colony. His anxieties were heightened by the devastating military reverses sustained by the British during what became known as 'Black Week'.

On 10 December, Gatacre lost a skirmish with Free State commandos at the key railway junction of Stormberg, in the Cape, in which 600 men were forced to surrender, while French barely managed to repel Boer invaders at Colesberg. Next day, Methuen was defeated at Magersfontein, near Kimberley, after launching an ill-advised frontal attack on De la Rey's forces, hidden in well-concealed trenches. However, the worst news of all was the rout of Buller's army by Louis Botha's much smaller force at Colenso, in Natal, in which the British suffered well over 1 100 casualties (killed, wounded or captured). In London, the news from the war front was received with incredulity.

From London, Milner's pen friend Bertha Synge reported that the state of tension in the capital was unique in her lifetime: 'The war affects all, rich and poor alike. All have friends and relations in it and it is no exaggeration to say we are all plunged in gloom ... The War Office is besieged – no one goes to the theatre – concert rooms are empty – new books fall flat – nothing is spoken of save the War.'[17] In reply, Milner wrote that 'one can only hang on grimly and hope for better things. The state of this Colony is awful. It simply reeks with treason ... I am sustained by my own belief in the soundness of the wholly misunderstood cause in which we are fighting. It is a war of liberation – from the rule of the Mauser.'[18]

It took Black Week to drive home to the War Office – and a complacent public – that Britain's 'small-war' army actually had a big war on its hands.[19] Yet in a perverse way, these early setbacks were a blessing in disguise for the British, unaware that their steadily growing troop numbers had already begun to turn the tide. The 'emotional spasm of astonishment, frustration, humiliation' caused by Black Week 'shook the British at home and throughout the Empire' and put an end to previous complacency.[20] It also brought much satisfaction to Britain's rivals on the Continent.

The unexpected tidings from South Africa, in turn, helped unite the British public behind the indecisive Salisbury government and brought political leaders together to reassure the country that the reverses on the veld were no more than tactical, and by no means a national disaster. Asquith, for the Liberals, pronounced the struggle to be much more than 'a question of asserting and maintaining our position in South Africa'. 'It is our title to be known as a world power that is now upon trial.'[21] Over at the War Office, Lansdowne responded to Black Week by announcing the immediate replacement of Buller as commander-in-chief in South Africa by Britain's most distinguished soldier, Field Marshal Lord Roberts, with Major General Kitchener as his chief of staff.

However gloomy the immediate outlook, Milner never abandoned his belief that Britain would eventually emerge victorious from the fighting: he had already begun to hatch plans for a civilian administration to steer the post-war reconstruction of the two republics. FitzPatrick had written from London asking for his permission to approach Chamberlain to discuss his (Milner's) schemes for immigration, irrigation and railway construction after the war.[22] His letter to Milner ended fawningly: 'You have practically all England at your back now and the future is your own. I cannot express my congratulations and gratitude to you for the magnificent handling – the patience, sagacity, courage and tenacity – of the past months.'[23]

In reply to FitzPatrick, Milner wrote that the war 'must have an end, and that end must be our victory … The *ultimate* end is a self-governing white community, supported by *well-treated* and *justly governed* black labour from Cape Town to Zambezi. There must be one flag, the Union Jack, but under it equality of races and languages. Given *equality* all round, English must prevail, though I do not think and do not wish that Dutch should altogether die out ... Though all South Africa should be *one Dominion* with a common government dealing with Customs, Railways and Defence, perhaps also with Native policy, a considerable amount of freedom should be allowed to the several States.'[24]

A 'godsend'

A temporary consolation for Milner amid the tumult was the almost daily presence at his side of a 'godsend', the much younger and 'extremely pretty' Lady Violet Cecil. The two would now take long walks of an early evening, and occasionally go horse-riding together.[25] An accident to Violet's foot in Kimberley on the way to Mafeking with her husband had required surgery, and she had returned to Cape Town where she found a friend in the like-minded Lady Charles Bentinck. Invited by Rhodes to stay at Groote Schuur ('in this lovely house, right away from the dust and racket of Cape Town'[26]) the two women became close companions over the ensuing weeks, making themselves useful by working for the Red Cross and helping to dispense rations to the thousands of war refugees. Violet also acted as Rhodes's hostess until the Colossus left for Kimberley, where he became locked down for weeks, complaining angrily to Milner all the while about the military's lack of urgency in relieving the besieged town.

Milner missed Violet's absence from his side at Government House and wrote to her saying, 'I *want you* to come back ever so much. The great gods will decide that and other things. Meanwhile, please know that you have been a great help indeed at a trying time. You will never quite know how much of a help. But I think whatever happens, I shall hardly ever again be in quite so tight a place as I was when you came to Cape T--& understood.'[27]

As more British troops arrived in Cape Town, so too did wives, relatives and hangers-on. After all, what could be a more worthy social endeavour for a young woman seeking excitement than a voyage to the fairest Cape to assist the war effort? Some of the visiting women did useful work, but others simply got in the way, driving up the prices of hotel rooms and occupying accommodation needed for soldiers.[28] After a few months, a frustrated Milner complained to Bertha Synge that 'apart from the war ... there is the most fearful bother here with lady visitors, their mutual jealousies, feuds, back-bitings and the total unsuitableness of a sort of quasi-Monte Carlo background to that grim tragedy going on in the Northern Veld. Bah! How I hate it. What between the stupidity of our generals and the frivollings of the fashionable females, I often feel desperately ashamed of my country.'[29]

Even Queen Victoria became aware of the trouble that society women were causing in the Cape. Chamberlain wrote to Milner saying the Queen 'regrets to observe the large number of ladies now visiting and remaining in South Africa and strongly disapproves of the hysterical spirit which seems to have influenced some of them to go where they are not wanted'.[30] He asked Milner to draw up an admonition notice for publication under the Queen's name, pointing out that 'for persons travelling merely for health or recreation, and above all for ladies so travelling, no place could be less suitable at the present moment than South Africa'.[31] When the notice was duly published, Milner came in for some mild abuse in social circles for having objected to the 'female invasion'.

New arrivals

On 10 January 1900, Lords Roberts and Kitchener arrived in Cape Town to take command of operations in South Africa from the much-criticised Buller, who was allowed to remain in charge in Natal. Milner's relief was palpable: 'I feel now that at least we shan't be shot sitting', he told Violet over a welcoming dinner for the two officers.[32] To his chagrin, however, the almost 70-year-old Roberts, grieving over the loss of his son at Colenso, had come with a clear plan of action of his own and was disinclined to take advice on military matters from any civilian. Nonetheless, a week after Roberts's arrival, Milner reported to Chamberlain that 'things are rather on the mend in this Colony and unless we have some hideous disaster in Natal, I look forward to a turn in the tide shortly ... there is, for the first time since trouble began, a

A portrait of 16-year-old Violet Maxse in 1888. She married Edward Cecil in 1894 and Alfred Milner in 1920. (*Wikimedia Commons/Noemi Guillaume*)

vigorous control of matters military – some sort of idea what we are driving at and a will behind it'.[33]

But a few more 'hideous disasters' lay ahead in Natal, where two more of Buller's attempts to relieve Ladysmith ended in humiliating defeats at the hands of Botha's commandos – at Spioenkop in late January 1900 and Vaalkrantz in early February. British war reporters – writing for a rapt audience at home – were unforgiving, calling Buller 'Sir Reverse' and referring to him derisively as the 'Ferryman of the Tugela'.

In a letter to Arnold Toynbee's widow, Milner wrote: 'Disaster after disaster has come upon us, but we hang on grimly, and hope to turn the corner yet. People at home have been magnificent, both in their patience with our blundering and in their grand rally to help us out of difficulties. It is a great country to serve. I am working 14 hours a day – have been for weeks and months. But strength is given one for the day's work. I am wonderfully well.'[34]

Of greater concern to Milner, however, were reports from home that 'pro-Boer' Liberal activists and journalists were agitating for the war to be ended by negotiation. Leading the pack was WT Stead, now an outspoken anti-imperialist and critic of his erstwhile friend Rhodes, as well as Chamberlain and his former assistant, Milner. Britain's aggression, according to Stead, 'was too inconceivably impolitic and criminal for me to sanction, even on Milner's authority'. Besides expressing his strongly held convictions in print, Stead had also launched a 'Stop the War' movement whose aim was the recall of Milner, whom he regarded as the principal obstacle to any attempt to bring about peace in South Africa.[35]

CHAPTER 14

Numbers Count
1900

It took Lord Roberts all of a fortnight to round off his preparations for the British Army to embark on a new and different kind of warfare in South Africa. Buller's slow-moving infantry battalions having proved no match for the Boers' mobile riflemen, Britain's most experienced commander had added a new cavalry division and other mounted units to a force that would grow, by the end of February 1900, to 180 000 men.[1] Deciding to rely heavily on the railway network to defeat the Boers,[2] Roberts's 'steamroller' campaign would take his much bigger army to the Boer capitals of Bloemfontein and Pretoria, via the most direct and expeditious route, while relieving Kimberley and Mafeking along the way. On 8 February, he and Kitchener left secretly for the Orange River area, where large numbers of British troops were mustering.[3]

A week later, before columns of infantrymen began marching across the Cape border eastwards, Roberts detached 6 000 cavalrymen under General French to outflank General Piet Cronjé's commandos defending the Free State and bring an end to the siege of Kimberley.[4] For 124 days, a large detachment of Boers under Chief Commandant CJ Wessels had hemmed in 500 British troops and some 2 500 local recruits in the diamond-rich town, blitzing its inhabitants from time to time with shells from 'Long Tom', a 155 mm Creusot siege gun.

There was never any real danger of Kimberley being overrun by the Boers, and its white inhabitants – thanks to Rhodes and the De Beers company's stock of fuel and food – had not suffered the acute food shortages of Ladysmith and Mafeking. Once again, it was the 30 000-strong African population that suffered most, often having to raid the surrounding Boer encampments to feed themselves.[5] In their township, malnutrition and typhoid ran rife throughout the siege.

While Kimberley was under blockade, there had been a fiery clash of wills between the long-suffering British military commander, Colonel Robert Kekewich, and an ailing, restless and querulous Cecil Rhodes, who threatened to overrule the military authorities and surrender Kimberley to the Boers if the British Army did not make greater efforts to liberate the town. Chamberlain observed that if there had been any other British commander in Kimberley but Kekewich, Rhodes would have been locked up.[6]

Inconvenient though the siege may have been to the De Beers company, the defence of Kimberley had pinned down some 7 000 Boers at various times, who might otherwise have sparked off what Milner feared most – an Afrikaner uprising in the far reaches of the northern Cape.[7] When the siege was ended on 15 February 1900, the news was greeted with euphoria by the British press and public. 'Kimberley is won', crowed Harmsworth's *Daily Mail*: 'Mr Cecil Rhodes is free, the De Beers shareholders are all full of themselves, and the beginning of the war is at an end.'[8]

Simultaneously, the main British force under Kitchener was advancing steadily towards the Modder River, where Cronjé's Boer force, with its 500 wagons, had retreated from Magersfontein eastwards along the river to defend the approaches to Bloemfontein. After ten days of artillery bombardment and infantry attacks on the Boer encampment at a drift near Paardeberg, Cronjé was forced to surrender – on 27 February 1900, the anniversary of Majuba. The general and 4 000 of his men were taken prisoner and transported to camps on the island of St Helena. With the route to Bloemfontein now open, Boer resistance melted away and morale crumbled as thousands of burghers left the capital for the sanctuary of the countryside.[9]

Ladysmith relieved

One day after Cronjé's surrender at Paardeberg, Buller's troops in Natal finally managed to lift the siege at Ladysmith, where the Boer ranks north of the Tugela had been thinned out by the need for reinforcements to be rushed hastily to the Free State. Cavalry under the command of Lord Dundonald, accompanied by embedded war reporter Winston

Churchill, entered the town in the afternoon of 28 February to end the 118-day siege. In a brief speech, General White told a hollow-eyed crowd of long-suffering residents, 'Thank God, we kept the flag flying.'[10] Three days later, General Buller arrived to take formal occupation of the town.

In Britain, where the little outpost in Natal had become a litmus test of her military endeavours in South Africa, huge crowds stopped the traffic in London streets, exulting at the news that Ladysmith had at last been relieved.[11] In Cape Town, there was much excitement too. A large multiracial crowd gathered in front of Government House, singing 'God Save the Queen' and 'Rule, Britannia!' and giving Governor Milner an enthusiastic reception when he came outside to address them.[12]

Gratified though he was by the change in British fortunes, Milner was still deeply concerned at the threat of an Afrikaner rebellion in parts of the Cape Colony that Roberts had denuded of troops. His fears materialised at Prieska, in the northwestern Cape, where 600 Free Staters joined forces with anti-British rebels from the Cape and occupied the little town, proclaiming it to be Free State territory.[13] Also under threat was De Aar, the key railway junction through which supplies for the British Army had to pass. Milner proposed that a small, mobile force of British troops be kept permanently in the colony to nip incipient rebellions in the bud, but Roberts refused to be deflected from the main task at hand. After crushing the uprising at Prieska and sending three columns under Kitchener to clear the De Aar district, the British commander continued his advance, ignoring Governor Milner's fears and brushing aside warnings of a potential uprising in the rear.

Having expected the war to be over in a couple of months if waged properly, a defiant Milner was not about to allow military strategy to override political considerations. His opinion of most British Army generals – excluding Roberts and Kitchener – was of an 'avalanche of military incompetence' that had nearly swept the Empire away.[14] And he was not going to concede turf – even to Roberts. Writing to Chamberlain in early March, an irritated Governor complained that the rebellion in the northwest had 'taken up all my days and (partly) nights ... Headquarters being 600 miles off ... it is extraordinarily difficult to get the military authorities to move ... The imperious necessities of Kimberley and Ladysmith have caused everything to be done in a hurry ... It is annoying to think that all this mess in the Colony might have been prevented by 500 men *permanently encamped* at Prieska, and that everybody knew this except the military chiefs whose eyes (naturally enough) were rigidly fixed on the main advance only. However, I suppose we shall muddle out of it somehow.'[15]

Bloemfontein falls

At midday on 13 March 1900, Roberts rode unimpeded into Bloemfontein, made his way triumphantly to the Presidency – vacated by Steyn a day earlier – and hoisted the Union Jack in the front garden.[16] Over the next few days and weeks, he did his best to ease burgher apprehensions by asking government officials to remain at their posts and inviting some of them to cocktail parties and other functions.[17] He shut down the local anti-British newspaper and used its printing press to launch a new, bilingual paper, *The Friend*, recruiting Rudyard Kipling from Cape Town to act temporarily as editor.[18]

Only eight days before Roberts arrived, presidents Steyn and Kruger had met in the Free State capital and issued a joint appeal for peace to Lord Salisbury personally, who had proclaimed less than a year earlier 'we want no gold, we want no territory'.[19] The two presidents repudiated the claim that the Boers had gone to war with aggressive intentions and asked for the independence of their republics to be restored. Their plea received short shrift.[20] In a cabled reply on 11 March, Salisbury stated curtly that Britain was not prepared to recognise the independence of either of the republics, which 'claimed to treat the inhabitants of extensive portions of Her Majesty's Dominions as if those dominions had been annexed to one or other of them'.[21]

Shortly after Bloemfontein fell to the British, Kruger and Steyn held a *krygsraad* (council of war) at Kroonstad, some 200 km north of the capital. Among the attendees were an ailing General Joubert; Louis Botha, Joubert's designated successor as the SAR's military commander; Christiaan de Wet, the soon-to-be-appointed overall commandant of the Free State forces; Koos de la Rey from the western Transvaal; and FW Reitz, the SAR's State Secretary. It was unanimously agreed that if the two republics were not to become 'mere appendages of the British empire', it was imperative to continue the war rather than sue for peace.[22]

However, since there were now too few Boers to confront the British by conventional means, an entirely new strategy was called for. From now on, there were to be no more Boer encampments or cumbersome and slow-moving wagon trains, and no more head-on confrontations with British forces; henceforth, the Boers' tactics would be hit-and-run, guerrilla-style raids on the enemy's communication links and supply chains. 'The hunter would become the hunted'[23] until the Salisbury government tired of spending huge amounts of money on the war and was ready to negotiate.

Two weeks after occupying Bloemfontein, Roberts played host to Milner, who arrived after a 14-day tour of inspection of the now rebel-free northeastern Cape, stopping off at Matjiesfontein, Victoria West, De Aar, Prieska, Stormberg and Aliwal North. Hearing the news of a further British setback at Mostert's Hoek, near Reddersburg, south of Bloemfontein, Milner noted, 'another bad day. The Boers are certainly dying extremely hard, if they are not coming to life again.'

From the Free State, he wrote to his old mentor, Goschen (now Viscount), to express his hope that nothing would induce the British government 'to relax now, even if the war should last another six months ... An irreconcilable enemy has tried to extinguish us as a power in South Africa. We must extinguish him. There is absolutely no compromise possible. An ultimate peace between the two white races is perfectly possible – I am sure of that – but possible only under one condition, that there shall be but one flag and one citizenship.'[24]

Writing also to Violet, he confided to being not much cheered by his journey through the Cape: 'The state of the Colony is awful, just reeking with treason. And the more I see of the Army, the more unhappy I feel about it. We have been saved by two men – especially one of them, that wonderful old creature [Roberts] with a heart of gold who alone seems untouched by jealousy, egotism, pettiness.'[25]

At a dinner in Milner's honour given by *The Friend*, a triumphalist Kipling proposed a toast to 'the health of a man who has taught the British Empire its responsibilities, and the rest of the world its power, who has filled the seas with the transports and the earth with the tramp of armed men, who has made Cape Town see in Table Bay a sight she has never seen before ... all in support of the Mother Country. Gentlemen, I give you the name of the Empire-builder – Stephanus Paulus Kruger.'[26]

Mafeking

Roberts delayed his departure from Bloemfontein for as long as seven weeks to enable his footsore and battle-weary infantrymen – many of them ill with enteric fever – to recover their strength before moving on. On 3 May, he headed northwards along the railway line to the Transvaal, confident that nothing could stop him now from bringing the war to a rapid conclusion.[27] His troop complement had grown to 170 000, with more men on the way, by comparison with the Boers' depleted and scattered force of some 30 000 men.[28]

By now, the only remaining town under siege by the Boers was Mafeking, which had held out (and tied down a Boer force) for more than six months but whose food supplies were almost exhausted. Baden-Powell's (and Cecil's) stout defence of the town and strict rationing of food supplies had enabled the white population to survive, but hundreds of Africans had succumbed to disease and malnutrition.

Mafeking's 'heroic' resistance for so long had gripped the imagination of British newspaper readers, fed daily with predictions of how long the little outpost could hold out before having to surrender. One of those holding her breath was Queen Victoria, who sent Baden-Powell a message in April expressing her admiration for his 'patient and resolute defence' of the town.[29] On 17 May 1900, a relief column from Kimberley finally broke through the Boer defences, bringing to an end the 217-day siege.

News of Mafeking's relief was greeted in Britain with an outpouring of nationalistic fervour seldom seen before, with huge crowds swarming through the streets of London and other cities, cheering, singing, dancing, waving patriotic flags and banners, and lighting bonfires. The celebrations went on for days, adding a new verb to the English language: to 'maffick' – to exult in an unseemly manner. Opponents of the war, both in Britain and South Africa, were disgusted by the displays of unbridled jingoism, and even supporters of imperialism were given pause for sober reflection.[30]

In their book on the Anglo-Boer War, the British historians Judd and Surridge describe the pandemonium over Mafeking as 'essentially pathetic: the relieved reaction of a nation fed on grandiose notions of imperial might, but underneath all the glitter, pomp and circumstance, insecure, resentful and embarrassed at the war's early fiascos'.[31] Milner, the anti-triumphalist, could not have expressed disapproval of the mafficking much better himself.

High jinks

In Cape Town, when Violet Cecil heard the news from Mafeking, she took to her bed with a headache.[32] Milner wrote her a note saying, 'There is nothing at all that I can say to you. I think you know what I should like to say. God ever bless you & give you all good & don't write. It is not a day for writing.'[33] Evidently, the return of Lord Edward to Cape Town was not a prospect that appealed to either of them. On 18 June, Milner sent his secretary, Ozzy Walrond, away for the night and the couple dined alone at Government House. According to Hugh and Mirabel Cecil, whatever happened that night will never be known, but Violet made a special note of the date in her diary and from then on 'Alfred had the supreme place in her heart'.[34] A week later she was reunited with her husband, who did not stay in the city for long before heading north on duty again.

Milner continued to deprecate the high jinks of visiting British women, who were 'sky-larking about under the noses of the enemy'. Present company was presumably excluded, since Violet and her friends were among the many who were thoroughly enjoying themselves in South Africa. She wrote regularly to a family friend, St John Brodrick, now at the War Office, giving him the social gossip from the Cape and claiming to be missing life in England. Disbelieving her protestations that life away from home was dull, Brodrick wrote to Violet saying, 'I am now a total disbeliever in the deserted, sorrowing grass widow – dragging along a dreary existence with longing for child and friends at home. Every returning friend brings me fresh evidence of a bustling, buoyant and beloved figure, dominating Cape Town society,

pervading South African politics ... I now record my deliberate conviction that, with intervals of depression, you are having the loftiest
and most antique time of your life; that you have not the least desire to
come home.'[35]

Also in Cape Town and hoping to persuade the military authorities to allow him to rejoin the army in the field was Winston Churchill,
now known around the world after his daring escape from captivity in
Pretoria and dash to freedom via Delagoa Bay. In his typically flamboyant style, *The Morning Post*'s star reporter wrote of Milner that 'only at
Government House did I find the Man of No Illusions, the anxious but
unwearied pro-consul, understanding the faults and virtues of both
sides, measuring the balance of rights and wrongs, and determined –
more determined than ever, for is it not the only hope for the future
of South Africa? – to use his knowledge and power to strengthen the
Imperial ties.'[36] Milner was so pleased with the description of himself
that he would occasionally sign off private correspondence as 'The Man
of No Illusions'.[37]

Rebels

Having rested for ten days at Kroonstad, Roberts's army set off again
towards Johannesburg and Pretoria. On 28 May 1900, before his men
crossed the Vaal River into the SAR, Roberts announced the Crown's
formal annexation of the Orange Free State, and the change of its
name to the Orange River Colony. The proclamation was backdated to
24 May, Queen Victoria's official birthday.

In a further notice on 1 June, Roberts announced that since the former Free State was now a British possession, any citizens who continued
to bear arms would be regarded as rebels. He was determined to curb
the activities of burghers who refused to surrender and had rejoined
the commandos attacking British supply routes along the railway line.
By further proclamation in August and September – applicable to the
Transvaal as well – Roberts tightened the screw by decreeing that former Boer combatants who declined to take the oath of allegiance to the
Crown were to be regarded as prisoners of war, and would be subject to
deportation. Any building harbouring Boer guerrillas would be razed
to the ground, and anyone failing to notify the British of the presence

of combatants on their properties regarded as aiding and abetting the enemy. The ensuing burning of farms and removal of livestock heightened Boer bitterness and aroused such an outcry in Liberal circles in Britain that Roberts's policy had to be quickly modified.[38]

With the war having relieved Milner of the burden of negotiating with Pretoria, his concern was the political situation in the Cape Colony. As High Commissioner, he still toyed with the idea of suspending the Cape constitution to enable him to govern all four colonies on the same footing, though he knew this would bring him into conflict with the Colonial Office.[39] His immediate difficulty was how to deal with 3 000 Afrikaner 'rebels', 'with another 3 000 more at least to come', who had laid down their arms after the Boer resistance in the north had collapsed. Trial by jury for political offences, he complained to Chamberlain, was not an option because every potential juryman in the colony was violently partisan. 'In one place, no jury could possibly convict; in another, the accused would stand no chance of acquittal.'[40]

As Governor, he demanded that his Schreiner-led ministry should make up its mind about the fate of several hundred rebel 'ringleaders' – among them MPs, mayors, army officers and others – telling the Cape Parliament it was 'not enough for you to grumble at martial law or preach clemency, and make excuses for treason ... We are showing great clemency to the rank and file, but you surely cannot maintain that we are to wipe the slate clean and let ... the instigators and leaders of rebellion go unpunished.'[41]

In trying to resolve the dilemma, Milner believed, the Cape government would split apart: 'The Prime Minister declines to be drawn one way or the other ... It is impossible to see how the ministry can be kept together, the members of which hold diametrically opposite views on all the most vital questions of the day.'[42] Writing to Hely-Hutchinson, Milner noted that 'the great crux here is the enormous number of rebels (5 000 at least). We cannot try them all for high treason. As a matter of fact, I don't want to try too many. Yet we must do something to them. I'd rather leave the country than accept Schreiner's proposal for a general whitewashing.'[43]

As Milner had predicted, Cape politicians proved unable to paper over their divisions over how best to deal with the thousands of rebels.

Dr Thomas te Water, a leading light in the Afrikaner Bond, demanded a general amnesty and a trial by jury for leaders of the rebellion. The rebels had taken up arms, he contended, only after 'vainly endeavouring, by all possible constitutional means to prevent what they, in common with the rest of the civilised world, believe to be an unjust and infamous war against their near kinsmen', one that had been forced upon them.[44]

To Te Water and other Bond members, even the British government's proposal to disenfranchise rebels for terms from five years to a lifetime was too extreme. In June, Schreiner was forced to step down as prime minister over the rebel issue and, in order to uphold the Cape constitution, the 70-year-old (and more pliable) Sprigg returned to lead another Progressive ministry, but with Schreiner, Rose Innes and some Bond members serving on it. Milner told Chamberlain that he was disappointed with Schreiner, who had 'fallen between two stools ... too imperialist for his followers, but not sufficiently strong in his advocacy of his own line to carry others with him. His going leaves things in an awful mess.'[45]

CHAPTER 15

Pretoria Falls
1900

Commandant-General Louis Botha and 3 000 Boers were all that stood between Roberts's massive war machine, advancing on either side of the railway line over a 40-km-wide front, and the gold mines of the Witwatersrand. After holding up the British at Klip River, outside Johannesburg, for two days, the outflanked Boers were eventually forced into headlong retreat. On 31 May 1900, Roberts marched into an almost deserted Johannesburg and raised the British flag over the courthouse. He would not have known of the drama playing out behind the scenes over the previous few days.

A group of Boer leaders, led by FW Reitz, had been intent on blowing up the gold mines, the richest prize of the war.[1] Sabotaging mine shafts, they felt, would be just retribution for the British who had caused the war, as well as for the wealthy mining 'capitalists' who had supported it.[2] Smuts was among those who opposed blowing up the mines while they were still in Boer hands but had changed his mind by the time the British took over the Witwatersrand. Kruger and others felt the mines should not be blown up, but the mere threat to disable them might somehow induce shareholders in Europe to come to the Transvaal's aid. A third group, led by Louis Botha and Fritz Krause – a Cambridge-educated lawyer – were totally against any plans to sabotage the mines.

Botha, as a former businessman and Volksraad member, understood the importance of gold revenues to the Transvaal and told Kruger that if the mines were to be damaged, he would order his commandos to stop fighting and protect the shafts. Kruger complied, ordering the Witwatersrand's military commander, the aforementioned Krause, to call off attempts to damage mining properties.[3]

On 30 May, anxious to avoid fighting in the streets of Johannesburg and to ensure that the mines were secure, Roberts sent an officer under a flag of truce to Krause's office to call for the town's surrender. Playing for time to enable Botha's hard-pressed commandos to retreat towards Pretoria with 'as much supplies, arms and gold as they could muster', Krause prevaricated, before yielding peacefully 24 hours later.[4] An appreciative Roberts wrote to Krause to thank him for his 'energy and vigilance' in maintaining law and order, and for the great courtesy he had displayed.[5]

As British troops approached the outskirts of Pretoria, 50 km away, there was widespread panic and a mass exodus of frightened citizens by train, cart and wagon and on foot. Two days earlier, the SAR's Executive Council had decided to abandon the capital in the face of impending defeat, moving Kruger and the seat of government by special train to Machadodorp, 216 km to the east. The defence of Pretoria was left in the hands of Louis Botha, whose orders were to hold up the British advance for as long as possible.

Shaken by the desertion of so many burghers, Botha called an emergency krygsraad of senior officers to consider whether or not to surrender. Smuts wrote of 'the bitter humiliation and despondency of that awful moment when the stoutest hearts and strongest wills in the Transvaal army were, albeit but for a moment, to sink beneath the tide of our misfortune'.[6] Stung by critical messages from the Free State, where De Wet was causing havoc, and encouraged by the determination of younger Boer commanders at the krygsraad, the gathering vowed not to engage in any peace talks with the British, but rather to beat a fighting retreat to the east in order to frustrate the enemy.[7]

On 5 June, Roberts – with Kitchener at his side – rode into Pretoria's central square and hoisted aloft the same Union Jack that had been hauled down after the British defeat at Majuba, 19 years earlier. A victory march-past followed, in celebration of the troops' exhausting 34-day trek from Bloemfontein. To the thousands of hensoppers (hands-uppers) who had already taken the oath of neutrality, Roberts was able to add, in the coming days, hundreds more burghers who responded positively to his promise of an amnesty for those who laid down their arms. Eventually about 5 500 hensoppers became active

The British commander-in-chief in South Africa, Field Marshal Frederick S Roberts, pictured in Pretoria in June 1900. (*Wikimedia Commons/George Grantham Bain Collection, Library of Congress*)

supporters of the British war effort, becoming known as 'joiners' (or collaborators). To the experienced Field Marshal, it seemed that the Boers had been vanquished. Apart from mopping-up operations, the war in South Africa was all but over.

Knowing that Roberts was anxious not to remain at his post for any longer than needed, Milner informed Britain's military commander that as soon as his responsibility for the two new colonies was at an end, he (Milner) was ready to take over the civilian administration. Not that he wanted to stay in South Africa, the High Commissioner insisted: he would much prefer to leave and rest his claim to fame on 'the fact that I precipitated a crisis, which was inevitable, before it was altogether too late. It is not a very agreeable, and in many eyes not a very creditable piece of business to have brought about a big war. Still, I think, in the distant future, people will say it was better than burying my head in the sand, as I might easily have done.'[8]

Help from home

As the overlord-designate of all four South African colonies, Milner had been giving careful thought, while confined to the Cape, to the reconstruction and future administration of the two ex-republics.[9] In August, he was given the assistance of two commissions sent out from London to look into the potential for post-war land settlement by British immigrants, and to examine the vexed question of monopolies and concessions in the former SAR. The first was headed by one Hugh Arnold-Forster; the second by another of Milner's old friends, the Honourable Alfred Lyttelton, better known as the first man to represent England at both football and cricket.

Lyttelton's wife, Edith, recorded in her diary her pleasure that the High Commissioner had unburdened himself with complete frankness to them and shared his plans for the future of the country. Like the two Violets, Edith was captivated by Milner, telling a relative she was 'immensely impressed by certain things in him. His ideas on the future are thrillingly interesting, so big and full of vision.'[10] Back in England, she became another of Milner's most devoted advocates and a moving spirit in the pro-imperial Victoria League.[11]

One of Milner's great concerns was that the Colonial Office might subject the two 'conquered territories' to a prolonged period of military government, to be followed by premature 'self-government'.[12] This was not going to happen if he, Milner, could prevent it. Writing to Chamberlain, he said he could not imagine a more perfect recipe for failure. What the Free State needed was a short period of military rule, followed by 'an autocratic civil government until the mess was cleared up'.[13] In the Transvaal, fundamental questions could not be settled by 'the methods of *party politics in their crudest form*. There must be a process of vigorous political sanitation before responsible government can be grown in that soil, *and there must be time for the British population to come back and qualify as voters* and in larger numbers, before we stake everything on a ballot-box.'[14]

In reply, Chamberlain said Milner was mistaken in thinking there were any plans for early self-government. There would be Crown Colony government 'until we are sufficiently assured of the goodwill of the Boers to grant full Colonial rights'.[15] In a further missive, the Colonial Secretary said he was waiting anxiously for a notification from Milner that he was ready to take up work at Bloemfontein or Pretoria: 'At present, we assume that you will be Governor of the Transvaal and High Commissioner [for South Africa], and Hely-Hutchinson Governor of the Cape.'[16]

Chamberlain's hopes that Milner might soon be able to assume his civilian responsibilities were to be dashed by the activities of Boer guerrillas across large swathes of the Orange River Colony and the entire southwestern Transvaal. And to Milner's dismay, regular attacks on trains were also preventing thousands of Uitlanders and other refugees from leaving the Cape and returning to their homes and businesses in Johannesburg.[17]

In the north

The Transvaal's new Governor-designate could not leave Cape Town safely until October 1900, when he undertook – with Chamberlain's approval, since Lord Roberts was formally still in charge – a short visit to assess the situation in Pretoria ('a lovely little spot – of water, trees and gardens, ruined by the most *horrible* vulgarities … of the German architecture of the Bismarckian era at its worst'[18]) and Johannesburg, where he met senior military and civilian figures. With him on the trip was a new aide, Lionel Curtis, set to become the leader of the Kindergarten, a group of talented young recruits, mainly from Oxford, eager to be involved in furthering the interests of Empire. While briefly in the Transvaal, Milner inaugurated the South African Constabulary, a new paramilitary police force for the two ex-republics under the command of Robert Baden-Powell, since promoted to major general after the relief of Mafeking. (The force was to be disbanded in 1908.)

Returning to the Cape by armoured train via Bloemfontein after his departure was delayed by more damage to the railway line,[19] Milner was able to witness at first hand the devastation caused by British farm-burning in the countryside. He complained to Chamberlain that while he was in favour of 'discriminating destruction' as a 'deterrent and punishment', he did not approve of the indiscriminate burning of all homes in a particular district simply to make it untenable for the enemy. When he took over the civilian administration, he intended to put an end to the 'wholesale destruction', which could lead, he believed, to the ruin of the entire country.[20]

One month earlier, an unwell Rhodes, suffering the after-effects of another heart attack during the siege of Kimberley, had returned to Cape Town, disavowing any intention of taking over the premiership. Although he could count on the support of almost 50 MPs, the Colossus proposed instead to stiffen Sprigg's ministry until he (Rhodes) was fit enough to run the Cape again. The entire country was still at war, he explained to his followers, and not yet ready to be transformed politically along the lines he envisaged. Confined to Cape Town, Rhodes could not visit his many fruit farms, factories and business premises around the colony as Boer guerrillas were now threatening towns and villages in the western Cape within 240 km of the city.[21]

From Pretoria, Roberts had sent Kitchener back across the Orange River to deal with De Wet's rebels, still threatening British encampments and facilities close to the railway line. Leading a by now much reduced force, the British commander pressed on along the railway line to the Lowveld to try to break through the Boer defensive line at Diamond Hill, about 30 km east of Pretoria. Occupying part of the hill by nightfall on 12 June, the second day of the battle, British troops woke next morning (13 June) to find that the Boers had stolen away in the darkness to avoid being encircled by General Hamilton's forces, which had broken through the Boer line in the south.

Six weeks later, between 21 and 27 August, at Bergendal, on the Dalmanutha plateau between Belfast and Machadodorp, the last great set-piece battle of the war took place, the hilly terrain offsetting the numerical imbalance between Botha's dwindling force and Roberts's much larger army. After fierce fighting, the Boers were compelled to fall back once again to avoid being encircled, thus allowing the British to capture Machadodorp.

For Paul Kruger, the war would come to a painful conclusion on 11 September, when he took a train from Nelspruit to Delagoa Bay and was picked up by the *Gelderland*, a cruiser sent by a sympathetic Queen Wilhelmina of the Netherlands to take him into European exile. Within days of the Boer figurehead's departure, Roberts announced the formal annexation of the Transvaal by the British Crown, and his intention to hand over command to General Kitchener.

British election

In Britain, the Unionist government sought to cash in on the British Army's successes by calling for a renewed mandate while the victorious Roberts was still in South Africa. Responding to Liberal complaints of the unfairness of trying to turn pride in a military victory into votes, the Unionists' Duke of Devonshire pointed out that the captain of a cricket XI, having won the toss, usually puts his own side in to bat rather than his adversaries.[22] Salisbury was in poor health and made no public appearances during the election campaign, but Chamberlain barnstormed around the country crying, 'A vote for the Liberals is a vote for the Boers', and suggesting that a Liberal victory would represent a political defeat for the British Army in South Africa. A prominent Unionist campaign poster depicted Liberal leaders kneeling in supplication before President Kruger.[23]

In the bitterly contested 'khaki' election of October 1900, the Unionists were returned to office with a decisive 134-seat majority but a much narrower lead in the popular vote. Since the 'South African War' was presumed to be over, the Unionist coalition's handling of the war did not come under much scrutiny. Selborne wrote to Milner to say the election was a ratification by the nation, 'to the hilt' of Milner's and the Colonial Office's policy in South Africa.[24] The election result was to give the Unionists another six years in power.

A new member of the House of Commons was the 25-year-old Winston Churchill, who had returned home in July after his exploits in South Africa and won a seat for the Conservative wing of the Unionists in the constituency of Oldham, near Manchester. Milner wrote to the young MP to congratulate him and to thank him for his supportive remarks while on the campaign trail. Speaking to an audience in Birmingham, Churchill had asserted that 'few British public servants in this century have been saddled with a heavier load of difficulty and responsibility ... or borne it with greater strength, than Sir Alfred Milner. The removal of Sir Alfred from his control of South African affairs at the present time would be a greater blow to Imperial interests than the defeats at Magersfontein, Stormberg, Colenso and Spionkop put together', declared the aspiring MP, one never given to understatement.[25]

Having won another vote of confidence, Prime Minister Salisbury took the opportunity to reshuffle his government, replacing Goschen and bringing into the cabinet his eldest son, Lord Cranborne, his son-in-law, Lord Selborne, and other relatives, causing the Liberals to accuse him of running a family business – the 'Hotel Cecil'. At the War Office, Lansdowne was replaced by Violet's pen friend, St John Brodrick, a man in whom Milner could confide with absolute frankness. As Pakenham recounts, Brodrick's feet were hardly under his desk when he received an extraordinarily emotional letter from Milner, predicting disaster in South Africa unless Britain adopted 'a more systematic military strategy'.[26]

Milner informed a startled Brodrick that the war in South Africa was far from over – as Lord Roberts unwisely claimed. It had erupted recently in a more virulent form – guerrilla warfare.[27] For this unanticipated development, he pinned the blame 'fairly and squarely' on Roberts, who had stayed on for too long. Milner had little confidence in Kitchener either, who had made no secret of his wish to hurry matters along so that he could leave for a more important assignment in

India. Suggesting that he might be able to do better than the generals himself, Milner told the new War Secretary that British strategy in South Africa had to be one of 'gradual subjugation'.[28]

Roberts leaves

In early December 1900, Roberts left South Africa, after paying a sorrowful visit to Natal to see the grave of his son Frederick, at Colenso. Stopping briefly in Durban, he repeated to an enthusiastic audience his belief that the war 'was practically over'.[29] According to Pakenham, despite Milner's high regard for 'the little man', no one felt a deeper sense of relief at Roberts's going than he did.[30] The commander-in-chief's misplaced optimism that the war was at an end, Britain's High Commissioner believed, was doing great damage both at home and in South Africa.[31]

At a farewell luncheon in Cape Town, the departing general paid generous tribute to Milner, whose kindness, forbearance and courage had 'immensely lightened my burden'.[32] Defending Milner against his critics, Roberts said he doubted that 'even those among you who see his daily work can appreciate how much he has done ... or what a deep debt of gratitude the country at large owes to him'.[33] Writing to Violet Cecil, who had returned home with Lord Edward in October, Milner said he was glad at the ovation given to Roberts when he set finally sail: 'We have all shouted ourselves hoarse over him and I am glad for his sake ... but there is something ill-omened and bizarre and almost repulsive in all this triumphing and congratulations – in the middle of war.'[34]

Roberts arrived in Britain to a rapturous welcome given only to conquering heroes. His warship was greeted with a 19-gun salute at Cowes, near the Isle of Wight, from where he left for a special audience with Queen Victoria, who raised his title from viscount to earl. He was subsequently made a Knight of the Garter and given the sum of £100 000 by a grateful Parliament, but when it became apparent that the war in South Africa was by no means over, a proposed service of thanksgiving at St Paul's Cathedral had to be hastily cancelled.[35]

CHAPTER 16

Scorched Earth
1900–1901

During Milner's brief foray onto the Highveld, the leaders of the two former republics, President Steyn and General Botha, joined Smuts and De la Rey at Cyferfontein, a secluded farm near Rustenburg, about 130 km northwest of Pretoria, to decide how best to counter the British Army's farm-burning tactics. (It should be recorded here that presidents Kruger and Steyn had vehemently rejected Roberts's annexations of their territories by proclamation, for being legally invalid.) While the ransacking of farms and looting of livestock might be keeping vengeance-seeking burghers in the field, untold hardship and misery were being inflicted on their women and children.

Ever the realist, Louis Botha harboured thoughts of suing for peace, but Steyn was vehemently opposed. Before the war, the Free State President had regarded it as foolhardy for the Boers to challenge the might of Empire; now he argued against any negotiations over peace. An autocrat and race-conscious patriot in the Milner mould, Steyn wanted to fight to the bitter end in order to preserve the 'chosenness' of the Afrikaner tribe. If the *volk* had believed at the outbreak of war that God was with them, what had changed since then, he wanted to know?[1]

Smuts was a temporary convert to Steyn's argument, and at Cyferfontein the Boer high command decided not only to prolong the guerrilla war but also to split what remained of their commandos into two separate forces – one to re-enter Natal and the other to invade the Cape Colony in the hope of arousing Afrikaner support for the republican cause.

Returning to the Cape from the north, Milner was in a deeply pessimistic mood. Reporting to Chamberlain, he described progress in South Africa as 'crablike'. He had been taken aback 'at the vitality and

President Marthinus Steyn of the Orange Free State. (*War Museum of the Boer Republics, Bloemfontein*)

ubiquity of the enemy, the staleness and dissatisfaction of our men, and the aimlessness and inconsequence of our present operations'.[2] He continued to keep his mind closed to the notion of using the split loyalties of Cape Afrikaners as a means of bridging the gap between the British and Transvaal governments, insisting on maintaining the division between 'sheep and goats'. As Marlowe comments, coming from an administrator in Milner's position, the increasing intemperance of his remarks about the Cape Dutch was 'astonishing'.[3]

Noting in his diary that the state of the Cape Colony was 'growing steadily worse', Milner complained to the Colonial Secretary that sedition was on the rise and a 'weak, divided cabinet, demoralized by a Bond-ridden Parliament', was unable to deal effectively with Afrikaner 'treason'.[4] Furthermore, the unbridled licence given to press and pulpit and the 'unchecked extravagance of the rebel party in the Assembly' were fostering racial hatred and prejudice. Besides martial law, the only other way to counter the twin threats of Afrikaner insurrection and guerrilla warfare was 'the formation of town and district guards in every part of the country under the Imperial authorities'.[5] But, as Governor, he had been unable to get the Progressive ministry, led by Rhodes's placeman, Sprigg, to agree.

Matters were not much better in the Transvaal, where a week after Roberts's triumphant departure, the British Army had suffered yet another calamitous defeat at the hands of Boer guerrillas, led by Smuts and De la Rey, at the farm Nooitgedacht on the road between Pretoria and Rustenburg. Even worse news was the invasion of the Cape by more than 2 000 Free State Boers, under Kritzinger and Hertzog, who had eluded British defences along the frontier and were now on the run in the colony.

Milner was especially concerned at the prospect of a widespread Afrikaner uprising in the Cape in support of the guerrilla campaign in the north. Though neither knew it, both he and Smuts shared the (mistaken) view that large numbers of Cape Afrikaners were ready for revolution.[6] While Roberts was in command in South Africa, Milner had kept silent, but with the war proper now over, he felt it his duty to speak out on British policy once again.

Among the measures he deemed urgent to quell a 'second rebellion' of Cape Afrikaners was suspending the constitution of the colony to put the Cape on exactly the same footing as the ex-Boer republics – that is, under his control. He also wished to impose martial law to deal with 'traitors' and hoped to persuade Kitchener to adopt a new and different military strategy. Sprigg was initially reluctant to reintroduce martial law, but after the invasion by Hertzog and Kritzinger's commando, he was prevailed upon to extend the measure to the entire colony – except for ports, a part of Cape Town and the 'native reserves'.[7]

Relations with Kitchener

Although determined to get along well with Kitchener, Milner chafed at the arrangement whereby he was effectively subject to Kitchener's authority while having to administer the two ex-republics from afar until civilian government could be established. Writing to Violet Cecil – in whom he was now confiding freely – he said it was fortunate he admired Kitchener in so many ways, and was therefore prepared to put up with a lot and never take offence: 'I am determined to get on with him and I think he likes me and has some respect for me … But shall I be able to manage this strong, self-willed man, dying to be off in time to take India, and turn his enormous power into the right channel?' 'I have a plan', Milner told Violet, 'but as yet [Kitchener] is unconvinced, or rather not sufficiently convinced.'[8]

Milner's plan was for the British Army to use the South African Constabulary to secure each district in the two ex-republics one by one, and the rural areas 'bit by bit' rather than by 'sweeping and scouring' the countryside.[9] Roberts's error, Milner believed, had been his misplaced optimism and failure to police each district properly before marching on to the next.[10] But neither British commander had been inclined to heed civilian advice, and the strategy Kitchener had implemented after Roberts's departure also deviated sharply from that of Milner.

If he could not catch the mobile Boers, Kitchener reckoned, he would enmesh the enemy in a spider's web of blockhouses – small fortifications linked by barbed-wire fencing – strung out along railways and roads and across the open countryside.[11] In January 1901, his troops embarked on a series of sweeping drives to force Boer guerrillas out into the veld and strip their districts bare of any means of support – horses, cattle, sheep and crops – as well as of women and children. Boer

Lieutenant General Horatio Herbert Kitchener succeeded Lord Roberts as British commander-in-chief. (*Wikimedia Commons/Duffus Brothers*)

wives were regarded by Kitchener as being as much of an obstacle to military victory as the commandos in the field: 'There is no doubt the women are keeping up the war and are far more bitter than the men', he once declared.[12]

Kitchener's troops herded together the hundreds of Boer families from burning farms, adrift in the veld and unable to fend for themselves, in hastily constructed 'protection' or 'concentration' camps, similar to those introduced by the Spanish during the Cuban War of Independence (1895–1898). The conditions in the camps were dire, with disease and malnutrition claiming the lives of many thousands of women and children, white and black alike. At one time, the camps contained as many as 160 000 inmates.[13] Not surprisingly, the effect of these 'methods of barbarism' (see Chapter 17) was to deepen the Boers' hatred of their imperial enemy.

Early in 1901, the war receded temporarily into the background at the news of the death of Queen Victoria on 22 January. 'The enemy have now marched two commandos through the Colony and they are hundreds of miles nearer Cape Town than they ever were before, but all that for the moment does not matter', Milner recorded. 'The only thought in everybody's mind is – the Queen. She kept the Empire together in the most critical half-century of its existence.'[14]

Chamberlain wrote to Milner to say the Queen had been convinced of the justice of the British cause in South Africa, and in its ultimate success. During the blackest days, she had refused to entertain any notion of defeat. 'I will tell you one thing', Victoria had declared after Black Week, 'I will have no depression in my house.'[15] Not long before she died, she had asked her daughter, 'What news is there from Lord Kitchener? What has been happening in South Africa these last days?'[16] Milner replied to the Colonial Secretary to say there was bitter disappointment in the Cape that the Queen 'did not live to see the pacification of South Africa'.[17] To a friend he wrote, 'The grief here has been very real – the manifestation of it impressive, and I am not easily impressed.'[18]

Middelburg

Milner's fears about Kitchener's readiness to call off the war too early were realised two months later when the general, off his own bat, initiated negotiations with Louis Botha at the eastern Transvaal town of Middelburg. Having ascertained from London that independence for the former Boer republics was non-negotiable, Kitchener nevertheless wished to end a conflict that was costing the British taxpayer at least £2 million a week. His scorched-earth tactics were having little discernible effect on the Boer commandos other than to deepen their hatred of the British.[19]

'It is a most difficult problem', he remarked, 'an enemy that always escapes, a country so vast there is always room to escape, supplies such as they want abundant almost everywhere.'[20] Disposed towards leniency himself, he put proposals before Botha that he felt might form the basis of a lasting peace, including a general amnesty for all Afrikaner rebels, the return of prisoners of war, an assurance that the white races would retain control in South Africa, eventual self-government under the Crown, equality between the Dutch and English languages, and compensation for war damage. In return, the Boers would surrender and hand over all their equipment to the British.[21]

The dialogue at Middelburg took place on 28 February 1901 while Milner was at last relocating from the Cape to the Highveld by train to take up his duties in the 'new colonies'. During the all-day discussion, the two generals got on well personally. Botha began by immediately raising the question of republican independence, only to be firmly rebuffed by Kitchener. The pair then got down to discussing settlement terms, with Botha putting forward a list of Boer demands, most of which had to be referred to London. The day ended with Kitchener teaching Botha how to play bridge, the new card game then at the height of fashion. Unfortunately for both men, their conduit to the Colonial Office in London was Milner, who had no intention of conceding any terms that would leave the Boers undefeated and able to make further claims on the British government in the future.[22]

On 2 March, Kitchener met Milner in Bloemfontein to brief him on the talks at Middelburg. He found the High Commissioner uncompromising – especially on the question of a general amnesty for Afrikaner rebels in the Cape and Natal, an issue on which he (Milner) had the backing of War Secretary Brodrick and most of the Salisbury cabinet. Writing to Violet after his session with Kitchener, Milner said the two did not 'see eye to eye' as might be expected: 'He is fearfully sick of the war, sees no possible credit in the continuance of it, and is ... rather disposed to go far in making things easy for the enemy. I feel that every concession we make now means more trouble later ... I foresee that I shall be driven to compromise – a thing I loathe. But I hope to save our policy from anything discreditable ... It is the price we have to pay for "regrettable incidents" and general military incompetence.'[23]

As go-between, Milner was able to temper most of Kitchener's proposals, so that when Britain's terms for peace were forwarded to Botha on 7 March, they were rejected by the Boer leader out of hand, without any explanation.[24] A disappointed Kitchener wrote to his confidante, Lady Cranborne, sister-in-law of Selborne, 'I was amazed that the Govt. was not more anxious for peace.'[25]

In private, Britain's military commander was furious with Milner and felt it was his political counterpart's obstinacy over amnesty that had caused the negotiations to go nowhere. He told Brodrick that although he had done his utmost to make Milner change his mind, the High Commissioner had chosen to be vindictive: 'I do not know of a similar case in history when, under similar circumstances, an amnesty has not been granted. We are now carrying on the war to put 2 or 300 Dutchmen in prison at the end of it. It seems to me absurd and I wonder the Chancellor of the Exchequer did not have a fit.'[26]

This was not the first time that Milner and Kitchener would disagree fundamentally over how the war should be run, or over the need for peace. While the military man had developed a grudging respect for an enemy fighting hard for survival, the diplomat who had never seen any battlefield action himself had no sympathy for the Boers and was as disinclined as ever to trust them. Milner harboured no regrets about the outcome at Middelburg, writing to Violet, 'The Botha negotiations have entirely failed. I hope we shall take warning and avoid such rotten ground in the future.'[27]

Before leaving Cape Town, Milner had obtained the military authorities' consent for a humanitarian social reformer from Britain, one Emily Hobhouse, to visit Boer internment camps south of Bloemfontein. The niece of an old-school Liberal politician, Lord Hobhouse, Emily had exploited her political connections to gain Chamberlain's approval for a mission to South Africa on behalf of a charity she had formed to ameliorate the hardships of Boer internees.[28] Her visit, Milner told a sceptical military commander at Bloemfontein, General Pretyman, was intended to be 'non-political'.

Hobhouse was horrified by the living conditions and high incidence of malnutrition, disease and death she encountered in the camps. In a scathing report, circulated to some of her influential friends at home, she put the blame squarely on the British Army's inefficient administration and the shortages of food, fuel, soap and other supplies, all made worse by 'ignorance, callousness and neglect'.[29] On returning to Britain, she shared her experiences with important politicians, including the Liberal leader, Sir Henry Campbell-Bannerman, who gave her a two-hour interview, and St John Brodrick at the War Office, who was not nearly as interested in her findings.[30] To supporters of the British Army, Hobhouse became known as 'that bloody woman', a soubriquet she bore with pride.

New broom

Arriving in the Transvaal in early March, Milner resisted advice from Chamberlain and chose to make Johannesburg, the business centre of the new colony, his place of residence rather than Pretoria, the political capital. A spacious and unoccupied property, the Sunnyside estate in Parktown, belonging to the American mining engineer Hennen Jennings, was acquired for the High Commission by Milner's young aide, Lionel Curtis. The mansion in which Milner was to live throughout the rest of his time in South Africa served as both his official residence and the administrative headquarters of the British government in the Transvaal. To a friend, Milner described Sunnyside as 'a villa which might be the residence of a prosperous London tradesman ... It is on the outskirts of Johannesburg, on the top of a hill to the north of the town, well away from the mines and places of business and looking over a magnificent rolling country north towards Pretoria. The climate is splendid, and we are nearly 6 000 feet above the sea.'[31]

In the same letter, he predicted that he would be much busier when the war was finally over: 'And that, I fear, is not yet. Indeed the war is never going to come to a definite end. It will just gradually die out as the resources of the enemy become more and more exhausted, and we shall have gradually to restart business, and may see the mines in full swing again before the last commandos have dispersed.'[32]

Due to depart on home leave in six weeks' time, Milner set about making key appointments to the Transvaal civilian administration with his characteristic vigour. Sir Richard Solomon, from the Cape, was chosen as his Chief Legal Adviser, Sir George Fiddes confirmed as Imperial Secretary, and a newcomer to South Africa, Patrick Duncan, his former private secretary at the Inland Revenue Board, recruited as the Transvaal's Colonial Secretary. Hurriedly putting a new municipal government in place to take over from the military authorities, Milner made Curtis acting Town Clerk of Johannesburg, an appointment made permanent less than a year later.[33]

From Bloemfontein in the Orange River Colony, Milner wrote to Violet Cecil: 'Things are going as well [here] as they can. Government is more or less a farce, with the country swarming with brigands and nothing but the railway line and a few towns really in our possession. But the little administration does well what little it has to do and will manage all the rest as it *falls* in.'[34]

Leaving Kitchener to act as High Commissioner in his absence from South Africa, Milner departed the 'new colonies' by train for Cape Town, his journey interrupted once more by Boer attacks on the railway line. On 8 May, he boarded the RMS *Saxon*, feeling 'mentally quite torpid' throughout the two-week voyage to Southampton.

CHAPTER 17

'Miracles are expected of me'
1901

Milner's return to England so soon after the failure of the Middelburg negotiations gave rise to a spate of rumours – spread by pro-Boer sympathisers – that he was being recalled because of his serious differences with Kitchener. Chamberlain decided the best way to halt the rumour mill was to stage an extravagant display of welcome for the High Commissioner, now regarded by the man on the Clapham omnibus as 'the Empire made flesh'.[1] Awaiting Milner in Madeira was a cable offering him a peerage and alerting him to a high-level reception planned for his arrival in London. Suspecting the message was a hoax, he took little notice, being more concerned about the presence aboard the *Saxon* of Emily Hobhouse, on her way home from her visit to the concentration camps. She had been most surprised to find Milner on the ship and was eager to bend his ear.

Told by the captain that the High Commissioner, sitting in solitary isolation on the upper deck, did not wish to mingle or converse with any lady, Hobhouse seized the opportunity to speak to Milner when she came across him admiring the view from the rail as the ship approached Madeira. Knowing that he had been receiving regular intelligence reports about her 'trouble-making' in the Free State, she assured Milner she had not been in South Africa for political reasons, and had resisted attempts by the military to provoke her. She gained the impression from a courteous Milner that he believed her.[2]

Writing to a friend, Hobhouse said she felt there were two Alfred Milners. There was 'the charming, sympathetic, gracious and cultivated man, whose abilities and culture found rather a desert in South Africa, and whose liberal leanings were in contrast to the military men surrounding him'. Then there was 'the politician who had given his word to carry out the ideas of English statesmen and felt bound in honour to do so. The clash must have given him dolorous moments of agony.'[3] The perceptive Hobhouse had put her finger unerringly on the duality in Milner's personality – his charm, in contrast to his single-mindedness.

By coincidence, the *Saxon* docked at Southampton on 24 May 1901. Awaiting Milner was another message from Chamberlain, proving the cable to Madeira had not been a hoax. It read that he and Prime Minister Salisbury would be at Waterloo station to greet him and convey him in an open landau through the streets of London for an audience with the King.

At Waterloo, almost the full Cabinet, as well as Lord Roberts, were on the platform to welcome Milner, before he was driven in triumph through cheering crowds to Marlborough House for a lengthy discussion with King Edward VII, who conferred on him the title of Baron Milner of St James's and Cape Town. Next day, Chamberlain presided over a welcoming lunch at Claridge's, London's finest hotel, during which he expressed the hope that the newly ennobled peer's reception had shown him that he had 'the unabated confidence of his Sovereign and of his fellow countrymen'.[4] 'His greatest work', the Colonial Secretary proclaimed, 'lay ahead – to unite and reconcile the two races and lay the foundation of a united South Africa, as free, as prosperous and as loyal as the sister federations of Canada and Australia.'[5] At the end of the month, Milner spent two days with the King and Queen at Windsor, during which he was given bridge lessons.[6]

The Times of Natal outdid other pro-imperial newspapers with its effusive tribute to 'this strong man from South Africa, with the kindly eyes and steel-wire determination, who has kept the faith of his country and upheld the honour of England in the hour of crisis … A man, too, of the sunniest temperament, the kindliest heart, the most liberal culture, the most attractive personality, who, in happier days, will live to see the completion of his task, the attainment of his high and pure ideal.'[7] The new baron was not taken in by this kind of adulation, complaining in a letter to George Fiddes, in Johannesburg, that he had been 'jumped' into the peerage. 'I should gladly have less honours and fuss, and more solid satisfaction in the shape of getting nearer to the end of the fighting',[8] he wrote.

After Windsor, Milner spent a few days in Birmingham with Chamberlain, where the two men held detailed discussions about the state of play in South Africa.[9] He told the Colonial Secretary that if Kitchener's aggressive strategy proved successful, troop withdrawals might begin in a matter of months. If not, Milner had a 'plan B' in mind: to use Baden-Powell's Constabulary to occupy 'protected districts' around towns garrisoned by British troops. A start had already been made outside Bloemfontein.

In these districts, he explained, where there would be no fighting, property owners could return to their homes and farms, and acts of war would be prosecuted. Mobile troops would scour the surrounding countryside for enemy dissidents, and these protected areas would be gradually extended over the whole country. This was a more humane policy than farm-burning, he asserted. He also asked for, and was given, a further £2 million for land settlement, £1 million for repatriating refugees and Chamberlain's approval for the state to take ownership of the railways, as a step towards unifying the four colonies into a South African federation.

Returning to London on 3 June for his investiture, Milner attended a spectacular military parade in Hyde Park at which, he, Roberts and 3 000 troops newly returned from South Africa were presented with medals by the King. Soon after, he was sworn in as a Privy Councillor along with Lord Cromer and Cecil Rhodes, and took up his seat in the House of Lords. In July, he was afforded the rare honour of the Freedom of the City by the Lord Mayor of London, in front of another large audience.[10] As Gollin notes, the only other civilian in living memory to be given such a reception was Benjamin Disraeli, when he returned in triumph from the Congress of Berlin.[11]

Liberal denunciations

The war in South Africa had not only made national heroes of Roberts and Milner but had also given rise to a serious division within the once-powerful Liberal establishment.[12] Party leader Henry Campbell-Bannerman, a Scottish barrister, and a radical faction led by the fiery young Welshman, David Lloyd George, were strongly opposed to the war and critical of Pushful Joe, and were in consequence pro-Boer, believing the war to have been motivated more by the interests of profiteering businessmen and glory-seeking generals and proconsuls than the noble cause of *Pax Britannica*.[13] 'Some people', Lloyd George declared, 'talk as if they have the British Empire in their own back yard. They put up a notice. No Admittance except on Business.'[14]

The praise lavished on Milner in Britain by press and politicians was far from universal. The pro-Boers, and their supporting newspaper editors, led by WT Stead, denounced Britain's envoy in South Africa as being 'heartless', 'bloodthirsty', 'narrow-minded', 'arrogant' and 'a prancing pro-consul'.[15] Also in London at the time were two of Milner's foremost critics in the Cape, John X Merriman and JW Sauer, regular speakers on the anti-imperialist, anti-Chamberlain lunch-and-dinner circuit. Merriman told audiences that allowing Milner, whose high commissionership had been an 'unmitigated and hopeless failure', to carry out the reconstruction of South Africa would be a 'suicidal and ruinous policy'.[16]

On 5 June, at a banquet given for Merriman and Sauer, the influential Liberal, Leonard Courtney, described the annexation of the two Boer republics as 'a wrong and a blunder' that the party would 'temper, if not abrogate' when it came to power.[17] A few days later, Merriman had a long talk with Campbell-Bannerman, who had been given a devastating account of conditions in the internment camps by Emily Hobhouse in person. According to Pakenham, what the Liberal leader was told dislodged him from 'his place on the tightrope between the two party factions'.[18] At a Liberal dinner at a Holborn restaurant on 14 June, C-B poured scorn on the notion that the conflict in South Africa had ended. 'If the war was over,' he asked, 'why were the Army's "methods of barbarism" continuing?'[19] Three days later he repeated his words, and a torrent of abuse from Unionists rained down upon his head. 'But C-B's three little words echoed around the world – especially on the Continent and in the two former Boer republics.

Lloyd George, even more outspoken than his leader, proposed formally to the House that 'consideration be given to the condition of the camps of detention in South Africa and the alarming mortality rate among women and children detained there'. Rather than being seen to support the Tory wing of the Unionist coalition in voting against the motion, fifty Liberal imperialists (or 'Limps'), whose ranks included the party's heir apparent, Asquith, as well as party heavyweights Edward Grey and Richard Haldane, abstained from voting.[20]

Double task

Milner found himself in a curious position in London. He had come back with the intention of stopping Chamberlain and the Limps from any 'wobbles' in the direction of leniency towards the Boers.[21] In Parliament, Winston Churchill, the only MP in either party to have had first-hand experience of the war, was urging the Unionist coalition, of which he was a member, to be conciliatory: 'I look forward to the day when we can take the Boers by the hand ... and say, "Go back and plough your fields".'[22] But the High Commissioner was also having to discourage the desire for retribution on the part of diehard anti-Boers on the Tory benches. In this respect, Britain's war was serving a useful political purpose – helping the Salisbury government to maintain the unity of the coalition while simultaneously keeping the Liberal opposition in Parliament divided.

Told repeatedly by Roberts that the war in South Africa was effectively over, the Salisbury cabinet – far removed from the action, and not privy to much military intelligence from an uncommunicative Kitchener – had little idea of what to do next. Except for vaguely hoping the Boers might unconditionally surrender, the Unionists had no policy to speak of but were nonetheless acutely aware of what the war was costing the Treasury.[23]

Unable to decide between the merits of 'scorched earth' versus 'protective districts' – after listening to Milner in person on 21 June, ministers were inclined to favour the second option but were fearful the popular Kitchener might resign in protest – Chamberlain, in the Limp camp himself, was privately of the view that the policy of 'sweeping and scouring' and herding women and children into detention camps was indeed 'barbarous'.

While in England, Milner made sure he kept up a cordial correspondence with the man standing in for him in South Africa. 'I have seen all sorts of people, statesmen, journalists, the man in the street', he told Kitchener. 'I have been doing nothing else since I came, but sucking in opinion ... The country is "*as sound as a bell*" ... The pro-Boer ravings produce astonishingly little effect. I don't believe we have ever had a big war in which the Opposition has had less weight.'[24]

'On the other hand,' Milner warned, 'there is a very natural impatience ... at the want of clearly visible progress ... [By] the end of August, people will want to see more [mining] stamps at work; some considerable district clear of the enemy; some reduction of the force within South Africa ... If these symptoms are not forthcoming ... they will want some of *our heads* on a charger, possibly yours, more likely mine ... But at present *there is not the smallest sign* of any loss of confidence in *you*. As regards negotiations, there is a general wish to see the war end without any more of them.'[25]

On 2 July, the Cabinet decided to ask an unwilling Roberts to inform Kitchener that he had until September to bring the war to a close, after which he should adopt Milner's proposals for getting the mines and farms working again. In private, Milner went to see Roberts, now supreme commander of the British Army, to propose splitting the South African command into three entities, each under a separate general. The war, Milner explained, no longer had any unity but had become a 'mass of scattered and petty operations which no single mind can grasp and the character of which varies considerably in the various localities'. As Le May records, Milner insisted to Roberts that civilian considerations should have equal weight with army requirements and asked to be given access to military intelligence.[26] He hoped a way might be found to hasten Kitchener's transfer to India.[27] Roberts made it clear, however, that until the Boers were finally defeated, there was no practicable alternative to Kitchener as the army commander in South Africa.

The Kindergarten

Another of Milner's purposes in London was to recruit a 'peace corps' of young men of talent and energy to help him carry out the reconstruction of the Transvaal and Orange River Colony. The group he assembled became known as his Kindergarten, though unkind critics called it a *crèche*. Besides JF (Peter) Perry, from All Souls, Oxford, already in South Africa as assistant Imperial Secretary, as well as the aforementioned Curtis and Duncan, Milner brought several other well-connected Oxford graduates into his orbit, among them Geoffrey Robinson from the Colonial Office (whose surname would change to Dawson in 1917 to take advantage of an inheritance), John Buchan, a journalist on the staff of *The Spectator*, and Hugh Wyndham (later Lord Leconfield), all three to serve as his assistant private secretaries. More *Kinder* were soon to join up, recommended by either Robinson or the war correspondent of *The Times* in South Africa, Leopold S Amery (generally known as Leo). All of them derived their passion for Empire from their association with the persuasive Milner.

While Milner was in London, Amery, another Balliol alumnus, was already at work on the monumental, seven-volume *The Times History of the War in South Africa*, and was unable to accept an invitation to return to Johannesburg as the proconsul's personal secretary. An unabashed admirer of Milner, Amery recalled years later his eagerness to accept the offer, 'both for the prospect of the adventure itself, and because of the great personal affection as well as admiration I had conceived for one who, unofficially or officially, was to be my spiritual chief for the rest of my days'.[28] To the awe-struck younger man, Milner was 'an Olympian figure' who became the dominant intellectual and moral influence throughout Amery's subsequent career in journalism and politics as one of the Empire's most forceful advocates.[29] (It was Amery who reflected that had the aeroplane been invented 20 years earlier, in such an open country the Anglo-Boer War could hardly have lasted as many months as it did years.[30] Both countries might have escaped much expense and human suffering.)

Before returning to South Africa, Milner also had a long meeting with Rhodes, who had ignored medical advice that he was not well enough to travel to London. Writing beforehand to Milner from a sanatorium in Kimberley, Rhodes said that his health was better, but since his heart was 'dicky', he wished to put his affairs in order. He had several 'big questions' to discuss with Milner, including an idea to buy 1 000 farms in the Transvaal on which to settle 'our own people', the financing of which would be 'up to Beit and others'.[31]

In London, the two men also discussed the Colossus's plan for his trust to carry on the imperial mission after his death, and his wish for Milner to replace his erstwhile friend WT Stead as a trustee of his estate. Milner wrote subsequently to Rhodes to say he was 'completely in sympathy with your broad ambitions for the race' and suggested that part of his legacy should be the support of a political party that would promote imperial endeavours and encourage British immigration to South Africa, especially by women.[32]

Warm welcome

During the busy ten weeks of a hot summer in England, Milner took time to enjoy weekend house parties at the homes of aristocratic friends. At Hatfield House, seat of the Cecil family, he visited the bed-side of Violet Cecil, recuperating after the difficult birth of a daughter, Helen. In a letter to his friend Clinton Dawkins in Egypt, Milner wrote that his time in London had been 'profitable': 'I have freshened up a lot of acquaintances of the better kind and have, I believe, done both the Government and the saner portion of the Opposition a lot of good. All this is encouraging and, though the military continues to show their complete incompetence in S Africa, I think we have now sufficient way on the ship to carry her well into port in spite of persistent bungling. But that does not alter my views of the total and ridiculous breakdown of our system, military, administrative, constitutional.'[33]

Milner also fitted in a luncheon meeting with the South Africa Expansion Committee, where he wove 'his usual personal spell' over a coterie of admiring female imperialists.[34] A few months later, he addressed an official letter of support to the Committee and set up a Women's Immigration Department in the Transvaal, which offered a £5 subsidy towards the travel expenses of each female immigrant, as well as her hostel costs in Cape Town and free railway passes. Chamberlain assisted by offering free travel in empty troop ships to prospective women emigrants, and the mining industry and other financiers also stepped in to help. According to Julia Bush, while ladies' imperialist associations basked in the glow of favourable publicity in the British press, for a time 'the spotlight on organised female emigration was intense.'[35]

On 10 August, after a series of farewell dinners, both formal and informal, Milner sailed for South Africa, arriving in Cape Town 17 days later to an enthusiastic reception. He was driven through an excited crowd of onlookers to a mayoral reception and then to Government House to meet his successor as Governor of the Cape, Sir Walter Hely-Hutchinson.

Writing to Violet, Milner – his feet on the ground as always – described his welcome in the Cape as 'really extraordinary – frantic. I don't over-estimate such things, but it would be dullness not to notice, and affectation to pretend not to be pleased by them … [But] it is ill-omened to be greeted with such a shout on *entering* the arena. Miracles are expected of me which I cannot possibly perform. The result cannot be equal to the anticipation.'[36]

CHAPTER 18

Falling Out with Kitchener
1901–1902

Since the failure of his peace initiative at Middelburg, Kitchener had become steadily more exasperated not only with Milner, whom he blamed for sabotaging the negotiations, but also with Chamberlain, for his lack of enthusiasm for the military's sweeping drives across the veld, now an indispensable element of British Army strategy.[1] The more successful these tactics, the less habitable the countryside became, and the bigger the internment camps grew. With 240 000 troops in the field against an enemy one tenth of the size of the British force, the proud hero of the Sudan was sensitive to the taunts of critics that the grinding war of attrition in South Africa was making the Army look ridiculous and draining Britain's Exchequer.[2]

Kitchener's frustration, and gloom, may be gleaned from his two private and confidential replies to Milner's missives from London. In the first, he wrote, 'I fear there is little doubt the war will go on for a considerable time unless stronger measures are taken. Hope [for] your support of my proposal.'[3] In the second, he reported, 'We are pegging away as hard as we can, but the Boers will not stand at all … After the recent decision to carry on the war, I do not expect there will be any serious peace again before September … I am not too enamoured of the army after six years' continual war, and would give a good deal to sink into oblivion and peace.'[4] The workaholic army commander was feeling the strain of a military burden that kept him working every day from early morning until late at night, with little time for recreation and no leave.[5]

On 7 August, Kitchener toughened his stance by issuing a proclamation that any Boer leaders who did not surrender by 11 September would be permanently banished from South Africa, and all burghers in the field would henceforward be charged a tax on their properties to pay for the cost of their families' upkeep in the camps. The Boers' response was a two-fingered salute, so the building of blockhouse lines continued apace. By the end of 1901, barbed wire stretched for almost 6 000 km across the veld, enclosing more than 80 000 sq km of the two former republics.[6] Denied their usual space in which to manoeuvre, the Boers felt the effects of a squeeze that began seriously to tell.

Inspired by the heroics of De Wet in the Free State, the Boer leaders persisted nevertheless with their plans, hatched eight months earlier, to invade the Cape and Natal. By the end of September, Smuts, with Deneys Reitz in his commando, was far down in the eastern Cape mountains, while Botha and more than a thousand men were being chased by British troops across northern Natal into Swaziland. In the Magaliesberg area of the western Transvaal, De la Rey was proving a constant thorn in the side of General Methuen.

Despondency

In the Cape, despite the enthusiasm that had greeted him on his return from London, Milner sensed a mood of despondency.[7] The war seemed never-ending and there was widespread resentment at the Sprigg ministry's arbitrary application of martial law. In the Governor's absence, a serious row had broken out between Sprigg and Kitchener over the extension of emergency measures to Cape seaports. Milner had no liking for martial law himself but recognised the justification of Kitchener's demand to be able to intercept 'treasonable communications' and munitions of war destined for the enemy.

Sprigg refused, however, to introduce measures that would amount to military rule and infringe the liberty of citizens of the colony. It took a meeting in Johannesburg in October between him, Kitchener and Milner before agreement was eventually reached over a limited application of martial law in specific circumstances. The accord was a minor triumph for Milner, who supported Sprigg in arguing that the Cape should be defended by its own troops rather than those under the command of Kitchener.

The presence of Boer commandos so close to Cape Town meant it was not safe for Milner to return by train to the 'new colonies', so he and his staff travelled by sea to East London and then overland to Bloemfontein and Johannesburg. Writing to a friend in England, Milner described the state of the Orange River Colony as 'horrible': 'death and destruction everywhere, as the continuance of this wretched and senseless guerrilla warfare has forced the military to sweep the colony from end to end'. The former republic was now 'virtually a desert, almost the whole population living in refugee camps along the railway line'.[8] Milner lamented that there were 'not more than 6000 Boers [the number was at least 10000][9] still in arms against us … ill mounted, ill clad, ill armed, the most wretched objects conceivable, and constantly on the run. Still they keep on, deluded by the persistent lying of their leaders, and it may take a long time to catch them, in twenties and thirties. It is a miserable business.'[10]

Back in Sunnyside again, the Governor travelled regularly to Pretoria to confer with Kitchener and the civilian administration, and to preside over meetings of the Executive Council. He continued to insist that 'neither the climate nor the tradition of Pretoria' gave it any special fitness to be the Transvaal's capital. Residing in Johannesburg, he told Chamberlain, enabled him to keep his hand on the pulse of 'the great dominant industrial centre'.[11] 'A great boon' was the installation of a telephone line between his office and Pretoria.[12] Impatient to get a move on with reconstruction and resettlement, Milner found himself frequently at odds with Kitchener, who insisted on going at his own pace when dealing with the return of refugees.[13]

Milner believed that for economic and political reasons, it was vital to set the wheels of industry on the Rand in motion again: if the mines were to reopen and business to return to normal, it would send a powerful message to the Boers. He also wanted the many Uitlanders who had fled to the coast to return to the Rand as soon as there was transport to carry them and enough produce to feed them.[14] But Kitchener, who listened politely to Milner and took no notice, had other priorities: his job was to end the guerrilla war, so he continued to monopolise transport facilities and supplies for his troops in the field. And, crucially, as the military commander he still had the rail network under his control.[15]

As Milner wrote impatiently to a friend, 'there is … a very little quickening in the process of resettlement. After prolonged controversy, I have succeeded in softening the stony heart of K. to the point of allowing the refugees to return in regular batches at a somewhat improved pace.'[16] Yet a fortnight later, Milner was again complaining that 'nothing is being done. Despite all my efforts, only 500 stamps are at work on the mines out of a possible 6000. Five-sixths of our people are still at the coast. The country is a wilderness, without inhabitants and almost without cultivation.'[17]

In London, Lord Roberts, his ear bent by Kitchener, had become alarmed that Milner might be undermining the military authority rather than the other way round. He told the cabinet that everything should be done to keep the army in South Africa in a thoroughly efficient state.[18] At the War Office, Brodrick had come round to a similar view, believing it essential that the Cape Colony be cleared of the enemy, even if it meant providing Kitchener with more men and money. Sensing the public and party mood, Chamberlain agreed that reducing troop numbers was not a good idea. Another loss to a Boer commando at Bakenlaagte, in the eastern Transvaal, where Colonel GE Benson, one of the army's best officers, was mortally wounded, lent weight to Kitchener's argument and caused opinions in cabinet to shift once more – away from Milner's proposals and back towards the general's much harsher strategy.[19]

In late October 1901, Milner was able to make an overdue visit to Natal, one of the most loyal outposts of Empire. Gratified by the warm welcome he received in Pietermaritzburg, he compared the relative prosperity and peacefulness of that British colony to the 'terrible conditions' in the rebellious parts of the Cape. He refuted the 'odious saying' that in South Africa, loyalty did not pay. What he and other imperial loyalists wanted, he stressed, was 'a peaceful and prosperous' country, 'one great community under the British flag'. But 'the people of South Africa must accomplish it for themselves. You must not approach the questions as Natalians, or Rhodesians, or Cape Colonists, or whatever it may be, but as South Africans.'[20]

In Durban, the High Commissioner told another enthusiastic audience: 'I wish I could have congratulated you on the fact that not only Natal but all South Africa was at rest. But I have come to the conclusion that it is no use waiting till the war is over. In a formal sense, it may never be over, but may just slowly burn itself out, as it is doing now.'[21]

Describing his visit to Natal to a Mrs Montefiore, Milner said that although most of his time had been taken up with meetings and functions, on the way back from Durban via Ladysmith he had managed to steal some time to visit the battlefields to see for himself where the clashes between Boer and British troops had occurred. After inspecting Colenso and its surrounds, he found it incomprehensible 'how anyone could have believed in Buller's generalship'.[22]

Milner's remark in Durban that 'the war might never be over' had an unexpected sequel in Britain, which revealed the extent of the confusion in top Liberal circles. Repudiating Campbell-Bannerman's allegations of 'barbarism' and his criticism of the army's tactics, Lord Rosebery, the Limps' leading pro-imperialist grandee, made a ground-breaking speech at Chesterfield in which he appealed for the founding of a new centre party in British politics. Pronouncing himself in favour of a vigorous prosecution of the war, he went on to denounce Milner, accusing him of pursuing a policy aimed at hunting the Boers to extermination.[23] His criticism might rather have been directed at Kitchener, who had just announced 'a new, model drive' to bring the war to an end.

Backtracking and dithering

At the end of October 1901, a frustrated Chamberlain – aware of the British public's irritation and impatience – wrote to Milner to complain that there had been little change in policy since their discussions in London: the army's great drives were continuing 'with disproportionate results': 'The war drags on, and there is no assurance that it may not continue for months and years. We still employ 200 000 troops and 300 guns to deal with 10 000 men without any guns at all.'

He wanted to know what had become of the plan to capture one or other Boer leader, such as Botha or Steyn, and then to apprehend another: 'We think the war will never end until the leaders are captured, and the surrender of one would be more important than all the drives, which only secure unimportant diminutions.'[24]

As for the concentration camps, 'the death rate [is] causing such anxiety here'.[25] The internees in the camps might be given the option of leaving voluntarily, Chamberlain suggested, thereby relieving the cost to the Treasury. Milner should discuss the situation with Kitchener and revert with the 'fullest possible report and explanations'. The Colonial Secretary was also anxious to know what been done to revive industry and agriculture in the two 'new colonies'.[26]

By now, Whitehall's dithering and backtracking had become almost too much for Milner to bear. On 1 November, he wrote to Chamberlain to suggest that Kitchener be removed from his post: 'It is impossible to guide a military dictator of very strong views and strong character'.[27] His memorandum, when put before the cabinet, resulted in a ministerial split down the middle, with Salisbury having to exercise a casting vote. The Prime Minister came down decisively on the side of Kitchener, an officer he had always admired. A disillusioned Milner was forced to accept finally that he could not exercise any influence over military strategy whatsoever.[28]

On 6 November, Milner sent a carefully measured report to Chamberlain, pointing out that in the Transvaal, despite repeated disasters, lines of communication were now seldom interrupted, and the most important districts had been cleared of the enemy. Unfortunately, these areas could not be reopened 'as Lord Kitchener does not see his way to resumption of industry and agriculture on any reasonable scale. I shall not cease to urge a bolder policy ... but I cannot press my personal view beyond a certain point ... Any view on [the] conduct of war which HM Govt. desires to impress upon Lord K. would be more effective from the War Office than coming through me.'[29]

A few days later, a more upbeat Milner wrote to Chamberlain to say, 'without being unduly optimistic, it is impossible not to be struck by two great changes for the better in the military position since I took up my position in the Transvaal just eight months ago. These are the now absolute safety and uninterrupted working of the railways and the complete pacification of certain central districts. Since my return from England, I have traversed the country from East London to Bloemfontein and Johannesburg and from Johannesburg to Durban and back, to say nothing of constant journeys between this place and Pretoria. On no single occasion has there been the slightest hitch or cause for alarm.

The trains have been absolutely up to time, and very good time.[30]

Another change for the better, he reported, was an improvement in conditions in the internment camps, which had come under civilian control in November 1901. After Emily Hobhouse's strictures, the Unionist government had sent out its own investigative commission under Millicent Fawcett, a leading suffragette and an old friend of Milner's. The report of her commission had largely confirmed Hobhouse's findings.[31]

On assuming responsibility for the camps, Milner had immediately sent a member of the Kindergarten, the newly arrived John Buchan, to investigate and improve the living conditions of internees. Buchan recorded that the camps had 'made my hair gray': 'When we took them over, they were terrible – partly owing to the preoccupation of the military with other things, partly to causes inherent in any concentration of people accustomed to live in the sparsely populated veld.' It was largely due to Buchan (and of course Emily Hobhouse) that the death rate in the camps dropped suddenly from an average of 344 per 1 000 in October 1901 to a figure of 20 per 1 000 only a few months later. It was too late to undo the damage to Britain's reputation, however, which would never be repaired.[32]

Full circle

Relations between Britain's two ruling autocrats in South Africa continued to be fraught. In early 1902, Milner reopened hostilities, telling Chamberlain that while his relations with Kitchener were friendly enough on the surface, 'co-operation in any true sense of the word is out of the question': 'Personally, I do not think there ever has been, or ever could be, co-operation between Lord Kitchener and any other man who was not either distinctly his subordinate or distinctly his superior. In our respective tasks, wherever they touch each other, we are always pulling different ways.

'As I see the position, things are constantly being done which will make our future task more difficult, while on the other hand golden opportunities of strengthening ourselves now in the deserted country are being thrown away. Kitchener won't go, unless he can do so with glory and saying that he finished the war. But the war can only be formally finished either by a compact – which Heaven forbid! – or by his catching the last Boer, which may take years.'[33]

As Le May observes, Milner's frustration had now come full circle. Kitchener could not beat the Boers, yet until the Boers were beaten, Milner could not make progress with his plans for South Africa's reconstruction.[34] To the Salisbury cabinet in London, the steady exchange of telegrams of complaint made it seem that the war in South Africa was less of a contest between Boers and Brits than between Kitchener and Milner.[35]

CHAPTER 19

Peace at Last
1902

'Before the Boer War,' Sir Edward Grey, a Liberal Foreign Secretary, later reflected, 'we were spoiling for a fight. Any Government could have had war by lifting a finger. The people would have shouted for it.'[1] That may have been true initially, but as the guerrilla war in South Africa dragged on into 1902, both sides had good reason to re-evaluate their participation in a conflict that had become ever more bitter, resource-consuming and painful.[2] In Britain, the conflict had cost the Exchequer nearly £200 million, without any prospect of outright victory in sight.[3]

The Unionist cabinet's war aim of 'unconditional surrender' became increasingly discredited, and pressure began to mount within the government and public for some form of peace settlement. The difficulty was that neither Kitchener, in supreme military command, nor Milner could agree on the way forward. The High Commissioner wanted negotiations to begin only after the Boers had surrendered unconditionally; the commander-in-chief, concerned about the effect of the war on the Army's morale, understood that a lasting settlement could only be negotiated by the Boer generals in the field, who would not surrender without inducement. Rumours of the fundamental clash in outlook between the two men began filtering back to Britain again.

The Boers had even stronger reasons for bringing the hostilities to an end. Having initially gone to war with 32 000 to 35 000 burghers under arms, over 30 000 were now prisoners of war and 1 118 had died in prison camps,[4] in addition to their thousands of suffering women and children. Not surprisingly, after more than two years of fighting, Afrikaner unity had begun seriously to fray. Historian Albert Grundlingh observes that another 5 464 Boers had switched sides to become 'National Scouts' or 'Volunteers' – agreeing to act as the armed eyes and ears of the British Army.[5]

On the islands of St Helena and Ceylon (Sri Lanka), Boer prisoners of war had indicated their willingness, if allowed to return home, to take the oath of allegiance to the King. Many more burghers were taking advantage of Kitchener's offer of amnesty to become *hensoppers*. Short of weapons, ammunition, horses, clothing and food, and with members of their families holed up in internment camps, even the most diehard Boers were struggling to survive.

It took a timely intervention from the Netherlands for the deadlock to be broken. On 25 January 1902, the Dutch Prime Minister, Abraham Kuyper, delivered a memorandum to the British Foreign Secretary, Lord Lansdowne, offering to mediate between the two combatants in South Africa. Lansdowne politely declined the invitation, pointing out that if the Boer leaders wished to negotiate, they should contact the British military commander in Johannesburg. A copy of the correspondence was sent to both Milner and Kitchener.

On 4 March, more in hope than expectation, Kitchener forwarded a copy of the Dutch offer and Lansdowne's reply – under a covering note – to Botha and Schalk Burger, acting President of the SAR, but not to the intransigent Free State patriarch, MT Steyn. To Kitchener's surprise, on 10 March he received a conciliatory reply from Burger saying he personally would be 'eager and willing' to consider peace proposals but first had to consult Steyn. Would Kitchener grant the Boers safe conduct for this purpose?[6] Three days earlier, at Tweebosch in the western Transvaal, De la Rey's commando had inflicted the biggest defeat on the British Army since Colenso, capturing a wounded General Methuen (later released for medical treatment at a nearby hospital).

Writing to Violet Cecil after receiving Lansdowne's correspondence, Milner was as implacable as ever: 'The Boers as a fighting force are quite done for … The best proof of this is that all the pro-Boers are once more shrieking loudly for "negotiations". Of course, there is nothing they hate like … being *simply conquered* and giving in, like other beaten people. We are at all costs to have *terms* – to be a source of embarrassment hereafter.[7]

'The stories of differences between Lord Kitchener and me are subsiding, I think', Milner continued. 'The differences are there – not personal but political. I do admire him in his own line. He is fearfully wrong-headed sometimes, but he is always *homme sérieux*, practising himself and enforcing upon others the highest standard of *workman-like* strenuousness, indefatigable industry and iron perseverance. Great qualities these in a wishy-washy world.'[8]

Melrose House

On 9 April, eleven Boer leaders – six Transvalers and five Free Staters – gathered in Klerksdorp, with Kitchener's prior approval. Ten months earlier, they had decided there could be no peace without independence.[9] This time, their choice was much starker: independence or Afrikaner survival. For three days, there was intense argument over whether or not to negotiate: De Wet, Steyn and Hertzog once again were far more intractable than Burger and Botha, but on one point there was eventual agreement: they had to find out from Kitchener exactly how much the British were prepared to concede.

On 12 April, Steyn, Burger and their advisers, Reitz and Hertzog, met Kitchener at his headquarters at Melrose House in Pretoria. They put forward a seven-point proposal, which in their opinion would prevent all future wars. To Kitchener's surprise, all seven points were based on the assumption that the Boers would regain their independence. Knowing this was out of the question, Kitchener did his best, 'as a friend', to persuade the delegation that surrendering and negotiating terms of eventual self-government were better options. After failing to make headway, he reluctantly helped the Boers to draft a telegram to the Secretary of State for War, setting out their proposals in a modified form. As expected, the Boer terms were summarily rejected by the Salisbury cabinet, but Kitchener was instructed to press for further proposals.[10]

Two days later, the two sides reassembled to discuss the response from London, and were joined this time by Milner, reluctant as ever to parley with the enemy. It was apparent that each of the four principals had a different objective in mind: Kitchener wanted a military victory, Milner unconditional surrender, Burger an honourable peace and Steyn independence.[11] On the British side, Kitchener had emerged as the 'dove' and Milner the 'hawk' – a divergence the Boers were quick to recognise.[12]

At various stages during the discussions, the differences between the two sides appeared unbridgeable. Kitchener skilfully used the telegraph to keep in touch with the British government, whose bottom line was non-negotiable: independence was not an option, and any settlement had to be based on Kitchener's proposals at Middelburg – or something similar. Without showing Kitchener's cable to the cabinet, Chamberlain sent a personal message to Milner, saying, 'the enormous cost of the war and the continuous strain upon the Army make peace most desirable, but we cannot buy it by concessions that may encourage future rebellion, or which would justify the loyal section in saying that they had been betrayed'.[13]

Steyn, initially addressed by Milner as 'Mr' and not 'President'[14] – to the Boer leaders' irritation – continued to insist that the Afrikaner people should 'not lose their self-respect', which Milner thought 'ridiculous', hoping all the while that the Free Stater would provide a reason for the talks to break down. But Kitchener pointed out tactfully that men who had fought so well in the field could not lose their self-respect by bowing to the inevitable.[15]

After withdrawing for further discussions among themselves, the Boers returned to Melrose House on 14 April for ask for a firm proposal of settlement from the British government that might compensate their people for their loss of independence, and be put before representatives of the commandos in the field for consideration.[16] By getting the British to acknowledge that only delegates chosen by Transvaal and Free State commandos – and no turncoat Afrikaners – could truly represent 'the people', the Boer delegates won a minor tactical victory.[17] (The *hensoppers*, National Scouts and the black inhabitants of both republics must have felt hard done by.) It was agreed that 30 delegates from each of the (former) republics would gather on 15 May 1902 on the banks of the Vaal River at Vereeniging.

Behind the scenes, Milner wrote to Chamberlain to express once again his mistrust of 'all negotiations': 'Personally … I should regard the future with more hope if the war was ended by a continuance of captures and surrenders, which continue, despite our frequently recurring

mishaps, to take place at a satisfactory rate … But as public feeling
at home evidently favours negotiations, we must do the best we can.
I am strongly of the opinion that we should not give an inch.'[18] It was
Milner's particular concern that Kitchener might go so far as to fix a date
for self-government in the ex-republics.

A week later, he again reminded the Colonial Secretary of the
'great difficulty' he was having with Kitchener: 'He is extremely adroit
in his management of negotiations, but he does not care what he
gives away.' 'He should be clearly told', Milner insisted, 'that the British government was not prepared to make any further concessions on
points of policy, and the sooner the better.'[19] So far, he complained,
Kitchener had 'practically held all the strings throughout. He was in
constant communication with the Boers and steered them into the
paths he chose.' In a revealing footnote, Headlam records Milner as
confiding to a member of his staff that at Melrose House he had felt as
if *he* was negotiating with Kitchener, 'whilst the Boers look on.'[20]

A few weeks earlier, on 26 March, Cecil Rhodes had died at the
age of only 48, at his small cottage on a hillside above the sea near
Muizenberg, along the Cape Peninsula. His heart had given in shortly
after his return from London to give evidence at the trial for forgery of
Princess Radziwill, a Polish-Russian fortune-seeker who had insinuat-
ed herself into his business affairs. His friend Sir Abe Bailey recorded
that Rhodes's last words to him were: 'They tell me I am going to die.
I must live five years. But you have Milner. But you have Milner.'[21]

Milner had written to Violet three days earlier to say that he had
been expecting to hear of Rhodes's death any day. 'One cannot but feel
the deepest sympathy for him in not living to see the object of his great
hopes accomplished. And there has certainly never been a time since
I first came to South Africa that I have wanted him more … It is like
the Evil Fate which has dogged us all along.'[22] As he had wished, Rhodes
was buried in the Matoppo Hills, near Bulawayo in Rhodesia.

In a codicil to his last will, the Colossus had added Milner to the
board of trustees of his huge estate. Writing to his fellow trustee and
friend, Earl Grey, Milner said that while he could not take any active
part in the administration of Rhodes's affairs for as long as he was
High Commissioner, he would have renounced the position if he had

not thought the Rhodes Trust 'may be of importance for the next 30 years'.[23] He advised Grey to separate the administration of the Scholarship Fund from the rest of Rhodes's estate; and if a capable man was required to run both, there was no one better than his pro-imperial Canadian friend, George Parkin, who was appointed in due course.

Vereeniging

Throughout April, armed skirmishes between Boer and British forces continued intermittently, mainly in the western Transvaal. Kitchener turned down the Boer request for an armistice but did what he could to enable their leaders to consult some 1 500 to 2 000 burghers[24] still at large in the veld and decide upon the delegates to represent them at Vereeniging. Writing to one of his confidantes, Lady Cranborne, in London, Kitchener said he felt 'things were going fairly well', but the Boers had 'a deadly loathing' for Milner, which made it difficult at times as 'he hardly recognised how much they detest him'.[25]

By mid-May, Smuts – accompanied by Deneys Reitz – had been recalled from his foray into the outer reaches of the Cape and given safe passage to Cape Town by sea and northward by rail. When his train reached Kroonstad, Kitchener went to meet him and the two men politely exchanged their hitherto irreconcilable views. Before sending Smuts on his way to rejoin Botha and his commandos in the Transvaal, Kitchener held out the prospect of British financial assistance to help rebuild the ravaged country.[26]

When Reitz arrived at Botha's camp, he was appalled at the sight of 3 000 starving burghers, clad in skins and sacking and covered in sores. 'Their spirit was undaunted, but they had reached the limit of physical endurance and we realised that if these haggard, emaciated men were the pick of the Transvaal commandos then the war must be irretrievably lost', he recorded.[27]

From the outset of the discussions at Vereeniging, there was a division of opinion between Free Staters and Transvalers, the former as inflexible as ever, the latter inclined towards conciliation and in search of a settlement. Led by De Wet, representing a very ill Steyn, the Free Staters repeated the arguments they had advanced at Klerksdorp: they had entered the war at the behest of the Transvaal, had borne the brunt of the devastation, were homeless, hungry and bereaved, and should not be deserted by those who had drawn them into the conflict in the first place.[28] In their opinion, the guerrilla war should be continued.

As they had done at Klerksdorp, the Transvalers advanced the contrary view, having concluded the war was lost, and that with every month that passed, Milner's hold on their former republic was tightening.[29] If for no other reason than the plight of women and children in the camps, the time had come to bring an end to the war in order to preserve and rebuild what was left of the Afrikaner *volk*.

After almost three days of heated argument, it was the yet-to-be defeated De la Rey whose intervention tipped the scales. Echoing Louis Botha's words, 'It has been said that we must fight to the bitter end, but no one tells us where that bitter end is', a sorrowful De la Rey asked whether the bitter end had not come.[30] He had arrived at Vereeniging with no intention of giving up, but after listening to the reports of the devastation and hardship, he agreed it was time for negotiations with the enemy.[31] On 17 May, the meeting resolved to send a delegation comprising Botha, Smuts and De la Rey, representing the Transvaal, and De Wet and Hertzog for the Orange Free State, to put a set of peace proposals before Kitchener and Milner.

At Kitchener's headquarters in Pretoria, there was more tough bargaining between the two sides. The five Boer leaders argued that if they were to conclude a peace treaty and recognise Edward VII as their lawful sovereign, they had to be officially recognised as representatives of the South African Republic and the Orange Free State, notwithstanding Lord Roberts's earlier proclamations. In return for the formal surrender of their independence, the former republics would be given compensation of £3 million for the rehabilitation of their territories, and loans would be made available at low rates of interest. As Edgar Holt points out, 'It must have been unprecedented for a victor to pay an indemnity to a vanquished.'[32] And, crucially, the enfranchisement of coloureds and Africans would not be decided before the introduction of self-government. At one point, the talks were about to break down, when Kitchener again saved the day by suggesting that the legal advisers should come up with the wording of an agreement. Drawing Smuts aside, he said that in his opinion a Liberal government might shortly come to power in Britain, and would be more likely than the Unionists to grant the Boers early self-government.

On 21 May, a set of peace proposals were cabled to London for cabinet approval. Privately, Milner told Chamberlain that the Boers were making 'preposterous demands'.[33] The proposals should not be accepted in a hurry, he said, as he needed time to present his views more fully. He believed the Boers were 'done for', and if the assembly at Vereeniging were to break up without any agreement, the delegates would surrender 'right and left': 'The men here are either personally anxious to upset negotiations or bluffing in reliance on our weakness, probably the latter.'[34]

As the Dutch historian Martin Bossenbroek records, Milner's lack of sympathy for the Boer leaders was not shared by the military men on the British side. On 24 May, Kitchener's chief of staff, General Ian Hamilton, was invited to a dinner in Pretoria to celebrate Smuts's 32nd birthday. The General was seated between Botha and De la Rey, with Smuts and De Wet on either side, and the company exchanged anecdotes about their various escapes. Writing to his close friend Winston Churchill afterwards, Hamilton said he'd had 'a splendid evening ... and never wish to eat my dinner in better company'.[35]

On 27 May, London's response came to hand. Ignoring Milner's strictures, Chamberlain and the Salisbury government agreed – with minor amendments – to the proposed terms. The Boers would lay down their arms and acknowledge the sovereignty of the British monarch; prisoners of war could return with their personal and property rights protected and no legal proceedings to face; the Dutch language could be taught in schools (but not allowed as a medium of instruction), and used in courts of law; and the possession of weapons for private protection would be permitted. Military administration would be replaced by civilian rule as soon as possible, and the first steps taken towards self-government. The critical 'native franchise' question would not be decided until after self-government, and special commissions would be appointed – and money made available – to restore the Boer people to their homes and embark on a programme of reconstruction. In a separate agreement between Milner, Kitchener and the Boer republican leaders (which did not form part of the final treaty), rebel

Afrikaners in the Cape were disenfranchised for a period of five years.

When the terms were made known to the Boer leaders on 28 May, Botha inquired whether the delegates at Vereeniging might propose amendments. Milner cut him short: 'This is an absolutely final document, and the answer must be Yes or No.' The Boers were given three days to return with an answer. After two more days of debate, during which the ailing and physically disabled Steyn tried to convince his fellow Free Staters to continue the war before resigning his presidency for health reasons, Botha and De la Rey eventually persuaded a reluctant De Wet to support a motion calling for acceptance of the British proposals, because of the impossibility of winning a victory. On the afternoon of 31 May 1902, the motion was carried by 54 votes to 6, with three Transvalers and three Free Staters voting against.

Shortly before 11 pm that night, a party of Boer leaders reached Melrose House from Vereeniging, to find Kitchener and Milner awaiting them. The formalities took no longer than five minutes, with Burger the first to sign the agreement, and Milner the last. A deathly silence ensued, broken by Kitchener saying, 'We are good friends now.'[36] De la Rey is said to have replied in his broken English, "We are a bloody cheerful-looking lot of British subjects!"[37]

A bitter and costly war, supposed to last three months, had dragged on into a third year before at last being brought to an end.

The aftermath

Milner was not pleased with the outcome, knowing he had been upstaged by Kitchener, but put on a brave face nevertheless. Writing to a friend, he said it had been 'an awful ten days but I saved more than I expected. I see things as they are, and recognise it's a fool's trick to waste the energy and devotion of 1000 men in trying to keep an Empire for people who are dead set on chucking it away ... Our political organisation is thoroughly rotten, almost non-existent.'[38]

'Never was there such an absurd waste of power,' he continued, 'such ridiculous inconsequence of policy – not for any want of men, but for want of any central authority or dominant idea to make them work together. Joe is a strong man ... But all he can do is maintain himself ... K is a strong man, but all he is doing is to paralyse me. Rosebery [the influential Liberal imperialist] is not a strong man, certainly. But he is a singularly gifted one. Yet his influence has been in the main, exceedingly mischievous.'[39]

The best Milner could bring himself to say was that he had prevented a disastrous peace, and stopped Kitchener from putting any date on the restoration of self-government to the Boers. He had bought himself and the Kindergarten time in which to transform the two former republics into British outposts. He had even developed a modicum of sympathy for the vanquished enemy. 'I have just come from signing the terms of surrender', he recorded. 'If anything could make me relent towards Boers, it was the faces of some of the men who sat around the table tonight. There was no mistaking the fact that some of them felt it deeply, with all their characteristic self-possession.'[40]

Whatever Milner's reservations, the coming of peace was greeted with cheers in England, though there was no 'mafficking' this time because of the public's war-weariness. Salisbury sent Milner a message saying, 'Heartiest congratulations on the glorious news', while Salisbury's son-in-law, Selborne, hailed Milner in a letter as 'Hercules': 'Your second labour is ended; the third (and last in South Africa) is about to commence; but is it not the biggest of all?'[41]

Less than a month later, Chamberlain notified Milner that the King had approved his further elevation in the peerage to 'Viscount of the United Kingdom', saying, 'In sincerely congratulating you on this mark of royal favour, I desire to add how greatly I appreciate the valuable work performed by you during a period of altogether exceptional strain and anxiety.'[42]

Now even more of a conquering hero to the British public, the man of iron who had held his nerve when others were losing theirs,[43] Kitchener lost no time in boarding a ship for home with a life-size statue of Kruger in the ship's hold.[44] On arrival in England, he was promoted to full general, given the Order of Merit, and elevated to the rank of viscount. He used the cash payment of £50 000, granted by Parliament on behalf of a grateful nation, to buy gold shares[45] – South African, of course.

CHAPTER 20

Going North
1902–1903

A vexed question requiring the British High Commissioner's attention during the final months of the war was what to do about the constitution of the Cape Colony. The Cape had been granted self-government by Britain back in 1872, but three decades later Milner concluded that the colony's self-governing constitution posed a threat to British colonial rule, and was an obstacle to the unification of the country.[1] As De Kiewiet notes, the grant of self-government in the Cape had greatly weakened Britain's authority and helped to thwart Carnarvon's plans for confederation in the 1870s.[2]

Ever the imperialist ideologue, Milner argued that all four colonies in South Africa should be placed on the same legal footing: the more power given to any one colony, the less likely it would be to take orders from London. The Empire's interests, he told Chamberlain, ought to be protected by the imperial authority itself, not a colonial parliament calling itself imperial.[3] Thus far, Milner had been unable to get his own way.

Before and after the Jameson Raid, the Cape remained the 'foundation stone' of British imperial influence in South Africa, but the Raid had thrown its internal politics into disarray. For the six years that Rhodes had been premier, supported by 'a solid Afrikaner political phalanx', imperial interests had been well protected.[4] But the Raid had put an end to that. Rhodes's replacement, Sir Gordon Sprigg, had thrown in his lot with the disgraced ex-premier and his jingo supporters, and had lost the support of Cape Afrikaners. After the parliamentary election of 1898, the SAP, led by WP Schreiner and comprising members of the Afrikaner Bond and its anti-jingo allies, had formed a new government, which increased its majority in April 1899 (see Chapter 9). However, in June 1900, Schreiner had been forced to resign over his opposition to the war, and Sprigg had stepped in again, without parliamentary sanction, to act as premier.

Throughout the war, Milner was at odds with Schreiner and Sprigg – and Chamberlain in London – over the Cape government's failure to protect the colony's borders effectively, or to take action against Afrikaners in the rural areas – including MPs – who had rebelled against the colonial administration and gone over to the Boer side.

Another Afrikaner rebellion in 1901 in the rinderpest-wracked Griqualand West had heightened Milner's fears that if a Bond-led government took power after the war, it would indemnify acts of defiance and treat Afrikaner rebels leniently.[5] Because he had always believed the political dice to be loaded against the colony's 'loyalists', he wanted the Colonial Office to intervene and either suspend the Cape constitution indefinitely or allow the rebellious districts of the Cape to be ruled under a separate authority.

With its constitution in de facto suspension throughout the war, the Cape was effectively being run as another Crown Colony.[6] Sprigg, appointed by Milner to replace Schreiner and not directly elected, had been allowed to rule without recourse to Parliament. Though normally obedient to the Governor, on one issue the premier had stood firm – his determination to uphold the sanctity of the colony's constitution. Proud of having a force of 18 000 town guards and another 1 800 loyalist troops under his command, Sprigg was not in favour of ceding powers to the military authority, maintaining that either his writ or the British Army's had to run in the colony: any hybrid form of civilian/ military rule would only lead to misunderstanding and confusion.[7] Chamberlain agreed, and advised Milner that only in extreme circumstances would an indefinite suspension be warranted. The Colonial Secretary was aware that other countries of the Empire were keeping a watchful eye on developments at the Cape, and believed the British public would be angered by 'so cavalier an action' as the suspension of a colonial constitution.[8] Saul Dubow records that at the 1902 Colonial Conference in London, Sprigg's opposition to suspension was supported by Dominion leaders who understood the implications for the autonomy of their own countries.[9]

Now that the war was officially over, however, the status quo in the Cape could no longer continue indefinitely: the government was unconstitutional and therefore unable to enforce the law. Parliament would soon have to reconvene, and when that happened, it was quite possible that Sprigg, now nominal leader of the Progressives, would be defeated and replaced by a government comprising people who, in Milner's view, were either rebel activists or sympathisers.

Sprigg and a minority of Progressives were not in favour of prolonging the suspension, and neither were Chamberlain and Selborne, who believed that any intervention in the affairs of a self-governing colony would set an unfortunate precedent. (The majority of Progressives supported suspension, and switched their loyalties to Leander Starr Jameson, who became leader of the party and in due course premier.) Milner was informed, via the office of the new Governor, Hely-Hutchinson, that it was not possible for the imperial government to intervene without a strong appeal from a majority of Cape citizens – and unless there was clear evidence that the existing state of affairs posed a threat to peace.[10] Since 1688, it had been the 'strongest rule of British constitutional practice that what the Crown had given, could not be taken away'.[11]

This flew in the face of Milner's hope to have the Cape (and Natal) run along the same lines as the two ex-republics. In his view, the question was no longer one of right or wrong but whether the Colonial Office was prepared to act in Britain's best interests in South Africa. Given Sprigg's love of power, Milner feared the premier would make further concessions to the Bond simply to stay in office, which would keep the Cape out of loyalist hands and make his post-war task of federating the country much more difficult.

Under pressure from the loyalist faction of the Progressives, who were demanding clarity on the Cape's constitutional future, Milner signed an unofficial letter of support for a petition to London to amend the constitution, which drew the signatures of more than 30 000 colonists. A copy of his letter was leaked to the *Cape Times*, published on 19 May and republished by *The Times of London* a week later. In the view of John X Merriman, the petitioners were now begging to surrender their constitutional rights in order to reduce the Cape Afrikaners to 'helots'. Lewsen records that Merriman, still the voice of the SAP but now in detention on his farm at Stellenbosch under martial law because of his outspokenness, was more shocked by Milner's letter than by the petition, as it was a direct act of imperial intervention in the politics of the Cape.[12] When Chamberlain saw the letter in print, he was furious, telling Milner he was 'dismayed and seriously embarrassed'. He had always supported his envoy with the utmost loyalty and was deeply hurt not to have been consulted before publication.[13] Selborne also wrote to Milner saying it was unwise to have written the letter.[14]

The veteran Cape politician John X Merriman, shown here circa 1910. (*Wikimedia Commons*)

On 1 July, the British cabinet formally rejected the loyalists' petition, thus ensuring that the existing uncertainly in the Cape would continue. A chastened but unrepentant Milner confided to his friend Jim Rendel that his 'indiscretion' had been 'a very deliberate, desperate, perhaps questionable attempt to prevent a tremendous blunder'. 'I hardly hoped to succeed, but I am glad I tried.'[15] To Chamberlain, he expressed remorse that he had caused him any annoyance or embarrassment, as he fully recognised the support the Colonial Secretary had given him 'in the past critical years'.[16] He also offered to resign on the grounds of poor health and exhaustion.

Never in robust health, Milner was worn out from his labours during the war. A friend from Balliol, the celebrated journalist HW Nevinson, described his impressions after visiting Milner a few days before the war ended:

> I found him looking older, nearly bald, and deeply wrinkled ...
> He cannot pronounce 'th' clearly, perhaps owing to his German education, and it gives him a tone of weakness. He was not so polished and 'superior' as I remember him in the old days ...
> He dwelt very much on the personal side of things, especially on his own career ... and described what a terrible five years he had been through; how he had been fighting all the time – with Boers, English, Colonials, everyone; how he expected to be flung aside ... soon after the war was over, and on this he spoke bitterly ... My general impression was of a perfectly honourable and very sensitive nature; rather inclined to introspection and examination of his own motives; perhaps inclined to exaggerate himself generally, like a man always on the defensive, without the calm assurance and unquestioning belief of a born conqueror in his cause.[17]

In reply to Milner's abject apology and offer to resign, Chamberlain held out an olive branch, saying he deeply regretted that any difference should arise over policy; he hoped that time and the progress of events would remove it, as such differences were inevitable in the difficult circumstances in which each found himself.[18] But on 6 September Milner told the Colonial Secretary he had not changed his mind. He felt 'out of touch with the prevailing sentiment in England' and was 'anxious to quit the field, while I can do so in peace, without discredit and with a really good pretext'.[19]

Well before that, in a powerful speech in the House of Commons, an anxious Chamberlain had declared that 'in Lord Milner we have a great administrator, whom no difficulty can daunt, no labour appal, and who is qualified in a special way to complete the work which Lord Roberts and Lord Kitchener have begun so well ... It will be Lord Milner's duty – there will be no one more competent to fill it – to lay the foundations of a great, free community in South Africa, to bury the animosities of the past, and to create those institutions under which a liberty-loving community may enjoy prosperity and the benefits which will be conferred by the British flag.'[20]

A month later, hoping to have persuaded Milner that he was indispensable to the cause of Empire and had to soldier on, Chamberlain announced that with the war now over, he wished to take 'a new step of a rather sensational kind', and visit all the self-governing colonies of the Empire – beginning with South Africa. A mollified Milner replied: 'It would be the best thing that could happen for all of us and I earnestly urge you to carry out your plan.'[21]

Fixing Johannesburg

'A great Johannesburg,' Milner had declared in early 1902, 'great in intelligence, in cultivation, in public spirit, means a British Transvaal.'[22] The task he faced on the Witwatersrand alone was daunting. Founded less than two decades earlier, the rapidly expanding mining centre had been described by one of the members of the Kindergarten as 'simply the veldt with the grass rubbed off by passing vehicles'.[23] Like all boom towns, 'eGoli' (place of gold) had sprung up overnight to serve the needs of a transient population bent more on making quick money than on laying the foundations of a settled community.[24] Worse still, its interests had usually been treated with contemptuous indifference by the republican administration in nearby Pretoria.

As soon as the responsibility for Johannesburg had been transferred to him in 1901, by a military authority for which he had little respect, Milner had been making preparations to establish municipal government and initiate better town planning across the Rand. Now ensconced in Sunnyside, and able to guide the hard-working but inexperienced Lionel Curtis, whose grasp of finance was limited, Milner brought in Lionel Hitchens from Egypt to be Town Treasurer. Another Oxford graduate and historian, Basil Williams, who had fought for the British in the recent war, was made assistant to Curtis, while Geoffrey Robinson, one of several imported private secretaries, was given responsibility for liaison between the municipal government and the High Commissioner's office.[25]

Curtis's master plan for Johannesburg extended the municipal limits to encircle the central business district, the residential suburbs adjacent to the mines and the mines themselves, with their company-owned labour compounds.[26] Run by a town council, Johannesburg would cover more than 200 sq km. The plan transformed a 'loosely-bound mining town into the second-largest municipality in the world, after Tokyo'.[27] The Chamber of Mines opposed any move to give the new administration control over mining properties, but Milner stood firm. As a believer in centralisation and efficiency, he regarded the Curtis plan as the best way of providing the greater Johannesburg region with an effective administration and enough tax revenue to pay for it.[28]

While on sick leave in Britain before Vereeniging, Curtis himself had recruited Richard Feetham, another friend from New College, Oxford, who became a key member of the Kindergarten. Feetham made such an immediate impact as Deputy Town Clerk that Milner was able to move Curtis to Pretoria as Assistant Colonial Secretary, responsible for improving municipal government throughout the Transvaal, and to appoint Feetham as Town Clerk of Johannesburg, a position he held throughout the rest of Milner's time in South Africa.[29]

In 1903, Basil Williams was moved from municipal affairs to take charge of education in the Transvaal, while Hitchens became Colonial Treasurer in place of Patrick Duncan, who had become the Colonial Secretary. A further significant addition to the Kindergarten's ranks was John Dove, also from New College, who was to succeed Feetham as Town Clerk of Johannesburg, and eventually become chairman of the Land Settlement Board.[30] With this bright and energetic, if inexperienced, team of young Oxford men in place, Milner felt better equipped to tackle the problems of reconstruction.

Priorities

On 21 June 1902, Milner formally took the oath as Governor of the Transvaal in the old Raadzaal, in Pretoria. His first act was to hold discussions with Botha and De la Rey on issues flowing from the agreement at Vereeniging. In Bloemfontein two days later, he was installed as Governor of the Orange River Colony as well. Now the time had come for which he had long prepared: to make the former Boer republics attractive to British settlers.

His right-hand men in the endeavour would be two lieutenant governors, Sir Arthur Lawley in the Transvaal and Sir Hamilton Goold-Adams in the Orange River Colony, each with an executive council to succeed the military authorities, as well as a nominated legislative council of leading citizens. Political rapprochement, Milner believed, would hinge on an economic revival, hence the importance of the mining industry to his reconstruction plans. Within days of peace being concluded, the new Governor had obtained authority from London to impose a ten per cent tax on mining profits to help fund economic recovery. Percy FitzPatrick, spokesman for the mining industry, and the Chamber of Mines were most unhappy, but there was little they could do about it.

Milner's immediate tasks were manifold: to bring the mines back into full production; to repatriate Boer prisoners of war; to return farmers to their lands; to restore the rail network in order to encourage the movement of goods and people; and to complete negotiations over a customs union between the colonies, which had been interrupted by the war.[31] Time was of the essence, he told Chamberlain: 'The next year or eighteen months may well decide the whole future. Our aim should be to get on as fast as possible with all recuperative work. This will both keep up the prestige of Government and help to keep in this country the thousands of splendid and willing British settlers who are anxious to find employment here ... The great thing is to restart the machine in time to catch them.'[32] He urged the Colonial Secretary again to come to South Africa and see for himself the scale of the challenges that lay ahead.

The repatriation of Boer prisoners alone would have daunted a less determined and efficient administrator than Milner. Besides the several thousand prisoners to be transported home from such far-off places as St Helena, Ceylon and Bermuda, 155 000 Boer men, women and children and 100 000 African labourers had to be brought out of the concentration camps and resettled on land denuded of buildings and livestock.[33] Much of the £3 million compensation agreed at Vereeniging was used for this purpose, and by March 1903 the whole burgher population had been returned to their homes.[34] In the end, ten times more than the promised amount was spent on war damages, grants and resettlement loans to displaced Boers, and in loans to rebuild the ravaged country.[35]

Resistance

With the mines up and running again, thousands of Uitlanders flocked back to the Rand, and it was from their ranks rather than from the Boers – who were intent on rebuilding their lives – that the first resistance to Milner's regime came. As Le May observes, the returning Uitlanders tended to think the war had been fought entirely for their benefit and did not take easily to being ruled by an autocratic administration, run by brash and inexperienced newcomers. As victors in the conflict, they expected some of the spoils of office to come their way and were quick to castigate the new regime for being aloof, expensive, wasteful and over-regulating.[36] Within weeks of their return, immigrants had formed the Transvaal Political Association to press for representative government – and for less 'Crown' and more 'Colony'.[37]

Lawley's arrival in September 1902 enabled Milner to spend most of the next three months trekking around his two new fiefdoms, travelling mainly on horseback, with an entourage in tow, and often overnighting in a tent on the open veld. His intention was to demonstrate to Boer farmers that their new government was neither aloof nor indifferent to their needs.[38] After his first foray – into the western Transvaal – Milner told Violet Cecil that he had found the countryside 'quiet … only it is a complete wreck'.

The most serious problem was a lack of draught animals: 'It is all we can do … to get the people just enough oxen to plough sufficient land to keep them alive; if the mealie crop fails, we shall have to feed nearly the whole population for another year.' He reminded Violet that two years earlier he had predicted that this would be the outcome of the military's 'evacuation' policy.[39]

In *South African Memories*, Sir Percy FitzPatrick, newly knighted for his services as adviser to the British government during the war, recorded Milner's impressions after his first encounters with rural Boers in their natural habitat. Over a fireside chat late at night, Milner confided that he could not feel certain that he understood the Boers or could see into their minds: 'The Boers are different. Their experiences and their history have given them an individuality and characteristics which, with the conditions and circumstances of South Africa, have made them a unique and very puzzling problem.'[40]

'Of course,' Milner continued, 'the men of the younger generation differ from the old Boer, but there are characteristics common to both. I confess that the genuine old Boer attracts me very much … These old fellows, quite uneducated in our sense, who have probably never read a book except their Bibles, and very frequently cannot write an ordinary letter, are yet … the landed aristocracy and gentlemen in the best sense: dignified, courteous and hospitable, and amazingly self-controlled. They think "behind their eyes" and give nothing away. One feels that deep down there is a stratum which one cannot penetrate, beneath which are hidden and sealed the secrets of the race and of the individual; their fundamental convictions; their abiding purposes and aspirations; their amazing oneness as a race to which all others are alien.'

As FitzPatrick reflected, 'I doubt if any or many had ever heard [Milner] let himself go like this. He was simply thinking aloud and revealing a side of himself entirely unknown to others.'[41]

By the end of November 1902, the indefatigable Governor had traversed every district in the Transvaal and Orange River Colony. With Chamberlain's arrival in South Africa imminent, Milner prepared a long memorandum for the Colonial Secretary describing the political situation and listing several fundamental matters that required resolution.[42] He warned Chamberlain that he might run into ill feeling, not only from irreconcilable Boers and their *predikante* (church ministers) who were angry at the imposition of English-language teaching in Afrikaner schools, but also from an immigrant community that, a little more than three years earlier, had been in 'absolute servitude' to the Boers and were now 'ready to applaud anyone who comes along and raises a cry for "Representative Government"'. 'I do not think the feeling for representative government is really strong among the majority of men', he told Chamberlain, 'but it is the fashion to express a desire for it, and nobody has the moral courage to run counter to that opinion.'[43]

CHAPTER 21

Chamberlain's Visit
1902–1903

Joseph Chamberlain's visit to South Africa was the first by a Colonial Secretary to a distant imperial outpost. His new Prime Minister, Arthur Balfour (nephew of the ailing Lord Salisbury), Field Marshal Roberts and half the Unionist cabinet were on hand to give 'Jingo Joe' (as he was now known) a grand send-off from London's Victoria station aboard the royal train. Chamberlain had deliberately chosen to sail down the east coast of Africa, via Egypt and Kenya, so that he could fly the Union Jack and visit British interests along the way. The message he was out to convey was that the Anglo-Boer War had not weakened Britain but made the Empire even stronger.[1]

Accompanied by his lively new American wife, Mary, 28 years his junior, Chamberlain was enthusiastically welcomed to Durban on Boxing Day 1902. He had come, he told loyalists who had flocked to hear the famous visitor speak, as 'a missionary in the cause of Empire'.[2] Having signalled in advance that his tour would be 'for business, not show', he was presented, in Pietermaritzburg, with a 20-page memorandum from Milner, listing seven matters requiring urgent decision by the imperial authority.[3] On 3 January, the Chamberlains were met at Charlestown, on the Natal/Transvaal border, by Milner and Lawley, who had ridden around the foothills of Majuba while awaiting the arrival of the train. From there, the visitors journeyed to Pretoria, where they stayed for a week before moving to Milner's Sunnyside estate in Johannesburg.

In a speech at a welcoming banquet on 6 January, Chamberlain declared that Britain's policy in the 'new colonies' would be one of 'union and conciliation' but warned that conciliation was not to be interpreted as a sign of weakness or a pretext for further demands.[4]

Seated in the audience were the Boer generals Botha and De la Rey, who, along with De Wet, had been given the same uncompromising message in person in London a few weeks earlier. Soon after Vereeniging, the so-called Glorious Trio had travelled to Europe to seek funds to rebuild the Boers' ravaged lands, and had annoyed Chamberlain by making an emotional appeal to the 'civilised world' for money to rehabilitate their women and children. Peeved at the trio's warm reception in Britain, and the virulent attacks on him by their Liberal supporters, the Colonial Secretary had brusquely refused to make any changes to the terms agreed at Vereeniging, or to sanction any increase in the £3 million promised as compensation.[5]

On 8 January, Chamberlain met a delegation of 100 Boers, led by Louis Botha, with Smuts as their spokesman. The Colonial Secretary welcomed Smuts's affirmation that 'we should stand together in the work of resettlement and restoration'. But when issues were raised that Chamberlain felt had been settled at the peace talks, he responded firmly. 'The Treaty of Vereeniging', he declared, 'is the charter of the Boer nation. You have every right to call on us to fulfil this in the spirit and the letter. But it is a little too early to try now to go behind or further than the terms thus concluded.'[6] The Boers also raised the language issue and let Chamberlain know of their strong objections to the treatment of Dutch in the civil service and schools.

Milner described Chamberlain's manner as 'inflexible, yet very courteous'.[7] Smuts, on the other hand, having joined in polite cheers for the Secretary on his departure, told an English friend, LT Hobhouse, that the visitor's speech had been considered insulting by every Boer present.[8]

During Chamberlain's two-week stay in Johannesburg, he held extensive discussions with Milner and approved a series of measures to speed up reconstruction. Among the matters dealt with were: railway policy and administration; the South African Constabulary; the repatriation from European exile of three prominent Boer leaders who had sought the financial help of France and Germany; the introduction of municipal administration as a step towards self-government; and the setting-up of a South African Native Commission, a Rand Water Board and a new Department of Forestry.

Milner is shown second from left, between Mary Chamberlain and Joseph Chamberlain, during the Chamberlains' visit to Johannesburg in January 1903. (*Wikimedia Commons/Duffus Brothers*)

On the vexing question of mine labour, Milner raised with Chamberlain the possibility of importing indentured Chinese workers to alleviate the serious labour shortage caused by the war. The Colonial Secretary was not in favour, saying that such a step might be extremely unpopular in South Africa, would raise a storm of protest in Liberal circles at home and could not be supported by the British government.

At a banquet held in his honour in Johannesburg on 17 January 1903, Chamberlain announced the raising of a loan of £35 million from 'a group of [mining] financiers who are specially connected with South Africa'.[9] The loan, to be secured over the combined assets of the Transvaal and Orange River Colony, would be underwritten by the imperial government and advanced in annual tranches of £10 million for the funding of reconstruction and rehabilitation. As it turned out, because of a decline in mining profits and objections to taxation without representation, the loan was never called up, and the money for reconstruction advanced by the British government in the meantime was eventually written off when self-government was granted to the Transvaal years later. However, as Worsfold points out, the political significance of the arrangement was that it had forced the mining magnates to acknowledge they owed a war debt to the 'mother country'.[10]

On many occasions in the Transvaal (and later in the Cape), Chamberlain brushed aside the contentious language question. His blunt message to Afrikaners was 'drop your language and become English': 'You must feel ... that any aspirations for a separate Dutch identity ... are absurd and ridiculous.'[11] In Potchefstroom, he expressed the hope that the Afrikaners would share 'our pride in being members of a greater Empire. The British nation had been strengthened by its fusion with other races.'[12]

From Johannesburg, the Chamberlains meandered through the veld of the two 'new colonies' via Krugersdorp, Potchefstroom, Ventersdorp and Lichtenburg to Mafeking and Kimberley, before being rejoined by Milner in Bloemfontein in early February. The reception given the Colonial Secretary in the former Free State was surprisingly friendly, despite his being harangued at a meeting by Hertzog and De Wet, who accused Britain of violating three of the terms of the Vereeniging agreement, including the language clause.[13]

At a formal dinner in Bloemfontein on 7 February, following a conciliatory address by Chamberlain, Milner announced the amalgamation of the railway systems in the Transvaal and the Orange River Colony, and the establishment of an Inter-Colonial Council (ICC) to manage the joint rail network, the Constabulary, and other matters common to the two colonies. He expressed the hope that the new ICC would 'open a wider political horizon' and 'create a South African habit of mind, as distinct from a colonial one'.[14] The ICC was eventually made up of 26 members and its operations overseen by yet another Oxford graduate, Robert Brand, brought out to join the Kindergarten and serve as the ICC's secretary.

One more year

Before taking leave of his host and heading on to the Cape, Chamberlain reached agreement with Milner on two other significant issues:

civilian representation on the Transvaal's Legislative Council, and the High Commissioner's personal future. In mid-1902, Milner had offered Botha, Smuts and De la Rey seats on the Transvaal's new 30-man council, but the invitation had been turned down because the Boer leaders believed it was far too early for even a nominated council. Encouraged by Chamberlain, Milner renewed his invitation to the three men.

Before responding, the trio went through the motions of consulting other Boer leaders about whether to serve in a legislature in which they would be outnumbered by British officials, or to stand aside in favour of more pliant Afrikaners who had sworn allegiance to the Crown. There was no disagreement that Boer interests would best be served by waiting for self-government and letting Milner's unpopular administration take the heat in the meantime. The only refusal that Milner really regretted was De la Rey's; he had once described the elderly general to FitzPatrick as 'a remarkably fine fellow; he is a man, every inch of him, and one of whom every country in the world would be justifiably proud'.[15]

Perhaps the most important item on Chamberlain's agenda was to convince a reluctant High Commissioner that he should prolong his service in South Africa. Bringing his formidable powers of persuasion to bear, Jingo Joe told Milner that it was his imperial duty to complete the task that he had undertaken: to leave the country at that time 'would be almost an act of cowardice'.[16] The two men struck a bargain: Milner would take a period of home leave a few months hence and then return to South Africa for one more year only. Chamberlain confirmed that Johannesburg could remain Milner's official place of residence, since Lawley was now based in Pretoria.[17] In every public speech, the Colonial Secretary paid tribute to Milner, denying claims that his envoy was a 'hard man inclined to arbitrary methods'.[18]

After the Chamberlains had departed the Free State, Milner wrote to a friend to say that their visit to the two 'new colonies' had been 'an unmitigated success', but he was anxious about Jingo Joe's reception in the Cape, where he might fall for the blandishments of Afrikaner Bond leaders. Already, 'Onze Jan' Hofmeyr had responded positively to Chamberlain's expressions of goodwill by declaring that members of the Bond were willing to work for the common good as loyal members of the Empire.[19]

Writing to Violet Cecil, Milner said: '[Y]ou can imagine my feelings if [Chamberlain] does forgive the Bond before he leaves South Africa. You may be kindly to the Dutch, even the rebels if you will ... But to have any truck with the fundamentally and incurably disloyal organisation which has caused all the mischief, and is as full of devilry as it ever was, would be an even greater blunder than the suspension mess. It is a blunder even to receive a Bond deputation. As many Dutchmen as you please, but not *as Bondsmen*.'[20]

In the Cape

Travelling by special train, sandwiched between a second train carrying the press and a third bearing a breakdown gang to repair the line if necessary, the Chamberlains made their 'semi-royal' progress down to the Cape via the loyalist outposts of Grahamstown and Port Elizabeth, their journey punctuated by official stops along the way. At Graaff-Reinet, the Colonial Secretary disregarded Milner's advice and received a deputation and loyal address from the Afrikaner Bond. At Middelburg, in the heart of the Karoo, the Bond's secretary, NR de Waal MP, second in line to Hofmeyr, said that while many of the 'Dutch' had differed from Mr Chamberlain in the past, 'they were prepared to clasp hands in sincere friendship'. He told Chamberlain that his name 'was now a household word in every Dutch homestead'.[21] Similar sentiments were expressed at Beaufort West, Worcester and Wellington, though not at Paarl, where the couple's reception was noticeably less welcoming than elsewhere.

On 17 February 1903, the Chamberlains eventually reached Cape Town, where they stayed at Newlands with Milner's successor as Governor of the Cape, Sir Walter Hely-Hutchinson. The next day, after an elaborate welcoming ceremony in the City centre attended by the great and good of the Colony, the visitors plunged into a busy week of engagements.

Hoping that the troublesome constitutional question might be resolved by an agreement between moderates within both parties, Chamberlain quickly discovered that the differences between Progressive loyalists and the Bond wing of the SAP were too wide to be bridged. The Progressives were convinced that if and when the vote was restored to thousands of Afrikaner rebels, they would be out of political power permanently.

Their concerns were heightened when the Colonial Secretary received a deputation of 150 members of the SAP, led by Merriman, who declared themselves descendants of the 'oldest pioneers of the colony' who 'intended, whatever happened, to identify themselves permanently with the country'.[22] Chamberlain was even more impressed by Hofmeyr's public manifesto, which denounced acts of discrimination against loyalists and promised to promote the unity of 'both the great European sections of our population under the flag which waves over all of us'.[23] The Colonial Secretary was able to rub along with Hofmeyr much better than Milner had ever done.

From Prime Minister Sprigg, now in disfavour with the loyalists over the constitutional question, Chamberlain exacted a promise that no attempt would be made to re-enfranchise any Afrikaner rebels before Parliament reconvened later that year and another election could be held. To the consternation of the Progressives, however, who felt slighted by Chamberlain's conciliation of the Bond, not long after the Colonial Secretary's departure 380 rebel prisoners in the Colony were freed, though not re-enfranchised.

On 24 February, Chamberlain took his leave of Cape Town with a farewell speech in the Drill Hall, in which he praised Milner's 'firm and sympathetic policy', which would make the two new northern colonies 'amongst the most prosperous and most contented of the imperial territories'. He looked forward to the growth 'of a new nation here in South Africa, as loyal in the true sense of the word, as Imperial in the best sense of the word, as any of the possessions of the British Crown'.[24]

During his two months in South Africa, the Colonial Secretary and his wife visited 29 towns, made 64 speeches and received 84 deputations. There was no precedent for a minister of the Crown making so lengthy a journey 'on the soil of a defeated enemy'.[25] Reinforcing his reputation as the Empire's foremost statesman, Chamberlain was greeted on his arrival at Southampton by a cheering crowd waving flags and banners, and in London by a parade of dignitaries led by Prime Minister Balfour.[26] Remarkably, despite being the most popular politician in the entire country, Jingo Joe was still the most mistrusted by the cabinet and his party colleagues. And the result of his South African visit was a revival of his prime ministerial ambitions. Within a few short weeks, Chamberlain set out on a course that would polarise British politics for the second time in his career.

Back in Cape Town, a disgusted Rudyard Kipling, summering in South Africa again despite disliking 'the Dutch' as much as Milner, recorded that the Colonial Secretary – whom he idealised for his imperialist enthusiasms – 'has come, he has seen; he has been spoofed. The Bond are almost stupefied by their good luck.'[27] Writing in reply to a personal letter of protest from Kipling, Chamberlain revealed that 'he had a higher opinion of Hofmeyr's sagacity, as well as of his sincerity, than some of our English friends at home and in South Africa.'[28] And as he explained to Milner's ally, the journalist Iwan-Muller, he had deemed it tactically wise to 'whitewash the Bond' and pin its leaders down, so that he could attack them if they should play false.[29] He thought Milner was 'a very great man, but he has his limitations. He does not suffer fools gladly and unreason makes him angry, while it only amuses me.'[30]

CHAPTER 22

Reconstruction
1903

Milner's aversion to the Cape's Afrikaner establishment was not assuaged by the cordial reception given to Chamberlain by most SAP members, with the notable exception of John X Merriman. The veteran politician thought the Colonial Secretary's speeches in South Africa were 'glib and boastful',[1] and complained to an English friend that while Chamberlain's visit had done less harm than expected, it had done 'no good' and 'left us with Milner'.

'Not one single act emanated from him that justified his absurd plea of being a pacificator', wrote Merriman. 'He owes much to the moderation of those who, in their desire for peace, have kept silence upon his antics out here.'[2]

Writing to Chamberlain in May, Milner said he was perfectly satisfied that whatever Onze Jan's own views might be, the bulk of his followers were just what they always were, only more embittered: 'They will keep their sheep's clothing on for the present ... but once firmly seated in the saddle, they will show their true colours. I know you do not quite share my views on this point, and I can only, with all respect, put on record my unshakeable conviction that the South African Party has no other object than to weaken, in the hope of ultimately dissolving, the tie which unites South Africa with Great Britain.'[3]

To a friend, Spenser Wilkinson, Milner confided, 'The South African struggle continues. It has changed its character; it is no longer war with bullets, but it is war still.' Chamberlain's speeches, 'excellent though they are in many respects ... are calculated to obscure this fact, and to encourage an optimism which is not justified. It is quite true that we now hold the winning cards, but it is not true that we have won the game, and we cannot afford to lose a single trick ... We are fighting for something immensely big ... of all the distant portions of the British Empire, this may become by far the most valuable ... We may lose South Africa yet, but if we keep it, we shall have kept it by developing here a spirit of wider British patriotism.'[4]

The decisions taken during his discussions with Chamberlain in Johannesburg enabled Milner to press ahead, 'with drums beating and colours flying', with his programme of reconstruction.[5] As always, he worked ferociously hard at it, rising at 6.30 am and spending the next six hours of every day at his desk, refusing to be interrupted by anyone except the most important visitors[6] and, according to Amery, also working night after night without ceasing.[7] His private secretary, John Buchan, described him as being able to 'control any number of wires at once, for he had all the terminals in his head'.

Milner, wrote Buchan, was the 'most selfless' man he had ever known: 'He thought of his work and his cause, much of his colleagues, never of himself. He simply was not interested in what attracts common ambition. He could not be bribed ... or deterred by personal criticism, for he cared not at all for fame and it would have been as easy to bully the solar system, since he did not know the meaning of fear. He was a solitary man; but his loneliness never made him aloof or chilly, and in his manner there was always a gentle, considerate courtesy. I have worked with him often', Buchan recorded, 'when he was desperately tired, but I never remember an impatient or querulous word. He was a stern judge of himself, but lenient to other people.'[8]

Depression and drought

Within days of Chamberlain's departure from the Transvaal, Milner – rising from a sickbed – had convened a Railway Extension Conference in Johannesburg aimed at developing a transport network to benefit the whole of southern Africa. It was a goal that no one, including Rhodes, had been able to accomplish.[9] Milner viewed the expansion of the railways as a prerequisite for economic development, as it would bring farms closer to towns, lower the cost of living and serve as a stepping-stone towards federation.

A week later, a Customs Union Convention was held in Bloemfontein. It succeeded – where all pre-war efforts had failed – in abolishing tariff barriers between the colonies and in setting rail rates across the whole of British-ruled southern Africa. A new tariff would give a 25 per cent imperial preference to goods from Britain and any other members of the Empire prepared to reciprocate – a concession pioneered by Canada and recommended to Milner by Chamberlain.[10]

Milner also gave special attention to agriculture, setting up technical departments to give scientific assistance to returning Boer farmers, who were supplied with ploughs, seed and rations until they were able to feed themselves. Veterinary services were introduced to combat stock disease. An especially difficult problem was what to do with the large number of landless *bywoners* (tenant farmers) in the Free State, who had gone over to the British side during the war and had no chance of being re-employed on farms belonging to Boer *bittereinders*. Many had to be given jobs on public works projects and housed in the former concentration camps. By the end of 1902, though, most of the *volk* were back on the land and planting food for the coming season.

Despite these far-reaching measures, prosperity was slow in returning to the two war-torn ex-republics: the first 18 months after Vereeniging were plagued by an economic depression brought on by southern Africa's worst drought in 40 years. Its severity hindered the government's ploughing programmes, caused severe livestock loses and generally made rural recovery much more difficult. The sustained drought (from 1903 to 1908) also set back Milner's plans to settle more British immigrants on farming land.[11]

To add to the Governor's problems, mineral production had been slow to increase after three years of war. In 1899, the mines employed some 100 000 African labourers, almost three-quarters of them from Portuguese East Africa; by 1903, that number had dropped by half as a result of the war's upheavals, low wages and the availability of other work on reconstruction projects. Mineral revenues over the same period had fallen from £15.5 million to £12.6 million.[12] With the labour shortfall on the mines assuming critical proportions, there were few alternatives to the importation of indentured labour from abroad.

As the core of his reconstruction policy was now under threat, Milner set up an inquiry into working conditions on the mines, and was shocked by what he found. After persuading the mine owners to make immediate efforts to bring down the number of fatalities, he went personally to Portuguese East Africa to see if he could step up the recruitment of unskilled labour.[13] Realising that African sources would never be sufficient, notwithstanding Chamberlain's warning he began reluctantly to reconsider the mining industry's plea to be allowed to import labour from Asia.

Writing to a correspondent in April 1903, Milner said he was coming to the conclusion that 'we must have some Asiatics – not necessarily Chinese – here for our industrial development. I am dead against the Asiatic settler and trader, but I do not believe the indentured Asiatic labourer would prove uncontrollable.' Without such help, he said, he felt unable to bring about 'that great influx of British population – for skilled work, trades, professions and agriculture – which is the ultimate salvation.'[14] His decision, in due course, to allow Chinese workers into the Transvaal was to have dire consequences for him personally – but more so in Britain than in South Africa.

Colour issues

Three days after an upbeat Chamberlain had declared, in a rousing report-back to his Birmingham constituents on 3 May 1903, that South Africa 'could become a model for the Empire as a whole',[15] Milner gave an important address to a municipal congress in Johannesburg on the issues of coloured and native rights, as well as Indian immigration. In what became known as his 'Watchtower speech', he nailed his racial colours to the mast by supporting the dictum that 'civilisation' not 'colour' should be the criterion for the granting of municipal voting rights.[16] Yet, although he wished to keep the door open to 'the native', the opposition of the white community to extending the vote to other races was so strong that he did not feel justified in forcing 'upon the white population a principle repudiated no less by the British inhabitants than the Dutch'.[17]

On the 'native' question, Milner asked what good there was in perpetually claiming that South Africa was a white man's country, when it patently was not: 'I am not speaking of the question of political rights. Those of the black men, the natives, have been relegated, and I think wisely relegated, to the future for decision ... by a legislature elected by the white population of this country alone. But I am speaking of other privileges accorded to civilised men. Can you, if you base the supremacy of the white man upon his civilisation, deny to other men who have attained his level in that respect, the same rights?' Was the well-educated and civilised native to have no voice whatever in municipal affairs? he asked.[18]

Milner claimed that for the 'coloured class' he had the deepest sympathy and would be sorry if one of the 'first fruits of our victory was to place an indelible stigma upon them'. Speaking for himself, and knowing that his opinion would not be shared by those present, he would think it 'an unhappy day when any large British community in South Africa completely and finally repudiates the doctrine of one of the greatest of South African statesmen – "equal rights for all civilised men" '.[19]

On the matter of Asiatic immigration, Milner asserted that whatever steps might be needed to restrict the indiscriminate inflow of settlers from India, any opposition should be based on 'strong and unassailable' social and economic grounds, 'and not upon the weak ground of colour'. 'How could we hope', he asked, 'to be regarded as anything but blindly hostile to men of colour if we are going to deny to the most educated and civilised Asiatic ... all the other privileges that other men enjoy? Is it justifiable to denounce Asiatics ... and take the view that all of them, whatever their degree of civilisation, must be unwelcome here, or if they come here, should be treated as pariahs?[20]

'I am the man on the watchtower,' he concluded, 'and the man on the watchtower may see further than the men on the veld, not in the least because he is a better man, but because of the mere accident of his topographical position ... I hope that what I have said might mitigate the savagery of the opposition ... towards certain sections of our fellow-creatures. It may or may not be right to give them certain privileges; it must be wrong to refuse them in a way which leaves an enduring sense of injury and oppression.'[21]

Four days later, Milner received a delegation from the British Indian Association, led by Mohandas K Gandhi, who came to protest about restrictions on their trading rights and the imposition of a registration fee upon their businesses. As on most racial matters, Milner chose once again – in the current jargon – 'to kick the can down the road', claiming that final decisions of this kind could only be taken once self-government had been established. All he could do was recommend patience in the hope that public opinion might shift, because he was only a 'temporary holder' of executive authority and had no mandate to make changes that a subsequent government might repudiate.[22] It was an evasive argument he had advanced before – during the peace talks at Melrose House.

At Vereeniging, he had resisted Chamberlain's insistence on extending the native franchise as one of the preconditions for self-government, rejecting the notion of political equality and endorsing the practice of blacks being represented in legislatures by nominated whites.[23] He had told Chamberlain that blacks should not be forced to change their way of life, or to work for whites, but should learn the habits of regular and skilled work instead, and be kept away from 'strong drink'.[24] Some historians today argue that people of colour were actually worse off under the Milner government than in the former Boer republics, being subjected to stricter laws firmly enforced by a more determined and efficient administration.

Another step that reflected Milner's propensity for forward planning was his appointment, in 1903, of a South African Native Affairs Commission to 'arrive at a common understanding of native policy in the four colonies', in preparation for a South African federation.[25] The Commission was chaired by Godfrey Lagden, Resident Commissioner of Basutoland (now Lesotho), who had apparently fought hard to keep the little protectorate out of the war and been appointed as the Transvaal's Native Commissioner in 1901, despite his unsuitability for the post. Held up by critics as a prime example of an official without the necessary knowledge and experience for the crucial position he had been given by Milner,[26] Lagden, who had been considered for a lieutenant governorship and then passed over, 'served truculently' as Native Commissioner.[27] He and the other British officials on the Commission endorsed the policies of Sir Theophilus Shepstone, who had first proposed the creation of 'native reserves' in African ancestral areas in order to make the administration of 'native affairs' easier.[28]

In support of its recommendation that the territorial separation of black and white should become a permanent principle of land ownership – as well as a means of reducing racial friction – the Lagden Commission advanced the spurious argument that African tribal chiefs, in administering the land on behalf of their people, had effectively transferred their sovereign rights – including the powers of administration over communal lands – to the Crown, through a process of 'peaceful annexation'.[29] The Crown had a duty, therefore, to administer the native reserves in accordance with tribal ways of governance.

The Lagden Commission's proposals, implemented from 1906, marked a significant departure from Britain's declared mission to 'civilise' its colonies, in favour of a policy of re-tribalising the black proletariat. As Davenport and Saunders point out, by reformulating the concept of segregation in a new way, Lagden introduced rigidities into South African thinking about race relations that had an immense influence on political debate from then on. It led directly to the Natives Land Act of 1913 and other segregationist legislation implemented by the Louis Botha-led government that came to power after Union.[30]

Asiatic labour

By mid-1903, the importation of Asiatic labour for the Rand mines – whether from India, China or Japan – had become a matter of growing public interest in Britain and South Africa. After consulting the Viceroy, Chamberlain ruled out India as a possible source of supply and Lawley immediately went ahead with the appointment of a Labour Commission to establish the actual number of workers required by both agriculture and industry in the Transvaal. Before going on leave, Milner told Chamberlain the issue was his 'one great anxiety', but he thought the man in the street's opinion, even among the Boers, was changing: 'It is sincerely to be hoped that the Chinese – since they are now our only hope – may come and come quickly. The mines have exhausted their efforts, by higher wages, better recruiting and much better arrangements in every respect – food, clothing, sanitation, etc. – to get natives, but, though they have got some thousands more, there are not nearly enough. The fact is they do not exist – not in these numbers.'[31]

After presiding over the first session of the new ICC, which he described to Chamberlain as 'a great success', Milner was ready to embark upon the home leave he had negotiated with the Colonial

Secretary. Notifying Chamberlain that would spend six weeks on the Continent, in absolute seclusion, and thereafter three or four weeks in London, he left quietly from Delagoa Bay on 7 August aboard a small steamer sailing up the east coast of Africa. From Mombasa, he made a quick detour into the interior of Uganda. At Suez, he was given the news of the death of Lord Salisbury.[32]

CHAPTER 23

Defying the King
1903–1904

On arrival in Europe, Milner disembarked at the then Austro-Hungarian port of Trieste, en route to Vienna where he spent four days, being given VIP treatment by the British and Austrian governments. Among the books he read on the long voyage was Christiaan de Wet's *Three Years' War*, which he thought 'genuine, but so badly written as not to be interesting'.[1] Having not felt well aboard ship, he took a detour to nearby Karlsbad for a rest cure at the famous health spa, whose mineral waters were popular among the English aristocracy.

His days there were enlivened by the presence of the novelist Elinor Glyn, an attractive redhead eleven years younger, well known for her romantic (and risqué) novels, and separated from her husband. Glyn was apparently attracted to 'real English gentlemen of the old school',[2] especially classical scholars like Milner. She also had a rarefied taste for imperial plenipotentiaries, for besides falling for Milner, whom she thought 'a reincarnation of Socrates', she had an even greater passion for Lord Curzon, the Viceroy of India. It was Curzon who gave her the tiger-skin rug that became her trademark and led to a celebrated piece of doggerel:

> Would you like to sin
> With Elinor Glyn,
> On a tiger skin?
> Or would you prefer
> To err
> With her
> On some other fur?[3]

As Glyn's biographer breathlessly records, Elinor and Milner would walk together in the pine forests surrounding the spa by day, sharing thoughts on the Greeks and their philosophers, while in the evenings he would read Plato aloud to her, especially the *Phaedo*, 'the closing page of which never failed to move him to tears'.[4] Elinor was inspired by Milner to write a little volume of satire called *The Damsel and the Sage* about their dalliance. What began as a holiday fling would ripen into a close and long-lasting friendship, which may not have led anywhere but succeeded in making Violet Cecil extremely jealous. Violet's daughter, Helen Cecil, recalled that her mother was infuriated whenever she caught her reading one of Glyn's novels.[5]

Chamberlain resigns

In mid-September, Milner's European idyll was rudely interrupted by the startling news from London that Chamberlain had resigned from the Unionist cabinet in order to campaign nationwide for his policy of tariff reform. At the height of his powers as the Unionists' 'weather-maker', Jingo Joe had concluded that the colonies needed commercial incentives to remain bound to Britain and was determined to bring the Empire's 'diffuse and decentralised authority' into his own hands.[6] He proposed the building of a tariff wall around the Empire: goods from outside the Empire would be taxed once they crossed the wall.[7] Imperial preference, he believed, would not only create a partnership between the Dominions, colonies, territories and 'mother Britain' that would pave the way to a federated Empire but would make him – if not prime minister – then indisputably the most powerful politician in the land.[8] Having split the Liberal Party once before over Ireland, he would now divide the Unionists over tariff reform versus free trade, and for the second time in his career leave a divided party with little chance of winning the next election.

The languid Unionist premier, Arthur Balfour, never one to be fazed by a crisis, was away golfing during the parliamentary recess, and took his time before dispatching a King's Messenger to Karlsbad to offer Milner the position of Colonial Secretary. The offer did not come as a complete surprise, as Milner had been forewarned that Balfour had him in mind as Chamberlain's successor. In his message, the Prime Minister said it would give the country confidence to know that the office would still be administered 'by a big man on big lines'. 'Am I at liberty to tell the King that your services would be available?' Balfour inquired. Even before Milner could reply, the Prime Minister, by then at Balmoral at the monarch's side, wrote again to emphasise that the King earnestly hoped he would accept the appointment.[9]

Not many men would have had the temerity to refuse such a summons from on high – but not many men were sticklers for principle like Milner. That night, he sat up late writing a letter of refusal to Balfour. Honoured though he was by being invited to succeed 'the greatest Colonial Secretary the country had ever had' – and after receiving 'the highest compliment that has ever been paid or is ever likely to be paid me' – he felt he might be 'leaving things at a loose end' by accepting, and could be of better service to his country by remaining in South Africa 'than in the higher office which you offer me'.[10]

Balfour was not easily deterred, and sent a cable back asking Milner to reconsider his decision, while the King told his Prime Minister he was 'extremely sorry Lord Milner has refused and does not think he ought to have done so'.[11] 'Very much upset by this', Milner sat up another whole night thinking, and next day replied to Balfour that he had not changed his mind but would come to London at once to see him. Accompanied by Elinor Glyn to Nuremberg, where they spent a 'joyous' day together, and also by Geoffrey Robinson, who had been taking the waters at nearby Marienbad, Milner arrived in London on 26 September, determined not to be persuaded to alter his decision.[12]

Despite being urged by Chamberlain to accept the Colonial Secretaryship because circumstances had changed since their 'bargain' in South Africa, Milner remained resolute. After consulting his closest friends, some of whom urged him to accept and others to refuse, he held two lengthy discussions with the Prime Minister before finally declining the appointment. 'The one great reason for my not coming in', he explained to Balfour, 'is that I do not think I ought to abandon the work, to which I have devoted so many years, at its present necessarily very incomplete stage.'[13] With that, Milner went back to Europe to resume his holiday and visit his parents' grave in Germany.

As O'Brien explains, the dedicated High Commissioner felt

morally committed to finishing the assignment he had been given, as well as obligated to the many British loyalists in South Africa who had been helping him do so.[14] Unstated at the time, though undoubtedly a factor in his decision, was his distaste for party politics in Britain, and his frustration with the shortcomings of the parliamentary system. Furthermore, he felt that he could hardly take the place of someone whose views on tariff reform he shared. Like the outgoing Colonial Secretary, he believed the Empire should be bound together by a federation of colonial nations that offered concessions to its members but denied them to foreigners.[15]

Seeking allies

During his six weeks in England, Milner's 'holiday' was the usual busy mix of work and play. Much of his time was spent at the Colonial Office, where he endorsed the appointment of his friend, the Honourable Alfred Lyttelton, as Chamberlain's successor. It was Lyttelton's first taste of public office and, being three years younger than Milner, he was to be more of a disciple than a superior.[16] On the Asiatic labour question, at the forefront of Milner's London agenda, Lyttelton was willing to be educated rather than to dictate.[17] On 16 November, he arranged for Milner to address the Balfour cabinet on the labour crisis in the Transvaal and other South African issues.

Warned by his political contacts that bringing indentured labour from either India or China onto the Rand was certain to invite strong censure from the pro-Boer section of the British press and public – some of it genuinely felt, but much of it manufactured – Milner went out of his way to persuade his political allies in the coalition government that the importation of foreign workers was essential to the economic recovery of the Transvaal – and the well-being of British immigrants. No one seemed much interested in the subject, but he was assured by the likes of Liberal imperialist heavyweights Asquith, Sir Edward Grey and Richard Haldane, staunch supporters of the war, that they would use their influence to prevent party political capital being made out of the issue.[18] Many mainstream Liberals, Campbell-Bannerman among them, were opposed to any land settlement or industrial development that might increase British numbers, and argued that the Transvaal should be given back to the Boers.[19]

On the social side, Milner was again in much demand, summoned to stay at Windsor and play bridge with the King, and invited to spend time at the homes of the Goschens and the Chamberlains. He saw much of Lady Cecil and a little of Elinor Glyn, spent weekends in the country with friends and entertained civil service colleagues and journalists.[20] Resolutely avoiding all public engagements, he reluctantly refused – for the second time – the offer of an honorary doctorate from Cambridge University.

On 28 November, Milner left Southampton aboard the *Dunottar Castle*, accompanied by Geoffrey Robinson and Ozzy Walrond, the latter soon to leave his side for reasons of ill health and to marry a South African. After a rough, storm-wracked voyage that confined him to his cabin for days on end, the High Commissioner stepped ashore in Cape Town on 15 December to be greeted by an enthusiastic crowd lining the city streets. Staying briefly in the Cape, he departed on a non-stop train journey to Johannesburg, where he was given a rousing municipal reception at the Wanderers' Club, paid for by public subscription.

In his address, Milner noted that it was the first time that several Transvaal municipalities, elected by popular vote, had acted together in arranging the function – an encouraging milestone along the road to constitution-making.[21] 'If the quiet people would only find a little time to examine things,' he noted, 'they would be astonished to realise how far the country had travelled in a short time.'[22]

Under fire

Milner's top priority on resuming his duties, shortly before Christmas 1903, was to forge ahead with the introduction of Chinese labour 'with all the energy, patience and tenacity which I may possess'.[23] He was soon under fire from various quarters, particularly Boer-Afrikaners countrywide. In the Cape, the Afrikaner Bond and some Progressives, hoping to secure coloured votes in the impending parliamentary election, were in outright opposition to any such scheme.[24] Agitation was rife in the Transvaal too, where a mass protest of Boers at Lydenburg in December demanded the holding of a plebiscite to test public opinion on the matter.[25]

Jan Smuts (left) and Louis Botha (right), circa 1905. *(both Wikimedia Commons)*

In early 1904, 15 Boer leaders (among them Schalk Burger, Botha, De la Rey and Smuts) signed a petition to the new Colonial Secretary, Lyttelton, protesting that the labour question 'had never been submitted to the approval of the people, the overwhelming majority of whom are unalterably opposed to the introduction of Asiatic labour ... The Legislative Council is in no sense representative of the Transvaal people ... We are most anxious that HMG ... shall not remain under the mistaken impression that the Boer population is in favour of a measure which it looks upon as a public calamity of the first magnitude.'[26]

Six months earlier, rumours of a 'capitalist plot to import Asiatic labour', which would mean adding another element to the Transvaal's already complex racial mix, had prompted Louis Botha to convene a large gathering of Boers at Heidelberg to protest against the measure and to denounce the imposition of English on Dutch/Afrikaans schools and the 'constitutional enormity' of being taxed without representation.[27] Among the assembled throng were many mineworkers, who feared the loss of their jobs to the Chinese or a reduction in their wages, as well as farmers anxious at the prospect of having to compete with the mines for labour.[28] Taking no chances, the administration sent no fewer than 500 special constables to Heidelberg to keep an eye on proceedings.[29]

When Lyttelton responded formally to the Boer leaders' petition by stating, unwisely, that he did not accept the claim of the 15 signatories to be the representative of their people, Botha and Smuts decided it was time to re-enter politics. In order to demonstrate to the British who the true representatives of the *volk* were, the two men set about laying the foundations of a new political party.

Given the stature of the Boer signatories, the Colonial Office cautioned Milner not to rely simply on the opinion of the Transvaal's British population, to which he responded by saying the absence of voting lists for the countryside meant it would take at least six months to organise a referendum on the issue. Moreover, he believed that as far as the Boers were concerned, any poll would not be a vote about importing labour but about the continuation of colonial government.[30]

Ever sceptical, Milner believed the racially prejudiced 'Dutch' population was set on exploiting the labour issue for all it was worth so as to advance the demand for self-government – which was partially true. But there were also many non-Afrikaners who honestly feared that if more 'Asiatics' were introduced, they 'would swarm over the whole country in enormous numbers, invading every trade and acquiring a permanent hold over the land'.[31]

While the Governor had been away in England, Lawley's Labour Commission had concluded that as many as 129 000 more workers were needed on the mines, 50 000 in industry and 35 000 on the railways.[32] The Commission's report coincided with the return of the Witwatersrand Native Labour Association's representative from the Far East, where he had established that Chinese workers would be suitable for work on the mines, and available in sufficient numbers if their conditions of service were acceptable.

Assurances from the president of the Chamber of Mines, Sir George Farrar, in the Transvaal Legislative Council that indentured workers from Asia would be employed in unskilled jobs only, helped to tip public opinion in favour of their recruitment. A petition in support of the measure gained more than 45 000 mainly English-speaking signatories – around half the number of 90 000 adult whites in the Transvaal, excluding some 15 000 civil servants.[33] On 28 December, the Legislative Council went ahead and approved a motion supporting the importation of unskilled labour by 22 votes to 4. On the strength of that vote, and particularly its support by Afrikaner representatives on the Council, Milner, Lawley and the Executive Council made preparations to introduce the necessary legislation without further delay.

Writing to Lyttelton on 3 January 1904, Milner said: 'I realise the gravity of the decision, but there can be no shadow of doubt as to its wisdom. The depression in business continues daily, people are without work, and unless the situation soon changes, a considerable exodus of whites is inevitable. The Legislative Council's adoption of the resolution faithfully reflects public opinion … I can remember no discussion in which the weight of argument was more completely on one side.'[34]

On 10 March, Milner reported to the Colonial Secretary that he had received a delegation of 'several hundred men' representing 30 public bodies, including the town councils of Johannesburg and surrounding towns, representatives of trade and commerce, and 40 mining companies urging him to impress upon the British government that without an adequate supply of unskilled labour, an increasing number of whites would have no jobs and the 'present acute financial and industrial depression will be intensely aggravated'.[35]

One delegate had declared that the unanimous opinion on the mines he represented was in favour of imported labour: 'It has been said that this is a capitalistic question, but I consider it is a working man's question.'[36] Only 12 months earlier, non-mining members of the Chamber of Commerce had decided by a large majority to vote against any measure to import foreign labour but had since changed their minds.[37] There was no doubt in Milner's mind that public sentiment on the Chinese question had shifted significantly.

CHAPTER 24

The Chinese
1904

In mid-1904, the first 600 indentured Chinese workers arrived in Durban from Hong Kong. On three-year contracts, they took up employment at the New Comet mine on the Witwatersrand a fortnight later. Their number increased to 40 000 within a year, and would eventually reach well over 60 000.

From recruitment to repatriation, the newcomers fell under the overall supervision of the Transvaal government, but their working conditions were laid down by the Chamber of Mines, a body formed primarily to protect the interests of mine owners. As temporary immigrants, the Chinese were given unskilled work, and could only terminate their employment contracts if they repaid the cost of travel to and from South Africa. In theory, they could bring their wives and children with them, but the expense of doing so was prohibitive.[1] When their first three years were up, they could opt to stay on for a further three, but thereafter repatriation was mandatory. On the mines, the Chinese were confined to cramped and ill-equipped compounds and given leave passes for a maximum of 48 hours. Desertion, laziness and inefficiency could be punished by fines, floggings or, in the worst cases, imprisonment.

Writing to the Bishop of Natal, Milner argued disingenuously that there was no more 'slavery' in employing Chinese on the mines than there was in a hundred forms of service based upon free contract – and certainly not as much as enlistment in the Army: 'It is true mining is not a healthy trade, but it will be carried on under conditions as favourable as Science can make them, and in all other respects the Chinese will be well cared for. They will earn here in a few years as much as they could at home in a lifetime and will return to their own country with what to

them appears a competency and even wealth. And this country absolutely requires some extraneous help to get along. Without it, there will
be a white exodus, and that of course, means a British exodus.'[2]

Although the cost of employing these foreigners – their recruitment, transport, wages, food and housing – exceeded that of hiring
Africans, their skills proved more than sufficient for the extraction of
lower-grade ores at ever-deeper levels. And as African workers also
began filtering back to the mines, the gold output of the Witwatersrand
began gradually to increase. By 1906, not long after Milner's departure, the Rand mines were in full production again, employing 163 000
workers – 94 000 of them Africans, 51 000 Chinese and 18 000 whites.
In 1907, South Africa's share of the world's gold output recovered
to over 30 per cent, which lifted the economy of the entire southern
African region.[3] As to why reluctant African workers had returned to
the mines in such large numbers, having shunned the industry for so
long, Milner's biographer Marlowe concludes that it was because the
mining companies had finally begun to pay better wages. Yet by introducing indentured mineworkers into the Transvaal, mine owners were
also able to keep a lid on the price of non-tied or 'free' labour.[4]

Ructions in Britain

Milner had been forewarned that importing Chinese labour into South
Africa would be a divisive issue in British politics, certain to be exploited by radical Liberals eager to embarrass the ineffective and tottering
Unionist government. For this reason, he had gone out of his way, while
in London, to gain the assurance of those Limps who had backed him
during the war that they would support a measure necessary to bring
about economic recovery in South Africa. On the understanding that
such support would be forthcoming, he had gone ahead with the
Chinese project.[5] But early in 1904, his like-minded friend Amery
alerted him to dangers ahead. 'The last week or two has been giving us
a splendid example of the impossibility of running the Empire by British democracy', wrote Amery. 'If you had not had a government already
very shaky, and an opposition thirsting for the spoils … you would
never have heard anything about the Chinese Labour Ordinance. As it
is, the thing has been worked with a vengeance.'[6]

But according to Gollin, when the details of the Transvaal Labour Importation Ordinance became public, there was an 'explosion of anger' in Britain. Fomented by the popular newspapers, a 'hymn of hatred and rage against Milner and the Unionist government swelled up in every section of the country', particularly among anti-capitalists and trade unionists fearful of their fellow miners in South Africa being deprived of jobs by wealthy, profit-seeking mine owners.[7] At Westminster, radical MPs denounced Milner for promoting 'Chinese slavery'. In the Commons, the Liberals' Herbert Samuel, egged on by the party leadership, proposed that royal sanction be withheld from the Transvaal legislation.[8] A motion to this effect was narrowly defeated by 281 votes to 230.

In the House of Lords, the Bishop of Hereford moved that 'this House disapproves of the importation of Chinese labourers into the Transvaal until the grant of full self-government'. His Lordship went on to assert that 'it would be a great boon for South Africa if Lord Milner were no longer there'. 'He has shown his disqualification for the position in two ways: (i) his temper constantly obscures his judgment and (ii) his language is constantly running away with him. Men of that temper and with that rasping journalistic pen should not represent the Empire in great positions.'[9] A furious Goschen rose to Milner's defence, and wrote afterwards to say he had given the Bishop of Hereford 'such a dressing down as I expect no Bishop had had for years in the House of Lords'.[10]

On the same day as the Lords debate, Campbell-Bannerman, in the Commons, deplored the Unionist government's approval of the Transvaal Labour Importation Ordinance. Toeing the party line, Asquith, who hoped to succeed C-B as Liberal leader, condemned the legislation because the House 'was the trustee of the liberty of the subject throughout the Empire' and had not been given sight of the legislation beforehand. An angry Amery told Milner, 'I did think you had got Asquith straight on the point, bit I am afraid the temptation, with office looming so near and wallpaper for 10 Downing Street already selected by Mrs A, was too much for him, and his performance was as bad as everybody else's, if not worse.'[11]

On 21 March, Campbell-Bannerman moved a vote of censure

against the Unionist government, which was lost by only 57 votes. Except for the Liberal imperialist Richard Haldane, all the other Liberals on whom Milner had been told he could rely voted for the motion – an example of the 'bald political opportunism' in British politics that so disgusted Milner.[12] It took the pro-Tory *Times* to point out that when the Liberals had been in government, they had allowed Asiatic labour to be brought into British Guiana, so the current 'Chinese slavery' cry was simply 'cant' on the part of 'pretending philanthropists' in the Liberal Party.[13]

The alleged unfairness of Milner's treatment at Westminster was recorded by Cecil Headlam with deep indignation: 'Politicians will be politicians, but in the whole history of party warfare there is not to be found anything more cynical or disgusting than the speeches, backed by banners and cartoons of flogged and fettered Chinamen, by which the anti-Chinese agitation was worked up in Parliament, by the Press, the Chapel and the street corner, by right revered prelates and non-conformist divines, by Hyde Park orators, and right honourable gentlemen who themselves sanctioned similar restrictions on indented labour.'

Writing to his friend Bertha Synge, Milner gave vent to his exasperation: 'What too *awful fools* the Liberals made of themselves about the Chinese. I suppose it paid like fun for the time being, but despite my age and cynicism, I do not believe that such pandering to popular prejudices can pay in the long run. Fortunately, I don't mind abuse in the very least, rather like it, from certain quarters. If C-B for instance were ever to praise anything I did, I should instantly resign, with a profound sense of failure.'[14]

The ever-contrarian WT Stead, by now an outspoken critic of imperialism, could not help being impressed by his former colleague's steely sense of purpose, which he described as 'heroic'. Wrote Stead: 'Lord Milner has neither wife nor child. He stands erect, alone, like a great monolith amid the arid sands of the desert, with no companion and no compeer, a solitary figure sustained alone by his unshakable belief in the wisdom of a policy the futility of which remorseless time is demonstrating day by day.'[15]

More encouraging news for Milner in early 1904 was the election result in the Cape, where the pro-British Progressives defeated the Bond-dominated SAP by 50 votes to 45, thanks to the disenfranchisement of Afrikaner rebels. On Rhodes's death, Sprigg had lost the party leadership (and the premiership) to the irrepressible Dr Jameson, who had been welcomed back to the colony in 1900 after being released, on medical grounds, from a brief spell of detention in Holloway Prison.

Milner refused to accept, however, that Jameson's victory undermined his argument for suspending the colony's constitution, to put the Cape on the same footing as the other colonies. Writing to his old friend Sir Clinton Dawkins, he claimed the election had provided 'the strongest argument' in favour of suspension: 'You have had to stir up all the old racial animosities, which under an impartial loyal government (not depending on elections, election violence, election dodges and the race hatred which electioneering excites to the highest pitch), would by now have been dying down ... Under your blessed Responsible govt. you have parties almost equally matched, fighting for power on the race issue alone, and the racial feud must soon spread to the other colonies.'[16]

In May, Kipling wrote to Milner to say he was leaving the Cape and asking if there was anything he could do for him in England: 'Things are not going so badly here. The Bond has been hurt ... which it dislikes; [it] has made itself ridiculous also and is quarrelling among itself ... in vituperating triangles. Dr Jameson's studious urbanity is driving the Dutch wild ... and they are working hard to remove any good impression he might make ... But to think that after such a war, we should be rejoicing here to have defeated "constitutionally" the declared aims of declared rebels. What a land it is!'[17]

Self-government

The outcry over 'Chinese slavery' – feigned or genuine – and the precariousness of the Balfour government brought home to Milner and Lyttelton the near certainty of a Liberal administration in Britain in under two years. This prospect, as well as Milner's need to retain the goodwill of the Transvaal's restive ex-Uitlanders, forced him to contemplate some form of self-government for the former republic. It had always been his intention to concede 'responsible government' when

English-speaking voters were in the clear majority, but time was no longer on his side.[18] He now feared that if some form of self-government
were deferred for too long, a large number of the British community
might throw in their lot with the Boers.[19] And a Liberal government,
once in office in Britain, would probably grant the Transvaal self-
government immediately – if only to evade responsibility for 'Chinese
slavery'.[20] That would bring a premature end to reconstruction – and
to Milner's hope of further imperial expansion.

On 2 May 1904, Milner sent the first of several secret dispatches
to Lyttelton on the subject of self-government: 'Every day that passes
impresses on me more and more the extreme undesirability of defer-
ring it for too long, especially in the case of the Transvaal. There is no
white population more impatient of control, or more lacking in the political experience and training which self-government is best calculated
to teach, than the people of that Colony, and in particular the British
inhabitants ...[21] The agitation for self-government will go on and it
would be impolitic to ignore it ... unless something is done, we shall
soon have to confront an organised movement which the bulk of the
British population will thoughtlessly welcome.'[22]

Lyttelton, who predicted that Parliament could be dissolved as early
as 1905, 'when almost inevitably we shall be beaten',[23] gave Milner the
authority to begin preparing the ground for self-government.

Milner also raised with the Prime Minister the question of his successor in South Africa. If an appointment were to come from within
the Colonial Service, he would recommend his deputy, Lawley, for
the job, but if a man 'of cabinet rank' were required, he would suggest
either Lyttelton, the Colonial Secretary, or Selborne, now First Lord of
the Admiralty. In a private and confidential letter to Balfour, he said he
regarded himself as merely holding on until a good man was found to
take his place. 'I have seen the "new colonies" through their immediate economic crisis, and I shall have my plans for constitutional change
ready by the end of the year', he promised.[24]

Divisions

The Unionist government's announcement, in mid-1904, of its intention to grant a form of representative government in the Transvaal

set off a chorus of disapproval in both Britain and South Africa, and a flurry of political activity in the Transvaal. In May, the founding congress of Het Volk (The People) was held in Pretoria, presided over by Botha and Smuts, and attended by nearly 200 delegates. In the Orange River Colony, a similar organisation, Orangia Unie (Orange Union), was formed. Formally inaugurated as a political party in January 1905, Het Volk proposed a policy of reconciliation between the two white groups that its founders hoped might appeal to Liberal politicians at Westminster. Milner, of course, was no more trusting of Het Volk's professed intentions than he was of the Afrikaner Bond's in the Cape.

On the English-speaking side of the divide, ex-Uitlanders, resentful at being passed over for some of the top posts in the Milner administration and believing they could run the colony as well as if not better than the Kindergarten, had also become more politically active. If Emily Hobhouse is to be believed, they had much to complain about. In a letter home in 1903, she wrote, 'Municipal taxation is far heavier. The Post Office is bad, slow and unreliable. The Railway is slow, unsure, constant thefts, dirty – even the Johannesburg paper devotes a stinging leader to it, complaining that military men are put in places to carry on work they know nothing about. Shop-keepers complain they cannot get their goods until the season has past – and so on. One looks in vain for any department that is well or satisfactorily worked. It all sounds very big and imposing in blue-books and newspapers, but the reality is failure and dissatisfaction with great squandering of public money.'[25]

During 1904, the Uitlanders formed themselves into two rival organisations, the Transvaal Progressive Association, supported by the mining industry, and the largely Johannesburg-based Transvaal Responsible Government Association, representing professional and commercial interests. They referred to each other derisively as the 'Retrogressives' and the 'Irresponsibles'. A third grouping of labour unions banded together as an Independent Labour Party.[26]

Unlike the Progressives, who wanted only representative (ie nominated) but not fully responsible (ie elected) government until English speakers were in the majority, the much smaller 'Responsibles' grouping demanded self-government immediately. Botha and Smuts envisaged an alliance between Het Volk and the Responsibles, led by

EP Solomon, brother of the Transvaal's Attorney General, Sir Richard Solomon, to fight 'the capitalists and the jingoes' in the Progressive Association, led nominally by Farrar but effectively by the indefatigable Sir Percy FitzPatrick.[27] Denoon records that Milner was paying a high price for his reliance upon the young men of the Kindergarten, who antagonised the British in the Transvaal by their manners, and 'brought the administration into disrepute by their shortcomings'.[28]

It took until December, however, for the details of a proposed new constitution for the Transvaal to be made public. A census in mid-1904 had indicated that in an election, Boer-Afrikaners would be in the majority.[29] Accordingly, a concerned Milner proposed throwing 'a sop to Cerberus' – a 'half-way house' in the form of an elected legislature to replace the existing nominated Legislative Council, combined with a 'Crown-colony' type of executive. If this hybrid system could last for three or four years, he explained to Lyttelton, 'immigration ought – if industry develops – to turn the balance in favour of the British' and render it possible to grant responsible government with less risk.[30]

In March 1905, Het Volk agreed to refrain from criticising the importation of Chinese, to which the Responsibles had been committed, in return for the latter's support for a white franchise and withdrawal of their backing for Milner's audacious – and objectionable – anglicisation of the education system in state schools, in which the medium of instruction had to be English. (A noted Afrikaner historian records that his generation grew up with the image of a primary-school Afrikaner child standing in the corner of a class with a placard around his neck saying, 'I am a donkey; I speak Dutch.'[31])

As has often been observed, those who do not learn from the errors of history are doomed to repeat them. In 1976, the imposition of Afrikaans as a medium of instruction in African schools sparked off the Soweto student uprising, which led to the loss of many lives.

In the view of Davenport and Saunders, the association between the Boers of Het Volk and the Responsibles was highly effective in undermining Milner's reconstruction plans, particularly after the Liberals came to power in Britain, as had been anticipated, in the election of early 1906.[32]

Death of Kruger

On 16 December 1904 (Dingaan's Day), the ceremonial funeral of Milner's bête noire, Paul Kruger – who had died some months earlier in Switzerland at the age of 78 – took place in Pretoria. His body had lain in state in Cape Town, from where it was accompanied by Louis Botha, on whom the mantle of Boer-Afrikaner leadership had descended, on its long journey by special train to the former republican capital. In a show of goodwill towards the Boers, in the spirit of 'we are good friends now', the Union Jack was flown at half-mast in towns along the railway line to Pretoria.

Milner gave permission for the equivalent of a state funeral for the former SAR president, the solemn occasion attended by many thousands of Boer mourners. The Governor did not attend the funeral in person but sent his military secretary in his stead, while the Transvaal government was represented by Sir Richard Solomon.

After the ceremony, Milner received a delegation of Boer leaders who respectfully informed the Governor that no constitutional proposals that fell short of 'responsible' government would be acceptable to their people. It was better, they suggested, that the present form of 'nominated' representation should continue until such time as the British were ready to grant the form of government promised in the peace treaty at Vereeniging.

It was not the shadow of self-government the Boers were after, but the substance.

CHAPTER 25

Successes and Failures
1904–1905

Now into his last lap in South Africa, a determined Milner was not going to allow the denunciation of his Chinese labour policy by British politicians, most of whom he regarded with contempt, to deflect him from his reconstruction project. In his view, a ready supply of un-skilled workers for the Transvaal's mines was as crucial to the economy of South Africa as the waters of the Nile were to the economy of Egypt.[1] Without cheap labour, he had no chance of regenerating the mining industry and using its substantial revenues to fund his modernisation programme.

At the top of his agenda were three highly contentious projects: settling more British immigrants on the land; making English the dom-inant language in the ex-republics; and preparing the way for limited self-government for the two 'new colonies' after his departure. On these issues, his aims had never changed, and were to be almost wholly frustrated.[2] Many of his secondary goals – remedying the finances of the Transvaal and Free State, revamping the rail network and improving farming methods and education standards – were more easily achievable. Other items on his 'to do' list included security and policing, native policy and Boer claims for war compensation.[3]

If the mines were to provide the 'overspill' of tax revenue needed to finance economic development, an efficient rail network was a pri-ority. No other agency, in his view, could produce 'social and industrial results of so direct and immediately beneficial a character' as efficient railways.[4] In London, the War Office was not making his task any easier, demanding the 'preposterous' sum of £1.5 million from the Transvaal government, allegedly spent by Britain on fixing damaged railway lines during the war.

Milner managed to have the payment reduced to £500 000 and exacted another £5 million from the British Treasury to extend the rail
network. The Customs Union Convention in Bloemfontein in 1903
had already led to the addition of new tracks connecting the Rand to
Kimberley, Zeerust, Ladysmith and Kroonstad, as well as doubling the
existing line between Witbank and Delagoa Bay.[5] On the once-fraught
question of inter-colonial rail tariffs, Milner's discussions with the Cape
and Natal governments had produced an agreement over the pooling of
receipts. The creation of the Central South African Railways, a public
utility that became the forerunner of South African Railways, must be
regarded as among his most successful reconstruction initiatives.[6]

Land resettlement

Milner had always looked upon a favourable (white) population balance as the key to the success of his rebuilding project. In 1901, he had
written to Asquith saying he attached the greatest importance to an
increase in the British population in South Africa: 'If ten years hence
there are three men of British race to two of Dutch, the country will be
safe and prosperous. If there are three of Dutch to two of British, we
shall have perpetual difficulty.'[7]

Post-war land settlement by English speakers from around the Empire was thus crucial to Milner, who hoped for 'a good class of settler,
with farming experience and a little capital'. He proposed to bring in
10 000 new colonists 'within a twelvemonth',[8] to be settled on land
schemes similar to the one at Westminster in the eastern Free State,
where his wealthy young ex-aide, Bendor, the inheritor of a dukedom at
the age of 18, had bought a large landholding.

Once again, Milner was doomed to disappointment: much of the
land inherited by his administration from the ex-republics proved either
unsuitable for cultivation or too expensive to purchase in the open
market, and the government lacked the power of expropriation. Only a
mere 700 British citizens were to settle in the Transvaal and 500 to 600
in the Orange River Colony after the war, the remnants of a much larger
number of aspirant farmers granted acreage by the Land Settlement
Board but unable to scrabble out a living from the harsh environment.

In his books *Imperiale Somer* and *Rekonstruksie*, Karel Schoeman recounts the first impressions of a 23-year-old Australian-born immigrant, one Leonard Flemming, who came out with his English father to South Africa, served in the Cape colonial army and was given 460 morgen of land in the Dewetsdorp district of the Free State[9]: '[On arrival] I remember going up a hill close by and taking stock of my surroundings. The silence was uncanny. I had never known or felt before what seemed to me the overwhelming sound of silence. There I was, a mere speck in the middle of the Universe. I could see for a hundred miles and more in every direction, and not one sign of life in all that enormous space around me.'[10]

Agriculture was always one of Milner's chief concerns, for he regarded farming as an area of common interest for Boers and British settlers and a means of breaking down the barriers of separation. Agriculturally, South Africa's land was poor: it required extensive capital to fund irrigation projects as well as more up-to-date farming methods and better transport facilities.[11] Any new approach to stock-raising and crop production had to go hand in hand with the redistribution of land and the education of first-time farmers. As soon as the war ended, Milner had sent a handful of newly released Boer prisoners of war to Canada, Australia and New Zealand to observe the latest farming methods at first hand.

He also gave encouragement to the informal alliance that grew up between the mines and the maize growers of the eastern and western Transvaal. Although his policies unambiguously favoured the mines, he gave extra support to farmers who directed their produce towards the Witwatersrand, and in particular to the labour compounds of the mines – the only assured market for large quantities of maize and meat. But what historians describe as 'the gold-maize alliance' also had another less worthy purpose: the maintenance of a stable and highly exploitable labour force that would keep the lid on black wages in other economic sectors.

The Milner administration took care to restore many Boer notables – including Louis Botha – to their farms and help them back on their feet, and gave favoured treatment to any 'progressive' farmers willing to modernise. Not as much relief was given to smaller landowners unable – or unwilling – to adopt modern farming methods.

Fewer troops

Milner fought a losing battle against the slimming-down of imperial troop numbers in South Africa after the war: under pressure from the Treasury, the British garrison had been reduced from 30 000 to well below 25 000. Besides his pipe dream of making the country a large-scale training ground for imperial troops, 'a second Aldershot', Milner had hoped to settle a large number of ex-soldiers on the land to help swell British numbers. Instead, he was forced to plan – in conjunction with his choice as Kitchener's successor, General Sir Neville Lyttelton – for the most effective deployment of the far fewer troops at his disposal. He also had to enlist the help of Lord Roberts, in overall command of the British Army, to put a stop to further force reductions.

The South African Constabulary, custodians of law and order in the 'new colonies' – except on the Rand and in Pretoria where there were municipal police forces – also had its numbers reduced by the Treasury: what had been a 10 000-strong force in 1902 became 6 000 in 1904. A year later, the SAC numbered only 4 500 and its military ranks had become civilian. Milner was no admirer of its founding Inspector General, Baden-Powell, and his unorthodox methods of leadership and soon managed to have the hero of Mafeking replaced by his second-in-command, the former Colonel JS Nicholson.

Emily Hobhouse was not impressed with the quality of recruits to the SAC, complaining that the British had enlisted ordinary farm labourers to police the Boers. 'Where on earth was such a low, rough almost criminal crew raked together?' she wrote.[12] One of the SAC's inspectors noted that 'the Boers certainly looked upon us as an occupation force rather than as police'.[13]

Reforms

Another of Milner's reforms was to introduce, for the first time, generally more competent civil administration and law reform in what had been a corrupt and inefficient SAR government supplanted by an inexperienced British military authority. Thanks to his efforts, the finances of the 'new colonies' were placed on a sounder footing, municipal and local authorities were introduced, and 'native affairs' was brought under the rule of district commissioners, on the advice of the Lagden Commission, and made 'a real part of the community'.[14]

Like Kruger, so short of skills that he had to rely on Hollanders such as Dr Willem Leyds to help him run the SAR, Milner also had a limited pool of administrative experience to draw on. His remedy, as we have seen, was to recruit an inexperienced but energetic cadre of budding imperial civil servants, whose influence before and after his departure from South Africa are described more fully in Chapter 27. Milner's most enduring legacy was the influence of his imperialist ideas on South Africa's education system – primarily but not only on English speakers. His planning of educational reform had begun well before he assumed responsibility for the ex-republics. In 1900, he had brought out an experienced English educationist, Edmund B Sargant, to organise the work of educational reconstruction. Sargant was an original thinker who combined the social concerns of Toynbee Hall with the imperialist enthusiasm of Milner himself, but he was 'a wretched administrator'.[15]

A chance visit to a Boer internment camp in Sea Point, Cape Town, gave Sargant the idea of schooling Afrikaner children stuck in the camps at Norvalspont on the Orange River. By the end of May 1901, there were 4 000 schoolchildren in camp schools in the two former Boer republics, as against 3 500 in town schools. To find suitable teachers, Sargant invited well-qualified young women from all over the Empire to volunteer their services. According to Worsfold, by the end of the war several thousand Boer children were being taught by mostly British teachers. These camp schools not only engendered a spirit of goodwill between the tutors and Boer children and their parents, but also bequeathed to the education departments of the two 'new colonies' a body of 500 carefully selected and experienced educators.[16]

After the peace treaty, the number of white schoolchildren in the Transvaal grew from a pre-war total of 14 000 to 29 000, and in the Free State from 8 187 to 12 187.[17] Fabian Ware, an older and more experienced member of the Kindergarten, was appointed Director of Education in the Transvaal, with Hugh Gunn as his counterpart in the Orange River Colony. Pupil numbers in the two 'new colonies' would have been even greater had the Dutch Reformed Church – outraged at the arbitrary imposition of English on Afrikaans-speaking pupils – not begun to set up rival schools of its own, offering 'Christian National Education' as an alternative to state schooling. Other educational advances in the Milner era included the establishment of two teacher training colleges, a technical institute and the expansion of Grey College in Bloemfontein.[18]

Under Milner, black education was also given attention for the first time. Before the war, the education of Africans had been left almost entirely in the hands of mission schools, with little help coming from the Transvaal's republican government. A similar situation prevailed in the Free State, though mission schools there were far more numerous. By 1903, 164 African schools in the Transvaal were teaching 10 640 children, and three years later 177 schools schooled 17 078 pupils. In the Orange River Colony, the number of children being educated in mission schools was more than 13 000. In both colonies, industrial schools for boys and girls as well as training colleges for black teachers were established for the first time.[19]

In the Transvaal, the Department of Education, under Sargant's overall direction, moved quickly after the war to set up the high schools that Milner regarded as a key element of his anglicisation policy. Modelled on leading British public schools, with their boarding establishments and sports fields, these institutions were intended to equip boys and girls to study at British universities such as Oxford or Cambridge and return home – imbued with the ideals of duty, loyalty and responsibility – for careers in the public service.

Four of the eight 'Milner schools' were in Johannesburg: King Edward VII School (initially the Johannesburg High School for Boys), Johannesburg Girls High School (now Barnato Park High School) and the two Jeppe high schools for boys and girls. Two more were located in the capital – Pretoria Boys High School (formerly Pretoria College) and the High School for Girls – and another two high schools for boys and girls were in Potchefstroom.

The Milner schools were staffed mostly by graduates brought out from Britain to establish what the liberal academic Peter Randall famously described as 'Little England on the Veld'. The founding spirit behind no fewer than five of them was Charles Hope, a Cambridge-educated Scot seconded from the eastern Cape to Pretoria, where there were no secondary schools for English-speaking pupils before the war.[20]

After 15 months in the Transvaal capital, Hope was transferred to Johannesburg to reopen the Jeppe High School (later split between boys and girls), closed during the war. He was subsequently asked to open a boys' school in the old republican stronghold of Potchefstroom, where he was to remain as headmaster for 22 years. His authorship of two textbooks on South African history prompted the University of Cape Town to offer Hope a professorship in 1912, which he turned down, choosing to stay in Potchefstroom until his retirement 12 years later.[21]

Hope was not a racial chauvinist in the Milner mould: during his time in Pretoria, he made a point of learning Dutch and becoming friendly with the Boer people. As an educationist, he believed that examination results were not the primary purpose of schooling: more important were character building and personality development, the encouragement of ideals and the inculcation of a work ethic. He left a permanent imprint on the Milner schools of the Transvaal, whose alumni and alumnae have made an immense contribution to the growth and development of English-speaking South Africa.[22]

CHAPTER 26

Going Home
1904–1905

For many months before his retirement as High Commissioner, Milner had given thought to the choice of his replacement. Knowing that Balfour's misfiring coalition was on its last legs, he was anxious that whoever succeeded him should share his imperialist ideals and not set about undoing his legacy. Writing to Colonial Secretary Lyttelton, he said that if he could in any way 'contribute to the selection of the right man, it would be the greatest service I can still render to the South Africa and the Empire'.[1]

Though initially favouring his deputy, Lawley, Milner now believed the new incumbent should be someone of cabinet rank, either Lyttelton himself or the First Lord of the Admiralty, Lord Selborne, whose views were closest to his own. But Balfour was still hoping he could dissuade his envoy, and friend, from leaving. 'The more I think of South African affairs,' the Prime Minister wrote in early 1905, 'the more convinced I become that the interests of the Empire will be best served by your continuance in office, like Cromer, for an indefinite period.'[2]

A mentally and physically exhausted Milner was not open to further persuasion, however, setting mid-March as his intended departure date. Balfour finally took the message and wrote resignedly to say, 'I do not presume to criticise your decision ... it is impossible for me not to lament the great loss which South Africa and the Empire will sustain by your withdrawal from the stage where you have won "name and fame". You will rejoice, I know, to hear that, as you were not available, we have succeeded in securing the services of Selborne.'[3]

Milner was delighted at the news and replied saying it was 'the greatest possible relief' to know that Selborne would be his successor. Geoffrey Robinson, a member of the Kindergarten, wrote to his father:

'Lord M. quite overjoyed. He had long given up all hope of getting anyone so good.'[4] For, besides Chamberlain and Milner himself, Salisbury's son-in-law was the Unionists' most ardent imperialist.

As Milner's term neared its end, the Boers and the Transvaal British took to the political hustings to make known their views on the proposed new constitution, the 'half-way house' devised by the Colonial Office in response to the clamour for self-government. On 28 January 1905, Het Volk was formally inaugurated as a political party at a rousing gathering in Pretoria. Its immediate aim was to prevent the soon-to-be-unveiled constitution from coming into effect. Party leader Louis Botha and the leading Pretoria lawyer Ewald Esselen toured the country areas of the ex-republic, forming Het Volk branches in all the old field-cornetcies.[5]

On the 'British' side, the Progressives and the Responsibles were agreed on a system of 'one vote, one value' in constituencies of an equal number of voters (in order to remove any imbalance between urban and rural votes), and on keeping the Transvaal as 'a white man's country', but on little else.[6] A visiting British trade union leader, Thomas Burt, was surprised at the level of dissatisfaction with the government that he encountered within the mining community. 'Of Lord Milner personally, of his high character, his great ability, his industry, his devotion to public duty as he sees it', Burt recorded, 'I heard the warmest admiration expressed, almost but not quite universally. But the condemnation of his policy and administration was equally general.'[7]

By the end of January 1905, even Milner no longer had any faith in the proposals he had put forward to Lyttelton a month earlier: 'I have no confidence', he wrote, 'that the lines on which we are at present going will command a sufficient amount of popular support to give even temporary stability to the proposed structure.'[8] He argued that further delay might be better than taking a false step, but found matters taken out of his own hands by an impatient Cabinet in London. On 31 March, the Colonial Office promulgated a constitution for the Transvaal by letters patent, its timing arranged to coincide with the announcement of Milner's imminent retirement as High Commissioner.[9]

Since it never came into existence, the proposed 'Lyttelton

Constitution' need not detain us further: suffice it to say that Het Volk's heated objections to it were based on the authority it gave a nominated executive (dominated by imperial officials) over an elected legislature, as well as the mooted 'one vote, one value' voting system, which would negate the Boers' advantage in rural constituencies. These reservations were shared by the Responsibles, with whom Het Volk finally concluded an electoral pact on 14 April.

The rival Progressives resembled an action group of the mining industry, at the helm of which were still Farrar and FitzPatrick, both members of the Reform Committee of 1895 sentenced for their involvement in the Jameson Raid. The Progressives' binding sentiment, according to Le May, was their fear of a resurgent Afrikaner nationalism, which made the party content to remain under the protection of the Crown, and reluctant to press for immediate self-government.[10]

Retirement

The announcement of Milner's impending retirement produced an outpouring of appreciation – and brickbats – from the usual quarters. The official release from the Colonial Office paid tribute to 'the steadfast courage with which Lord Milner had confronted the issues of war, and scarcely less momentous, the problem of the ensuing peace', and asserted that he 'had laid deep and strong the foundation upon which a united South Africa will arise to become one of the great states of the Empire'.[11] London's *Daily News*, on the other hand, commented that Milner's retirement 'was as inevitable as the coming Liberal victory. His retention of office a day after the accession of the Liberals to power would be impossible ... He represents the war and all the waste and the ruin and bloodshed it created.'[12]

In South Africa, criticism of the High Commissioner abated briefly while friends and enemies took stock of his eight-year term in the country, before there was a deluge of letters and messages – public and private – from supporters thanking Milner for his achievements and acknowledging his dedication. An effusive Sir Percy FitzPatrick, who had written to *The Times* a month earlier to urge support for the Lyttelton Constitution, said that some Mark Twain of the future would judge that 'the Almighty [had] fashioned South Africa upon plans supplied by Lord Milner … Of course, the Boers hate you, it is their certificate of your success … The greatest trial – to me – was the failing of faith and patience among our own folks. It was sad and it used to make me hot with shame and sick with anxiety.'[13]

A former sworn enemy took a more measured view. In an extraordinarily magnanimous letter that Milner only came across after leaving South Africa, Jan Smuts wrote, 'Will you allow me to wish you "Bon Voyage" now that you are leaving South Africa for ever? I am afraid you have not liked us; but I cherish the hope that, as our memories grow mellower and the nobler features of our respective ideals become clearer, we shall more and more appreciate the contribution of each to the formation of that happier South Africa which is surely coming, and judge more kindly of each other.

'At any rate, it is a consolation to think what is noble in our work will grow to larger issues than we foresaw, and that even our mistakes will be covered up ultimately, not only in a merciful oblivion, but also in that unconscious forgiveness which seems to me to be an inherent feature of all historical growth. History writes the word "Reconciliation" over all her quarrels and will surely write it over the unhappy differences that have agitated us in the past … Who knows but that our respective contentions will reach a friendly settlement?'[14] It is not known whether Milner ever replied to the olive branch that Smuts had belatedly extended.

Saying goodbye

In the course of three valedictory speeches before he left, Milner reminded his listeners of the accomplishments of his government. As Denoon notes, he was intent on emphasising the 'non-partisan and universally beneficent nature of his work', playing down the political purpose behind economic and material development, and trying to shield the institutions he had created and the appointments he had made from public criticism. A praise-singing Amery wrote of Milner's efforts that 'what was achieved in that brief space was not a mere series of useful reforms, but the creation of a new country'. Thanks to Milner, 'Britain had brought a higher degree of civilisation to a backward corner of the world.

Hardworking technocrats working for the progress of all South African humanity were contrasted with politicians who exhibited all the worst features of human nature.' That, Denoon concludes, was the image of himself that Milner sought earnestly to propagate – in Egypt, at Inland Revenue, in South Africa and later, as we shall see, in British politics.[15]

To an audience in Germiston, Milner reviewed his work in the Transvaal and surveyed the colony's financial and industrial prospects. Here, and in Pretoria a week later, he defended his administration against conflicting charges of 'extravagance and recklessness' after the war, when things had to be done in a hurry, and of 'parsimony and sloth' during the years of drought and depression. 'I for one', he declared, 'have no fear whatever of the verdict which any impartial chronicler will pronounce on our work as a whole.'[16] 'The one thing essential ... when we took over this country, a total wreck, with half its population in exile, with no machinery whatever, and as far as the plant of government was concerned, with the scantiest equipment of any civilised country in the world, was to make it a going concern again as soon as possible.'[17]

Milner blamed whatever failures he was accused of on matters outside his control: the growth of rival political movements, criticism that had turned into agitation and the perverseness of his opponents – especially the British, who might have been more moderate in their strictures and 'perpetual fault-finding'.[18] The only error he came close to confessing was his inability to implement 'Mr Rhodes's principle of "equal rights for every civilised man"'.[19] But he now felt free, he said, 'as a civilian-soldier of the state' to give way to new leadership before his failing health led him to become a nuisance and detriment to South Africa's reconstruction.[20]

The departing High Commissioner's last and longest address was reserved for an almost 1 000-strong audience in the Drill Hall, Johannesburg, on 31 March, where he spoke for an hour and 20 minutes. According to Headlam, he pulled no punches, 'his thoughts so tight-packed that they left no room for rhetorical flourishes'. He spoke of the 'fads of Milner', the issues to which he had given personal attention – land settlement, afforestation, irrigation, scientific agriculture, the ICC, the SAC and railway amalgamation – all of which were still under threat.

'If you believe in me,' he pleaded, 'defend my works when I have gone. I care for that more than I do for [any] eulogy, or indeed for any personal reward ... I shall live in the memories of people here, if I live at all, in connection with the great struggle to keep this country within the limits of the British Empire.'[21]

'When we who call ourselves Imperialists', Milner continued, 'talk of the British Empire, we think of a group of States, all independent in their own local concerns, but all united for the defence of their own common interests ... in a permanent organic union.' Only such a consummation, he asserted, could solve the 'most difficult and persistent' of South Africa's problems – how to unite its white races: 'The Dutch can never own a perfect allegiance merely to Great Britain. The British can never, without moral injury, accept allegiance to any body politic which excludes their motherland. But British and Dutch alike could, without loss of integrity, without any sacrifice of their several traditions, unite in loyal devotion to an Empire-State, in which Great Britain and South Africa would be partners and could work cordially together for the good of South Africa as a member of that greater whole. And so, you see, the true Imperialist is also the best South African.'[22]

As a hard-headed realist, though, Milner would have understood by now that his ambitions in South Africa were unachievable. As Le May observes, for all the remarkable achievements his administration could point to, the Transvaal had not become a British outpost, the Boers were as determined as ever to rule themselves, the colony's English speakers were disunited and argumentative, and the personal admiration Milner had inspired among his colleagues no longer extended far beyond the limited confines of his administration. Privately, he still regarded Boer-Afrikaners as 'an enemy of the Imperial connection', so the best he could do before leaving, Le May concludes, 'was to exhort British and Boers to sublimate their quarrels in a higher loyalty.'[23]

On the colour question, notwithstanding his rhetorical support for an extension of the franchise, Milner had been unable, or unwilling, to move much beyond the 'colonial settlement' negotiated at Vereeniging. As Breckenridge points out, Milner's distaste for liberal democracy had shaped his attitude to the black vote, and to local representative government in general.[24] Despite his crocodile tears about the denial of the vote to 'civilised' Africans, his preferred solution while in South Africa was for a separate Council of 'Natives elected by Natives', with legislative powers limited to 'matters affecting Natives only and within their own districts'.[25] This, in theory, was not far removed from future government policy after Union.

Although he had exempted educated Africans from having to carry passes, Milner made no real effort to define, or refine, the term 'native' as used in the Vereeniging treaty. He had redrafted the Transvaal's municipal council regulations in 1903 to exclude all non-whites from the franchise, including 'civilised Indians', who were not given the vote on the grounds that this would be a 'slap in the face' for coloured people in the Cape.[26] Like most British and Boer politicians of his time, he found it easier to rock the boat only gently on racial issues, and to defer the solution of an admittedly difficult problem to future generations.

When Winston Churchill became the Under-Secretary in the Colonial Office a year later, he formed his own assessment of Milner's activities in South Africa derived from the notes of permanent officials there:

> British authority in South Africa must stand on two legs. The inherent vice of Milner's policy was that it stood on one leg. [As Governor of the new colonies] no more unsuitable agent could have been chosen ... Being regarded after the war as the inveterate enemy of the Dutch ... he was condemned to fall back entirely on the support of the British; and of the British party the mining interest is of course the only formidable fighting part. The mining interests were, therefore, the only friends upon whom he could rely, and to preserve that allegiance, scarcely any expedient seemed too desperate.[27]

Departure

On Sunday 2 April 1905, Milner left Johannesburg by train for Delagoa Bay, en route to Britain via Egypt and Italy. Despite being deluged by a typical Witwatersrand thunderstorm, thousands of people lined the streets to wave farewell as the departing High Commissioner was escorted by a guard of honour to Park Station in the city centre. 'As the train steamed out,' he wrote to a friend, 'I was standing on an open *stoep* at the end of the last carriage – the great crowd rushed down from the platform into the centre of the line, and the last thing I saw of Johannesburg was a dense mass of frantically excited people, waving hats and handkerchiefs, which filled railway, platform and everything from embankment to embankment and stretched as far back as my eyes could carry me.'[28] He was not to return to South Africa until nearly 20 years later.

Milner was accompanied on the first part of his sea voyage by Geoffrey Robinson, who had recently succeeded Basil Worsfold as editor of *The Star*. As High Commissioner, Milner had personally arranged for Robinson's appointment in the hope of having his pro-imperial ideas perpetuated after his retirement. In a sweltering Egypt, the two men went sightseeing together before Robinson returned to his newspaper, leaving Milner to journey on to England via Lake Como, where his old friend Sir Clinton Dawkins lay dying.[29]

While on the long sea voyage, Milner compiled a 35-page memorandum to Selborne to warn him what he might expect in South Africa, to which another 16 pages were added in Venice: 'People think that the war decided that South Africa should remain for good and all part of the British Empire ... [but] it only made that result possible, at most probable.' 'Making it certain', he told Selborne, 'requires years of strong patient policy, the principal danger to this, as in all our Imperial problems, being at home. Without the tomfoolery of home party politics interfering with a sane Imperial policy, we should be safe.'[30]

Milner went on to caution his successor about the Boers, with whom 'it had become almost a point of honour to oppose me and all my works', and for whom every phrase had a double meaning: 'Their creed and ideal is that of a separate Afrikaner nation and state comprising ... men of other races who are ready to be Afrikanerised ... although some of them are prepared to see their object realised, for a time at least, under the British flag.'[31]

After five weeks in Italy, an unheralded Milner arrived in England in July 1905. As to his future, well before leaving South Africa he had written to Dawkins saying that after being released from 'this dungeon', he would not resume political life 'in the ordinary sense of the word'. 'What I may do is quite uncertain ... but I am too far, too increasingly out of sympathy with our political system and the political attitude of the bulk of my countrymen, to be a successful politician in the ordinary sense. I am an anachronism. It may be that I was born too late, it may be I was born too soon ... I may be of some use as an outsider, though never again as an active participant in the fray.'[32]

Britain's retiring proconsul was only 51 years old.

CHAPTER 27

The Kindergarten
1905–1909

Milner may have failed personally in his quest to unify South Africa under the British flag, but his mission was accomplished not long after his departure with the help of his Kindergarten – although the outcome was not as he had intended. Within two years of his departure, the Boers he had fought so bitterly were back in the saddle in the Transvaal and the Orange River Colony at the head of administrations swearing allegiance to the British Crown. His youthful accomplices, believing that by making South Africa economically attractive to British immigrants, the country could become a key component of some future imperial federation, had seized upon the foundations he had laid and embarked on a unification project of their own.

'Kindergarten' (nursery school) was a German term first used derisively by one of Milner's critics, Sir William Marriott, an eccentric British barrister living in Johannesburg, to describe the group of young men drawn from Britain to abet Milner in his post-war reconstruction programme. The term was given greater currency in the Cape Parliament by John X Merriman, who complained that the British High Commissioner was 'setting up a sort of kindergarten of Balliol young men to govern the country'.[1] The slightly inaccurate description was adopted by the group as a badge of distinction. For of the dozen or so Oxford graduates who gathered round Milner, only three had actually been at Balliol: the others were recruited mostly by Lionel Curtis from New College, his (and Milner's) alma mater.

Four of the brainiest *Kinder* (Peter Perry, Robert Brand, Geoffrey Robinson and Dougal Malcolm) were also fellows of the intellectually exclusive All Souls College, while two other Oxford men, John Buchan and the journalist Leo Amery, were closely associated with the Kindergarten but not regarded as members. Along with Milner's various private secretaries, these young men of the gentry were the kindred spirits among whom the High Commissioner could relax – on the rare occasions he chose to – while in Johannesburg.

Members of Milner's Kindergarten. In the front row are (left to right) John Dove, Philip Kerr and Geoffrey Robinson (later Dawson). Seated in the middle row (left to right) are Hugh Wyndham, Richard Feetham, Lionel Curtis, Patrick Duncan, F (Peter) Perry and Dougal Malcolm. Shown standing are (left to right) Robert Brand, architect Herbert Baker and Lionel Hichens. (*Wikimedia Commons/Terence O'Brien*)

Milner once told FitzPatrick that he had been advised by Cromer to leave behind, after he had gone home, 'young men with plenty of work in them'.[2] Of his non-Oxford recruits, most came from contacts in the

Colonial Office or on the recommendation of friends whose judgement he trusted. Complaints of nepotism did not deter Milner: 'first-class men of position and experience' were scarce in Johannesburg, where there were much better prospects in the mining industry than in the service of the Crown. His solution, therefore, was to import young graduates and civil servants of promise, whose intellect and character (and incorruptibility) would make up for their almost total lack of experience. According to Amery, Milner was determined to enlist the very best brains and bring the greatest possible energy and adaptability to the unique task before him.[3]

The one characteristic that united most of the *Kinder*, besides their privileged backgrounds, shared experiences at Oxford and admiration for Milner, was a desire to be of public service. To a man, they were interested in world affairs, economic issues and politics, and in promoting the fortunes of the world's largest Empire. As AL Rowse, a distinguished fellow of All Souls, wrote of his colleagues: 'There was nothing they would not do if they were convinced it was their duty. This was the air they breathed.'[4] Some were no doubt keen, too, to exchange the rigours of the English winter for the sunshine of the Highveld, but they all understood that behind Milner's plan to make South Africa British was a far greater purpose – creating a federal Empire. As Gollin observes, the opportunity was of a kind that young men could only dream about.[5]

Besides Lionel Curtis, the earliest recruits to the Kindergarten – Lionel Hitchens, Basil Williams, Richard Feetham, their barrister friend from New College, and John Dove – were formally employed by the City of Johannesburg, whose foundations they helped lay. These five were distinct from the trio who worked directly for the High Commission – Perry, Duncan and Robinson.[6] Also part of the brotherhood were Milner's private secretaries, John Buchan, Hugh Wyndham and, in due course, Robinson.

When Milner was on leave in England in 1903, Ozzy Walrond, his aide of long standing, suffered a breakdown and had to be replaced by Robinson, who, after serving for a year as liaison between the High Commission and municipalities, became Milner's private secretary for his last two years in office. Robinson was the only member of the

Kindergarten who became a close friend of his demanding employer: on leaving the country, Milner launched his young aide on what would become a long and controversial career in journalism. As editor of *The Times* of London in the 1930s, Geoffrey Dawson was to become notorious for his appeasement of Hitler.

Three of the *Kinder*, Duncan, Perry and Brand, were appointed to senior positions in the Transvaal administration. Duncan, brought out by special request in 1901 to become Colonial Treasurer, went on to serve as Colonial Secretary, and for a time as acting Lieutenant Governor. Throughout Milner's last two years in office, Duncan was the former republic's chief administrative officer, and remained in that key post until the coming of self-government in 1907.

Peter Perry, the only member of the Kindergarten to marry while in office – his bride personally escorted from Britain by Milner[7] – was given the crucial role of supervising the administration of native affairs, at the heart of the government's drive to provide sufficient labour for the mining industry. It fell to Perry to recruit African workers from Basutoland and Swaziland and, when these sources proved inadequate, to bring in extra workers from Portuguese East Africa. Perry eventually resigned from Milner's staff to become chairman of the Witwatersrand Native Labour Association, and in that capacity was directly involved in the negotiations between London and Beijing over the importation of the Chinese. He became a key figure in what Breckenridge describes as the most enduring element of Milner's state-building project – the grafting of the state onto the administrative fabric of the gold-mining industry.[8]

Though Milner himself presided over the 24-strong ICC, whose chief tasks were to coordinate railway amalgamation and policing, he required a full-time secretary to relieve him of the administrative burden. To this end, he recruited one of Perry's close friends from New College and All Souls, Robert Brand, who arrived in South Africa in 1902 and remained in charge of the ICC until the coming of Union. As ICC secretary, Brand won the respect of all its members, Boer and British alike, as well as of his fellow *Kinder*. When Milner left, he told Selborne that Brand was 'a fellow of real ability, who has this particular business at his finger's end. You can safely lean on him, for he has not only a great mastery of all the rather complicated details, but a good grasp of the general policy.'[9] Brand was to become a central figure in the drafting and adoption of the Union constitution.

By the time of Milner's departure, Brand had found railway matters taking up so much of his time that he required an assistant secretary. On his advice, Milner appointed one of Brand's friends from New College and All Souls, Philip Kerr, to fill the post. Kerr had come out earlier to work for Lawley in Pretoria, but after three months in an unchallenging position was pleased to make a switch to Johannesburg. His keen intellect and capacity for hard work were to make him invaluable as Brand's assistant.[10]

The last significant member of the Kindergarten, Dougal Malcolm, arrived in South Africa from the Colonial Office only days after Milner's departure, and took up duty as Selborne's private secretary. Malcolm had made a favourable impression on Milner in London in 1903, yet it had taken him longer than usual to join his friends in Johannesburg, despite intensive lobbying by Perry and Robinson. In time, Sir Dougal Malcolm was to become a noted colonial administrator.

The Moot

According to Milner, South Africa was the most expensive place he had ever lived in, and the Transvaal the most over-priced part of the country, 'and this it will continue to be for years to come – for civilized Europeans'.[11] Most of the *Kinder* were impecunious and thus obliged to pool their resources and go into 'digs' together near the Sunnyside estate. A few lived in Hugh Wyndham's rented house, until Milner left office and their landlord went off to become a farmer near Standerton. By then, Feetham had acquired a piece of land on the Parktown ridge and commissioned Herbert Baker to build a large stone house to accommodate him and his friends. Completed in July 1906, the 'Moot House', designed as a place where 'moots' (mock courts in which law students could argue) could be held, became the home of Feetham, Brand, Kerr and Dove. The 'Moot', as it was called, served as the unofficial headquarters of the Kindergarten until the coming of Union. (Today, Moot House, distinguished by a blue plaque, is a private home in Parktown.)

From 1906 to 1908, the Moot also became the main venue for meetings of the Fortnightly Club, an association of some 40 young like-minded imperialists who would gather regularly to discuss papers by members on the future of 'empire, race and statehood'.[12] The question they grappled with was how to formulate a future structure that would accommodate the Empire's many diverse colonies in a way that took account of their significant racial and ethnic differences. South Africa was regarded as a laboratory – a place where a new concept of the empire could be tried, tested and, if successful, exported to other parts of the world.[13]

Among members of the Fortnightly Club, there was general agreement that self-government for whites in South Africa not only accorded with their liberal ethics but was also consistent with the country's political needs. However, as Dubow points out, racial segregation was not regarded as an end in itself but as a means of 'persuading white South Africans to bury their political differences'.[14] Every member took the view that the solution to South Africa's racial problem was for white immigration to be substantially increased.[15]

Discussions at the Moot were not confined to South Africa, however, but ranged across the wider Anglophone world, including the United States. As Thakur and Vale observe, the club became the forerunner of international relations institutes that took root and grew up in other parts of the English-speaking universe. Thanks to Lionel Curtis, the Fortnightly Club was also the genesis of today's British Commonwealth of Nations. These various entities may be said to have originated from the discussions that took place in Feetham's Moot House in Parktown, Johannesburg.[16]

Outside working hours, the Kindergarten's lively bachelors – most of them unable to find socially acceptable young women in Johannesburg – revelled in the sunshine and enjoyed a vigorous outdoor lifestyle, following Milner's example of exercising in the saddle and becoming part-time mounted reservists and/or polo players. When not called upon to help the High Commission entertain a stream of post-war visitors to Johannesburg, the *Kinder* would be invited to lunches and dinners by leaders of the city's business community. To preserve their spirit of camaraderie, members held regular 'Oxford dinners' in full evening dress.[17] On Boat Race Night in 1903, Denoon records, Milner and 50 others attended the Oxford dinner, while Lawley and 23 others attended the victorious Cambridge dinner. On other special days on the Oxford calendar, the Moot would play host to an eclectic group of politicians, lawyers, churchmen, journalists and civil servants. The new stone house was soon one of the most desirable destinations in the social life of Johannesburg.

Admiration for the *Kinder* was no means universal, however. Many Uitlanders who had settled in the Transvaal had been hoping for choice positions in the Milner administration after their side's 'victory' in the war, and resented being ruled by the very 'toffs' from whom they had hoped to escape by emigrating. Thomas Burt, the visiting trade unionist, observed that his fellow miners had two main complaints about Milner: he followed the lead of the mining houses too slavishly, and had appointed inexperienced people to responsible, well-paid jobs in the civil service. 'These men were admittedly highly educated in the technical sense, but they were unfitted by previous training and experience for the great positions they hold,' Burt recorded.[18] A junior bureaucrat in the Colonial Secretary's department, unimpressed by the earnestness of the *Kinder*, recounted how he and his friends used to pray, 'From Winchester, New College and Balliol, Good Lord deliver us'.[19]

Initially, Boer leaders also took a jaundiced view of Milner's young men. After Joseph Chamberlain's visit, Smuts commented sarcastically to Emily Hobhouse, 'it is such a comfort to have a little "kindergarten" show of dolls – all your own, moving at your sweet will, not asking inconvenient questions, not making factious opposition ... That is the way we are ruled here by the "finest flowers of Varsity scholarship".'[20] In due course, Smuts had second thoughts and was to put the *Kinder* to a useful purpose by harnessing their energies in the drive for South Africa's unification.

Selborne

Milner's replacement, William Palmer, Lord Selborne, was no less of an imperialist than his predecessor, but of a more amiable and conciliatory disposition.[21] It was said of him that he 'shared Milner's views,

William Palmer, 2nd Earl of Selborne, Milner's successor as High Commissioner for Southern Africa. (*Wikimedia Commons/Bassano Ltd*)

but not his enemies'.[22] Arriving in the Transvaal in May 1905, with Milner's warnings ringing in his ears, Selborne was drawn initially towards the mining-dominated Progressive camp – to the dismay of the Responsibles, Het Volk and Labour. He did not take long to conclude, however, that it was too early for self-government for the former republics and that the Lyttelton Constitution that he had been instructed to put into effect was destined for failure. While he regarded its provisions as having the merit of providing a period of apprenticeship prior to self-rule, he could see no point in preparing the Transvaal for a system that was never going to be implemented.[23]

While the new High Commissioner pondered his options, he was rapidly overtaken by events at home, where Balfour resigned the premiership in December 1905, to be replaced by the Liberals' Campbell-Bannerman. Lord Elgin succeeded Lyttelton as Colonial Secretary, and Winston Churchill, who had caused outrage among Tories by crossing the floor to the Liberals, became Elgin's understudy and spokesman in the House of Commons. Elgin, a former Viceroy of India, was an aristocratic politician with his own views and not afraid to differ from his thrusting young deputy. On one occasion, Churchill scribbled on a memo, 'These are my views', to which Elgin replied tersely, 'But not mine', and insisted on getting his own way.[24] As the new Colonial Under-Secretary, Churchill was immediately confronted by demands from various quarters for responsible government for the Transvaal.

Het Volk, for its part, lost no time in pressing the case for self-rule, sending Smuts to London early in 1906 to parley with Churchill and Campbell-Bannerman. Smuts returned with an assurance that the Lyttelton proposals would be jettisoned, and a Royal Commission appointed to determine how to establish responsible government for the two ex-republics.

As Le May records, 1906 was a year of 'conscious transition' in the Transvaal: everyone knew that change was coming, but no one from the High Commissioner down knew what the new dispensation might look like: the Boers were cautiously optimistic, while the British were apprehensive – and flustered. In the meantime, the Kindergarten – free from Milner's 'immediate gaze' and all-consuming personality –

had begun their efforts to keep the Transvaal, and South Africa, under British influence by reviving Milner's plans for using the surplus from mining revenues to promote economic development. A prerequisite for any economic growth was the consolidation of the four colonies into one unified nation.

Although the Kinder realised that the Boers' numerical majority would almost certainly bring Het Volk to power, they understood that unification of some kind – and not necessarily federal, as had been widely assumed to be the way forward – was essential for the political stability and security that had been lacking in South Africa since the war ended. A growing economy and the prospect of money-making were necessary to attract British immigration in far greater numbers than had proved possible under Milner. Assuming a constitution that guaranteed a fair franchise and a sufficiently anglicised population, a Boer-led national government might conceivably keep South Africa within the Empire. Unification of the four colonies ran counter to the immediate plans of political leaders, Boer and British, however.

It was to be Lionel Curtis ('the Prophet'), whose enthusiasm for the cause of Empire was to remain with him for the rest of his life, who once again led the way, becoming the draughtsman for a subcommittee of *Kinder* set up to examine how unification could take place. The historian Leonard Thompson describes Curtis as probably 'not the wisest member of the Kindergarten', but he had the sort of mind which produces powerful propaganda once convinced that a cause is important and becomes obsessed by it.[25]

According to Dubow, Curtis had come across an 'original and provocative' study of colonial nationalism published by a fellow Oxford alumnus, Richard Jebb, which had a profound effect on him and his fellow Kinder, and also on Lord Selborne. The essence of Jebb's argument was that the growth of Empire depended as much on the recognition of colonial 'self-respect' as loyalty to the British Crown: 'As the evolution proceeds, the Empire is valued less for its own sake, and more in proportion as it subserves the interests and ideals of separate nationalisms.'[26]

Travelling to South Africa in 1906, Jebb advised Boers and Brits alike to unite on the basis of mutual interests and a common patriotism, and to commit to 'a closer union of the Empire in any form'. His advice was interpreted by the Kindergarten as justification for their changing views on a federal structure as the best way forward.[27]

The Egg

For three years, the unification project became Curtis's overriding passion, and he resigned from his official positions to devote himself fully to the task. In December 1906, his draft memorandum, known as 'the Egg', was refined, amended and presented to Selborne. A few months earlier, Curtis had written a long letter to Milner explaining the purpose of the Egg and hoping for his approval (and financial assistance). 'I have always told you that I am much more of a pro-Boer than you',[28] he told his former mentor, who was less than enthusiastic about the plan but agreed to give it the support of the Rhodes Trust for one year in an amount of £1 000 only.[29]

As the Transvaal and Free State moved closer to holding elections, Selborne's support for unification grew from tentative to whole-hearted. He agreed with the argument that closer union might eventually produce a British majority in South Africa but was concerned also by the growing possibility of a war between Britain and Germany, which made it desirable to consolidate Britain's hold on South Africa before any conflict broke out. The new High Commissioner made a few amendments to the Egg before adopting it as his own plan and declaring himself fully in favour of unification. The 'Selborne Memorandum' carefully soft-pedalled its imperialist objectives and was couched in terms that called upon white South Africans to come together and unite in their own future interests.[30]

But how was the memorandum to be presented to local politicians and the public without its appearing to have been authored by the Colonial Office? Once more, Curtis produced the solution. He prevailed upon the Cape premier, Dr Jameson, supported by a member of the Afrikaner Bond, FS Malan, to publicly request the High Commissioner to review the current situation in South Africa and report on the feasibility of unification. The latter was by no means a new idea; unification had been under discussion for several years by the likes of Smuts, Merriman and Steyn, but not in as much detail as in the

Curtis-inspired memorandum. Dubow observes that the formative role of the Kindergarten was vital, and without their intervention, it is uncertain whether unification would have been achieved.[31]

In January 1907, Selborne sent a copy of the document to each of the colonial governments, obscuring its origin and giving the assurance that it was not in any way an attempt to force unification upon the people of South Africa. Generally well received by politicians, public and press alike, the Selborne Memorandum was subsequently used by Smuts and others at the National Convention of the four colonies, held in Durban in 1908–1909, to bolster the case for Union.

The Round Table

Having succeeded in their mission to help unify the country, members of the Kindergarten not intending to settle in South Africa drifted back to England, most of them destined for greater things. Emboldened by their success as imperial strategists, Curtis, Kerr and Dove embarked on another ambitious exercise in empire-building, hoping to create an organic unity among members of the Empire along federal lines.[32] In 1909, with Milner's encouragement and Rhodes's money, Curtis and Kerr established the Round Table movement, an imperial version of the Kindergarten, aimed at promoting closer union between Britain and her self-governing Dominions and Crown colonies (see Chapter 28). John Dove took over from Kerr to become the long-serving editor of a quarterly publication, The Round Table, the first journal of its kind devoted to international issues.

The energetic Curtis took upon himself the role of imperial missionary, travelling widely to promote the gospel of imperial unity. In 1916, he wrote The Commonwealth of Nations, which became a blueprint for the British Commonwealth, the successor to the Empire. In 1919, he founded the Royal Institute of International Affairs, headquartered at Chatham House in London, and in due course inspired an American equivalent, the Council on Foreign Relations. The South African Institute of International Affairs, modelled on 'Chatham House', was to follow in the late 1920s.

In 1939–1940, Philip Kerr became the 11th Marquis of Lothian and British Ambassador to the United States. John Buchan, famous as a novelist and war historian, was ennobled as Baron Tweedsmuir and served from 1935 to 1940 as Governor General of Canada. Robert Brand, later Lord Brand, headed the British Food Mission to the US between 1941 and 1944 and was the Treasury's representative in the US from 1944 to 1946. Basil Williams became an author and a distinguished professor of history in Canada and Scotland, while Geoffrey Dawson, as noted, was twice editor of *The Times*.

Of the three *Kinder* who stayed in South Africa, Hugh Wyndham, later Lord Leconfield, became a farmer, parliamentarian and co-architect of the South Africa Defence Act of 1912; Richard Feetham went on to become a distinguished Judge of Appeal, chairman of the Irish Boundary Commission and Chancellor of Wits University. The most prominent of the three, however, turned out to be Sir Patrick Duncan, a long-serving member of the Union Parliament, cabinet minister and eventually Governor General of South Africa. It was Duncan who played the decisive role in the nail-biting parliamentary debate of 1939 that took South Africa into the Second World War on the side of Britain and the Commonwealth in the fight against Nazi Germany.

CHAPTER 28

A Mixed Reception
1905–1907

Arriving in England in May 1905, Milner went to ground in a hotel, under an assumed name, to deal with a mound of correspondence and reply to invitations from all quarters. On 19 July, he returned to his old bachelor quarters at 47 Duke Street, St James's, and the next day his arrival in London was announced in the press. The King and Queen sought to see him, as did Balfour, Chamberlain and Margot Asquith, as well as a score of his friends.

In August, he gave indifferent health as his reason for turning down the Empire's most glittering prize: the viceroyalty of India, which Curzon had resigned after a power struggle with Kitchener. Milner told his friend St John Brodrick, now at the India Office, that he was exhausted by his long period of service in South Africa and intended to rest for a year before he took on any new assignments.[1] He went public nonetheless in support of Chamberlain's campaign for tariff reform and Lord Roberts's call for the introduction of compulsory national service.

Now retired from the civil service, Milner had to earn a living, since he refused on principle to accept a pension from the state. He joined the boards of the London Joint Stock Bank (later acquired by Midland Bank), the Bank of British West Africa, the Rio Tinto mining company and a mortgage company in Egypt.[2] His old mentor, Goschen, reintroduced him formally into the House of Lords, to which he showed no great desire to return in a hurry.

Looking to the future, Milner found himself in a bind. Unwilling to accept the evasions and compromises of party politics, he was nonetheless eager to further the interests of Empire: one way of doing so was to become active as a Rhodes trustee. In early December, he was devastated by the death of his friend of long standing, Sir Clinton Dawkins, aged only 46. Milner wrote in his diary that 'it was one of the worst days of my life'.[3] In low spirits, and in order to escape the 1906 election campaign, he took himself off on holiday to France from where he viewed with dismay the overwhelming defeat of Balfour's Unionists at the hands of the rejuvenated Liberals.

Writing to a friendly journalist, EB Iwan-Muller, he expressed his disgust at 'the utter uselessness of doing anything for such a pack of fools as the British people ... If I was beginning my life afresh, the last thing I should touch with the end of the tongs would be public service or anything remotely connected with public affairs. A nation which is capable of giving the largest majority on record to Campbell-Bannerman may be everything that is excellent and desirable, but it's no master for the likes of me.'[4]

Second only to tariff reform as an issue in the 1906 election was the hullabaloo over 'Chinese slavery'. Ever since his home leave in 1903 to garner support for the forthcoming Transvaal labour legislation, Milner had been held up by radical Liberals as the willing tool of mining capitalists and betrayer of the working men of Empire. From then on, Unionist cabinet ministers were regularly interrogated about allegations that Chinese workers on the Rand were being mistreated and subjected to corporal punishment. In mid-1905, Colonial Secretary Lyttelton had been obliged to give Parliament an assurance that floggings were only inflicted after conviction by a magistrate and a subsequent confirmation of sentence by the Supreme Court of the Transvaal.

During August 1905, however, Lyttelton had been astounded to learn that some Chinese had indeed been caned by compound managers, without any recourse to courts of law. He was even more astonished to be told that Milner himself had sanctioned the practice. When Balfour resigned in advance of the general election and Elgin temporarily took over the Colonial Office a month or two later, the Liberals lost no time in making it known that Lyttelton and the Unionist cabinet had been party to the misleading of Parliament.

On the election hustings in early 1906, no one quite knew what Lord Milner was alleged to have done, but the slogan 'Slavery under the British Flag' was used to great effect by Liberal candidates on public platforms. A furious Balfour found himself having to defend his administration for actions he described to friends privately as 'stupid, illegal and immoral'.[5] The treatment of the Chinese became a significant factor in the Liberals' crushing victory, which brought many of the party's radical wing into Parliament for the first time.

Maiden speech

The tone of the debate during the King's Speech at the opening of Parliament in late January 1906 may be gleaned from the remarks of a new Liberal MP that the policy of the Unionist government in South Africa had been 'engineered ... by bloodthirsty money-grubbers, mostly of foreign extraction, without honour, without conscience, without country, without God'.[6] A radical amendment to the Royal Address expressed regret that the King's ministers should have brought the reputation of the country into contempt by allowing the introduction of Chinese 'slavery'. When the Liberal government also gave notice that it was about to reveal its plans for self-government in the Transvaal and Orange River colonies, a provoked Milner, who knew South Africa better than anyone else in Britain, decided most unwisely to intervene. On 26 February, he made his maiden speech in the House of Lords – and in so doing brought down an avalanche of criticism upon his head.[7]

Henry Campbell-Bannerman, the new prime minister, had become increasingly resentful of the *religio Milneriana*, the blind belief of liberal imperialists in Milner and all his works. Although pro-imperialist himself, C-B had argued – in contrast to Milner – since 1900 that the sooner self-government was granted to the Boers, the sooner they would become citizens of a liberal Empire.[8] He considered Milner – not even a party member – and Joseph Chamberlain to be the prime causes of the disunity in the Liberal Party's ranks between radicals, centrists and the Limps, led by the heir-presumptive, HH Asquith. The Prime Minister had privately marked Milner down as a threat to party unity, to be dealt with when circumstances permitted.[9]

In his address to the House of Lords, Milner declared it was 'only with the greatest reluctance and from a strong sense of public duty' that he had been moved to speak. In tones tinged with bitterness, he defended his policy in South Africa and argued that there was nothing morally wrong with it.[10] A loyal and prosperous Transvaal was key to 'the whole South African situation' and it was prudent for Britain to pursue 'a cautious line in constitutional development'.[11] He hoped that Lord Elgin would dispel the alarm of those 'who did not sympathise with the enemy during the war, and do not want to see all the hard and costly work accomplished since its conclusion, mutilated or undone'.[12]

Liberal lords were far more interested in making political capital out of the Chinese labour issue, however. Lord Portsmouth invited Milner to declare whether or not he had condoned the unauthorised flogging of 'Chinese coolies'. Milner rose immediately to take the 'whole responsibility' for allowing 'light corporal punishment for acts of violence and disturbance to order' on the mines – thereby implicitly admitting the charge against him. He said he now realised, on looking back, that he had been wrong to do so. But shortly before leaving the Transvaal, he had been informed by his deputy as Governor, Lawley, that unauthorised floggings that had taken place at one or two mines had immediately been stopped. If he had known of it earlier, Milner said, he would have done the same.[13]

That was enough to enable the radical-supporting *Morning Leader* to carry the banner headlines, 'THE FLOGGING OF CHINESE', 'LORD MILNER'S GRAVE ADMISSIONS' and 'SANCTIONED ILLEGALITY', leading to a pious statement from Colonial Under-Secretary Churchill in the Commons that he would not 'put myself to any undue or excessive exertion to defend Lord Milner from any attacks that might be made upon him'.[14]

When the House debated a motion by a radical MP, William Byles, that Milner be censured for his conduct in South Africa, the brash young Churchill, now in the embarrassing situation of having to defend actions he had once supported as a Tory, famously described the word 'slavery' as a 'terminological inexactitude'. Moving an amendment to Byles's motion, he proposed that the House 'while recording its condemnation of the flogging of Chinese coolies in breach of the law, desires in the interests of peace and conciliation in South Africa to refrain from passing censure on individuals'.[15]

Churchill then went on to make an astonishingly patronising

'defence' of Milner, who, he declared, had 'gone from South Africa, probably for ever'. 'The public service', Churchill intoned, 'knows him no more. Having exercised great authority, he now exerts no authority. Having held high employment, he now has no employment. Having disposed of events which have shaped the course of history, he is now unable to deflect in the smallest degree the policy of the day ... he is today poor, and honourably poor. After 20 years of exhausting service under the Crown, he is today a retired civil servant, without pension or gratuity of any kind whatever ... Is it worthwhile to pursue him any further? Lord Milner has ceased to be a factor in public life.'[16] A justifiably outraged Milner would never forgive him.

From King Edward VII downwards, there was furious indignation at Churchill's choice of words. In the Commons, Chamberlain rose to Milner's defence, referring to 'a single error of judgement' in a long course of public service. Balfour told the House that 'if I were Lord Milner, there is no Boer I would not prefer as an enemy to some of the gentlemen who attack him in this country'.[17] Voting on the amended motion – in effect a vote of censure on Milner – was split along party lines and the amendment was adopted by 355 votes to 135. Liberal imperialist MPs who voted in favour included Milner's former friend Asquith. The Times pointed out that while a mistake had been made in South Africa, the whole affair was 'comparatively trivial'. Despite the triviality, the House of Commons had censured 'one of the greatest and most devoted of England's public servants'.[18]

In the Lords, Earl Halifax moved that the House should place on record 'its high appreciation of the services rendered by Lord Milner in South Africa'. He quoted tellingly from Churchill's words six years earlier that the removal of Milner from South Africa would be 'a greater blow to Imperial interests than the defeats at Magersfontein, Stormberg, Colenso and Spionkop put together'.[19] Others to come to Milner's defence were Goschen, Roberts and Lansdowne. In a sharp rebuff to the Commons, the Lords approved a motion thanking Milner by the huge majority of 170 votes to 35.[20]

On Empire Day, 24 May, a well-attended banquet was held in Milner's honour in London, at which Chamberlain described the former proconsul as 'one of the Empire's great assets'. An address signed by 370 000 of Milner's supporters recorded their appreciation of his services to 'Crown and Empire', while in the Cape a similar address drew 25 000 signatures. In Johannesburg, Patrick Duncan wrote that the censure motion in the British Parliament had made people angrier that at any time in his experience.[21]

In June, Cambridge University conferred a doctorate of laws on Milner, 'our *Scipio Africanus*'. Marlowe records that Campbell-Bannerman and Elgin were honoured at the same ceremony and must have been embarrassed by the 'exceptionally prolonged applause' given to Milner.[22]

Political 'Ishmaelite'

By his unceasing support for imperial unity and tariff reform, Milner had come to personify the struggle between the defeated Unionists and Liberal Radicals, now led by a fiery young Welshman, David Lloyd George, that raged in Britain from the Anglo-Boer War until the First World War (or Great War). To his supporters, Milner was the epitome of integrity, intent on championing his country against socialism, class war and the weakening of Empire.[23] His opponents, on the other hand, chose to depict him as the enemy of free trade and the opponent of domestic reform and social improvement – which was far from the truth, though not a difficult case to make.

On 11 July 1906, three days after his 70th birthday, Joseph Chamberlain suffered a stroke that would debilitate him for the rest of his life and leave the tariff reform movement without its leading advocate. Leo Amery immediately tried to persuade Milner to take the stricken Chamberlain's place. He declined the invitation but agreed instead to make two public speeches on the importance of imposing tariffs on non-imperial goods before the year was out.

In Manchester, Milner told a large audience that imperialism was not the opponent of social reform at home but a precondition for it. 'You cannot have prosperity without power', he asserted: 'The maintenance and consolidation of the British Empire ("not a cry but a creed") should be the highest of all political objects for every subject of the Crown.' If Britain were to remain a power of the first rank, able to keep up with Russia, the United States and Germany, and not become a poor country, social reform would depend upon imperial strength, otherwise it would be a case of 'building castles upon the sand.'[24]

Three days later, Milner spoke at a Unionist meeting in Wolverhampton, declaring himself a freelance, 'a sort of political Ishmaelite' who had fallen out with the dominant faction of the Liberal Party because of their suspicion – or dislike – of Empire, which they connected with war, the need for a large army and navy, and military conscription. 'If you have an Empire, you have to fight for it', he asserted. Unlike the free traders, he was 'not large-minded enough to be interested in the total wealth of the world ... his ideal was to see the greatest number of people living healthy and independent lives by means of productive work in our own country.'[25] While he was unable to join the 'hue and cry' against socialists, on the other hand he had no time for the 'odious form of socialism that attacks wealth and lives upon the cultivation of class hatred.'[26]

The *National Review*, well-regarded by Conservatives, and owned and edited by Violet Cecil's pro-imperial brother, Leo Maxse, was so impressed with Milner's views that it published them in full under the title *Imperial Unity: Two Speeches.*

In the summer of 1906, Milner began working in the City again and rented a small house at Sutton Courtenay, on a beautiful backwater of the Thames, to indulge in another of his favourite forms of exercise – rowing. Among his acquaintances at the time were the pioneering Fabian socialists Sidney and Beatrice Webb, who had known him since his Treasury days and supported his efforts as a social reformer and moderniser. A year earlier, Beatrice Webb had observed that the returning Milner had grown 'grey and bitter and obsessed with the idea of a non-party government, without having invented any device for securing it'. He seemed to her to be 'harder and more intolerant, and more distinctly the bureaucrat than when he left England'. He blamed the party system for having forced 'half the political world to be against him.'[27]

After cycling to visit Milner at Sutton Courtenay, Webb recorded that the unpretentious house seemed 'a fit setting for that stern, rigid man, brooding over South Africa. We tried to cheer him up ... but he would not be comforted. He practically admitted the mistake of Chinese labour, given the stupidity of the British electorate and the wicked lies of radical agitators, but defended its introduction as inherently right in that you had to create material wealth before you could give a start to higher things.

'Though a public-spirited, upright and disinterested man', Webb continued, 'Milner does not believe in the spiritual, or even in the relevance of the spiritual, side of things – goodness is something to be arrived at after a course of money-getting by whatever means, and any blood-letting that may be necessary ... As I listened to his feeble, forceful voice, watched his rigid face and wrinkled brow, noted the emphasis on plentiful capital, cheap labour and mechanical ingenuity, I thought that ... a God and a wife would have made Milner, with his faithlessness, persistency, courage, capacity and charm, into a great man. Without either, he has been a tragic combination of success and failure.'[28]

Self-government

In late 1906, Milner purchased the home in which he was live for the rest of his life. Sturry Court – 'a ridiculous name for a little old tumbledown manor house' – was a small estate of 160 acres in Kent, two miles from Canterbury. Violet Cecil, whose marriage to Edward was now in ruins – he no longer required her presence in Egypt, where he was posted – helped him redecorate the manor. She had also bought a home, Great Wigsell, 64 km away and close to the Kiplings. Until the Great War, Violet, Milner and the Kiplings would celebrate Empire Day together at one or other of their houses and rail against the 'Little Englanders' now ruling Britain.

Still feeling personally responsible for the British immigrants he had encouraged to settle in South Africa, Milner continued to make frequent speeches in the Lords and to lobby his friends privately in the hope of delaying the advent of self-government. In February 1907, the Transvaal elections duly took place, in which Het Volk won an absolute majority. A reluctant Selborne was obliged to invite Louis Botha to form a government, but appointed a majority of FitzPatrick's Progressives to seats in the nominated Senate. A month later, it fell to Botha to represent his new administration at the Colonial Conference in London. In mid-1907, Orangia Unie won 28 out of 39 seats in the legislature of the Orange River Colony.

Contemplating the election outcome in the Transvaal, Milner commented to a former member of his secretariat at Vereeniging, Major JF Henley, that his 'feelings about what has happened in South Africa are not capable of description in any language [in] which it would be decent to write. So I will spare you. But I must add, that as far as many decent people are concerned, I think they made an extraordinarily good fight of it. They never had a chance, as it would have taken something like a miracle to get a genuine British majority ... And with these swine in office here, throwing their whole weight into the scale in favour of the Boers ... the conclusion was of course more than foregone ... [But] the best men are now in and no doubt the new Govt. will not have a bed of roses.'[29]

CHAPTER 29

Freelancing
1907–1910

As one of only three living imperial proconsuls, Milner now occupied a special place in the British political firmament. His unrelenting pursuit of imperialist aims would involve him, in one way or another, in every major controversy over the next decade. Chamberlain had succeeded in making tariff reform the dividing line between mainstream Liberals and Unionists, even though many Tories in the Unionist coalition were not persuaded that imposing a duty on non-imperial imports was the best way to finance social upliftment, or to keep the Empire intact.[1] Outside Parliament, the anti-free-trade lobby continued to regard Milner as the stricken Chamberlain's obvious successor.

For a time, the defeated prime minister, Balfour, feared that Milner might abandon his 'Olympian aloofness'[2] and mount a challenge for effective control, if not the titular leadership, of the Unionist coalition. Both men, who knew each other well, shared a friendship with the journalist EB Iwan-Muller, to whom Balfour expressed his concern about Milner's intentions. Iwan-Muller, who had been secretly briefing Balfour from South Africa, dined alone with Milner in January 1907 and reported back that he (Milner) was determined to remain a 'freelance' in order to impress his views on public opinion, and would lead no movement against the Unionists or attempt to unseat its leadership.[3]

Among Milner's friends and supporters outside Parliament, no one tried harder than Leo Amery, now a journalist on *The Times* and an aspiring Conservative politician, to persuade him to take the helm of the influential, non-party-political Tariff Reform League, a pressure group formed in 1903. The fervently imperialist Amery believed that if Milner, a man whose intellect and moral influence he admired more than any other, would only head the League, its clout would increase substantially.

Though Milner was tempted, after several months of consideration, he thought better of accepting, saying he did not feel his strength was equal 'to the direction of so great an enterprise'.[4] Never an effective orator in public, he realised he lacked the temperament and qualities required of a successful politician in a democracy.[5] As one of his most devoted admirers observed perceptively, Milner never sought official power for himself: '[H]e wielded power because it had been conferred upon him by men who had themselves acquired it, and wanted his assistance.'[6]

Colonial matters

The Colonial Conference of 1907 presented Milner with an opportunity to steer the new Liberal government, and British public opinion, in a more pro-imperial direction.[7] In an article for the April edition of the *National Review*, reproduced at length by *The Times* and *The Morning Post*, he suggested that the forthcoming meeting of prime ministers should be more than the 'display of friendly feeling' expressed at the three previous gatherings over 20 years. This time, he insisted, the Conference should create some permanent machinery for coordinating imperial affairs, and for securing the defences of the Empire from external attack.[8] He warned, however, that if the 'mother country' wished the colonies to contribute to imperial defence, they would have to be brought more closely into the policy-making process.

Two of the colonial prime ministers at the Conference, representing opposing viewpoints, stood out above the others: they were Alfred Deakin and Wilfrid Laurier, leaders of Australia and Canada, respectively. Deakin was a champion of the 'New Imperialism', arguing that each member of the Empire should be prepared to surrender some individual sovereignty to the authority of an Imperial Council; Laurier, the doyen of the Conference and representing the most powerful colony, took the contrary view, claiming that the Empire's future lay in the freedom and independence given its component parts, and not in any unwieldy centralisation.[9] The other Anglo-Saxon premiers present – Joseph Ward from New Zealand and Jameson from the Cape – supported Deacon's wish for closer unity and a permanent secretariat, while Louis Botha took the side of Laurier, a French Canadian.

Milner, who was kept abreast of the conference proceedings by his friends in the press, commented sourly to Amery that he was getting bad reports that Botha had not lived up to his promises after the recent Transvaal election, but supposed that the British public, nonetheless, would 'lick his boots and go into paroxysms of delight over him. We do so love humbug.'[10]

Opened by Campbell-Bannerman on 15 April and presided over by Lord Elgin, the Colonial Conference fell far short of the hopes of Milner and the pro-imperialists.[11] Tariff preference was opposed by free traders in the new Liberal government, the proposal to enhance common policy-making was resisted by Laurier and Botha, and no progress was made on the coordination of defence. There was agreement only on changing the name of the conference from 'Colonial' to 'Imperial' and on regarding Canada, Australia and New Zealand henceforth as 'dominions' rather than 'colonies'. It was also decided to hold future Imperial Conferences every four years, rather than five.[12]

If Milner felt frustrated at the lack of progress at the Colonial Conference, he was equally exasperated by the narrow focus of the Unionists' domestic policy programme, which seemed to him to be based mainly upon opposition to the Liberals' 'socialism'. To his disciple Amery, he confided that he was 'going into the wilderness' and would offer – in a series of speeches – his own vision of a 'constructive policy' that would combine tariff reform, the Empire and social improvement at home as an alternative to radical Liberal proposals for a national old-age pension.[13]

Amery urged him on, as did another devotee, Violet Markham, who encouraged Amery to get Milner to 'commit himself up to his neck in something' – she didn't care what. 'For I think his frame of mind is critical, and if he persists, he will be, not as we hope a great man with a great future but a great man with a past – the most tragic of spectacles.' Like Amery, Markham hoped that contact 'with a big, fresh, vigorous country' would have a stimulating effect on Milner's outlook.[14]

The 'fresh and vigorous' country both had in mind was Canada, the key to any scheme for imperial federation. A trip that Milner planned in 1907 had to be called off, but in September 1908, with the encouragement of the Governor General, his imperialist friend Earl Grey, Milner set off for Canada to further his own, independent crusade for closer imperial cooperation.[15] Before his departure, he spent the weekend at Great Wigsell with Violet Cecil and her two small children, Helen and George, to whom he had become known as 'Uncle Alfred'.[16]

Milner eventually spent seven weeks in Canada, making speeches in Vancouver, Winnipeg and Toronto and more than one in Montreal, where he declared himself to be a believer in federalism but unable to conceive of effective cooperation between self-governing states without a common executive organ belonging to all of them.[17] He stressed the importance of equality and cooperation on practical matters to precede the setting up of more formal imperial ties.[18]

At Government House in Ottawa, Milner met up again with John Hanbury-Williams, his former military secretary at the Cape, and his wife, whom he assured that in South Africa there was 'no question of the black population ever becoming a danger to the supremacy of the whites'.[19] In his final speech in Canada, he predicted that imperial tariffs would eventually be introduced in Britain. Reverting to his favourite theme of the link between imperialism and social reform, he declared that patriotism could not thrive in the 'squalor and degradation of the slums of our great cities ... You cannot expect a casual labourer in an English town to set much store on being the citizen of a great Empire.'[20]

Grey described his friend's visit as 'a great success', as did Northcliffe's *Daily Mail*, which hailed Milner as the person 'on whom Chamberlain's mantle had unmistakeably fallen', and 'the brain-carrier of Imperial policy for the next twenty years'.[21]

People's Budget

After turning down an invitation to join the board of *The Times* and spending another six weeks visiting his old haunts in Egypt, Milner returned to England to participate in the thunderous parliamentary battle over Lloyd George's revolutionary 'People's Budget' of 1909. In order to finance the building of more dreadnought battleships so as to

Britain's leader in the First World War, David Lloyd George. (*Wikimedia Commons/Harris & Ewing*)

counter the growing German naval threat, the radical Chancellor had decided to increase income tax, impose inheritance and land taxes on the wealthy, and levy duties on liquor and other goods. 'This is a War Budget: it is for raising money to wage implacable warfare against poverty and squalidness',[22] the combative Welshman declared. Instead of funding social improvements through import duties – as Milner and the tariff reform movement were demanding – Lloyd George, with Churchill in support, insisted on upholding the principles of free trade, which, in their view, kept prices lower and promoted economic growth. The Unionists were outraged by the imposition of the new taxes. Outvoted in the House of Commons, they resolved to defeat the 'socialist' budget in the House of Lords.

By long-standing parliamentary tradition, the Lords could overrule the Commons on all matters except money bills, but on this occasion an aristocratic 'old guard' in the upper house argued that Lloyd George's budget was radical social change artfully dressed up in fiscal clothes. Among the most uncompromising of the Lords was Milner.[23] In a speech in Glasgow, in the tones of someone wearied by the underhanded tactics of politicians, he declared that when confronted by an evil scheme of 'such exceptional magnitude, with such far-reaching consequences', it was the duty of men like him to try to prevent it and 'damn the consequences'. 'All we claim to do', he asserted, 'is to refer the question to the nation ... Let the people decide.'[24] It had taken him more than half a lifetime to discover some virtue in democracy.

Both Balfour and Lloyd George were delighted at Milner's outspokenness – for contrary reasons: the Conservative leader because he had ordered his party to vote down the budget; the Chancellor because he was able to depict his opponents as out-of-touch reactionaries, ready to do anything to preserve their narrow class interests.[25] Milner's vehement denunciations of the Liberal government, now led by Asquith after the untimely death of Campbell-Bannerman a year earlier, meant that their once-close political relationship was now well beyond repair.

In response to the Lords' crushing rejection of Lloyd George's budget by 350 votes to 75, Asquith was forced to call for the dissolution of Parliament. In two bitterly contested and indecisive elections in

1910, the premier managed to keep a tenuous hold on power, threat-ening to overwhelm the Unionists' majority in the Lords by creating hundreds of new Liberal peers. It took the intervention of the new King, George V, to calm the waters and persuade a majority of the Lords to accept the loss of their permanent veto on decisions of the Commons. The Parliament Act of 1911 brought an end to the House of Lords' traditional dominance of British politics, though the upper house has maintained its importance ever since. A group of 114 die-hard peers, known as the (Last) 'Ditchers', held out against the provisions of the Parliament Act to the bitter end. Prominent among the 'bitter-enders' was Lord Milner.

The road to Union

In the Cape, meanwhile, the fall of Jameson's Progressives to Merri-man's Afrikaner Bond administration in 1908, largely because pre-viously disenfranchised rebels were able to vote once again, had brought the unification of South Africa much closer. A National Convention of delegates from the four colonies had come together to settle on a constitution for the country, their deliberations enhanced by the preparatory work done by Milner's Kindergarten. The tireless Lionel Curtis had previously set up 'Closer Union Societies' around the country, whose sole purpose was to promote the concept of a common statehood and political union. In 1908, he and Philip Kerr had launched *The State/De Staat*, a monthly journal financed by Sir Abe Bailey and printed in English and Dutch, to promote the case for unity. The Kindergarten also published two books, *The Government of South Africa*, a two-volume tract, and *The Framework of the Union*, to bolster the case for unification.[26] Although the Milnerites had once set out to create a federal system of government, Robert Brand and Patrick Duncan were to actively assist Smuts at the National Convention with his designs for union.[27]

The Kindergarten's relationship with Smuts had been through sev-eral phases: at first, it was one of disaffection on either side. Recognising that the Boer politician was an implacable adversary of Milner's poli-cies but also the most able of the opponents, the *Kinder* used to refer to Smuts sneeringly as 'Slim Jannie' (meaning 'clever Jannie'), a nickname

that followed him all his life. Smuts, for his part, was initially disparag-
ing of the work of Milner's young disciples. Eventually overcoming his
reservations, the chief architect of the South African constitution began
gradually to cooperate with the likes of Curtis, Kerr, Brand and Duncan.
It was via Smuts that the *Kinder* were able to exercise an influence over
the country's unification.[28] In 1909, Brand and Duncan were invited
to accompany the National Convention delegation to London for the
passing of the South Africa Act by the British Parliament.

Having achieved their objective in South Africa – and worked
themselves out of government employment – *Kinder* such as Brand,
Perry and Malcolm returned home to take up lucrative positions in
business. But Curtis and Kerr, as mentioned earlier, decided to follow
Milner's example and devote their energies to the cause of a greater
imperial federation. Most of their colleagues stayed on in South
Africa, however, and kept in touch with one another, attending when
they could the various 'moots' in England that became the core of the
former Kindergarten's pro-imperial activities.[29]

Writing to Amery in 1909, Curtis described his ambitious ideas
for tackling the issue of greater imperial unity.[30] He had in mind putting together a comprehensive memorandum, another Egg, to initiate
discussions on 'a common policy, and for getting a number of minds to
move automatically in the same direction'.[31] Besides forming a group
dedicated to 'organic unity' within every dominion, he proposed also
to launch another journal, so that everyone 'from Lord Milner downwards would have at their disposal a medium through which the same
train of thought could be set in motion through all the self-governing
colonies of the Empire at the same time'.[32]

Amery discussed Curtis's plan with Milner, who thought there was
'a great deal to it', especially the proposal for a 'first-rate magazine', and
agreed to provide financial assistance for it from the Rhodes Trust. In
September 1909, an inaugural meeting of the Round Table took place
at a country mansion, Plas Newydd, on the island of Anglesey in north
Wales. It was attended by many ex-members of the Kindergarten, as
well as Milner, Jameson, Selborne (on home leave), a few well-heeled
prospective patrons and, in spirit, by an unwell Leo Amery.

Also present was a key supporter of the Round Table initiative, the wealthy Scottish businessman and apostle of federalism, FS Oliver, author of a ground-breaking biography of the American federalist Alexander Hamilton. Oliver's book, discovered by an excited Curtis after Milner had left South Africa, had renewed the enthusiasm of the *Kinder* for the notion of an imperial federation. Oliver and Milner had since become close friends, the Scot even more contemptuous than Milner of the shortcomings of parliamentary democracy.[33]

Following the Plas Newydd gathering, Curtis and Kerr departed on a tour of Canada, reporting back to Milner and company at a Round Table 'moot' before Curtis went off to Australia and New Zealand, via South Africa, where he attended the final session of the Transvaal Legislative Council, of which he was a member.[34] In his absence, Kerr forged ahead with preparations for the publication of *The Round Table*, the first edition of which appeared in November 1910. Subtitled 'A Quarterly Review of the Politics of the British Empire', the journal was distributed in Britain, Canada, South Africa, New Zealand, Australia and India. Its declared aim was to 'present a regular account of what is going on throughout the King's dominions ... entirely free from the bias of local political issues'.[35] *The Round Table* did not seek a large circulation, confining its readership to a select audience of what today would be called 'influencers'. And it did not disclose the identity of its financial backer – South Africa's Sir Abe Bailey.

Between 1910 and 1914, *The Round Table* exerted a significant influence on political thought in every outpost of the Empire. However, as the Imperial Conference of 1911 was to demonstrate, most Dominions remained reluctant to cede more of their powers to a centralised organisation based in London. Hampered by the outbreak of war in 1914, the Round Table movement failed to make any appreciable headway with its proposals for imperial unification. In the view of the Hoover Institution academics LH Gann and Peter Duignan, 'the Round Table group failed to understand either the force or the divisiveness of dominion nationalism; within the context of Africa, they never understood the Afrikaners, much less the Africans.'[36]

Like Milner, the Round Tablers shunned party politics and sought to exercise influence elsewhere than in Parliament. Their 'moots' were conducted in private and articles in *The Round Table* were kept anonymous, which led to allegations that the movement was a secretive cabal intent on exercising power without responsibility.[37] Lloyd George was to add to the Round Table's mystique after the war by referring to the extra-parliamentary organisation as 'perhaps the most powerful in the country.'[38]

Regular 'moots' of the Round Table ceased in 1916 upon Milner's appointment to the War Cabinet, after which its eponymous journal continued to be financed by the Rhodes Trust and others, and published as a high-quality magazine without any propagandist intent. In 1931, the steam eventually went out of the imperial movement after the passing of the Statute of Westminster, which gave the Dominions greater independence from 'Mother' Britain. Today, *The Round Table* is still published as the *Commonwealth Journal of International Affairs*, testimony to the vision and enthusiasm of its young founders more than a century ago.

CHAPTER 30

Irish Troubles
1910–1914

As Milner approached his sixties, an issue of more pressing concern to him than tariff reform, national service or 'creeping socialism' was the threat that Home Rule for Ireland posed to the unity of Britain, and by extension to his beloved Empire. As Gollin records, the Irish crisis of 1912–1914 was more terrible than any other in recent British history. Parliamentary democracy, so long accepted as the traditional method of British politics, was shaken to its foundations, and notwithstanding Milner's reputation for level-headedness, he was to become deeply involved in its shaking.[1]

The parliamentary stalemate between Liberals and Unionists in two successive elections in 1910 had resulted in Asquith having to call on the support of Irish nationalists in order to carry on as prime minister – as Gladstone had done decades earlier. (Winston Churchill reflected that it was 'the sinister influence of eighty Irish votes, making and unmaking governments, swaying the fortunes of both great political parties, which poisoned nearly forty years of our public life'.[2]) The price the Liberals had to pay was to put Irish Home Rule at the forefront of the political agenda again.[3] For Milner and the Round Table, the key question was the form that any devolution might take: would a separate Ireland become in effect a British province behind a tariff fence, and remain within the Empire, or would it be granted full sovereign independence?

The Irish nationalists in the House of Commons had one purpose only: to establish an Irish parliament in Dublin, no longer beholden to British rule from Westminster. Irish Protestants, on the other hand, many of them landowners with close ties to the English gentry, were terrified at the prospect. Heavily outnumbered by the Catholics, they had always been able to express their opposition to Home Rule in Parliament. And in the northeast of Ireland, where Protestants outnumbered Catholics, the Ulster Orangemen – led by the barrister Sir Edward Carson – were ready to fight to keep their ties to Westminster. Given the threat to the unity of the kingdom, many Unionists were ready to resort to extreme measures to put down rebel Irish 'terrorism' in order to preserve the status quo.

Milner, who had joined the Liberal imperialists back in 1886 in opposition to Gladstone's Home Rule plans, was fiercely against full independence for Ireland: it meant another step towards the disintegration of Empire – whose unification in one form or another had been his life's great mission. He had hoped that tariff reform might bind Ireland to the United Kingdom in a manner compatible with some kind of autonomy, but that was no longer feasible. His abiding fear was that Asquith and his Liberals were prepared to dismember Britain in order to prolong their tenuous hold on power.[4]

The position of the Ulster Protestants, in Milner's view, was similar to that of the Uitlanders in Kruger's Transvaal. And the current Liberal government still contained many of the pro-Boer, anti-imperialists who had given him so much trouble in South Africa. 'These people are capable of any treachery', he wrote to Violet Cecil. 'They are crawling today, but unless we are wary and give them no chance, they may jump up again tomorrow.'[5] The principal target for his anger was his former soul mate, Asquith, scornfully referred to as 'Squiff' by the Milnerites[6] because of his well-known fondness for alcohol.

In April 1912, Squiff introduced the Government of Ireland Bill, based on similar lines to devolved legislation in other parts of the Empire. The absence of any special provisions for Ulster in the Bill aroused huge passions on both sides of the Irish Sea. In the face of furious opposition in the House of Commons, the Liberals could only advance the Bill by frequent use of the parliamentary guillotine. Tempers ran high: on one occasion, Winston Churchill was hit on the head by a book flung by an irate Unionist MP.[7] After eventually passing through the Commons, the Bill was thrown out by the Conservative-dominated House of Lords by 326 votes to 69. For the next two years, Britain teetered uneasily on the brink of civil war.

1911 Imperial Conference

A year earlier, a weary and disillusioned Balfour had resigned as Unionist leader, fed up with arguing with Milner and like-minded colleagues in the Lords, who had resolved to 'die in the last ditch' but were too few to resist the passage of the Parliament Act, which reduced the powers of the upper house. Balfour was replaced by the Canadian-born businessman Andrew Bonar Law, the most effective of the tariff reformers in the House of Commons. Law had concluded, however, that the unity of the Unionist coalition could not be preserved unless tariff reform was abandoned: the policy might have served Chamberlain's imperial purposes but had become a handicap in British elections.[8] The abrupt scrapping of tariff reform as Unionist policy made Milner more distrustful than ever of party politics.

Law's U-turn on tariff reform caused an outraged Amery to try again to persuade Milner to step forward and seize control of the movement: 'We are absolutely paralysed ... what are you going to do about it? You are the one and only man who can give us life and coherence. What we want is a Graaff-Reinet speech, or rather a campaign to do for England what Graaff-Reinet did for South Africa.' But Milner would not be drawn. Replying to Amery, he refused to make any new commitments: 'Anything that is done or planned must be planned *as if I did not exist*. As long as I continue to exist, I *may*, at times, be useful, but that will be a windfall. I have got absolutely to paddle my own canoe.'[9]

Paddling his own canoe meant, among other things, giving more attention to the affairs of the Round Table in advance of the Imperial Conference of 1911, timed to celebrate the coronation of George V. At a 'moot' in January, a subcommittee of Round Tablers had been appointed to draft an imperial constitution and suggest to the Conference what powers an imperial parliament might exercise. As Milner had predicted, however, despite the Round Table's best efforts, the Imperial Conference went the way of its predecessors. Sir Wilfrid ('Won'tfred') Laurier, with South African support, once again countermanded proposals put forward by New Zealand's premier Ward to advance the organic unity of Empire. Louis Botha declared that 'decentralisation and liberty have done wonders ... It is the policy of decentralisation which has made the British Empire.'[10]

As he did each year, Milner spent the first few months of 1912 in Egypt, returning in time for a well-attended memorial service on 25 April for his former colleague and later adversary, WT Stead, who had been among the hundreds drowned on the maiden voyage of the ill-fated *Titanic*. Despite their estrangement, Milner wrote a generous tribute to Stead in a special edition of *The Review of Reviews*, in which he declared that his old colleague had been 'endowed with courage, physical and moral, in as great a measure as any man I have ever known ... If Nature had gifted him with judgment in anything like proportion to his other qualities of mind and character, he would have been ... simply irresistible.' Looking back to his days of intimate companionship with Stead, Milner 'could not remember one human being – man, woman or child, within the circle of his radiant personality, who did not regard him as a friend'.[11]

Encouraged by the election, in Canada, of the pro-imperial Robert Borden as prime minister in place of Laurier, Milner paid another visit to the country in 1912 to take in the Maritime Provinces, which he had not been to previously. While in Canada, he paid his one and only visit to the United States, calling on friends in Massachusetts and New York.[12] Back in England, he busied himself with the affairs of the London Joint Stock Bank, of Toynbee Hall – of which he was now chairman – of the Rhodes Trust and, as always, of the Round Table.[13] Among those he brought to 'moots' or dinners of the Table were Bonar Law and Robert Borden, and a new press baron, Waldorf Astor, whose multimillionaire American father, William W Astor, had bought *The Observer* from Lord Northcliffe and given editorial control to his son. Many Round Table 'moots' were held at Cliveden, Waldorf Astor's mansion on the Thames, or at his house in London.

Two further extensions of the Kindergarten's influence were the appointment of Lionel Curtis to the key position of Beit lecturer in Colonial History at Oxford, and the elevation of Geoffrey Robinson to the editorship of Northcliffe's *The Times*, the voice of Britain's ruling class. Milner wrote to his protégé saying he had been 'praying hard for this consummation for months past and while I realise all the difficulties of your position, I have the greatest confidence that you will make a success of it ... I don't know that there is a finer chance in the whole sphere of public affairs.'[14]

Ulster

In mid-1913, Milner received a letter from Lord Roberts, Britain's foremost military figure, of Anglo-Irish stock himself and a keen supporter of Ulster's Protestants. Roberts had been in discussion with Bonar Law and both agreed the time had come for Milner 'to take a more prominent part than you have of late in politics'.[15] Once again, Milner temporised but in late 1913 wrote to Sir Edward Carson to ask for a meeting, saying, '*I am completely in accord with you about Ulster* and what I want to know is whether there is not something which men like myself who disbelieve in mere talk at this juncture can do to help you?'[16] He also wrote to Amery saying the time had come for action at last.[17]

In January 1914, Milner was invited by Lord Willoughby de Broke to join the committee of the Union League for the Support of Ulster, an organisation De Broke had founded himself in 1907 to oppose Home Rule. Milner hurried back from a visit to Spain on Rio Tinto business to propose to De Broke, Roberts, Law and others the drawing up of a British Covenant, an idea suggested to him by Amery.[18] The object of the Covenant would be to force the Liberal government to call a general election before any Home Rule Bill could become law. 'Our job', Milner wrote, 'is to make the coercion of Ulster difficult if not impossible if the Government should be driven to attempt it'. He proposed 'action … falling short of violence or actual rebellion, *or at least not beginning with it*'.[19]

As an experienced administrator, Milner knew that as time was short, any new movement would need the machinery of an existing organisation, and he persuaded De Broke to put his staff at the Covenant's disposal.[20] With as much energy as he could muster, Milner threw himself into raising mass support for the Covenant, telling Violet Cecil that 'for the last 3 or 4 months, *I have really worked hard* – at public things – for the first time since South Africa.'[21]

In February, the Round Table held another 'moot' to discuss the future of Ulster. For once, not everyone went along with Milner's plans for mass action. Curtis, Kerr and Oliver all declined to support the Covenant movement because they believed in a federal solution to the Irish problem. But nearly two million members of the public pledged their support for the Covenant, including Lords Roberts, Balfour,

Halifax and Desborough, as well as Rudyard Kipling, the composer Sir Edward Elgar and the famous legal scholar and constitutional expert Professor AV Dicey. A tract titled *The Covenanter* duly appeared in May, carrying articles by Milner, Kipling, Carson and Amery, with the defiant motto of 'Put your trust in God and keep your powder dry'. On 4 April, Milner, Balfour, Carson and Amery addressed a huge open-air gathering in Hyde Park to rally support for the Covenant. In addition to these public activities, Milner and some wealthy friends began secretly raising a substantial war chest to buy weapons for the under-armed Ulster Volunteer Force,[22] a loyalist militia who were having to practise their drills with broomsticks.

On 3 March, the formal launch of the British Covenant was announced by most of Britain's leading newspapers. Milner had made full use of his press contacts to drum up editorial support for the movement, writing personally to the editors of all pro-Unionist newspapers and journals. Robinson replied to say he hoped Milner had found *The Times* 'adequately docile', and stressed the need to have 'a dozen good names to add tomorrow – from mugwumps, merchants and the middle classes'. JL Garvin of *The Observer* wrote to say that he would help in every way, but an immense roll of signatories was necessary: 'As soon as your arrangements for general signing are ready, I will give every prominence to them.'[23]

Six days later, Asquith proposed a compromise, devised by Lloyd George and accepted with reluctance by the Irish nationalists: each of the six counties of Ulster would be given the option of remaining outside Home Rule from Dublin for six years. If a Unionist government were to come to power in the interim, it could scrap the legislation or make permanent the exclusion of any or all of Ulster's counties.[24] Carson rejected the proposal out of hand, declaring that Ulster had no desire 'to accept a sentence of death with a stay of execution for six years'.[25]

Milner was also dismissive of Asquith's proposal. Believing the Liberals would be unable to use force to get their way in Ulster, he and Amery began to consider ways of activating plans for a provisional government in Ulster, set up by Carson, to wait in the wings. Its purpose would be to keep the peace but also to take over the administration of

Ulster if settlement attempts failed. AV Dicey, among the first to sign the Covenant, cautioned Milner that once the Home Rule Bill became law, defiance of it by any Englishmen would be 'a crime, and probably treason'.[26]

Once again, Milner found himself in a position uniquely his own. Unlike politicians engaged in the Irish struggle, he was able to advance a course of action that many of his friends believed was too extreme, too disruptive of national life or too contrary to parliamentary tradition to be supported.[27] But Milner had little respect for parliamentary tradition, was dedicated to the United Kingdom, and – as always – had great difficulty in putting himself into the shoes of people who did not agree with him. As Amery wrote later, 'if the Government had been demented enough to precipitate civil war, he [Milner] would almost inevitably have found himself the real leader of the resistance'.[28]

The Curragh 'mutiny'

Many officers in the British Army were drawn from the Anglo-Irish gentry, hence the widespread sympathy among the upper ranks for the Unionist cause. On 18 March, Carson wrote to Milner asking if the Covenanters would set up a fund for 'officers in the army who resign rather than violate their consciences'.[29] Two days later, Asquith and the Liberals were shaken to the core – and the Ulster Unionists greatly encouraged – by a near mutiny at the Curragh, the British Army's main base in Ireland, when 57 officers resigned rather than obey orders to put down any potential rebellion in Ulster. The incident shook Parliament and the nation. Conservatives accused the Liberals of being prepared to sacrifice Ulster; Liberals accused the Tories of encouraging a rebellion against the Crown.[30] Churchill was particularly shocked at the challenge to the Liberal government by senior officers, which he believed could endanger the future security of the Empire.[31]

On 24 April, the Irish situation took a more serious turn when 30 000 rifles were smuggled in from Germany to arm a substantial number of the Ulster Volunteer Force's 100 000 members. The weapons had been purchased from funds raised by signatories of the Covenant. In the south, there was a corresponding rush of men to join the well-armed Irish Volunteers. At Westminster, politicians on both sides of the divide realised they could not enforce their will on Ulster without bloodshed, and began considering further compromise.

On 12 May, Asquith introduced another amendment to the Home Rule Bill that would offer Ulster an indefinite rather than a six-year suspension of rule by Dublin. The Bill passed through the Commons and was sent to the Lords for approval. Milner remained intransigent, warning of the danger of the Unionists' abandoning 'the firm ground of principle'. The correct solution, he suggested, should be either a referendum or a general election.[32] Behind the scenes, he was working in the strictest secrecy on plans for a new currency system in Ulster should the provisional government declare 'UDI' – a unilateral declaration of independence.[33]

On 24 June, the day on which Asquith's amending Bill reached the Lords, Milner made a fighting speech in which he urged Unionists not to forego the chance, however slight, of preventing a disaster from which the Empire might never recover. 'I am not a Jingo', he declared, 'but I will not be led by Jingoes nor always by Orangemen … Ulster is not asking to dominate, but to remain as they are and not part of a state which might result in a total severance from the United Kingdom.'[34]

On 2 July, the day the news reached London of the assassinations of Archduke Franz Ferdinand and his wife at Sarajevo, Joseph Chamberlain died at the age of 78, after many years of infirmity. Incredibly, even though he was unable to sign his name and had to be carried into the Commons each day, he had twice been returned to Parliament unopposed by his Birmingham constituency.[35] Paying tribute in the Lords to his 'incomparable chief', Milner described him as 'a great leader of men, who was successful in winning not only the admiration and respect but the affection of those who were brought most closely into contact with him … The confidence which they felt in him gave them greater confidence in themselves and thus he got the best work out of them of which they were capable.'[36]

In mid-July 1914, almost at his wits' end, Asquith called on the King to convene a conference at Buckingham Palace in the hope of finally resolving the Irish crisis. Milner expressed to Bonar Law his hope that the conference would fail: 'If we had to deal with anything like honest people, I might be differently inclined, but I know we shall be tricked in any bargain.' In a letter to Carson, Milner wished the Ulster leader 'well out of the Buckingham Palace trap. What an eel Asquith is … he has actually secured another week for "wait and see".'[37]

After three days of negotiation, the Buckingham Palace conference broke down over a disagreement between the Catholics and Protestants of Ulster's two southern counties. Only days later, however, a much larger threat loomed to which British politicians had thus far paid scant attention. The reverberations from Sarajevo were being felt throughout Europe. For Britain, civil war would be averted by a far greater international conflict. And fortunately for Milner, he had been spared the likely consequences of his own impetuosity.

CHAPTER 31

War
1914–1916

At 11 pm on 4 August 1914, the day on which the Kaiser's forces invaded Belgium, King George V declared the United Kingdom to be at war with Germany. As Lawrence James points out, the war was another and bigger imperial conflict. Every European power involved was out to accumulate land, economic advantage or political influence. The fighting was an extension of the partitioning of the world by the Great Powers.[1]

Although Milner was a private citizen without any formal party affiliation, he was involved from the outset in Britain's frantic war preparations. Worried by Asquith's tendency to procrastinate, he hurried over to see Kitchener, on home leave from Egypt, to urge his old adversary to offer his services as Secretary of State for War. The two men were among the few who realised that an under-equipped Britain would be in for a long and costly conflict; most people mistakenly assumed that – as in South Africa – the hostilities would be over 'by Christmas'.

At the time, Kitchener's status in the public's mind was that of a 'martial demi-god'[2], a superior being and brilliant soldier to whom the safety of the nation could readily be entrusted. Whatever their past differences, Milner considered Kitchener to be the only man with the necessary single-mindedness and drive to direct Britain's war effort. Fearful that Asquith might delay the deployment of the British Expeditionary Force (BEF) across the Channel to confront the Germans, Milner urged Kitchener to press for an immediate appointment with the Prime Minister, which he reluctantly did. Two days later, the Field Marshal's appointment as Secretary of State for War was announced, greeted by the newspapers as a masterstroke by the Liberal government.

Within days, the reality of war was brought home to Milner when his estate at Sturry Court was temporarily requisitioned by the West Kent Yeomanry. Army officers took over the house, horses filled the barn and other ranks pitched tents in his field, the property soon showing the signs of its rough treatment by the military. But of far more concern was the fate of Violet Cecil's 18-year-old son, George, newly commissioned in the Grenadier Guards and caught up in the fighting at Mons, in Belgium. On 8 September, the young man was reported to be among the wounded and missing. Spending the weekend at Great Wigsell trying to comfort Violet, Milner recorded that 'the uncertainty about George hangs like a pall over everything here'.[3] He pulled every string he could to prise information out of the military authorities in Britain and France, but it was not until November that confirmation was received that young George had been killed, along with most of his battalion. The Cecils' distress at their loss was to be repeated in countless homes across the length and breadth of Britain over the next few years.

Not wishing to hamper Kitchener's appeal for volunteers to join the BEF, Roberts and Milner agreed to suspend temporarily their campaign on behalf of the National Service League (NSL), a pressure group founded in February 1902 to campaign for the introduction of compulsory military training. When, on 14 November 1914, the 82-year-old Roberts died suddenly after a visit to the war front, the leadership of the NSL devolved upon Milner,[4] who revived the League's lobbying almost a year later.

Enmeshed in the Irish crisis, the Asquith government had given insufficient attention to how the war against the Central Powers (Germany, Austria-Hungary, Bulgaria and the Ottoman Empire) should be fought, hoping the country could fall back – as it had done for the past 100 years – on the strength of the Royal Navy to defend the homeland. Without the navy, the British Isles – an importer of food and without a large standing army – was extremely vulnerable to blockade and invasion.[5] It was Kitchener who jolted the politicians out of their complacency: he asked Parliament to approve a call-up of 500 000 men, and the War Office appealed for volunteers by papering the country with posters of the moustachioed Field Marshal pointing an accusing finger and saying pointedly, 'Your Country Needs You'.[6]

Of the four divisions of the BEF sent to France under the command of Sir John French, no fewer than 40 000 men were killed, wounded or missing within the first month of fighting. After an encouraging Anglo-French victory at the River Marne, which halted the German advance on Paris and ushered in four years of trench warfare, Milner noted that 'our people *have fought magnificently* under the leadership of men who are, I think, without exception our South African warriors. What would have happened to us if we had not had the experience of the South African War, or the men which that war brought to the front, God only knows.' He was thinking of seasoned officers such as French, Haig, Methuen and Hanbury-Williams, the latter now a major general on secondment to the Russian imperial forces.[7]

Early in the war, Milner was saddened by the news from South Africa that General Koos de la Rey had been killed in a shooting accident in Johannesburg, writing, 'I always regarded him as the finest of the Boer leaders, both as a soldier and a gentleman.' He would have been displeased to hear that the veteran Boer leader was actually being driven by car through a police roadblock on his way to a rally against his government's support for the imperial war effort.[8]

Two schools

By the spring of 1915 – after six months of war – Allied forces had become bogged down in the mud along the Western Front, entrenched behind a line of barbed-wire entanglements extending from Switzerland to the sea. With high-explosive shells and other armaments in short supply, Anglo-French attempts to break through the German lines at Loos and Neuve Chapelle had failed, with heavy casualties on both sides. In the Middle East, the Ottoman Empire had joined the Central Powers, cutting off the Allies' supply route through the Dardanelles and the Black Sea to Russia, and threatening the approaches to the Suez Canal.[9]

Milner also kept an anxious eye on the South African incursion into German South West Africa at Britain's request, writing a letter of congratulation to the Prime Minister, General Louis Botha, who had personally gone into the field and brought the campaign – the Allies' first outright victory in the war – to a successful conclusion. Botha wrote in reply, 'Dear Lord Milner, It is indeed kind of you to write and congratulate me on the success of our German South West African campaign. Let me assure you it is very highly appreciated.'[10]

The British public's disquiet over the war's slow progress was fuelled by rumours of dissension within the Asquith cabinet, resulting from the furious row that had broken out between Churchill, First Lord of the Admiralty, and his tempestuous First Sea Lord, Sir John Fisher, over Churchill's plan to strike at the Ottoman Empire through the Dardanelles, the strategically vital sea channel separating Europe and Asia. Asquith responded to growing criticism by inviting leading members of the opposition to join a coalition cabinet consisting of 12 Liberals, 8 Unionists and one Labour member. His up-and-coming rival within the party, Lloyd George – the Liberals' most vociferous internal critic – was given the key post of Minister of Munitions, and Churchill was sent packing from the Admiralty, to be replaced by Balfour. Although Milner's friend Selborne was made Minister of Agriculture, for Milner himself there was no place. Excluded from the inner circle, he now became the new cabinet's most formidable critic.[11]

By this stage, Asquith and Milner had come to represent the two opposing schools of thought in wartime British politics.[12] Many Unionist MPs and military leaders thought that a man of Milner's experience and administrative ability was more likely to achieve victory in the war than anyone else. Squiff was widely regarded as an old-style peacetime politician, more intent on papering over the cracks within his party than energetically prosecuting the war.[13] Dissident army officers and politicians alike made a habit of writing to Milner to vent their concerns, making him a focus of opposition to the coalition's handling of the war.

Though seething with impatience over Asquith's tactics of delay and compromise,[14] Milner was hesitant at first about re-entering the public arena in wartime, knowing he was disliked by many in the country at large and not wishing to condemn the Prime Minister publicly or undermine the unity of the newly formed coalition. Instead, he accepted an invitation from Selborne to chair a commission into food production, a matter about which he had formed definite views while in war-torn South Africa.[15] In a rapidly produced report, Milner recommended the introduction of a guaranteed minimum-price scheme to encourage farmers to grow more crops for military needs – and was 'fearfully disgusted' when the government did nothing to implement his proposals.[16]

Manpower shortage

On 27 May 1915, Geoffrey Robinson gave prominence to a letter from Milner, published on the editorial page of *The Times*, expressing concern at the lack of firm leadership by the coalition and declaring that 'the State ought not to be obliged to tout for fighting men. It ought to be in a position to call up the number it wants … It is high time that the whole of our able-bodied manhood … should be enrolled … And the nation is ready to obey the order. It only needs the captain on the bridge to give the signal.'[17]

In August, as losses on the Western Front mounted, Northcliffe's newspapers threw their weight behind Milner's renewed campaign for conscription, explaining that as circumstances had changed, the NSL was ending its voluntary suspension, since the safety of the entire Empire was now under threat.[18] Liberal newspapers, on the other hand, criticised the temerity of militarists who presumed to tamper with the freedom of Englishmen to decide for themselves, with the *Daily News* warning Lloyd George that the British people would not 'take the message of Milner even from your lips'.[19] The King himself was distressed at the agitation for enforced national service, believing it could endanger the unity of the British people.[20]

By now, and not for the first time, Milner had come to view Kitchener as a problem rather than a potential war-winner: the prickly War Secretary seemed to regard complaints about manpower shortages as a reflection on his recruitment campaign, and complained about a lack of equipment for new volunteers. His notorious secretiveness was also proving a serious hindrance, for by keeping his views from the public (and the cabinet) and banning war correspondents from the battlefields of France, he was causing rumour to flourish and morale to plummet. On 6 September, Milner went to see Kitchener to voice his concerns but found him as disinclined as ever to accept a civilian's view of military matters, as had been the case in South Africa.

From late 1915 into 1916, Britain's tally of wartime disasters mounted. The attempt to force a passage through the Dardanelles had collapsed at Gallipoli, while on the Western Front – where Haig had replaced French as commander-in-chief – the army lost 60 000 men in the first day of fighting on the Somme. During the indecisive Battle of Jutland, off the Danish coast, the Royal Navy suffered heavy losses at the hands of a much smaller German fleet. To the east, Bulgaria had joined the war on the side of the Central Powers.[21] The most devastating blow to public morale, however, was the mid-year death by drowning of Kitchener, whose warship, HMS *Hampshire*, was sunk while the Field Marshal was on his way to Russia to discuss how to supply the Tsar's army with munitions.

Upon Kitchener's death, the critically important position of Secretary of State for War – second only in importance to the prime minister – fell vacant. Two politicians were eager to fill it: Lloyd George and the Conservative leader, Bonar Law. Yet some of Northcliffe's newspapers regarded Milner as the most suitable candidate.[22] At *The Times*, Robinson was conflicted: he was convinced that Lloyd George and Milner in tandem were the best men to save the country but did not want to offend either, so he expressed doubt that Milner would accept the appointment but hoped that he might somehow join Lloyd George inside the government: 'The two of them would either control affairs within the cabinet or would bring it down with a run if they were to resign together.'[23] Lloyd George let it be known to *The Times* that Asquith would not countenance the presence of Milner in the cabinet and that he (Lloyd George) intended to make the War Ministry his own.[24]

In January 1916, at the urging of Amery, a determined Milner began to host a series of Monday-night dinners at his London home, the aim of which was to plot the overthrow of the Asquith government. It was his way of exercising influence along with men he respected and who were able to get things done. Regulars at the table were Sir Edward Carson, the most powerful opposition MP in the Commons, Robinson, Waldorf Astor, FS Oliver, Lloyd George, Philip Kerr and, from time to time, Amery (then in the army). The presence of two powerful newspapermen in Astor and Robinson made the 'Monday night cabal' effectively the 'general staff' of the opposition to Asquith. Both Carson and Oliver were keen to invite Churchill to join the group, but Milner was unable to overlook what his bumptious critic had said about him a decade earlier.[25]

Continuing to denounce the government publicly by means of frequent speeches in the House of Lords, Milner condemned the decision to abandon the Dardanelles and urged that military men rather than politicians should run the war.[26] At Robinson's behest, he and Lloyd George, now the War Secretary, met secretly for lunch on 30 September 1915 – a momentous encounter between the former pro-Boer, who had been so critical of Milner in South Africa, and the target of his vitriol in person. Robinson wrote afterwards that 'it had taken a little scheming, but each obviously wanted to get in touch', without the meeting becoming known publicly.[27]

The discussion over lunch was cordial and ranged widely. Lloyd George viewed conscription as the only way to regulate the supply of skilled labour, agreeing with Milner that the war could not be won without it.[28] The War Secretary insisted that to prosecute the war successfully, a small inner cabinet of four or five was necessary, but nothing would happen until after the British offensive at Loos (in France) upon which Kitchener and Asquith 'were gambling'.[29] In October, Milner lent his house for another secret meeting, this time between Lloyd George and the pro-conscription press lord, Northcliffe.[30]

In mid-1916, calculating that a study of the recent past might distract his cabinet from criticism of the present, the vacillating Asquith set up various committees of inquiry into the wartime campaigns that had ended in failure.[31] Via Bonar Law, the Prime Minister invited Milner to chair the high-level inquisition into the Dardanelles campaign. Although it might have enabled him to level scores with Churchill, Milner declined the offer without hesitation. He thought the request curious, as he was already working on a task of huge significance to the war effort – coordinating the work of three ministerial committees responsible for the distribution of coal supplies within Britain and the export of coal to the Allied nations.

In his report to the cabinet, Milner proposed an immediate freezing of coal prices and miners' wages, as well as the setting up of a Royal

Commission to examine the future of the coal industry. Once again, his recommendations were far too radical for coalition politicians, but this time were not dismissed outright. Asquith invited Milner to become the country's new Coal Controller, an offer he did not immediately refuse but sought time to consider. Before Milner could reply, Asquith was no longer Britain's premier.

In late 1916, at the invitation of Haig, Milner spent a strenuous ten days visiting British forces on the Western Front, where the fighting on the Somme had ended at last with huge loss of life and no strategic gain on either side.[32] He also visited the headquarters of the South African Brigade, and the scene of the Battle of Delville Wood, returning home convinced that the German army could not be beaten on the Western Front but much taken 'by the possibility of air power becoming the decisive factor in the war'.[33]

Asquith goes

Throughout 1916, there were attempts by the 'Monday night cabal' to induce either Bonar Law or Lloyd George – the twin props of the coalition – to resign and bring down the Asquith government. The cautious Law proved difficult to persuade, so the cabal concentrated instead on Lloyd George, with whom Milner and Carson were now in regular contact.[34] As Marlowe records, the last days of November were 'full of intrigue', with Lloyd George angling to take control of the war while still leaving Asquith nominally in charge of the government, and Churchill trying to inveigle his way back into government.[35]

In mid-month, Lloyd George had returned from a meeting of Allied military commanders in Paris in a fury: he had wanted to abandon the war of attrition on the Western Front, where the lives of thousands of troops were being wasted, and move the conflict eastwards by providing the Russians with better equipment and more men. But he had been outmanoeuvred by wily generals, led by the Frenchman Joffre who had already decided on a series of Western offensives planned for 1917. Calling the Paris conference 'a complete farce' and inclined at first to resign, the War Secretary decided instead to suggest to Asquith and Bonar Law an alternative scheme for conducting the war.[36]

On 4 December, *The Times* reported that Lloyd George had

proposed the appointment of a small War Council, of which Asquith would not be a member but an adviser, to operate as a super-cabinet and take ultimate responsibility for the direction of the war. The chairman of the council had to be 'tough, resilient and energetic',[37] that is, either Bonar Law or himself. Correctly surmising that his scheming cabinet colleague was colluding with the proprietor of The Times to increase the pressure upon him, the Prime Minister broke off discussions with Lloyd George and Law, both of whom promptly resigned from the government.

Not believing that either dissident could put together an administration of his own, Asquith tendered his resignation to the King, declaring that he and most of the cabinet would not serve under a government led by either Law or Lloyd George. As arranged beforehand, Law declined the King's invitation, and advised the monarch to send for Lloyd George instead. To Asquith's surprise – and fury – most of the leading Unionists in the cabinet agreed to serve under the combative Welsh radical.

Milner, who had played no part in these manoeuvrings, was not enthused by the outcome. While he had got the War Council he wanted, it was not the clear-out of the old guard he had been hoping for. Writing to Violet Cecil, he complained that the 'unexpected firmness of Bonar Law, while it certainly gave the coup de grâce to Squiff, has resulted in the return of the old Unionist tail – A. J. B. – and all the rest of them – so that the new Govt. is really old Unionist hordes, L. G. and and some new men'. He continued: 'So we have not, after all, completely sloughed off the old party skin ... My own disposition is strongly against being in the government at all unless I am part of the Supreme Direction.'[38]

On 8 December, Lloyd George summoned Milner to offer him the post of Minister without Portfolio in a five-man War Cabinet comprising himself, Law, Milner, Curzon and Arthur Henderson, the representative of the Labour Party. This time Milner did not hesitate. At the age of 63, he had been bidden to return to the epicentre of power at a time of great national crisis. He sensed the weight of the burden that would be laid upon him but was resolved to do his duty. At long last, he had triumphed over the politicians and party hacks and brought an end to his bitter decade in exile since returning home from South Africa.[39]

CHAPTER 32

War Cabinet
1916–1918

Temperamentally, the new Prime Minister and his Minister without Portfolio were a study in contrasts. A politician of genius, Lloyd George was impulsive, mercurial and sharp-tongued, while Milner – the anti-politician – was measured and methodical. Yet, as Lloyd George told his newspaper-owning friend, Lord Riddell, the two had much in common: 'Milner and I stand for the very much the same things. He is a poor man and so am I. He does not represent the landed or capitalist classes any more than I do. He is keen on social reform and so am I.'[1] Despite Milner's occasional irritation with the Welshman's 'harum-scarum ways', he was to serve Lloyd George diligently and with exemplary loyalty until well after the war.[2]

The Prime Minister was later to write that Milner 'was much the best all-round brain that the Conservative Party contributed to our councils. He had none of Curzon's brilliancy or Carson's dramatic oratory … he had no flow of words, he had no colour, his voice had no resonance, his delivery was halting … But in constructive power and fertility of suggestion, he surpassed them all … He was at his best when I invited him, as I often did, to a quick talk in the Cabinet room on the perplexing questions which continually rose during the war.'[3]

Lloyd George's purpose in appointing a five-man inner cabinet was to avoid the lack of direct control over war policy that had hampered the Asquith government. The new War Cabinet would be in supreme command of policy-making, able to put the government's directives into immediate effect. The principle of collective responsibility applied to the five-man executive only; no other cabinet minister would be answerable for the government's actions. At the outset, the War Cabinet met two or three times daily, and later at least once every weekday for the rest of the war.[4]

Milner's appointment was met with delight by his friends and admirers. Jingo Joe's son Neville Chamberlain, Lord Mayor of Birmingham and a future prime minister, wrote that 'the knowledge that at last you are in a position where your judgment, determination and organising ability can have scope, gives me more confidence in the ultimate success than any other fact in the change of ministry ... Thank God "wait and see" is over ... and it is not too late to retrieve the situation. With you there, I am sure we will turn over a new leaf.'[5] After sending Milner a telegram saying simply, 'At last thank God', Sir Percy FitzPatrick wrote to Amery expressing his pleasure at the 'long-delayed but most splendid coming-in of our man" ... It looks as if Milner and the Milner men are going to run the Empire.'[6]

Amery himself was recalled from the army to become one of two political secretaries to the War Cabinet, under the eye of a sceptical cabinet secretary, Colonel Maurice Hankey, who suspected at first that the newcomer had been put there to keep an eye on him. Hankey had not known Milner, and instead of encountering a 'rash, impetuous, "damn the consequences"' character, found someone rather slow to make up his mind, but 'very sure' of himself thereafter. Up to then, he had always disliked Milner's politics, but found the new cabinet member an attractive personality, 'and we got on like a house on fire'.[7]

Needing a separate secretariat for himself, Lloyd George turned to Milner for help and, taking his advice, found places for the Round Tablers Astor and Kerr and other close associates of Milner, including John Buchan, who was brought in as Director of Information. The imperial connections of the PM's young secretariat – housed in temporary huts in the garden of 10 Downing Street and known as the 'Garden Suburb' – aroused radical suspicions. The Liberal journal *The Nation*, referred contemptuously to the 'little body of *illuminati* ... travelling empirics of Empire, who came in with Lord Milner and whose spiritual home is fixed somewhere between Balliol and Heidelberg'. 'Reactionary Imperialism', the journal complained 'has seized the whole body of liberal and democratic doctrine and is making off with it under the cover of war.'[8]

At the suggestion of Milner and Kerr, Lloyd George also took the bold decision to invite Dominion leaders and a representative from India to attend cabinet meetings when in London for the Imperial War Conference of March 1917. The War Cabinet itself, it was decided, would deal with British business only, but an Imperial War Cabinet would be brought into all matters relating to the wider conduct of the war. The Imperial War Cabinet duly met intermittently until the armistice.

The Imperial War Cabinet, 22 March 1917. Seated in the front row are (left to right) Arthur Henderson, Milner, Lord Curzon, Bonar Law, Lloyd George, Robert Borden, William Massey and Jan Smuts. (*Wikimedia Commons/Bain News Service*)

On 13 March, Milner gave a welcoming dinner for Jan Smuts, representing Louis Botha, who had felt unable to leave South Africa because of the opposition of Hertzog's anti-war Nationalists. Amery reflected upon the warmth of sentiment that developed over dinner between the two former arch-foes in the Anglo-Boer War. 'It was great fun', he wrote later, 'to see Lord M and Smuts hobnobbing like the best of old friends ... It was nice to see Smuts taking Lord M's arm with the sort of affectionate deference that one would pay to a favourite uncle. *Oom Alfred!*'[9]

Hankey predicted that whatever their past differences, Smuts and Milner would have little trouble in working together.[10] Smuts himself put Milner 'in a different class' to the rest of the War Cabinet in intellect and administrative ability.[11] And it was Milner who persuaded Lloyd George to invite South Africa's Defence Minister to stay on after the Imperial War Conference in order to become the sixth member of Britain's War Cabinet.[12]

Throughout 1917, Milner and Smuts met regularly, either in their respective offices or over dinner with Lloyd George, Curzon, Bonar Law, Hankey and others. A typical entry in Milner's diary in May reads, 'Home very late to dress for dinner at the Savoy, where Selborne took the chair in a great entertainment to Smuts. The latter made an excellent speech about S African problems.' On 6 June, Milner was visited by Rider Haggard and later dined with Smuts at the Savoy. Also present were Lionel Phillips, Brand and Amery.[13]

On 26 December, Milner recorded being met on an inspection visit to France by Captain Botha, son of the South African premier and now an aide to General Haig, who drove him to Transportation HQ. Next day, Botha drove him back through the snow to Boulogne, and the two men discussed 'South African matters' along the way.[14]

At the Imperial War Conference of 1917, a historic agreement was reached – after 12 years of debate – on the vexed question of imperial preference. Each member agreed to give favoured treatment to goods and produce from other parts of the Empire, thus partially fulfilling Milner's aim of forging closer links between the Dominions. An agreement on tariffs, he hoped, might lead after the war to a more permanent organic structure for the Empire.[15]

Ironically, the establishment of the Imperial War Cabinet had exactly the opposite effect, and brought an end to the aspirations of Milner, Curtis and others that the Great War might pave the way to an imperial federation. The Conference resolved instead that the Dominions would henceforward enjoy all existing powers of self-government and be given 'full recognition as autonomous nations of an Imperial Commonwealth'.[16] As Thompson observes, that resolution turned out to be the epitaph for a federal empire, the desire for autonomy that motivated it carried forward into the Statute of Westminster (1931).[17]

Mission to Russia

By the end of 1916, the British Army had sustained over a million casualties, mostly on the Western Front, resulting in a critical manpower problem that made it essential to sustain and bolster the Tsarist Russian forces in Eastern Europe. For if Russia collapsed, the Germans would be able to divert even more divisions to the west. The War Cabinet needed to know urgently what it had sent Kitchener to find out: what munitions did the Russians require, and how would these be supplied and financed? And who better than the cabinet's troubleshooter to lead an Allied mission to establish how to keep Russia in the war? Milner was warned by friends not to undertake an exercise that was both militarily and politically dangerous. But he understood how important the Russian mission was to Lloyd George's strategic outlook and accepted the challenging assignment.

One who thought Milner was quite the wrong choice was Samuel Hoare, then a young MI6 officer (he was Britain's Air Minister during the 1920s) heading an intelligence operation in Petrograd (St Petersburg), the imperial capital. Hoare was on hand when Milner and an assortment of 51 elderly Allied generals and ex-ministers arrived in Murmansk in early 1917. He thought that Milner's 'reserved manner, precise mind and colourless personality' would cut no ice with Tsar Nicholas II, who had disliked the idea of an Allied mission from the start. The Tsarist army and bureaucracy were equally unenthusiastic because the mission would expose the incompetence and weakness of the Russian war effort.[18]

Milner and his mission spent most of February in Russia and found the country's military machine in an abject condition thanks to high casualties, a shortage of munitions, rampant corruption, official ineptitude and a lack of fighting will. The blinkered Tsar was not prepared to discuss his country's internal dynamics with anyone else but his wife. But, according to Hoare, 'poor Milner was from the start completely disoriented. The confusion and corruption were beyond the reach of his well-ordered mind. "The whole thing was exceedingly ill-arranged" was his plaintive understatement of the conditions in which he was supposed to work. The Russians, not having wanted the mission at all, determined to drown it in vodka. Banquet followed banquet, and each in succession made Milner more ill and dejected.'[19]

Britain's Consul General in Moscow, however, formed a far more favourable impression of Milner. The 29-year-old Robert Bruce Lockhart later became famous as a diplomat, a spy and the author of *Memoirs of a British Agent*, an internationally best-selling account of his attempt, in 1918, to sabotage the Bolshevik Revolution. Lockhart wrote that he found Milner extraordinarily well-informed about facts and figures, 'which he seemed to carry in his head without effort'. And 'his nobleness of mind, his entirely natural charm of manner, his lofty idealism, the complete absence of any ambitious scheming or of anything approaching self-conceit in his character, and his broad and vigorous patriotism made him the ideal inspirer of youth … I must have been one of the last young men to worship at his feet and there I have remained … he stands out as an example to the country of the ideal public servant … Among all the so-called great men of the world whom I have met, there has been none who in this respect is fit to hold a candle to Milner.'[20]

In his report to the War Cabinet, Milner estimated the Russians to have sustained more than six million war casualties and feared the army's disarray might have grave political consequences. Nonetheless, he had worked out a scheme for the supply and distribution of war material via a British military mission. 'There is a great deal of exaggeration in the talk of revolution', his report continued, 'and especially about the alleged disloyalty of the army … [But] the danger which threatens Russia is not so much deliberate revolution as chaos. If an upheaval were to take place, its effect on the course of the war might be disastrous.'[21]

Lloyd George expressed initial satisfaction with the report's main conclusions, regarding Milner as a valuable ally in the ongoing fight with his generals. But shortly after the mission's return, revolution broke out, and before long the Tsar – inflexible to the last – abdicated. Russia's new Provisional Government had no further interest in an

Allied victory. In view of the mission's prediction that revolution was only a 'possibility' after the end of the war, Milner and his colleagues came in for much disparagement.

In his *War Memoirs*, written well after Milner's death, Lloyd George wrote critically of the man he had personally chosen, with what Hoare described as 'cynical ruthlessness': 'The head of the British delegation, Lord Milner', the ex-premier wrote, 'was by training and temperament, a bureaucrat. He knew nothing of the populace that trod the streets outside the bureau.' As for the rest of the mission, 'having regard to the warnings which were blaring at them in every direction, it is incomprehensible that they should have been so deaf and blind. It is one more proof of the way in which the most intelligent human judgment has always been misled by the tapestries of an established order without paying sufficient regard to the condition of the walls they hide and on which they hang.'[22] Such scathing judgements, never uttered at the time, are always much easier in hindsight.

Troubleshooting

Early in 1917, the Germans adopted a new policy of unrestricted submarine warfare, in the hope of cutting off the flow of supplies to the Allies from across the Atlantic.[23] The Royal Navy was charged with countering this new menace, and Milner was given the overall responsibility for shipbuilding.[24] As Lloyd George's aide, Lord Addison, recorded, 'Lord Milner, after his return from Russia, was the war minister to whom the difficult and thankless task was allotted of dealing with the many inter-departmental conflicts that ensued, and the most tantalising among them was the conflicting claims of the shipyards for labour, and the army for men. It was a favourite device of the War Cabinet to saddle Milner with tasks of this sort, but ... he was so grandly efficient and had such well-balanced constructive faculties that he stood out as the man for the work.'[25]

The direct outcome of Germany's U-boat onslaught on Allied merchant shipping was America's belated entry into the First World War. The Germans miscalculated that submarine warfare would bring Britain to its knees before American troops could arrive in such numbers as to alter the balance of forces in Europe. But thanks to a new convoy system, which Milner helped devise, the U-boat campaign failed to have the effect the German high command intended.

The activities of German submarines did, however, result in temporary food shortages in Britain, which necessitated an increase in agricultural production and the diversion of 100 000 men to farms. Milner's proposal to increase grain supplies, previously rejected as too drastic, was dusted off and implemented. By now, as Minister without Portfolio, he was in virtual charge of the country's wartime economy, besides having to stimulate, coordinate and settle disputes between the various business chiefs brought in to run the ministries of munitions, shipping, coal, food and national service.[26] The most difficult problem he faced was how to allocate manpower most effectively for Britain's varied wartime requirements.

Milner also served as Lloyd George's bulwark in his continuing battle with the armed services over who was actually in charge of the war – the War Cabinet or the admirals and generals. Worried about the Admiralty's apparent inability to curb German submarine activity, the Prime Minister seized on Milner's suggestion that Carson be invited to join the War Cabinet and take charge of the Royal Navy.[27] On the war front, where Lloyd George had little faith in Haig's dogged and costly tactics, it was Milner who successfully persuaded the War Cabinet to appoint a four-man war policy committee, comprising Lloyd George, Curzon, Smuts and himself, to override the generals where necessary. This committee endorsed the far-reaching decisions that brought about Anglo-French unity at Doullens and the key appointment of General Foch as the Supreme Allied Commander on the Western Front (as described in the Prologue to this book).

On 26 November 1917, Milner recorded in his diary that 'to my great grief, Starr Jameson, after a short illness, passed away today'.[28]

Not long after returning from Doullens, Milner grew anxious at reports from France that another of General Erich Ludendorff's offensives was under way. The German spring offensive began on 21 March 1918. Checked in his effort to divide the Allied armies at Amiens, Ludendorff swung north, breaking through the British line near the Belgian border and advancing steadily along a 40 km front until his capture of the Channel ports seemed inevitable. On 13 April, Haig issued to all British ranks this memorable Order of the Day: 'There is no other course open to us but to fight it out. Every position must be held to the last man; there must be no retirement. With our backs to the wall and believing in the justice of our cause, each one of us must fight to the end.'[29]

Next day, Lloyd George asked Milner to go back to France to see Clemenceau and spend several days at the front monitoring the relationship between Foch and Haig. On Milner's return to London, Lloyd George decided to make a much-overdue change at the War Office, previously in the hands of the ineffective Lord Derby. Instead of taking the post himself, he decided to make Milner Secretary of State for War, the most important office besides his own as prime minister.

War Secretary

For his first three months as War Secretary, Milner spent much of his time in France, conferring with Clemenceau, Foch and Haig on behalf of the War Cabinet, and mediating between the fractious generals. The French thought the British were not pulling their weight sufficiently on the battlefield; the British felt the French were not recognising their contribution to munitions and coal production, and at sea. On 4 June, Hankey recorded gloomily that the Germans were fighting better than the Allies, 'and I cannot exclude the possibility of a disaster'.[30]

An end to the war came quite unexpectedly. Boosted by the addition of 180 000 American troops under General Pershing, the Allies embarked on a series of counteroffensives in early August 1918. The so-called Hundred Days Offensive pushed the Germans back beyond the River Marne and ended their hopes of capturing Paris. A furious battle at Amiens on 8 August, in which Ludendorff lost 30 000 men, took the last resistance out of an exhausted and demoralised German army, whose members began to melt away. By the end of September, the armies of the Central Powers were in retreat on every front.

No one had foreseen that the Royal Navy's blockade of German ports would bring about food shortages and a worsening of price inflation. By October, public order in Germany had begun to break down and there were riots, strikes and a naval mutiny. The Kaiser's army faced stark choices: civil war or a truce and peace negotiations.[31]

By this time, the forces on both sides had been severely affected by the worldwide pandemic known as the 'Spanish flu', which eventually affected one-fifth of the world's population and killed some 50–100 million people. Given their levels of fatigue and stress, lack of cleanliness and unhealthy living conditions, the soldiers fighting in the trenches were particularly vulnerable to the disease.

In late October, the Germans accepted US President Woodrow Wilson's Fourteen Points, a programme for peace based on considerations of justice and democracy rather than reparations. The idealistic American leader insisted that everyone in the world had the right to belong to a sovereign state under the government of their choice. Haggling over the spoils from the empires of the defeated Central Powers, Lloyd George, Clemenceau and other Allied leaders had no intention of complying with such sanctimony.[32] Milner thought privately the American president's intervention was unnecessary, and the harsh damages the Supreme Allied War Council intended to foist on the Germans 'absurd'. The argument over reparations went on until 10 November, when the Kaiser abdicated and fled to the Netherlands, never to return.

At 7 am on 11 November 1918, 'a wonderful day', Milner was woken by a dispatch from the War Office announcing the signature of the armistice by the Germans at 5 am, to come into force that day at the 11th hour of the 11th month of the fifth year of fighting. His diary records: 'At 9 30, I was sent for to Downing St, where I found the PM, Barnes, Bonar Law, Geddes, Smuts and Wilson. We discussed certain doubtful aspects of the situation, such as the attitude of the German navy and arranged for the immediate public announcement of the armistice.'[33]

At 11 am, as the bells of Westminster Abbey rang out and Big Ben struck again after four years' silence, Milner made his way through a huge, celebrating crowd to Buckingham Palace, where he was received by the King and Queen. In the afternoon, he began making preparations for troop demobilisation. At 7.30 pm, he was summoned again to a meeting in Downing Street, at which Lloyd George, Bonar Law and Smuts were present. Later, he noted, 'Lady Edward dined with me. I walked home with her to 69 Grosvenor St through crowded streets of rejoicing people. Very orderly. Walked home again, and sat up working until 2 am.'[34]

On 9 December, Milner recorded the attendees at dinner given for him at Claridge's by 25 of his 'old South African friends'. Lawley was in the chair, and among those present were Lionel Phillips, Brand, Dove, Kerr, Curtis, Williams, Fiddes, Dawson, Sir Abe Bailey, and the only outsider, FS Oliver.[35]

During the final stages of the war, Milner's performance in office had been widely lauded. Northcliffe wrote in a memo to the editorial staff of his newspapers: 'The War Cabinet is feeble enough at present. It needs no more politicians, but one or two men of inflexible determination and untiring energy. Having to deal with the War Cabinet, I know very well that there are only two people in it who do anything, the Prime Minister and Lord Milner.'[36] To his brother, Lord Rothermere, Northcliffe wrote: 'Milner is doing extraordinarily well. He is the best executive member of the War Cabinet.'[37]

Lloyd George, with whom Milner (along with Smuts and Botha) was soon to disagree strongly over the question of German reparations, recalled in his war memoirs his gratitude to 'the Milner of 1917', who 'lent me the constant aid of a mind rich in suggestion, resource and courage'. From the army, Sir Douglas Haig, no admirer of politicians, wrote to Milner to express the hope that he might carry on in office as War Secretary: 'We know what great anxieties and responsibilities you have had as a member of the War Cabinet ... and realise that you must just long for a period of rest and freedom from cares of office. On the other hand, it is so vitally important that there should be no change in the supreme direction of the army in the very critical period which must supervene between a state of war and the time when the army assumes a peace footing. We all therefore venture to hope that you will stay on at the War Office, even at some personal sacrifice.'[38]

CHAPTER 33

Colonial Secretary
1918–1920

Even before the signing of the armistice, however, the relationship between Milner and Lloyd George had begun to deteriorate. The Prime Minister was tired, irritable and anxious about having to face a general election soon after war was over.[1] Two days into the peace, Milner had to plead by letter for a meeting of the cabinet to discuss demobilisation and the future of the army. Understandably, Britain's soldiers were eager to shed their uniforms and return to their families as soon as possible, yet with much of Europe in the grip of anarchy enough men had to be retained in the armed services to help police a world in disarray.[2]

Lloyd George was particularly nervous of labour unrest in the run-up to an election. On 6 December, he lost his temper with his War Secretary, in front of senior civil servants, over the army's slow release of miners from army service. As Gollin comments, it was outrageous for the Prime Minister to berate a colleague of such high standing.[3] Next day, Milner wrote a stiff letter to Lloyd George tendering his resignation, saying he would not accept a position in which he was exposed to 'such vehement charges of dilatoriness and neglect as you made yesterday in the presence of a large number of people, many of them not ministers.'[4] It took all of Lloyd George's fabled charm to persuade Milner to swallow his pride and soldier on in cabinet, which he agreed to do at least until the election was over.

Instead of relying on his stature as the 'Man Who Won the War' to implement the post-war reforms he had promised his supporters, Lloyd George decided that continuing his wartime alliance with Bonar Law was more important than putting re-election at risk. The Tory leader, for his part, defended his decision to continue supporting the

Prime Minister as necessary to ward off the looming threat of 'Bolshe-vist radicalism'.[5] During the election campaign, a disaffected Milner complained privately to Violet Cecil that Lloyd George never stopped 'scheming, cajoling, bribing and wrangling, and trying to rig the press'. He predicted that once re-elected, the PM would 'have to spend all his time in trying to reconcile the inconsistent policies to which he has committed himself'.[6]

The general election of December 1918 – in which women over the age of 30 were able to vote for the first time – became known as the 'coupon' election, because candidates standing for the coalition were given a letter (or coupon) of support, signed by Lloyd George and Bonar Law. When the votes were counted, the Conservatives' 'coupon' candidates had won 379 seats and Lloyd George's Liberals 127, against Labour's 57 seats and the Asquith Liberals' 36.[7] Milner played no part in an election that had reinforced his distaste for populist democracy, with vindictive crowds chanting 'Hang the Kaiser' and demanding that the Germans be 'squeezed until the pips squeak' at the forthcoming peace negotiations.[8]

In the midst of the election campaign, Milner was shocked to hear of the death of Lord Edward Cecil, who had succumbed to the Spanish flu. When the first phase of the Anglo-Boer War was over, Cecil had left South Africa on secondment to Egypt, where he resigned from the army to serve in the Egyptian civil service, eventually filling Milner's old position as financial adviser to the government. Over the years, his marriage to Violet had come under increasing strain because of his lengthy absences from Britain and the couple's widely differing inter-ests. His young, art-loving and socially active wife had been disinclined to make a family home for him and their children in dusty, far-off Cairo.

With divorce unacceptable in post-Victorian society, Edward sol-diered on in lonely exile, missing his family and – after young George's much-lamented death – returning only intermittently to England to stay with Violet and their daughter, Helen, at Great Wigsell, which he disliked for being 'too old, dark and damp'.[9] As the Great War drew to a close, he was struck down with tuberculosis, from which he was recuperating in a Swiss sanatorium when he died from the flu on 13 December 1918. He was only 51 years old.

As Hugh and Mirabel Cecil reflect in their lively account of the Edward-Violet-Alfred relationship, Lord Edward had regarded his life-long imperial service – first as a soldier, then as an administrator – as a duty that no patriotic Englishmen should shirk. Like his father, Lord Salisbury, he believed that British imperialism was justified by the better living standards it brought people and not by high-sounding arguments about 'national destiny or mission'. In this respect, Salisbury father and son were quite different from diehard imperialists such as Joseph Chamberlain, the Maxses, Rudyard Kipling, and most of all, Alfred Milner.[10]

New responsibilities

Worn out by his onerous wartime responsibilities, Milner was not the right man to soothe the impatience of a restive – and occasionally riotous – soldiery, and his last days as War Secretary could not come quickly enough. Having won re-election, Lloyd George made public his new coalition cabinet on 10 January 1919: Winston Churchill was to be War Minister and Milner was offered the position he had turned down 15 years earlier – Secretary of State for the Colonies. He took the job with reluctance, and only on condition that Leo Amery MP would become his parliamentary under-secretary. On learning at the last minute that Lloyd George and Bonar Law intended to renege on that agreement, Milner refused to carry on until Amery was appointed as promised. As Gollin notes, few politicians would have acted as Milner did, and it was standing on principle that led to his being regarded with such devotion by the men who served under him.[11]

The New Year began socially for Milner with 'a huge party' given by Sir Abe and Lady Bailey, at their London home at 38 Bryanston Square. Among those present, he noted in his diary, were 'General and Mrs Botha, Sir Douglas and Lady Haig, Selborne, Kipling, Winston Churchill, the Graaffs, Schreiners and a number of others'.[12]

The new Colonial Secretary's friends and political supporters hoped that, as a peacetime cabinet member at long last, he might bring his influence to bear on the causes closest to their hearts – imperial uni-ty, tariff reform, social upliftment and national service – but important colonial matters had to be given preference. Milner's first five months in office were taken up with frequent trips to Paris, not as a member of the British Empire's five-man delegation to the peace talks but as a support for Foreign Secretary Arthur Balfour.[13] Many Unionists had been dismayed at Milner's omission from the official team in France, which meant that negotiations over German reparations would be conducted almost exclusively by the more hard-line Lloyd George and Balfour.

Despite complaining to his diary about not being able to make out clearly 'what I am supposed to be here for',[14] Milner played a notable part in the proceedings in Paris. Before the peace conference, he had urged publicly that while Germany should be prevented from future war-making, its people should not be punished by the imposition of swingeing economic sanctions. His reason was not – as unkind critics suggested – his own part-German ancestry but because, like Smuts and Churchill, he was fearful of the spectre of Bolshevism (communism) and what its rapid advance might mean for a ravaged Europe, as well as for the Empire.

Milner's views on German reparations brought him furious opposition from an unexpected quarter – the presses of his erstwhile supporter, Lord Northcliffe. A tough-minded outsider who had clawed his way up to the commanding heights of the newspaper industry, Northcliffe was determined that Britain should enforce a 'hard peace' in Paris and make the German people foot the bill for war damage. His populist *Evening News* wrote disapprovingly of Milner: 'His German origin is not forgotten, and the man in the street declares that he is acting as a Prussian.'[15]

Though he admired Milner's contribution to the War Cabinet, Northcliffe was also annoyed by the influence that members of the 'Monday night cabal', such as FS Oliver and rival newspaper owner Waldorf Astor, exerted over the editor of his flagship daily, *The Times*. Milner often exploited his friendship with Geoffrey Robinson (now Dawson) and Northcliffe resented any tampering with the allegiance of his editor.[16]

When another newspaper in Northcliffe's stable attacked Milner over his alleged plans for 'peace with the Hohenzollerns', Dawson had had enough of his overbearing proprietor – and promptly resigned. After Northcliffe's death in 1922, and the purchase of *The Times* by the

Astor family, Dawson was to return as editor, fortified this time with a memorandum defining his status and responsibilities, drawn up jointly by himself and his mentor, Milner.[17]

Milner's other role at the Paris Peace Conference, which he regarded as a 'circus', was to help settle the question of mandates over the German colonial territories captured by the Allies during the war. In his Fourteen Points, the basis of the negotiations in Paris, President Wilson had recommended that ethnic self-determination be adopted as a guiding principle, and endorsed a system of trusteeship over former German possessions, devised by Smuts among others, exercised under the auspices of a League of Nations. To Milner's disgust, yet another unseemly 'scramble for Africa' broke out in Paris, with Britain, France, Belgium, Australia, New Zealand, Japan and South Africa all laying claim to one of three classes of mandates. Instead of the Great War being a war to end wars, Milner complained, it was becoming 'a Peace to end Peace'.[18]

On 23 March 1919, Milner celebrated his 65th birthday, reflecting gloomily, 'A year ago, we were in the middle of the great German offensive. Now there is "Peace". But I am not sure the outlook for this country and the world is not even blacker today than it was then.'[19] At Versailles he often crossed swords with his (and Violet's) old friend Clemenceau, survivor of an assassin's attack during the Peace Conference and utterly determined to ensure that Germany would never again be able to invade or devastate his homeland.

The French leader complained that dealing with Milner over reparations – and the future of Syria – was extremely difficult: 'If he does not agree with you, he closes his eyes like a lizard, and you can do nothing with him.' Their differences in Paris, however, were not to affect their friendship. When the tensions of 1919 had died down, the sensitive Clemenceau wrote affectionately of Milner's 'brilliant intellect, crowned with high culture, extreme gentleness and extreme firmness ... who, on a night journey from London to Versailles, at one of our most trying moments, paused to speak of the loveliness of the moonlight and the young spring grass.'[20]

Frequently travelling to and from Paris in the company of Smuts and Botha, with whom his relations were now extremely cordial, Milner supported South Africa's claim to a 'C' mandate over the former German South West Africa, a territory regarded as not yet ready for independence. He took care to ensure that Britain was given responsibility for ex-German East Africa, to be brought into the Empire as Tanganyika, as well as for part of Togoland and a sliver of the Cameroons.

At this time, Milner took what appears to be his first-ever air flight, 'in the cabin of a DH-4', destined for Paris: 'We had a very fine and rapid flight – lovely over the channel – and alighted … just beyond Versailles. The only discomfort I felt … is a little deafness, due to the terrific noise of the machines. I was stone deaf when I landed, and tho' gradually recovering am still rather deaf with my left ear.'[21]

On 17 May and 20 May, Milner recorded a 'much perturbed' Smuts coming to see him to discuss the harshness of the peace terms to be imposed on Germany.[22] As a member of the British cabinet, the Colonial Secretary found himself in disagreement with Lloyd George but at one with the South Africans, and also with John Maynard Keynes and Churchill, in arguing – as Smuts put it – for 'a fair and generous peace, a peace of understanding which might be lasting and which would heal the dreadful wounds the war had caused'.[23] The dissenters could only watch in dismay, however, as Wilson was outmanoeuvred by the other Allied leaders and hopes for a humane post-war settlement gave way to a vindictive peace.

According to Sir Percy FitzPatrick, it was in the Hall of Mirrors at Versailles that the famous scene took place when Louis Botha rose to his feet, put his hand on Milner's shoulder, and reminded delegates that on the same day (1 June) 17 years earlier, Britain had imposed terms on his defeated people that were hard but generous, enabling his Boers to accept peace terms and rebuild their shattered country.[24] (Sir John Evelyn Wrench, on the other hand, suggests that Botha's oft-quoted remarks were made at a meeting of the British Empire Delegation in Paris.[25]) Unfortunately, in the light of subsequent history, so great was the pressure on British and French leaders for revenge that Botha's (and Milner's) pleas at Versailles for magnanimity fell on deaf ears and went unheeded by the assembly.

The latter pair were to disagree, however, over the role the Empire should play in future international conflicts. Botha had extracted from

Lloyd George a promise that the Dominions would not be obliged to ratify any British undertaking to come to France's aid in a future European conflict. Milner was strongly opposed to the notion of Dominion neutrality, and wrote to Lloyd George to remind him any such agreement would be 'incompatible with the existence of the British Empire as a political unit'.[26]

In July, Milner recorded his attendance at the funeral in Golders Green, London, of the visiting WP Schreiner, noting that there was a large attendance, including Botha, Smuts and many other South Africans. Little over a month later, the Colonial Office rang him 'with the bad news of the death of General Botha', shortly after his return home. 'It may be the beginning of serious trouble in S Africa', he noted in his diary.[27]

Back to Egypt

After the signing of the Treaty at Versailles on 28 June 1919, Colonial Secretary Milner was free to concentrate on one of three matters (besides Ireland and India) pressing upon the Lloyd George government: the troublesome post-war situation in Egypt, a country Milner knew well from his past service there and regular visits on business. Although legally still part of the Ottoman Empire at the end of the war, Egypt was effectively an imperial possession. Yet America's insistence on applying the principle of self-determination indicated that British control over the protectorate could not be maintained indefinitely.[28]

Shortly after Versailles, Milner spent almost three months in Egypt at the head of a mission charged with making recommendations as to the future relationship between the protectorate and Britain.[29] His difficulty was that most Egyptians wished to see an end to British rule, and neither of the opposing nationalist leaders, Saad Zaghlul or Adly Yeghan, would recognise the Milner delegation – hence the decision to move negotiations from Cairo to London.

After painstaking 'unofficial' talks with the two men, Milner proposed an ingenious formula that would give greater independence to Egypt but also preserve Britain's interests in an area of the world of 'vital importance to our Imperial system'.[30] To a deeply divided cabinet, he recommended a pact between the two countries that would give Egypt greater independence over its own affairs in return for allowing Britain to guide its foreign relations and maintain a military presence in the country.[31]

Initially, Milner's proposal for a treaty relationship with a protectorate was too much for 'old guard' Tories in the cabinet such as Foreign Secretary Curzon to stomach, but after Milner had retired in 1922, his plan was eventually adopted and imposed unilaterally. The treaty with Egypt set the pattern for Britain's gradual retreat from the Middle East over the next three decades. Milner's biographer Marlowe comments on the irony of the arch-exponent of an assertive imperialism in 1899 being the first to sound the signal for the retreat from Empire 20 years later.[32] Milner had learnt some lessons over the years, however, and his formula enabled Egypt to be kept under imperial control for the next quarter century and provide a strategically vital base for Allied operations in the Middle East during the Second World War.

On 1 January 1920, Milner wrote to 'My dear Smuts' from Cairo to say that not a week had passed since he had left England without 'my realising the great need of a closer touch between you and us than telegrams can supply'. The Colonial Secretary was concerned that the changes wrought by war and the peace treaties had left relations in the Empire 'at sixes and sevens'. He felt that the only basis on which the connection between Britain and the self-governing Dominions could be maintained was as 'a union of equals'.

'As soon as we had dispersed [after the Imperial Conference and the British delegation in Paris]', Milner wrote, 'difficulties had arisen which were almost hopeless to try and resolve by correspondence between five different governments at all ends of the earth, even if each one of them was not preoccupied with the solution of its own domestic problems.' He went on to urge the holding of another imperial conference, preferably in the coming year, to deal with issues including the 'tangle' over legislative jurisdiction in respect of the mandated territories.[33]

Milner also asked Smuts for his opinion about a new governor general for South Africa to replace the outgoing Sydney Buxton: 'The ideal seems to be a man of the world, of high social position, with some experience of public affairs who would try … to use his influence quietly … to get over such difficulties as must from time to time arise

between S Africa and other parts of the Empire – such as the Indian Question, as well as in the local relations of the Union with the
Native Territories.' 'Believe me, my dear Smuts, the letter ended, 'with
the heartiest good wishes for your prosperity and success in the New
Year. Yours very sincerely, Milner.'[34]

In due course, the man chosen to be South Africa's third governor general was Prince Arthur of Connaught, a military officer and
grandson of Queen Victoria.

Time to go

Milner's onerous responsibilities as Colonial Secretary, and long
stretches away from home, would have taxed the energies of a much
younger and healthier man.[35] Soon after returning from Egypt, he
decided the time had come to consider retirement. Although still
loyal to Lloyd George, his desire to serve in cabinet was no longer
there. Having always regarded himself as 'a man for a crisis', and with
private matters now requiring his attention, he saw no need to carry on
in office indefinitely and gave the Prime Minister advance notice of his
intention to step down at the year-end.[36]

Until then, he had several weighty colonial issues to occupy him:
the future of Palestine; post-war emigration schemes from Britain to
far-off imperial outposts; plans for indigenous education in the colonies; and the establishment, in London, of an Institute for the Study of
Tropical Diseases; as well as the development of agriculture and railways in every corner of the Empire. Most of his last weeks as Colonial
Secretary were spent preparing for the next Imperial Conference, held
in the summer of 1921, but by the time the Dominion leaders gathered
in London for their get-together, Milner had already returned his seals
of office to the King.

At the end of 1920, the Cabinet had taken a decision – over Milner's
objections – to establish a Middle Eastern department in the Colonial
Office to supervise the mandates over Iraq, Palestine and Transjordan.
Asked by the Prime Minister to stay on to implement an arrangement
of which he disapproved, Milner put his foot down and insisted instead
on being given a date for his release. Realising he could procrastinate
no longer, on 14 February 1921 Lloyd George announced Milner's

resignation as Colonial Secretary and his replacement, once again, by Winston Churchill. Before long, Curzon was complaining to Milner that Churchill was 'already spreading his wings over the entire universe'.[37]

On 24 February, the Prime Minister wrote to Milner saying he had been asked by members of the cabinet to express their 'huge appreciation' for his counsel and assistance during the past four years: 'They earnestly hope that the services you have given so unstintingly and so selflessly will not be lost to the Empire and that, after a rest, you will be able to devote time and energy to public affairs for many years to come.'

'May I also say personally', Lloyd George added, 'how much I regret your resignation. I could not have had a more hard-working, a wiser or a stauncher colleague during the War Cabinet days ... They were great days to have lived through and I shall never forget your loyal and most efficient cooperation which contributed enormously to the victory of the Allies.'[38]

The retiring Milner received a shoal of letters regretting his departure from public office and expressing the hope that he might one day return. Curzon wrote to say that he would deeply deplore Milner's absence from the Cabinet and the House of Lords, while from South Africa Smuts cabled that Milner's gifts were indispensable to the coming discussion of international relations.[39] In recognition of his service to the nation, Milner received from King George V one of the highest honours the Crown could bestow – the Order of the Garter, never given to more than 25 people at any one time.

CHAPTER 34

A Busy Retirement

1921–1925

On 26 February 1921, only a few days into retirement, Milner put an end to his long-standing reputation as one of London's most eligible bachelors by marrying Lady Violet Cecil. He was almost 67, and she, a widow for the past two years, was nearly 50. During her unhappy marriage to Edward Cecil, Milner's new wife had been his close friend, staunch political supporter and regular confidante for more than 20 years. As O'Brien records, their admiration for one another, shared tastes, mutual friends and interests in politics and economics, art and travel, and houses and gardens had been the foundation of their long relationship.[1]

Although both were non-believers, Lord and the new Lady Milner were married at St James's Church, Paddington, in the presence of a handful of friends. Keeping their intentions secret, the couple left unobtrusively by train from Charing Cross to Dover for a honeymoon in France, after sending a brief notification of their marriage to the Press Association. Milner was in buoyant mood, telling a friend, the Standard Bank's Lewis Michel, that he was proud of having brought off his nuptials so successfully, 'in spite of the constant prying of the Press'.[2] He had failed, he admitted, to prevent 'all the Sunday papers giving a more or less sensational account of our "secret wedding"'.[3]

After a few carefree weeks in the French countryside, and some time in Paris, where he and Violet called on the recently retired Clemenceau, Milner returned to London and was as busy as ever again.[4] He resumed most of the directorships he had laid down upon entering government and became chairman of Rio Tinto, whose mining activities involved frequent negotiations in Spain. He also maintained his interest in public affairs by making an occasional speech in the House of Lords. He told a friend he was 'back again and fit for anything'[5] but declined invitations to join the new government even though remaining keenly interested in political developments, particularly in the imperial and economic spheres.[6]

Now the last of the original Rhodes trustees – the only honorary post he retained while in the cabinet – Milner was able to devote more time to the affairs of the Trust. Following his breach with Northcliffe, Geoffrey Dawson had temporarily become its secretary, as well as editor of *The Round Table* (and a director of Consolidated Gold Fields).[7] Milner arranged a payment of £2 500 to keep *The Round Table* in print,[8] but by this time the journal had lost some of its *raison d'être* because of the growing independence of the Dominions and enthusiasm for the new League of Nations.

Loyal friends from his South African days such as FitzPatrick still came to see him, as did Rudyard Kipling. The three men would talk of launching a new drive for tariff reform and lamented, as always, the iniquities of Boer nationalism and the decline of Britain's imperial influence. Milner and his wife took up the challenge of raising funds for the 1820 Memorial Settlers League in South Africa, the forerunner of the present-day Grahamstown Foundation.[9]

Though not a participant in the Imperial Conference of 1921 that he had helped organise, Milner met all the visiting Dominion prime ministers at various dinners and ceremonial functions during the gathering and was a guest at 'one of Sir Abe Bailey's immense parties'.[10] Presided over by Lloyd George, the Conference went on for almost five weeks behind closed doors and produced little of substance other than an agreement that Britain would not renew its alliance with Japan. At more than one meeting of the Moot, members of the Round Table were given an insider's account of the proceedings, which must have failed to excite them. In a farewell message to Milner on leaving for home, Smuts reported that the Conference 'had avoided making mistakes, even where no positive work was done'.[11]

In March-April 1922, Milner and his wife paid a two-month private visit to Palestine, Syria and Transjordan, after stopping off in Paris to see Clemenceau again. They disembarked briefly in Egypt, where Violet noted with pride that 'the whole of Cairo appears to be flocking to meet Alfred at Port Said'.[12] As was his habit, Milner kept a detailed diary of the trip, recording meetings with deputations from the Zionists and the anti-Zionist Christian-Muslim League, both aware that as a member of the Imperial War Cabinet in 1917, their visitor had been party to the drafting of the Balfour Declaration, in which the British promised to support the creation of a Jewish national home in Palestine. Amery, his aide at the time, had helped with the actual wording of the Declaration.

Though revelling in the beauty of the countryside, Milner left the Holy Land – then home to some 80 000 Jews, mostly from Eastern Europe – thoroughly fed up with both Zionists and Arabs. 'I have no doubt', he noted, 'that the chief cause of all the fuss is the tactlessness with which some of the Zionists have boosted their cause and which has frightened the Arabs. But the latter are crying out before they are hurt, and their ceaseless denunciation of the Balfour Declaration and the Mandate are really not denunciations of what either the Declaration or the Mandate really contain, but of what the Zionists and the Arabs themselves have chosen to read into them.'[13]

A year later, in a House of Lords debate initiated by an opponent of a Jewish homeland, Milner rose vigorously to defend the Balfour Declaration at a time when the government was harbouring doubts about it. Acknowledging his share of responsibility for the document, he insisted that its terms were not incompatible with pledges given to the Arabs. There was room in Palestine for considerable Jewish immigration, he averred, 'without bringing the smallest prejudice to the existing Arab population: on the contrary, the Arabs will, in many respects, benefit from it'.[14]

In November 1922, a public outcry over the sale of honours by Lloyd George and a diplomatic defeat for his coalition over Turkish policy precipitated yet another general election in Britain. In 'a land fit for heroes', as the Prime Minister had been proudly asserting, too many heroes were out of work. Milner did not believe that Lloyd George had lost any of his political agility, but 'where the devil he'll spring next is more unpredictable than ever'. He confessed that although he 'still loved Lloyd George for what he did in 1916–18, I have hated almost everything he has done since, except his masterly handling of last year's Dominion Prime Ministers' Conference.'[15]

Led by an ailing Bonar Law, the Conservatives campaigned as a separate party in 1922, and romped to victory at the poll, their tally of 344 seats giving them an absolute majority of 88 seats over all the other parties combined. For the first time, Labour became the official opposition in Parliament by winning 142 seats. The Liberals, split down the middle between supporters of Lloyd George and Asquith, came third with 115 seats, marking the beginning of the Liberal Party's precipitous decline as a force in British politics.

Asquith's tart-tongued daughter, Violet Bonham Carter, unkindly described the election as a contest between a man with sleeping sickness (Bonar Law) and one with St Vitus's Dance (Lloyd George). The unfortunate Law was to serve as premier for only seven months, the shortest term in British history, before falling victim to cancer. He was succeeded not by Milner's friend Lord Curzon, as everyone including Curzon himself, expected, but by Stanley Baldwin, son of a prosperous Worcestershire ironmonger, the man who had precipitated the Tory revolt against Lloyd George's coalition.[16]

As if he did not have enough on his plate, Milner returned, in early 1923, to his old occupation of journalism. Having refused overtures to return to politics and serve in the new Tory cabinet, he still felt a need to impress his views upon a wide audience, especially on what he considered were the government's misguided economic priorities.[17] In a series of five essays for Waldorf Astor's Sunday newspaper, *The Observer*, Milner argued that although saddled with an enormous war debt, the United Kingdom was not as poor as it kept claiming: the watchword for economic recovery ought to be expansion rather than austerity. There were so many opportunities, and such crying need in Britain and the Empire, that it was time for the evolution of a new political creed.[18]

These and more of his well-received opinion pieces were published in book form, under the title *Questions of the Hour*, which went into a reprint two years later. Milner's final excursion into politics was to accept an invitation from Baldwin to chair a committee on tariff reform. Before the committee could complete its work, however, the Conservative government had fallen from power.

Return to South Africa

In March 1924, Milner turned 70, a milestone he celebrated quietly at Sturry Court while his wife successfully fended off newspaper reporters.[19] On 'a black day' in June, he learnt with concern of Smuts's election defeat in South Africa at the hands of a Nationalist-Labour coalition headed by General JBM Hertzog. In November, despite some misgivings about their reception by the new government, the Milner couple embarked on the *Walmer Castle* for a long-planned private return to the Union, after an absence, in his case, of almost two decades. During the voyage, Milner was pleased to hear that his disciple Amery had become Britain's Colonial Secretary, though less pleased at the news that Churchill was now Chancellor of the Exchequer.[20]

In a note in his diary at the beginning of the trip, Milner explained that he intended to record his South African experiences more thoroughly in a different journal. But he subsequently wrote that he had abandoned his intention of keeping a 'special diary' of the visit, as he had been unable to find the time. We are thus left with his usual terse account of the events of each day, with only an occasional reflection on the people he encountered. Violet's diaries, however, are more forthcoming.

The Milners arrived in Cape Town on 17 November 1924, to be met by a flood of letters and telegrams, and a warm onboard welcome from old friends, for a brief stay at the Mount Nelson Hotel.[21] That night the couple were given a welcoming dinner by the former Unionist leader, Sir Thomas Smartt, attended by some 70 people, at which Milner noted that his reception had been 'extremely cordial'.[22] Next day, the visitors were driven along the western shore of the Cape Peninsula: 'It was a lovely day, and the views all along the road – about 22 miles – are unequalled by any in the world.' The couple were also shown over the impressive new memorial to Rhodes on the mountainside above Groote Schuur, driven down to the sea at Muizenberg, not far from Rhodes's cottage, and given a dinner by the Rose Inneses.[23]

From Cape Town, a special train laid on by the Hertzog government took the Milners to Kimberley, to be the guests of De Beers. Two years earlier, Milner had turned down an offer to become chairman of the famous diamond company. After a few days in Kimberley, the couple were forced by the extreme heat to cancel their proposed visit to Rhodesia. 'It is too late in the year and 3 weeks hard travelling would be too much for V. This involves a complete reconstruction of all our plans', Milner recorded.[24] Violet noted that it was 'a great upset. I had never seen Rhodesia and A[lfred] had never seen the Falls.'[25]

Moving to the Highveld, the Milners were met in Johannesburg by Patrick Duncan and friends, and taken to see his old home at Sunnyside – now a hostel for girls from nearby Roedean School. They were shown the impressive new barrage across the Vaal River at Vereeniging and paid visits to the farms of British settlers in the Transvaal. Headlam records Milner's terse reflection: 'We have made this country for the Boers. They could never have done it for themselves.'[26]

After a meeting with Colonel Cresswell, Minister of Labour in the Hertzog government, Violet noted tartly: 'He has split the English vote and is as responsible as any individual can be for the continued Dutch government South Africa has. He has been very coy about coming to see Alfred – had made excuses and the like. But when ordered by Government House, he turned up.'[27]

During a stay with the Governor General, the Earl of Athlone, in Pretoria, the Milners were shown over the 'magnificent' new Union Buildings, 'one of [Herbert] Baker's best works'.[28] At lunch, they met Prime Minister Hertzog, 'who was rather embarrassed at first meeting me, but quite civil', Milner noted.[29] (Their last meeting had been during the peace negotiations at Melrose House in 1903.) Violet wrote in her diary: 'I was told afterwards that when he [Hertzog] was first asked to meet us, he replied that he had nothing to say to Alfred and did not wish to see him. To which the Governor General replied with some asperity that he had been asked to lunch and was expected to come.'[30]

Lunch with the Smutses at the family farm at Irene, outside Pretoria, was more convivial. Milner observed that Smuts lived 'like a yeoman farmer, in a very simple style, tho' in perfect comfort … The conversation was interesting, and we were sorry to leave sometime after 3.'[31] Violet's account of the occasion, published almost 30 years later, was more enlightening.

At the lunch, she recorded: 'Alfred and G. Smuts talked high politics – European – I could see that Smuts was hungry and thirsty for talk about the great affairs he had been so closely concerned with during the war and about which no one in SA knows anything. I was very anxious that they should have a time together, so after the lunch I engaged Mrs Smuts and as many others as I could talk to while A[lfred] and Smuts went at it hammer and tongs on the sofa in the sitting room. They had so much to ask and hear about each other's continents.

'I had regretfully to tear Alfred away ... otherwise we should have stayed for hours – we greatly liked our time at the Smuts' and were only very sorry we could not go and stay there for the weekend as they suggested. Smuts is very impressive in his own house. He is an excellent host. Mrs Smuts said several times we must take them as we found them ... Smuts is much too great a gentleman even to think of making a difference between one set of people and another. He gives you his whole attention ... and is immensely quick to know what is in your mind.'[32] (See also Afterword.)

From the Transvaal, a slow train journey took the visitors to Bloemfontein for two nights, via the British farming outpost at Westminster, named after Bendor, where dozens of 'Milner Settlers' came from near and far to greet him. On Boxing Day, the Milners reached Ladysmith, in Natal, where he visited the Natal battlefields once more, and climbed Spioenkop. By the time the couple reached Durban, however, Milner was feeling far from well, but attended a mayoral reception nonetheless and undertook a full programme of engagements.[33]

Throughout Natal, the Transkei and the eastern Cape, the warmth of the Milners' reception increased the further they travelled: 'The British people in these parts, not being outnumbered by the Dutch, were much more demonstrative in their welcome and our visit was much more of a public event than in other parts of the country.'[34] In Grahamstown, Milner showed much interest in the boys' private school, St Andrew's College, and the future Rhodes University College.[35]

By late January, the Milners were back in the western Cape for another fortnight, staying at the Muizenberg home of Sir Abe Bailey, where the social pace, Milner recorded, 'grew if possible more fast and furious as we neared the end.'[36] After a drive to Cape Point, a climb up the slopes of Table Mountain and many encounters with old friends, the couple attended the formal opening of Parliament by the Earl of

Athlone. Every government speaker, Milner noted, made a point of speaking in Afrikaans, though the Speaker ensured the proceedings were conducted in both official languages:[37] 'It was noticeable that Boers of the old type, the big-bearded burghers … who were so conspicuous in the Cape Parliament of old days, were little in evidence. Their places have been taken by men of such a different type (lawyers etc) … a much more common-place crowd.'[38]

Milner was careful not to express any criticism of the Hertzog government in public but confided to the likes of Patrick Duncan that he was 'very depressed' by the political situation he found: 'Thinks the racial [Afrikaner-English] division is accentuated and that the Govt is thoroughly untrustworthy as far as their relations to the Empire are concerned.'[39] Sceptical as always of bilingual education, he noted that 'the British race' were having difficulty in getting a decent education in state schools, 'where even the English language was no longer being taught properly.'[40] He continued: 'In schools in which the medium of instruction is Dutch, the teachers are in many cases violent nationalists and more concerned to imbue their pupils with racial prejudice than to make them good scholars,' and the history being taught in South African schools was 'a highly coloured and very anti-British version of S African history.'[41]

Two days before the Milners sailed for home on 21 February 1925 aboard the passenger liner *Saxon*, Smuts travelled to Cape Town for a last long talk to Milner. Smuts was relieved that Milner's visit had gone off without mishap. 'Old enemies combined with old friends to make the tour agreeable', he wrote later.[42] As he had done 20 years earlier, he sent Milner another farewell message to be read on the boat: 'Bon voyage to you and Lady Milner. I trust your visit has been as agreeable to you as it has been helpful and encouraging to your friends.'[43]

As the ship left Table Bay 'on the most lovely afternoon conceivable', Milner recorded, 'we watched the beautiful mountain landscape till it was lost to sight, wondering whether we should ever see it again.'[44]

Last lap

Arriving home on 2 March, after a brief stop at Madeira, a travel-weary Milner plunged immediately into his usual busy round of private and public engagements. Geoffrey Dawson thought his mentor looked 'rather aged', as did Rudyard Kipling.[45] Soon after returning, Milner was saddened by the news that his old friend and colleague, Curzon, five years his junior, had died.

On 24 March 1925, he celebrated his 71st birthday working quietly at home, and a few days later underwent a thorough medical examination to be told he had 'nothing particularly wrong' with him.[46] Unbeknown to the doctor, his patient had picked up encephalitis lethargica (cerebral malaria or 'sleeping sickness') while in South Africa, for which there was no effective remedy.

Curzon's death had left vacant the chancellorship of Oxford University, and Milner was invited to put his name forward as his successor. After initially declining, telling an old friend he was determined not to stand, since 'though physically quite strong and well, my mind is ... *more easily tireable*', he was persuaded to change his mind and become a candidate.[47]

On 12 May, Oxford University announced that, in default of other nominations, 'the Rt Hon Viscount Milner, MA (Hon.) DCL, KG, GCB, GC, MG was deemed to be duly elected as Chancellor'.[48] Sadly for both Oxford and Milner himself, it was not to be. A week earlier, the Chancellor-designate had lapsed into semi-consciousness. At 11.30 am on 13 May, one day after the university's announcement, Milner died peacefully at Sturry Court, in the presence of Violet and her married daughter, Helen.

The next day, Prime Minister Stanley Baldwin used the occasion of a speech at Oxford to extol the virtues of public service, holding up Lord Milner as a prime example of dedication and devotion to the nation.[49] *The Times* led the tributes to Milner in the mainstream British newspapers, with Geoffrey Dawson commenting that when 'the story comes to be fully written, it may be found that nothing even in the South African chapter has left a more decisive mark on history than Lord Milner's work at Doullens and in Downing Street'.[50] The French press observed that Milner's passing had stirred a deep chord in the hearts of the French people, 'who recognise his signal service to the Allied cause during the Great War'.[51] From Cape Town, *The Scotsman* reported that General Smuts had paid 'a handsome tribute' to the memory of Lord Milner, and was immensely grateful that he had visited South Africa to see how the old wounds had healed, and the great material progress achieved'.[52] Afrikaner-Nationalist press comment in South Africa, understandably, was far less friendly.

On 16 May, Milner's funeral service was held in Canterbury Cathedral, his coffin draped in the Union Jack. Conducted by the Archbishop of Canterbury, the formal service was followed by a private burial in the presence of Violet's relatives and a few intimate friends, including the Kiplings and Amerys, in the Maxse family's graveyard in the village of Salehurst, near Great Wigsell. Two days later, Milner was honoured by a memorial service in Westminster Abbey, attended by the Prime Minister and his full cabinet. Simultaneous services were held at New College, Oxford, and at St George's Cathedral in Cape Town.

Credo

Always in the habit of putting his thoughts on paper, shortly before he died, Milner had written a note for posterity, headed 'Key to My Position'. Discovered by Violet among his papers, she arranged with Dawson for its publication in *The Times* of 27 July 1925. Milner's 'Credo' reads in part:

> I feel myself a citizen of the Empire. Canada is my country, Australia is my country, New Zealand is my country, South Africa is my country, as much as Surrey or Yorkshire ... I am a Nationalist and not a Cosmopolitan ... I am a British (Indeed primarily an English) Nationalist. If I am also an Imperialist, it is because the destiny of the English race, owing to its insular position and long supremacy at sea, has been to strike fresh roots in distant parts of the world. My patriotism knows no geographical but only racial limits. I am an Imperialist and not a Little Englander, because I am a British Race Patriot ... It is not the soil of England, dear as it is to me, which is essential to arouse my patriotism, but the speech, the tradition, the spiritual heritage, the principles, the aspirations of the British race. They do not cease to be mine because they are transplanted ...
>
> The time cannot be far distant when this practical aspect of

Imperial unity will become apparent to everybody. The work
of British Imperialists during my lifetime has been to hold the
fort, to keep alive the sentiments which for so long appealed
only to the far-seeing few … [until they] become the accepted
faith of the whole nation.[53]

When he penned these words, Milner was not to know that only
a decade later, Adolf Hitler would bring sinister new meaning to any
notion of a 'master race' and the concept of 'racial patriotism'.

CHAPTER 35

Summing Up

'I never knew a man who had better motives for all the trouble he caused.'
Alden Pyle, in *The Quiet American*[1]

In a message of condolence to Violet Milner on her husband's death, King George V lamented the loss of a man who had devoted his whole life, in peace and war, to the cause of the British Empire. Milner's work at home and overseas, the King predicted, would be gratefully remembered forever. Alas for Empire loyalists, the monarch was mistaken: the Treaty of Versailles and the new League of Nations had put paid to Milner's pipe dream of an integrated, worldwide federation of English speakers under Britannia's rule. And in South Africa, the country with which he was most closely associated in the public mind, Milner is remembered today without much gratitude or appreciation.

It is difficult for a modern audience to appreciate that little over a century ago, even well-intentioned idealists regarded war as the appropriate means of establishing political order and making material progress. War-making was an intrinsic part of the international system and the normal way in which a nation enhanced its power and prestige. It required, however, popular support and the willingness of men and women to lay down their lives in the cause of flag and country. As Margaret MacMillan explains, among European countries, 'an exaggerated respect for their own militaries and the widespread influence of social Darwinism encouraged a belief that war was a noble and necessary part of a nation's struggle for survival'.[2] The rush for land was defended in Darwinian terms: only the fittest and most adaptable of the Great Powers would survive and grow stronger, at the expense of the enfeebled.[3] Central to the task of empire-building, from which men like Milner (and Rhodes) insisted that all mankind would benefit, was the use of force as a natural, inevitable process, although one that might also impose a moral duty.

In fomenting war in South Africa, Milner revealed, not for the first time, the dualism in his character, as well as his genius for arousing passions and attracting controversy. On his retirement as High Commissioner in 1905, Britain's leading Liberal newspaper, the *Daily News*, editorialised that 'Lord Milner stands for everything this country abhors … It is a happy omen that that sinister rule is over … South Africa has proved the graveyard of his, as of so many other reputations.'[4] The political journal *The Outlook*, by contrast, claimed that in Milner, Britain had brought forth someone who, 'in intellectual strength and moral force had no equal among the politicians of his generation.'[5] These qualities had saved the Empire in South Africa. As AM Gollin rightly observed, where Milner is concerned, there exists no middle ground: many people thought his beliefs, methods and policies were 'harsh, brutal and un-English', yet for others 'these same designs had the simplicity and straightforwardness of genius'.[6]

John Buchan was one who concluded, rightly, that Milner was the wrong man to be sent to South Africa to undo the damage caused by Rhodes and the Jameson Raid. For all his administrative excellence, the situation required someone flexible and broadminded, not a man described as 'that rare phenomenon' – a brilliant Englishman 'with a doctrinaire cast of mind',[7] whose rigid opinions were derived from an authoritarian temperament and a disinclination to compromise.[8] In Milner and his bête noire, Paul Kruger, two hedgehogs came face to face in South Africa, each knowing one big thing: Milner, that war with the Transvaal was necessary to advance British interests; Kruger, that any concession to Milner would mean the loss of republican independence. The unwillingness of either man to yield to the other was to cost both their countries dearly in blood and treasure.

Milner had not come to South Africa with the express purpose of waging war, but the prospect was never far from his mind. After Bloemfontein, he worked towards a 'great day of reckoning', when the Transvaal would be forced to give in to his demands or face the consequences. Yet he was not solely responsible for the armed conflict that ensued. To appropriate Iain Smith's cooking metaphor, Milner stirred the pot, but Chamberlain, the Uitlanders, the Transvaal government and the mining industry all helped to supply the ingredients. When all was said and done, the ultimate decision to wage war was neither Milner's nor Chamberlain's but that of Lord Salisbury's cabinet.[9]

Despite Milner's insistence to Lord Roberts that he had merely 'precipitated a crisis which was inevitable, before it was too late',[10] a war over the Transvaal was by no means inevitable – or necessary. Chamberlain did not want such an outcome, nor did most Boer leaders: it was primarily Milner's belligerence that led Britain into its most expensive and humiliating conflict in a century. Four times as many British troops were involved in South Africa in 1899–1902 as in the Crimea 40 years earlier, and the cost to the Exchequer was three times as much.[11] On the South African side, the price paid in lost lives, the suffering in the concentration camps and the devastation of the countryside was several times greater.[12]

In a recent study of Rudyard Kipling, the historian David Gilmour tries to reconcile the two facets of Milner's double-sided personality – his Dr Jekyll ('brilliant, courteous, high-minded and urbane') with his Mr Hyde ('racist, bigoted and almost fanatic'). As Britain's proconsul in South Africa, Gilmour concludes, Milner played both roles in equal measure. Believing the country to be 'the weakest link in the Imperial chain',[13] his ambition was to establish 'a self-governing white community, supported by well-treated and justly governed black labour from Cape Town to the Zambesi', under the British flag.[14] It was a goal comparable to that of Rhodes's for its overstretch and unfeasibility.

To do justice to Milner, after the Anglo-Boer War was over he did his considerable best to undo and repair some of the damage he had wrought. No one could have approached the task of post-war reconstruction with more determination or energy. The youthful Buchan was awed by the High Commissioner's dedication to the task at hand, and by his capacity for hard work. In his memoirs, he described Milner as being as 'infallible as Cromer in detecting the centre of gravity in a situation, as brilliant as Alfred Beit in bringing order out of tangled finances, with Curzon's power of keeping a big organisation steadily at work'.[15] Leo Amery also writes of how Milner 'worked day after day, night after night without ceasing, whether at his desk at Sunnyside or in the veld inspecting the work of restoration. The one thought always with him, ever conquering weariness and ill health, was the need of haste.'[16]

Unsurprisingly, Milner's grasp of the realities of post-war South Africa, where capital and enterprise had finally caught up with and overtaken the effects of the Great Trek, fell far short of his reach: Afrikaners continued to comfortably outnumber English speakers in three of the four colonies; immigration from Britain remained well below expectations; and his attempts to anglicise Afrikaner society succeeded only in provoking a furious reaction. The *volk*'s nurturing of the memory of the war united it far more than anything Kruger had ever done.[17] Milner's belated efforts to bring 'responsible' government to the Transvaal led directly to the rise of Het Volk and the return to power of the Afrikaner leaders he had tried to vanquish. And he failed to substantiate Salisbury's pre-war protestations that the British government desired 'no territory, but equal rights for men of all races, and security for our fellow subjects and for the Empire'.[18] Milner's defence of the rights of non-whites was always contingent upon his calculation of the political and economic consequences: '[He] had never been prepared to move far in advance of colonial sentiment, and colonial sentiment was hardly prepared to advance at all.'[19]

Although his chief objectives may not have been met, what Milner achieved after the war within a short time was nonetheless remarkable: the building of new railways, the development of the city of Johannesburg, laying the foundations of local government throughout the Transvaal, improving the quality of education, introducing new methods of farming and irrigation, and setting up better policing, prisons and communications networks.[20] On retiring as High Commissioner, he could justifiably point with pride to the improvements he had wrought, and plead – as he did in his farewell speech in Johannesburg – that his works should be 'defended' after he had gone.[21]

❖

It remains surprising that Milner, being a self-declared 'race patriot', had such little appreciation of the patriotism of others, and that he ever thought he could convert Afrikaners into faux Englishmen. His suspicion of the 'Dutch' stemmed from his early encounters in the Cape, when he found to his surprise that not all Afrikaners wished to be brought out of their cultural isolation or shared his faith in the good intentions of the British Empire. Being so single-minded, he failed to comprehend that Afrikaner colonists such as Jan Hofmeyr were quite capable of dual loyalties. On leaving South Africa, Milner warned his successor, Selborne, that no Afrikaner politician was to be trusted, which tells us more about his own prejudices than the 'Dutch' he was supposed to conciliate.

History was to prove Milner right in one respect, however: his conviction that the majority of Boer-Afrikaners would never willingly abandon their efforts to regain republican status, or that their acceptance of imperial ideals was anything other than temporary.[22] Fifty years later, the celebrated English historian AJP Taylor observed that while the Boers may have gone to war in order to preserve their independence, they also had a less admirable aim – to preserve their 'tyranny over the natives'.[23] 'It is clear', Taylor wrote in his usual coruscating style shortly after DF Malan's Nationalists had come to power in 1948, 'that victory has gone to the worst elements on both sides. Milner got his war without achieving his vision; the Boers won their independence without being won for progress and civilisation.'

To Milner's legacy must be added the activities of the Kindergarten, the cadre of young imperialists he inspanned to assist in modernising the infrastructure of the Transvaal and Free State, and who helped pave the way politically for the unification of South Africa. For decades after the coming of Union, members of the group, as well as 'fellow-travellers' such as Buchan and especially Leo Amery – who became a lifelong friend of Smuts's – maintained their interest in South Africa by their continuing involvement in the 'moots' of the Round Table.

Under Milner's direction, the Rhodes Trust created the famous scholarship programme that has brought hundreds of young American, German and Commonwealth scholars to Oxford to further their studies before returning to their own countries. Inspired by Milner, after cutting their teeth in South Africa, former *Kinder* such as Curtis, Kerr and others devoted years of their lives to furthering the aims of imperial unity. Although the Great War brought a premature end to the activities of the Round Table as originally conceived, the organic union that Milner's young protégés first proposed at the Fortnightly Club in Johannesburg has morphed into today's Commonwealth of Nations, comprising 54 member countries of equal status, under the symbolic aegis of the British Crown.

Perhaps Milner's most puzzling characteristic was his desire to propagate the British system of governance around the world, given his own disaffection for Parliament, party politics and democracy in general. It was his distaste for the partisanship at Westminster – deepened by his humiliation in the Commons after returning from South Africa – that made him decline to become Chamberlain's successor as Colonial Secretary, lead the tariff reform movement, accept the Viceroyalty of India, or seek a prominent role in either of Britain's main political parties. To the disappointment of his friends and admirers, his unwillingness to ally himself with either the Liberal or Conservative camps precluded him from fulfilling the role for which they believed he possessed most of the attributes – that of Britain's prime minister.

However, from the one and only election he contested, Milner knew better than anyone that he did not have a platform presence, and could never 'put himself across' to a popular audience. Had he been alive today, he would not have had a Facebook account or communicated his views via Twitter. His lack of the common touch required of most successful political leaders, allied to his anti-democratic instincts and inability to compromise, made him unable to fit comfortably into a leadership role within the British political system.

In an appraisal of Milner's proconsular career, AJP Taylor described one of his great 'flaws' as his lack of 'luck': 'Things always went wrong at the point of triumphant success.' As examples, Taylor points to South Africa, where Milner successfully manoeuvred the Boers into war, only to find the British Army unprepared for it; to his work of reconstruction in the two ex-Boer republics being thwarted by the coming to power of a Liberal government; to his public humiliation by Lloyd George after his loyal service in the Great War; to his unsuccessful courtship of Margot Tennant; and finally to his death only one day after being chosen as Chancellor of Oxford.

Yet Taylor overlooks one of Milner's greatest strokes of luck – the timing of the outbreak of war in 1914, which diverted attention from the Irish crisis, in which he had been advocating policies so extreme as to raise the eyebrows of the most defiant Ulstermen. Unlike Edward Carson and others, Milner was prepared to countenance acts of resistance that amounted to sedition. As J Lee Thompson reflects, perhaps Milner would have come to his senses at the moment of extremity. 'The Great War', he concludes 'not only saved Milner from possible treason over Ulster' but also afforded him the opportunity of redemption after a decade in the wilderness.[24] His wilful preparedness to disregard British constitutional tradition in Northern Ireland was yet another example of how different Milner was from the other public figures of his day.

Whatever one's view of Milner's life and work, it must be acknowledged that he was one of a kind. Besides his intellectual brilliance and administrative excellence, what set him apart from other men was his acute sense of duty to country and 'race', his lack of narrow personal ambition and his dogged adherence to 'principle'[25] – even if his principles were sometimes of his own making. As is evident from the succession of high appointments he turned down, Milner's reason for seeking power was not to enjoy the trappings of great office but to be of service to Britain and the Empire. What made him exceptional, O'Brien observes, was his unswerving addiction to the causes he believed in – the Empire, Egypt, his mission in South Africa, Northern Ireland, national service and victory in the Great War: 'His loyalty to these knew no limits in terms of exertion, and sometimes of prudence.'[26] As James Morris observes, after Milner's death, and that of his friend Curzon, there would never be imperialists like them again: 'No men of their calibre, in future generations, would see in the Empire a proper arena for their talents, or satisfaction for their profoundest hopes ... [for the Empire had] lost its power to fascinate men of great ambition.'[27]

The great paradox of Milner's involvement in South Africa was that although the British won the Anglo-Boer War, it cost them control of the country. And, as De Kiewiet and other historians observe, even though the war was to bring all South Africans together in one nation for the first time, it left the nation more politically divided and disunited than ever.

Milner had not much liked South Africa or its people, and, notwithstanding Headlam's efforts to convince us of the contrary, these feelings were reciprocated. The ruinous consequences of the Anglo-Boer War, the Anglophobia he stoked among Afrikaners, the unrealistic expectations he aroused among English speakers and his acceptance of the racial status quo meant that for all his nobly expressed intentions, Milner did far more harm than good and added to the country's difficulties in building a more stable and humane society.[28]

There are few men in our history of whom Mark Antony's lament about Brutus in Shakespeare's *Julius Caesar* is truer than of Alfred, Lord Milner: 'The evil that men do lives after them; the good is oft interred with their bones.'

AFTERWORD

Preserving the Legacy
1925–1958

No account of Alfred Milner's life would be complete without a description of his wife's resolute efforts after his death to protect his reputation and perpetuate his imperialist legacy. Throughout his life, Milner wrote prolifically – and often at great length – and bequeathed to posterity a trove of diaries, letters and memoranda. Most of his papers were given by his widow to New College at Oxford, which passed them on to the Bodleian Library, where they may be found today.

In furthering her post-marital mission, Violet hoped to build a side chapel to Milner's memory in the little church at Salehurst, but ran into unanticipated opposition from the vicar, so she settled for a 'rather fortress-like' white stone tomb in the graveyard, designed by Sir Edwin Lutyens.[1] Her late husband's property at Sturry Court, with its Tudor house, barn and six surrounding acres, was given to the junior wing of King's School, Canterbury, housed until then in the cramped surrounds of Canterbury Cathedral. Some years later, a further 70 acres were added to King's by a Milner memorial committee, headed by Leo Amery. The school was further endowed with five Milner Scholarships, awarded each year to the sons of men engaged on colonial service.[2]

In addition to his own writings, the *religio Milneriana* – that blind faith in Milner and all his works[3] – was revived in the years following his death by the more fervent of his disciples. Pro-imperial opinion-makers such as Dawson, Astor, Kerr, Curtis, Amery, Williams and Worsfold helped to sustain the myths that had grown up around their former mentor and the influence of the Round Table on the history of those times.[4] Yet, in hindsight, Milner's main contribution to British political thought was the passion he brought for a time to the concept of a unified Empire, painted pink on the map, bound together by an imperial parliament, military and system of tariffs. His belief in the virtues of Empire and unabashed racial credo would not survive him for long.

It was Violet who undertook the laborious task of assembling and organising Milner's papers as her way of keeping up her own imperial faith and staying in touch with the memory of her husband.[5] In the belief that his labours in southern Africa had never been fully acknowledged, she commissioned the journalist Cecil Headlam to compile a comprehensive, two-volume record of Milner's eight years of service as British Governor and High Commissioner.

Determined to keep affairs of the heart strictly private, especially any letters that might reveal the depth of her relationship with Milner while she was married to someone else, Violet spent countless hours going through their mutual correspondence to make sure that every hint of intimacy was removed, before releasing the papers to Headlam. Her own copies of letters to and from Milner she burnt, in order to keep them from the prying eyes of future historians.[6]

In 1931, Violet decided to offer Milner's papers, decorations, gold boxes, portraits and other memorabilia to New College, Oxford, where they may be found today in a 'Milner Room' dedicated to his memory. In a little chapel in Westminster Abbey, there is also a memorial plaque to him, along with Curzon and Rhodes, three of the great figures of Empire. An Abbey history notes that these once-famous names have been almost forgotten today, 'the sentiment of the Empire only haunts the place as a ghost'.[7]

In widowhood, the Francophile Violet's links with Georges Clemenceau became stronger than ever, and she visited the ageing former leader as often as she could, in Paris and at his seaside home on the Brittany coast. She regarded the Frenchman's attitude to life, and politics, as similar to Milner's: 'When you have done your *utmost*, then you can do no good by being miserable over your failure.'[8] In late 1929, she paid a last visit to Clemenceau a few days before his 87th birthday, realising her old friend was slowly slipping away, as he did a few weeks later.[9]

Violet was unable to attend Clemenceau's funeral because her brother, Leo Maxse, publisher and editor for four decades of the *National Review*, was dying of cancer. Stepping in temporarily to help, she was to fill Leo's shoes for the next 18 years, not only planning the content of the *Review*, soliciting advertising, sourcing contributions and preparing copy for the printers, but also writing many of the political commentaries herself. Under Leo, the 'Nat', as it was known, had adopted a radical, right-wing stance, and Violet continued to reflect her brother's (and Milner's) views on issues such as tariff reform, imperialism and the need for vigilance about Germany's ambitions and intentions. Curiously, she never campaigned for women's rights. Confident of the behind-the-scenes influence of women such as herself, she regarded the political status of women as an irrelevance.[10] As Julia Bush confirms, many upper-class women within organised female imperialism in Britain held firmly conventional views on gender differences.[11]

By the 1930s, as a peeress, widow of an eminent statesman and now a political commentator in her own right, Violet, Lady Milner, had become formidable and opinionated, another of that distinctive breed of superior-minded Englishwomen who might not have ruled the world but felt they ought to. According to her relatives by marriage, Hugh and Mirabel Cecil, as the crisis in Europe gathered momentum throughout the decade, and as she grew older, Violet became most comfortable with like-minded friends, 'to whom she gave lunches at her London club, where she expected everyone to be well-informed and eloquent – a stimulating if alarming experience'.[12]

Her racial views had not undergone much change since her early days in South Africa, when, as Bush records, she had displayed 'no particular interest in the native question'. In later years, as a prominent member of the Victoria League, she took the lead in resisting the League's attempt to open its doors to male visitors from India.[13]

While editor of the *National Review*, she kept up an interest in South African affairs, lamenting the loss of British influence at the hand of successive prime ministers who had all been Anglo-Boer War generals, and deploring moves in the Cape to deprive Africans of the vote. 'No barrier of race, colour or creed should be applied to citizens of the British Commonwealth', the *Nat* declaimed piously, its editor seemingly oblivious of the racism that underlay her own imperialist beliefs.[14] In the journal, she applauded the government's belated adoption in the 1930s of Chamberlain's and Milner's prescriptions in imposing a levy of ten per cent on all foreign imports, except meat and grain, and the granting of free entry to produce from imperial sources. The move came far too late, however, to have the unifying effect on the Empire that her late husband and other tariff reformers had hoped for.

Among the *National Review*'s prime targets was the League of Nations, whose most fervent advocate happened to be Edward Cecil's elder brother, Robert, one of Britain's most highly esteemed Conservatives. Decrying the League's vague 'internationalism', Violet equated the international body with woolly-headedness and weakness. She had many arguments with 'Bob' Cecil, who used to dread meeting her at Hatfield and being subjected to the outspokenness of 'the most tiresome woman I know'.[15]

As Hitler's behaviour began to cast a growing shadow over the affairs of Europe, Violet gave free expression to her anti-German and anti-Nazi sentiments. She was particularly incensed by the treatment of German Jews and in November 1938 joined in the great protest rally at the Albert Hall after the Kristallnacht pogrom. She also became bitterly critical of two of her husband's most faithful disciples, Philip Kerr (now Lord Lothian) and Geoffrey Dawson, among the most prominent figures in the pro-appeasement lobby. Once evangelical imperialists, the pair were now even more fervent in their desire to keep Britain from going to war again and on the right side of Hitler. Dawson, editor of the newspaper often regarded as the mouthpiece of the British government, confessed to a friend: 'I do my utmost night after night to keep out of the paper anything that might hurt [German] susceptibilities' and 'drop in little things which are intended to soothe them.'[16] A member of the Cecil family, Lord Cranborne, commented: 'The idea of Philip Lothian and *The Times* that by beaming seductively on the present German government, we shall persuade them to moderate their attitude is to my mind pure bunkum.'[17]

Another Round Tabler in her sights was Lionel Curtis and his Institute of International Affairs. In 1938, she described a discussion she had attended at the Institute as 'worse than I thought possible ... I walked nearly the whole way home, feeling the need for decontamination after the really dreadful atmosphere of Chatham House.'[18]

The Second World War years were especially difficult for Violet.

During the late summer of 1940, the Battle of Britain took place in the skies directly above Great Wigsell. On one occasion, part of the house was set ablaze by a German incendiary bomb, which she, her house guests and staff managed to extinguish only with difficulty. Four days later, a Spitfire crashed nearby, the loss of its young pilot reminding her – as she scattered flowers upon his remains – of the loss of her own beloved George two decades earlier.

She had little confidence in Winston Churchill's early conduct of the war and was dismayed by his promise that India would be granted Dominion status when the conflict was over, as it would pave the way, she feared, for an imperial break-up. Her grandson George, newly enlisted in the Royal Navy, found it hard to understand the opinions she inflicted upon him about national pride and the need to preserve the by now diminished Empire.[19]

On VE Day, 8 May 1945, Violet was able to rejoice at the news that the war in Europe was over, wishing only that her late husband, Kipling and brother Leo could have celebrated the defeat of Germany with her at Great Wigsell.[20] As soon as it was safe to do so, she hastened over to her beloved France, returning home after the huge shock of a Labour victory in the 1945 general election. In Britain's new welfare state, she realised, her world, the old order, the aristocracy and especially the Empire would never be the same again.

Now in her mid-seventies, Violet was told by her physician that despite lifelong headaches and periodic fits of depression, she had the heart and blood pressure of a much younger woman. In 1948, she took the decision to sell the *National Review* to a family friend, and three years later published a memoir, *My Picture Gallery*, an account of her early life from 1872 until leaving South Africa in 1901. The book contains many vivid reflections of her time as a young married woman in the Cape and her experiences with Edward in the western Transvaal. 'It was a pang', she recorded, 'to leave South Africa. Such a crowded fourteen months of my life had been lived in that beautiful country.'[21] Of her affair with Milner, there is no mention.

In 1951, Violet published some recollections of her second visit to South Africa 30 years earlier, shortly after becoming Lady Milner. Taking the cue from her late husband, she managed to cause offence in

South Africa once again by displaying her abiding mistrust of Afrikaners. Although Milner had long since made a friend of Smuts, Violet seems never to have warmed to 'the General'. Her recounting of the lunch at the Smuts family farm at Irene contained several patronising observations, to which Smuts's son Jannie responded with indignation in the biography of his father, published in 1952. '[Lady Milner] refers to my mother as "a plump Boer woman", though at the time my mother weighed only 107 pounds. She says we seemed awed by the presence of a great man. Doornkloof has seen many great men, and we are not easily awed. And the "scrub cattle" she saw were prize studbook Frieslands. However, my father was very pleased to see Milner and to show him hospitality. It was an informal, enjoyable occasion,'[22] the younger Smuts wrote.

In her 1951 reminiscences, Violet actually described 'Ouma' Smuts as 'a short, stout, active-looking woman, with black curly hair cut short all over her head – she has very bright, intelligent eyes and is evidently a ruling spirit'. She seemed 'a little flustered' when the Milners arrived, having been for years very anti-British, 'though she had changed her views'. She (Violet) liked her hostess's 'naturalness' and thought 'the whole household was a lesson in simple life and abundant warm-hearted hospitality'. Their lunch, a Malay-style *babootje*, had been accompanied, to Violet's surprise, by a 'very good champagne'.[23]

When Milner died, despite Smuts's warm tribute to him in an interview with the *Cape Times*, published in several British newspapers, Violet took offence at something Smuts said. 'I was not surprised', she recalled, 'when my husband died … General Smuts should have given to the press a very inaccurate account of the talk he had had [at Irene] and the views he [Milner] held on the South African question – views dramatically opposite to those he had actually held and expressed.'[24] Hugh and Mirabel Cecil conclude that both parties were acting in character here, Smuts being not entirely 'on the level' and Violet sardonic as usual, seeking belated revenge on a former enemy.[25]

On 10 October 1958, 33 years after her husband's death, Violet, Lady Milner, passed away peacefully at Great Wigsell, at the great age of 86. On her desk were the papers she had gathered in preparation for a second volume of memoirs, which were to have covered her time in Egypt, the experiences of two world wars, the tragic loss of her son, her two marriages and the happiness she found with Alfred Milner. It would have made for fascinating reading. She might even have reflected on the Suez debacle in Egypt two years earlier, a strategic and diplomatic misadventure that brought closer the demise of her – and her beloved husband's – much-cherished British Empire.

Acknowledgements

One of the few benefits of the long COVID-19 lockdown in 2020 was the opportunity it provided for writing the first draft of this book. The downside, however, was that every research library in South Africa and the UK was closed and overseas travel proscribed. This left me no choice but to rely on published sources and the internet until some of the restrictions were lifted.

My earlier books on Jan Smuts and Louis Botha had aroused my interest in the character of Alfred Milner, whom I knew only as a shadowy individual, detested and vilified by many South Africans. Yet it struck me as odd that no South African had written a book about him. As far as I am aware, no local historians, of whom I am not one, have attempted an account of the life of this complex character, whose influence – for good or ill – was felt throughout the British Empire, and who left an indelible imprint on the history of South Africa. As a journalist, I fell for the temptation to rush in where academics had feared to tread.

When I raised the subject of a biography of Milner with Eugene Ashton, managing director of Jonathan Ball Publishers and a keen student of South African history, he needed no persuasion. Eugene subsequently became my sounding board for each chapter of the manuscript. My brother, Chris, another history buff, was also prevailed upon to read the manuscript and tell me whenever his eyes began to glaze over. Jeremy Boraine, Annie Olivier and Alfred LeMaitre also read an early draft, identified shortcomings and made many helpful suggestions. Unable to leave South Africa because of the pandemic, I was fortunate in obtaining the assistance of Dr Stephen Massie, an Oxford-based historical researcher with a special interest in the career and legacy of Cecil John Rhodes, who combed through the relevant sections of Lord and Lady Milner's papers at the Bodleian Library for me. I am also greatly indebted to Professor Fransjohan Pretorius, a leading expert on the Anglo-Boer War, for his helpful advice on how to add balance to the text. At the last minute, the British author Duncan Campbell-Smith kindly sent me some reflections on Milner by Samuel Hoare that he had come across in his researches. I owe my deep gratitude to everyone mentioned.

I also record my appreciation to Sally MacRoberts and the staff of the Brenthurst Library, and especially to Jennifer Kimble, for their ready assistance at all times, and for enabling me to consult some important reference books during the lockdown. And my thanks, too, to Professors Sarah Nuttall and Keith Breckinridge of WISER, the Wits Institute for Social and Economic Research, for enabling me to spend long hours in the William Cullen Library, whose staff were helpful at all times.

Once again, my editor, Alfred LeMaitre, was of immeasurable assistance and encouragement. My publisher, Annie Olivier, was equally generous with advice and the sourcing of photographs. On the production side, I record my thanks also to book designer Martine Barker, cover designer Sean Robertson, indexer George Claassen and proofreader Paul Wise. Sadly, Jonathan Ball himself fell ill and died before he could cast his eye, as he usually did, over the final manuscript.

Finally, I end with the usual *mea culpa* for errors in the text. As I cannot attribute them to anyone else, I reluctantly acknowledge my own responsibility.

Richard Steyn

Notes

Preface

1 Amery, LS (ed), *The Times History of the War in South Africa 1899–1900, Vol 1* (Sampson Low, Marston and Co, 1900), p vi.

2 De Kiewiet, CW, *A History of South Africa: Social & Economic* (Oxford University Press, 1966), p 138.

3 Nutting, A, *Scramble for Africa: The Great Trek to the Boer War* (Constable, 1994), p 306.

4 Brendon, P, *The Decline and Fall of the British Empire 1781–1997* (Vintage, 2008), p 215.

5 Smith, IR, *The Origins of the South African War, 1899–1902* (Longman, 1996), p 27.

6 Ibid, p 148.

7 Roberts, A, *Churchill: Walking with Destiny* (Penguin, 2019), p 976.

8 Bush, J, *Edwardian Ladies and Imperial Power* (Cassell, 2000), p 1.

9 Ibid.

10 Roberts, B, *Cecil Rhodes: Flawed Colossus* (WW Norton, 1988), p 27.

11 O'Brien, TH, *Milner: Viscount Milner of St James's and Cape Town* (Constable, 1979), p 83.

12 Morris, J, *Farewell the Trumpets: An Imperial Retreat* (Penguin, 1978), p 116.

13 Ibid.

14 Buchan, J, *Memory Hold-the-Door* (Read Books Ltd, 2013, ebook), pp 99–100.

15 Ibid.

16 Ibid.

17 Roberts, *Cecil Rhodes*, p 274.

18 Rotberg, R and Shore, M, *The Founder: Cecil Rhodes and the Pursuit of Power* (Oxford University Press, 1988), p 620.

19 Denoon, D, *A Grand Illusion: The Failure of Imperial Policy in the Transvaal Colony during the Period of Reconstruction 1900–1905* (Longmans, Green & Co, 1973).

20 Duminy, A and Guest, B, *Interfering in Politics: A Biography of Sir Percy FitzPatrick* (Lowry, 1987), p 95.

21 Ibid.

22 O'Brien, *Milner*, p 220.

23 Ibid, p 222.

24 Weaver, JRH (ed), *The Dictionary of National Biography 1922–30* (Oxford University Press, 1937), p 602.

25 Schoeman, K, *Rekonstruksie: Die naoorlogsjare in Suid-Afrika, 1902–1905* (Protea Boekhuis, 2021), p 101.

Prologue

1 Wrench, JE, *Alfred Lord Milner: The Man of No Illusions* (Eyre & Spottiswoode, 1958), p 343.

2 Ibid, pp 344–345.

3 Ibid, p 340.

4 Gollin, AM, *Proconsul in Politics: A*

Study of Lord Milner in Opposition and in Power (Anthony Blond, 1964), p 501.

5 Ibid, pp 502–503.

6 Weaver (ed), *The Dictionary of National Biography*, p 600.

7 Wrench, *Alfred Lord Milner*, p 341.

8 O'Brien, *Milner*, p 297.

9 Wrench, *Alfred Lord Milner*, pp 341–342.

10 Gollin, *Proconsul in Politics*, p 505.

11 Wrench, *Alfred Lord Milner*, p 341.

12 Ibid, p 343ff.

13 O'Brien, *Milner*, p 298.

14 Wrench, *Alfred Lord Milner*, p 342.

15 Reid, W, *Five Days from Defeat: How Britain Nearly Lost the First World War* (Birlinn, 2017, ebook), p 201.

16 Crankshaw, E, *The Forsaken Idea: A Study of Viscount Milner* (Longmans, Green & Co, 1952), p 11.

Chapter 1 Youth

1 Wrench, *Alfred Lord Milner*, p 23.

2 Quoted by Marlowe, J, *Milner: Apostle of Empire* (Hamish Hamilton, 1976), p 2.

3 O'Brien, *Milner*, p 22.

4 Thompson, JL, *Forgotten Patriot: A Life of Alfred, Viscount Milner of St James's and Cape Town* (Fairleigh Dickinson University Press, 2007), pp 22–23.

5 O'Brien, *Milner*, p 22.

6 Thompson, *Forgotten Patriot*, p 24.

7 Ibid.

8 Wrench, *Alfred Lord Milner*, p 30.

9 Headlam, C (ed), *The Milner Papers, Vol II: South Africa 1899–1905* (Cassell, 1933), p 3.

10 Picard, HWJ, *Lords of Stalplein: Biographical Miniatures of the British Governors of the Cape of Good Hope* (HAUM, 1974), p 146.

11 Smith, *The Origins of the South African War*, p 145.

12 Marlowe, *Milner*, p.3.

13 Thompson, *Forgotten Patriot*, p 25.

14 Headlam (ed), *The Milner Papers, Vol II*, p 4.

15 Thompson, *Forgotten Patriot*, p 27.

16 Headlam (ed), *The Milner Papers, Vol II*, pp 5–6.

17 O'Brien, *Milner*, p 36.

18 Wrench, *Alfred Lord Milner*, p 38.

19 Thompson, *Forgotten Patriot*, p 26.

20 Ibid, p 28.

21 Ibid, p 29.

22 Ibid.

23 Ferguson, N, *Empire: How Britain Made The Modern World* (Penguin, 2004), pp 248–249.

24 Morris, *Farewell the Trumpets*, p 122.

25 Thompson, JL, *A Wider Patriotism: Milner and the British Empire* (Routledge, 2016), p 1.

26 Thompson, *Forgotten Patriot*, p 30.

27 Ibid.

28 Morris, *Farewell the Trumpets*, p 116.

29 Marlowe, *Milner*, p 14.

30 Breckenridge, K, 'Lord Milner's Registry: The Origins of South African Exceptionalism', seminar paper, University of KwaZulu-Natal, 2004, p 5.

31 O'Brien, *Milner*, p 42.

Chapter 2 Early Career

1 O'Brien, *Milner*, p 49.

2 Ibid, p 51.

3 Thompson, *Forgotten Patriot*, p 34.

4 Wrench, *Alfred Lord Milner*, p 62.

5 Thompson, *Forgotten Patriot*, p 34.

6 Gollin, *Proconsul in Politics*, p 10.

7 Buchan, *Memory Hold-the-Door*, p 101.

8 O'Brien, *Milner*, p 51.

9 Thompson, *Forgotten Patriot*, p 41.

10 Ibid, p 38.

11 Ibid.

12 Thompson, *A Wider Patriotism*, p 16.

13 Ibid.

14 Thompson, *Forgotten Patriot*, p 44.

15 O Brien, *Milner*, p 60.

16 Picard, *Lords of Stalplein*, p 147.

17 Ibid.

18 Marlowe, *Milner*, p 14.

19 Weaver, *DNB*, p 590.

20 Headlam, C (ed), *The Milner Papers, Vol I: South Africa 1897–1899* (Cassell, 1931), p 20.

21 Thompson, *Forgotten Patriot*, p 49.

22 Headlam (ed), *The Milner Papers, Vol I*, p 20.

23 Ibid.

24 Wrench, *Alfred Lord Milner*, p 80.

25 Ibid, p 82.

26 Ibid.

27 O'Brien, *Milner*, p 71.

28 Wrench, *Alfred Lord Milner*, p 89.

29 O'Brien, *Milner*, p 84.

30 Picard, *Lords of Stalplein*, p 148.

31 Wrench, *Alfred Lord Milner*, p 93.

32 Ibid.

33 Ibid, p 94.

34 Ibid.

Chapter 3 Egypt

1 James, L, *Empires in the Sun: The Struggle for the Mastery of Africa* (Jonathan Ball Publishers, 2016), p 80.

2 Ibid, p 78.

3 Ibid, p 82.

4 Brendon, *The Decline and Fall of the British Empire*, p 174.

5 Lloyd, T, *Empire: The History of the British Empire* (Hambledon and London, 2001), p 113.

6 Thompson, *Forgotten Patriot*, p 66.

7 Hardy, R, *The Poisoned Well: Empire and its Legacy in the Middle East* (Hurst, 2016), p 126.

8 Wilson, AN, *The Victorians* (Arrow, 2003), p 467.

9 Ferguson, *Empire*, pp 267–268.

10 Wrench, *Alfred Lord Milner*, p 97.

11 Morris, J, *Pax Britannica: The Climax of an Empire* (Penguin, 1968), p 246.

12 Hardy, *The Poisoned Well*, pp 126–127.

13 Wrench, *Alfred Lord Milner*, p 98.

14 O'Brien, *Milner*, p 89.

15 Thompson, *Forgotten Patriot*, p 65.

16 O'Brien, *Milner*, p 89.

17 Thompson, *A Wider Patriotism*, p 27.

18 Ibid.

19 Wrench, *Alfred Lord Milner*, p 98.

20 Thompson, *A Wider Patriotism*, p 26.

21 Wrench, *Alfred Lord Milner*, p 98.

22 Bush, *Edwardian Ladies*, p 108.

23 Ibid.

24 Massie, RK, *Dreadnought: Britain, Germany and the Coming of the Great War* (Jonathan Cape, 1992), p 191.

25 Ibid, p 240.

26 Morris, *Pax Britannica*, p 249.

27 Brendon, *The Decline and Fall of the British Empire*, p 201.

28 Thompson, *A Wider Patriotism*, p 26.

29 Wrench, *Alfred Lord Milner*, p 118.

30 Ibid, p 103.

31 Ibid, p 104.

32 O'Brien, *Milner*, p 94.

33 Thompson, *Forgotten Patriot*, p 75.

34 Ibid, p 107.

35 Rotberg and Shore, *The Founder*, p 282.

36 Thompson, *Forgotten Patriot*, p 75.

37 Ibid. p 76.

38 Ibid, p 77.

39 Ibid, p 81.

40 Gollin, *Proconsul in Politics*, p 25.

41 Picard, *Lords of Stalplein*, p 148.

42 Wrench, *Alfred Lord Milner*, p 122.

43 O'Brien, *Milner*, p 107.

44 Ibid.

45 Wrench, *Alfred Lord Milner*, p 136.
46 Thompson, *Forgotten Patriot*, p 83.

Chapter 4 **Tax Gatherer**

1 Marlowe, *Milner*, pp 19–20.
2 Headlam (ed), *The Milner Papers, Vol I*, p 25.
3 O'Brien, *Milner*, p 109.
4 Thompson, *Forgotten Patriot*, p 66.
5 Ibid, p 88.
6 Thompson, *A Wider Patriotism*, p 35.
7 Ibid.
8 O'Brien, *Milner*, p 107.
9 Thompson, *Forgotten Patriot*, p 76.
10 O'Brien, *Milner*, p 115.
11 Wrench, *Alfred Lord Milner*, p 148.
12 Thompson, *Forgotten Patriot*, p 95.
13 Ibid.
14 Hattersley, R, *The Edwardians* (Abacus, 2006), p 38.
15 Thompson, *Forgotten Patriot*, p 96.
16 O'Brien, *Milner*, p 118.
17 Wrench, *Alfred Lord Milner*, p 149.
18 O'Brien, *Milner*, p 119.
19 Wrench, *Alfred Lord Milner*, p 150.
20 O'Brien, *Milner*, p 119.
21 Ibid., pp 119–120.
22 Ibid, p 121.
23 Massie, *Dreadnought*, p 558.
24 Thompson, *Forgotten Patriot*, p 100.
25 Wrench, *Alfred Lord Milner*, p 154.
26 Pakenham, T, *The Scramble for Africa, 1876–1912* (Jonathan Ball Publishers, 1991), p 489.

Chapter 5 **A New Challenge**

1 O'Brien, *Milner*, p 124.
2 Ibid, p 125.
3 Wrench, *Alfred Lord Milner*, p 158.
4 Marlowe, *Milner*, p 23.
5 Evans, RJ, 'The Victorians: Empire & Race', Lecture at Museum of London, 2011.
6 Crosby, T, *Joseph Chamberlain: A Most Radical Imperialist* (IB Tauris, 2011), p.174.
7 Smith, *The Origins of the South African War*, p 72.
8 Baxter, P, *Gandhi, Smuts and Race in the British Empire: Of Passive and Violent Resistance* (Pen & Sword Books, 2017), p 115.
9 Pakenham, *The Scramble for Africa*, p 489.
10 Ferguson, *Empire*, p 240.
11 Heffer, S, *The Age of Decadence: Britain 1880 to 1914* (Random House, 2017), p 45.
12 Hattersley, *The Edwardians*, p 414.
13 Ibid.
14 Ibid.
15 Ferguson, *Empire*, p 258.
16 Ibid, p 256.
17 Brendon, *The Decline and Fall of the British Empire*, p 194.
18 Marais, JS, *The Fall of Kruger's Republic* (The Clarendon Press, 1961), p 329.
19 Clarke, P. *Hope and Glory: Britain 1900–2000* (Penguin, 2004), p 17.
20 O'Brien, *Milner*, p 130.
21 Marais, *The Fall of Kruger's Republic*, p 325.
22 Smith, *The Origins of the South African War*, p 148.
23 O Brien, *Milner*, pp 130–131.
24 Pakenham, T, *The Boer War* (Futura, 1988), p 25.
25 Thompson, *Forgotten Patriot*, p 105.
26 Wrench, *Alfred Lord Milner*, p 158.
27 O'Brien, *Milner*, p 127.
28 Ibid.
29 Wrench, *Alfred Lord Milner*, p 160.
30 Picard, *Lords of Stalplein*, p 149.
31 Thompson, *Forgotten Patriot*, p 105.
32 Wrench, *Alfred Lord Milner*, p 161.
33 Thompson, *Forgotten Patriot*, p 107.
34 Ibid.

35 O'Brien, *Milner*, p 133.
36 Ibid, p 127.
37 Marlowe, *Milner*, p 42.
38 O'Brien, *Milner*, p 138.
39 Lowry, D (ed), *The South African War Reappraised* (Manchester University Press, 2000), p 98.
40 O'Brien, *Milner*, p 131.
41 Smith, *The Origins of the South African War*, p 107.
42 Rotberg and Shore, *The Founder*, p 548.
43 Thompson, *Forgotten Patriot*, p 108.
44 Rotberg and Shore, *The Founder*, p 548.
45 Smith, *The Origins of the South African War*, p 107.
46 Massie, *Dreadnought*, pp 213–231.
47 Ibid.
48 Thompson, *Forgotten Patriot*, p 108.
49 O'Brien, *Milner*, p 131.
50 Headlam, *The Milner Papers, Vol 1*, p 42.
51 Wrench, *Alfred Lord Milner*, p 165.

Chapter 6 **Playing Himself In**

1 Headlam (ed), *The Milner Papers, Vol I*, p 41.
2 Ibid, p 42.
3 Ibid, p 43.
4 O'Brien, *Milner*, p 138.
5 Rose Innes, J, *Autobiography* (Oxford University Press, 1949), p 165.
6 Headlam (ed), *The Milner Papers, Vol I*, p 43.
7 Knox, C & Coetzee, C, *Victorian Life at the Cape 1870–1900* (Fernwood Press, 1992), p 94.
8 Headlam (ed), *The Milner Papers, Vol I*, pp 43–44.
9 James, *Empires in the Sun*, p 56.
10 Rose Innes, *Autobiography*, p 177.
11 Marlowe, *Milner*, p 41.
12 Smith, *The Origins of the South African War*, p 61.
13 Tamarkin, M, in Lowry (ed), *The South African War Reappraised*, pp 120–121.
14 Giliomee, H and Mbenga, B (eds), *New History of South Africa* (Tafelberg, 2007), p 197.
15 Giliomee, H, *The Afrikaners: Biography of a People* (Tafelberg, 2003), p 241.
16 Smith, *The Origins of the South African War*, p 62.
17 Tamarkin, in Lowry (ed), *The South African War Reappraised*, p 122.
18 Michell, Sir L. *The Life of the Rt Hon Cecil John Rhodes, 1853–1902, Vol 1* (Edward Arnold, 1910), p 75.
19 Ibid.
20 Smith, *The Origins of the South African War*, pp 31–32.
21 James, *Empires in the Sun*, p 101.
22 Smith, *The Origins of the South African War*, p 44.
23 James, *Empires in the Sun*, p 102.
24 Smith, *The Origins of the South African War*, p 47.
25 James, *Empires in the Sun*, p 102.
26 Baxter, *Gandhi, Smuts and Race in the British Empire*, p 142. 2017
27 James, *Empires in the Sun*, p 108.
28 Thompson, *Forgotten Patriot*, p 109.
29 Ibid.
30 Smith, *The Origins of the South African War*, pp 151–152.
31 O'Brien, *Milner*, p 138.
32 Headlam (ed), *The Milner Papers, Vol I*, p 226.

Chapter 7 **Widening Horizons**

1 Allen, C, *Kipling Sahib: India and the Making of Rudyard Kipling* (Abacus, 2008), p 341.
2 Gilmour, D, *The Long Recessional: The Imperial Life of Rudyard Kipling*

(Farrar, Straus and Giroux, 2002), pp 120–123.

3 Headlam (ed), *The Milner Papers*, *Vol I*, p 49.
4 Ibid, p 180.
5 Lewsen, P, *John X. Merriman: Paradoxical South African Statesman* (Yale University Press, 1982), pp 182–183.
6 Ibid, p 191.
7 Thomas, A, *Rhodes: The Race for Africa* (Penguin/BBC Books, 1997), p 349.
8 Judd, D & Surridge, K, *The Boer War: A History* (IB Tauris, 2013), p 45.
9 Headlam (ed), *The Milner Papers*, *Vol I*, pp 85–87.
10 Ibid, p 87.
11 Thompson, *Forgotten Patriot*, p 116.
12 Headlam (ed), *The Milner Papers*, *Vol I*, p 100.
13 O'Brien, *Milner*, p 144.
14 Headlam (ed), *The Milner Papers*, *Vol I*, p 130.
15 Ibid, p 132.
16 Ibid, p 134.
17 Thompson, *Forgotten Patriot*, p 117.
18 Headlam (ed), *The Milner Papers*, *Vol I*, p 140.
19 Ibid.
20 Smith, *The Origins of the South African War*, p.60.
21 Ibid.
22 Headlam (ed), *The Milner Papers*, *Vol I*, p 140.
23 Ibid, p 141.
24 Thompson, *Forgotten Patriot*, p 118.
25 Ibid.
26 Knox & Coetzee, *Victorian Life at the Cape*, p 94.
27 Thompson, *Forgotten Patriot*, p 113.
28 Knox & Coetzee, *Victorian Life at the Cape*, p 94.
29 Thompson, *Forgotten Patriot*, p 113.

Chapter 8 Choosing Sides

1 Marlowe, *Milner*, p 46.
2 Headlam (ed), *The Milner Papers*, *Vol I*, p 212.
3 Marais, *The Fall of Kruger's Republic*, pp 329–333.
4 Headlam (ed), *The Milner Papers*, *Vol I*, pp 220–222.
5 Ibid, p 226.
6 Ibid, p 229.
7 Smith, *The Origins of the South African War*, p 189.
8 Ibid, p 190.
9 Ibid.
10 Nutting, *Scramble for Africa*, p 379.
11 Headlam (ed), *The Milner Papers*, *Vol I*, p 216.
12 Ibid, p 240.
13 Rose Innes, *Autobiography*, p 179.
14 Headlam (ed), *The Milner Papers*, *Vol I*, p 241.
15 Smith, *The Origins of the South African War*, p 195.
16 Headlam (ed), *The Milner Papers*, *Vol I*, p 244.
17 Ibid, p 245.
18 Ibid, p 246.
19 Smith, *The Origins of the South African War*, p 196.
20 Ibid, pp 196–197.
21 Ibid, p 197.
22 Headlam (ed), *The Milner Papers*, *Vol I*, p 246.
23 Thompson, *Forgotten Patriot*, p 121.
24 Smith, *The Origins of the South African War*, p 198.
25 Headlam (ed), *The Milner Papers*, *Vol I*, p 159.
26 Ibid, p 163.
27 Ibid, p 160.
28 Ibid, p 161.
29 Cartwright, AP, *The First South African: The Life and Times of Sir Percy FitzPatrick* (Purnell, 1971), p 93.

30 Smith, *The Origins of the South African War*, p 199.
31 Ibid, p 200.
32 Ibid.
33 Duminy, A & Guest, B, *Interfering in Politics: A Biography of Sir Percy FitzPatrick* (Lowry Publishers, 1987), p 49.
34 Ibid, p 50.
35 Smith, *The Origins of the South African War*, p 202.

CHAPTER 9 **The Rhodes Factor**

1 Nutting, *Scramble for Africa*, p 366.
2 Thomas, *Rhodes*, p 350.
3 Rotberg & Shore, *The Founder*, p 603.
4 Nutting, *Scramble for Africa*, p 366.
5 Rotberg & Shore, *The Founder*, p 608.
6 Thomas, *Rhodes*, p 351.
7 Rotberg & Shore, *The Founder*, p 607.
8 Rose Innes, *Autobiography*, p 170.
9 Thomas, *Rhodes*, p 351.
10 Rose Innes, *Autobiography*, p 166.
11 Smith, *The Origins of the South African War*, p 178.
12 Headlam (ed), *The Milner Papers*, *Vol I*, p 282.
13 Rotberg & Shore, *The Founder*, p 614.
14 Ibid.
15 Headlam (ed), *The Milner Papers*, *Vol I*, p 232.
16 Ibid, pp 234–235.
17 Ibid, p 236.
18 Smith, *The Origins of the South African War*, p 157.
19 Ibid.
20 Ibid, p 158.
21 Ibid, p 159.
22 Ibid.
23 Ibid.
24 Ibid, p 160.
25 Headlam (ed), *The Milner Papers*, *Vol I*, p 267.
26 Ibid, p 268.

27 Smith, *The Origins of the South African War*, p 39.
28 Ibid, p 207.
29 Ibid.
30 Ibid, p 209.
31 Ibid.
32 Thompson, *Forgotten Patriot*, p 124.
33 Ibid.
34 Thompson, *Forgotten Patriot*, p 127.
35 Ibid.
36 O'Brien, *Milner*, p 153.

CHAPTER 10 **Tensions Rise**

1 Headlam (ed), *The Milner Papers*, *Vol I*, p 299.
2 Ibid.
3 O'Brien, *Milner*, p 152.
4 Smith, *The Origins of the South African War*, pp 213–214.
5 Ibid, p 214.
6 Ibid, p 213.
7 O'Brien, *Milner*, p 152.
8 Smith, *The Origins of the South African War*, p 222.
9 Picard, *Lords of Stalplein*, p 151.
10 Smith, *The Origins of the South African War*, p 224.
11 O'Brien, *Milner*, p 153.
12 Thompson, *Forgotten Patriot*, p 128.
13 Headlam (ed), *The Milner Papers*, *Vol I*, p 301.
14 Ibid, p 302.
15 Smith, *The Origins of the South African War*, p 227.
16 Ibid, p 173.
17 Rogers, O, *Lawyers In Turmoil: The Johannesburg Conspiracy of 1895* (Stormberg Publishers, 2020), p 30.
18 Judd & Surridge, *The Boer War*, p 49.
19 Smith, *The Origins of the South African War*, p 218.
20 Ibid, p 220.
21 Ibid.
22 Ibid.

23 Ibid, p 45.
24 Headlam (ed), *The Milner Papers,* *Vol I,* p 328.
25 Ibid, p 329.
26 Smith, *The Origins of the South African War,* p 231.
27 Headlam (ed), *The Milner Papers,* *Vol I,* p 340.
28 Smith, *The Origins of the South African War,* p 259.
29 Ibid, p 260.
30 Ibid, p 160.
31 Headlam (ed), *The Milner Papers,* *Vol I,* p 353.
32 Gilmour, *The Long Recessional,* p 139.
33 Ibid.
34 Thompson, *A Wider Patriotism,* p 45.
35 Headlam (ed), *The Milner Papers,* *Vol I,* p 353.
36 Smith, *The Origins of the South African War,* p 267.
37 Headlam (ed), *The Milner Papers,* *Vol I,* p 359.
38 Ibid, p 378.
39 Ibid, p 385.
40 Ibid, p 400.
41 Ibid.

Chapter 11 Bloemfontein and Beyond

1 Meintjes, J, *President Paul Kruger: A Biography* (Cassell, 1974), p 225.
2 Meredith M, *Afrikaner Odyssey: The Life and Times of the Reitz Family* (Jonathan Ball Publishers, 2017), p 69.
3 Meredith, M, *Diamonds, Gold and War: The Making of South Africa* (Simon & Schuster, 2007), pp 405–406.
4 Marlowe, *Milner,* p 69.
5 Smith, *The Origins of the South African War,* p 279.
6 Ibid.
7 Meredith, *Afrikaner Odyssey,* p 68.
8 Baxter, *Gandhi, Smuts and Race in the British Empire,* p 124.
9 Meredith, *Afrikaner Odyssey,* pp 68–69.
10 Picard, *Lords of Stalplein,* p 152.
11 Marlowe, *Milner,* p 71.
12 Smith, *The Origins of the South African War,* p 282.
13 Ibid, p 285.
14 Meredith, *Afrikaner Odyssey,* p 71.
15 Marlowe, *Milner,* p 72.
16 Nutting, *Scramble for Africa,* p 402.
17 Pakenham, *The Boer War,* p 68.
18 Marlowe, *Milner,* p 73.
19 Ibid, p 75.
20 Headlam (ed), *The Milner Papers,* *Vol I,* p 424.
21 Marlowe, *Milner,* p 75.
22 Welsh, F, *A History of South Africa* (HarperCollins, 1998), p 379.
23 Thompson, *Forgotten Patriot,* p 140.
24 Fisher, J, *The Afrikaners* (Cassell, 1969), p 155.
25 Thompson, *A Wider Patriotism,* p 47.
26 Ibid, p 49.
27 Quoted in Thompson, *Forgotten Patriot,* p 140.
28 Marais, *The Fall of Kruger's Republic,* p 288.
29 Thompson, *Forgotten Patriot,* pp 131–132.
30 Cartwright, *The First South African,* p 98.
31 Ibid.
32 Ibid, p 102.
33 Smith, *The Origins of the South African War,* pp 274–275.
34 Ibid, p 275.
35 Ibid.
36 Headlam (ed), *The Milner Papers,* *Vol I,* p 509.
37 O'Brien, *Milner,* p 160.
38 Headlam (ed), *The Milner Papers,*

Vol I, pp 425–426.

39 O'Brien, *Milner*, p 160.

40 Thompson, *Forgotten Patriot*, p 141.

41 Marais, *The Fall of Kruger's Republic*, p 276.

42 Smith, *The Origins of the South African War*, p 297.

43 Ibid, p 304.

44 Headlam (ed), *The Milner Papers*, *Vol I*, p 468.

45 Ibid, p 469.

46 Ibid, p 466.

47 Thompson, *Forgotten Patriot*, p 144.

48 Smith, *The Origins of the South African War*, pp 321–322.

CHAPTER 12 Build-Up to War

1 Smith, *The Origins of the South African War*, p 317.

2 Rotberg & Shore, *The Founder*, p 619.

3 Ibid.

4 Smith, *The Origins of the South African War*, p 339.

5 Ibid, p 341.

6 Ibid, p 342.

7 Ibid, p 344.

8 Bossenbroek, M, *The Boer War* (Jacana, 2015), p 118.

9 Smith, *The Origins of the South African War*, p 351.

10 Ibid.

11 Headlam (ed), *The Milner Papers*, *Vol I*, p 490.

12 Smith, *The Origins of the South African War*, p 353.

13 Thompson, *Forgotten Patriot*, p 147.

14 Thompson, *A Wider Patriotism*, p 51.

15 Headlam (ed), *The Milner Papers*, *Vol I*, p 493.

16 Jeal, T, *Baden-Powell* (Pimlico, 1991), p 208.

17 Pakenham, *The Boer War*, p 90.

18 Milner, Lady V, *My Picture Gallery 1886–1901* (John Murray, 1951),

p 125.

19 Ibid.

20 O'Brien, *Milner*, p 161.

21 Bush, *Edwardian Ladies and Imperial Power*, p 45.

22 Cecil, H & M, *Imperial Marriage: An Edwardian War and Peace* (John Murray, 2002), p 114.

23 Bush, *Edwardian Ladies and Imperial Power*, p 47.

24 Smith, *The Origins of the South African War*, p 326.

25 Ibid, pp 329–330.

26 Ibid, p 329.

27 Headlam (ed), *The Milner Papers*, *Vol I*, p 536.

28 Ibid, p 545.

29 Ibid.

30 Marlowe, *Milner*, p 88.

31 Smith, *The Origins of the South African War*, p 380.

32 Nutting, A, *Scramble for Africa*, p 435.

33 Ibid.

34 Meredith, *Diamonds, Gold and War*, p 423.

35 Lewsen, *John X Merriman*, p 216.

36 Ibid.

37 Headlam (ed), *The Milner Papers*, *Vol I*, p 559.

CHAPTER 13 Strategic Blunders

1 Headlam, C (ed), *The Milner Papers*, *Vol II*, p 8.

2 Pakenham, *The Boer War*, p 116.

3 Bossenbroek, *The Boer War*, p 145.

4 Headlam (ed), *The Milner Papers*, *Vol II*, p 12.

5 Ibid, p 15.

6 Lewsen, *John X Merriman*, p 219.

7 Marlowe, *Milner*, p 92.

8 Lewsen, *John X Merriman*, p 218.

9 Ibid, p 216.

10 Pakenham, *The Boer War*, p 166.

11 Ibid, p 158.

12　Ibid, p 117.

13　O'Brien, *Milner*, p 167.

14　Kruger, R, *Good-Bye Dolly Gray: The Story of the Boer War* (Pan Books, 1977), p 101.

15　Headlam (ed), *The Milner Papers, Vol II*, p 32.

16　O'Brien, *Milner*, p 168.

17　Headlam (ed), *The Milner Papers, Vol II*, p 43.

18　Ibid, pp 23–24.

19　Pakenham, *The Boer War*, p 246.

20　Ibid, p 247.

21　Ibid, p 248.

22　Headlam (ed), *The Milner Papers, Vol II*, p 35.

23　Ibid.

24　Ibid, p 35.

25　Pakenham, *The Boer War*, p 166.

26　Milner, *My Picture Gallery*, p 144.

27　Thompson, *A Wider Patriotism*, p 57.

28　Ibid, p 58.

29　Headlam (ed), *The Milner Papers, Vol II*, p 74.

30　Ibid, p 73.

31　Ibid, p 74.

32　Milner, *My Picture Gallery*, p 161.

33　Headlam (ed), *The Milner Papers, Vol II*, p 55.

34　Wrench, *Alfred Lord Milner*, p 213.

35　Thompson, *Forgotten Patriot*, p 159.

CHAPTER 14 Numbers Count

1　Meredith, *Afrikaner Odyssey*, p 109.

2　Samson, A, *Kitchener: The Man not the Myth* (Helicon & Co), p 83.

3　O'Brien, *Milner*, p 171.

4　Meredith, *Afrikaner Odyssey*, pp 109-110.

5　Judd, & Surridge, *The Boer War*, p 146.

6　Roberts, *Cecil Rhodes*, p 278.

7　Judd & Surridge, *The Boer War*, p 146.

8　Meredith, *Diamonds, Gold and War*, p 441.

9　Meredith, *Afrikaner Odyssey*, p 110.

10　Judd & Surridge, *The Boer War*, p 174.

11　Ibid.

12　Wrench, *Alfred Lord Milner*, p 217.

13　Headlam (ed), *The Milner Papers, Vol II*, p 53.

14　Ibid, p 61.

15　Ibid, pp 65–66.

16　Meredith, *Afrikaner Odyssey*, p 111.

17　Meredith, *Diamonds, Gold and War*, p 443.

18　Ibid.

19　Pakenham, *The Boer War*, p 388.

20　Headlam (ed), *The Milner Papers, Vol II*, p 92.

21　O'Brien, p 177.

22　Meredith, *Afrikaner Odyssey*, pp 114–115.

23　Ibid.

24　Headlam (ed), *The Milner Papers, Vol II*, p 72.

25　Ibid, p 68.

26　Gilmour, *The Long Recessional*, pp 148–149.

27　Meredith, *Diamonds, Gold and War*, p 444.

28　Ibid.

29　Ibid, p 445.

30　Judd & Surridge, *The Boer War*, p 182.

31　Ibid.

32　Thompson, *Forgotten Patriot*, p 164.

33　Ibid.

34　Cecil, *Imperial Marriage*, p 159.

35　Bush, *Edwardian Ladies and Imperial Power*, p 48.

36　Wrench, *Alfred Lord Milner*, p 219.

37　Headlam (ed), *The Milner Papers, Vol II*, p 104.

38　Ibid, p 79.

39　Marlowe, *Milner*, p 92.

40　Headlam (ed), *The Milner Papers, Vol II*, p 106.

41　Ibid, pp 106–107.

42 Ibid.
43 Ibid.
44 Ibid, pp 109–110.
45 Thompson, *Forgotten Patriot*, p 165.

CHAPTER 15 **Pretoria Falls**

1 Meredith, *Afrikaner Odyssey*, p 118.
2 Ibid.
3 Ibid, p 119.
4 Ibid, p 120.
5 Rogers, *Lawyers In Turmoil*, p 457.
6 Meredith, *Diamonds, Gold and War*, p 446.
7 Trew, P, *The Boer War Generals* (Jonathan Ball Publishers, 1999), p 8.
8 Thompson, *Forgotten Patriot*, p 166.
9 Headlam (ed), *The Milner Papers*, Vol II, p 141.
10 Thompson, *A Wider Patriotism*, p 63.
11 Ibid.
12 Headlam (ed), *The Milner Papers*, Vol II, p 142.
13 Ibid.
14 Ibid.
15 Ibid, p 145.
16 Ibid, p 151.
17 Thompson, *Forgotten Patriot*, p 167.
18 Headlam (ed), *The Milner Papers*, Vol II, p 156.
19 Ibid.
20 Thompson, *Forgotten Patriot*, p 171.
21 Rotberg, & Shore, *The Founder*, p 662.
22 Massie, *Dreadnought*, p 288.
23 Massie, p 289.
24 O'Brien, *Milner*, p 182.
25 Thompson, *Forgotten Patriot*, p 168.
26 Pakenham, *The Boer War*, p 468.
27 Ibid.
28 Ibid, p 469.
29 Ibid, p 458.
30 Ibid, p 485.
31 Ibid.
32 Thompson, *Forgotten Patriot*, p 169.

33 Ibid.
34 Headlam (ed), *The Milner Papers*, Vol II, p 191.
35 Holt, E, *The Boer War* (Putnam, 1958), p 246

CHAPTER 16 **Scorched Earth**

1 Thomas, RD, *Two Generals: Buller and Botha in The Boer War* (AuthorHouse, 2012), p 156.
2 Headlam (ed), *The Milner Papers*, Vol II, p 166.
3 Marlowe, *Milner*, pp 92–93.
4 Headlam (ed), *The Milner Papers*, Vol II, p 170.
5 Ibid, pp 171–172.
6 Pakenham, *The Boer War*, pp 485–486.
7 Headlam (ed), *The Milner Papers*, Vol II, p 174.
8 Ibid, p 166.
9 Jeal, *Baden-Powell*, p 335.
10 Pakenham, *The Boer War*, p 487.
11 Meredith, *Diamonds, Gold and War*, p 453.
12 Ibid.
13 Judd, & Surridge, *The Boer War*, p 194.
14 Headlam (ed), *The Milner Papers*, Vol II, p 188.
15 Ibid, p 189.
16 O'Brien, *Milner*, p 184.
17 Thompson, *A Wider Patriotism*, p 66.
18 Headlam (ed), *The Milner Papers*, Vol II, p 188.
19 Meredith, *Diamonds, Gold and War*, p 453.
20 Ibid.
21 Judd & Surridge, *The Boer War*, p 202.
22 Royle, T, *The Kitchener Enigma* (Michael Joseph, 1985), p 182.
23 Headlam (ed), *The Milner Papers*, Vol II, p 211.
24 Royle, *The Kitchener Enigma* p 182.

25 Judd & Surridge, *The Boer War*, p 204.

26 Thompson, *Forgotten Patriot*, p 175.

27 Headlam (ed), *The Milner Papers*, Vol II, p 215.

28 Thompson, *A Wider Patriotism*, p 67.

29 Thompson, *Forgotten Patriot*, p 179.

30 Ibid.

31 Headlam (ed), *The Milner Papers*, Vol II, pp 235–236.

32 Ibid.

33 Nimocks, W, *Milner's Young Men: The 'Kindergarten' in Edwardian Imperial Affairs* (Hodder & Stoughton, 1970), p 30.

34 Headlam (ed), *The Milner Papers*, Vol II, p 238

Chapter 17 'Miracles are expected of me'

1 Pakenham, *The Boer War*, p 502.

2 Brits, E, *Emily Hobhouse: Beloved Traitor* (Tafelberg, 2016), p 70.

3 Ibid.

4 Headlam (ed), *The Milner Papers*, Vol II, p 253.

5 Ibid.

6 Thompson, *Forgotten Patriot*, p 177.

7 Headlam (ed), *The Milner Papers*, Vol II, p 250.

8 Ibid.

9 Ibid, pp 254–255.

10 O'Brien, *Milner*, p 186.

11 Gollin, *A Proconsul in Politics*, p 38.

12 Hattersley, *The Edwardians*, p 93.

13 James, L, *Churchill and Empire: Portrait of an Imperialist* (Weidenfeld & Nicolson, 2013), p 39.

14 Hattersley, *The Edwardians*, p 93.

15 Headlam (ed), *The Milner Papers*, Vol II, p 252.

16 Thompson, *Forgotten Patriot*, p 179.

17 Headlam (ed), *The Milner Papers*, Vol II, p 262.

18 Pakenham, *The Boer War*, p 508.

19 Ibid.

20 Massie, *Dreadnought*, pp 554–555.

21 Pakenham, *The Boer War*, p 510.

22 Le May, GHL, *British Supremacy in South Africa 1899–1907* (The Clarendon Press, 1965), p 112.

23 Judd, & Surridge, *The Boer War*, p 208.

24 Headlam (ed), *The Milner Papers*, Vol II, p 258.

25 Ibid.

26 Le May, *British Supremacy in South Africa*, p 113.

27 Pakenham, *The Boer War*, p 512.

28 Nimocks, *Milner's Young Men*, p 27.

29 Louis, WR, *In the Name of God, Go! Leo Amery and the British Empire in the Age of Churchill* (WW Norton, 1992), p 39.

30 Amery, LS, *My Political Life, Vol 1: England Before the Storm 1896–1914* (Hutchinson, 1953), p 161.

31 Thompson, *Forgotten Patriot*, p 181.

32 Ibid.

33 Headlam (ed), *The Milner Papers*, Vol II, p 266.

34 Bush, *Edwardian Ladies and Imperial Power*, p 52.

35 Ibid, pp 52–53.

36 Headlam (ed), *The Milner Papers*, Vol II, p 269.

Chapter 18 Falling Out with Kitchener

1 Pakenham, *The Boer War*, p 535.

2 Royle, *The Kitchener Enigma*, p 184.

3 Headlam (ed), *The Milner Papers*, Vol II, p 257.

4 Ibid, p 259.

5 Kruger, *Good-Bye Dolly Gray*, p 438.

6 Judd & Surridge, *The Boer War*, p 214.

7 Headlam (ed), *The Milner Papers*, Vol II, p 269.

8 Ibid, p 273.

9   According to Anglo-Boer War expert Professor Fransjohan Pretorius.
10 Headlam (ed), *The Milner Papers, Vol II*, pp 274–275.
11 Ibid, p 275.
12 Ibid, p 274.
13 Ibid, p 277.
14 Marlowe, *Milner*, p 114.
15 Le May, *British Supremacy in South Africa*, p 121.
16 Headlam (ed), *The Milner Papers, Vol II*, p 277.
17 Ibid, p 278.
18 Judd & Surridge, *The Boer War*, p 212
19 Ibid.
20 Headlam (ed), *The Milner Papers, Vol II*, p 286.
21 Ibid.
22 Ibid, pp 291–292.
23 Ibid, p 287.
24 Ibid, p 293.
25 Ibid.
26 Ibid.
27 Judd & Surridge, *The Boer War*, p 213.
28 Ibid.
29 Headlam (ed), *The Milner Papers, Vol II*, p 294.
30 Ibid, pp 294–295.
31 Thompson, *Forgotten Patriot*, p 184.
32 Ibid.
33 Le May, *British Supremacy in South Africa*, p 124.
34 Ibid.
35 Marlowe, *Milner*, p, 122.

CHAPTER 19 Peace at Last

1   Morris, *Farewell the Trumpets*, p 125.
2   Judd, & Surridge, *The Boer War*, p 270.
3   Le May, *British Supremacy in South Africa*, p 125.
4   Hobhouse, E, *Die Smarte van die Oorlog en wie dit Gely het* (Nasionale Pers, 1941), p 399.
5   Warwick, P (ed), *The South African War: The Anglo Boer War, 1899–1902* (Longman, 1980), p 264.
6   Bossenbroek, *The Boer War*, p 394.
7   Headlam (ed), *The Milner Papers, Vol II*, p 326.
8   Ibid.
9   Bossenbroek, *The Boer War*, p 394.
10 Judd & Surridge, *The Boer War*, p 278; Le May, *British Supremacy in South Africa*, p 135.
11 Bossenbroek, *The Boer War*, p 396.
12 Le May, *British Supremacy in South Africa*, p 134.
13 Ibid, p 136.
14 Judd & Surridge, *The Boer War*, p 279.
15 Headlam (ed), *The Milner Papers, Vol II*, p 331.
16 Le May, *British Supremacy in South Africa*, p 137.
17 Ibid.
18 Headlam (ed), *The Milner Papers, Vol II*, p 334,
19 Ibid, p 339.
20 Ibid, p 340.
21 Ibid, p 411.
22 Ibid.
23 Thompson, *Forgotten Patriot*, p 188.
24 Bossenbroek, *The Boer War*, p 398.
25 Judd & Surridge, *The Boer War*, p 285.
26 Bossenbroek, *The Boer War*, p 397.
27 Reitz, D, *Commando: A Boer Journal of the Boer War* (Faber & Faber, 1929), p 320.
28 Le May, *British Supremacy in South Africa*, p 131.
29 Ibid.
30 Ibid, p 144.
31 Bossenbroek, *The Boer War*, pp 399–400.
32 Holt, *The Boer War*, p 290.
33 Headlam (ed), *The Milner Papers, Vol II*, p 349.
34 Ibid.

35　Bossenbroek, *The Boer War*, p 401.

36　Pakenham, *The Boer War*, p 569.

37　Judd & Surridge, *The Boer War*, p 296.

38　Headlam (ed), *The Milner Papers*, *Vol II*, p 364.

39　Ibid.

40　Ibid, p 365.

41　Ibid.

42　Ibid, p 366.

43　Royle, *The Kitchener Enigma*, p 195.

44　O'Brien, *Milner*, p 195.

45　Pakenham, *The Boer War*, p 570.

CHAPTER 20 **Going North**

1　Marlowe, *Milner*, p 123.

2　De Kiewiet, *A History of South Africa*, p 144.

3　Headlam (ed), *The Milner Papers*, *Vol II*, p 407.

4　Ibid.

5　Marlowe, *Milner*, p 123.

6　Headlam (ed), *The Milner Papers*, *Vol II*, p 406.

7　Worsfold, WB, *Lord Milner's Work in South Africa* (John Murray 1906), p 485.

8　Gollin, *Proconsul in Politics*, p 47.

9　Dubow, S. 'Colonial Nationalism, The Milner Kindergarten and the Rise of "South Africanism", 1902–101', *History Workshop Journal* 43(1) (1997), p 56.

10　Headlam (ed), *The Milner Papers*, *Vol II*, p 423.

11　De Kiewiet, *A History of South Africa*, p 144.

12　Lewsen, *John X Merriman*, p 255.

13　Headlam (ed), *The Milner Papers*, *Vol II*, p 417

14　O'Brien, *Milner*, p 196.

15　Ibid.

16　Headlam (ed), *The Milner Papers*, *Vol II*, p 418.

17　Gollin, *Proconsul in Politics*, p 39.

18　Headlam (ed), *The Milner Papers*, *Vol II*, p 419.

19　Ibid, pp 420–421.

20　Thompson, *Forgotten Patriot*, p 204.

21　O'Brien, *Milner*, pp 199–200.

22　Nimocks, *Milner's Young Men*, pp 30–31.

23　Ibid.

24　Ibid, p 31.

25　Ibid.

26　Ibid, p 32.

27　Thakur, V and Vale, P, *South Africa, Race and the Making of International Relations* (Rowman & Littlefield International, 2020), p 2.

28　Nimocks, *Milner's Young Men*, p 32.

29　Ibid, p 33.

30　Ibid, p 34.

31　Davenport, R & Saunders, C, *South Africa: A Modern History* (Macmillan/St Martin's Press, 2000), p 237.

32　Headlam (ed), *The Milner Papers*, *Vol II*, p 370.

33　Ibid.

34　Ibid, p 375.

35　Bossenbroek, *The Boer War*, p 407.

36　Le May, *British Supremacy in South Africa*, p 155.

37　Ibid, p 156.

38　Headlam (ed), *The Milner Papers*, *Vol II*, p 384.

39　Ibid, pp 384–385.

40　FitzPatrick, P, *South African Memories* (Cassell, 1932), p 194.

41　Ibid.

42　Headlam (ed), *The Milner Papers*, *Vol II*, p 428.

43　Ibid.

CHAPTER 21 **Chamberlain's Visit**

1　Crosby, *Joseph Chamberlain*, p 167.

2　Thompson, *Forgotten Patriot*, p 222.

3　O'Brien, *Milner*, p 202.

4　Headlam (ed), *The Milner Papers*,

Vol II, pp 432–433.

5 Ibid.

6 Meintjes, J, *President Paul Kruger: A Biography* (Cassell, 1974), pp 117–118.

7 Headlam (ed), *The Milner Papers, Vol II*, p 433.

8 O'Brien, *Milner*, p 203.

9 Ibid.

10 Worsfold, WB, T*he Reconstruction of the New Colonies Under Lord Milner, Vol 1* (Kegan Paul, Trench, Trubner & Co, 1913), p 187.

11 Steyn, J C, '*Ons Gaan 'n Taal Maak: Afrikaans sedert die Patriot-jare* (Kraal Uitgewers 2014), pp 63–65.

12 Ibid.

13 Worsfold, *The Reconstruction of the New Colonies Under Lord Milner, Vol 1*, p 198.

14 Headlam (ed), *The Milner Papers, Vol II*, p 440.

15 FitzPatrick, *South African Memories*, p 193.

16 Thompson, *Forgotten Patriot*, p 222.

17 O'Brien, *Milner*, p 204.

18 Ibid.

19 Headlam (ed), *The Milner Papers, Vol II*, p 443.

20 Ibid, p 442.

21 Worsfold, *The Reconstruction of the New Colonies Under Lord Milner, Vol 1*, p 217.

22 Ibid, p 224.

23 Marlowe, *Milner*, p 145.

24 Thompson, *Forgotten Patriot*, p 223.

25 Crosby, *Joseph Chamberlain*, p 156.

26 Ibid.

27 O'Brien, *Milner*, p 205.

28 Gilmour, *The Long Recessional*, p 159.

29 O'Brien, *Milner*, p 205.

30 Ibid.

Chapter 22 Reconstruction

1 Lewsen, *John X Merriman*, p 260.

2 Ibid, p 262.

3 Headlam (ed), *The Milner Papers, Vol II*, p 444.

4 Ibid, p 449.

5 Ibid.

6 O'Brien, *Milner*, p 205.

7 Amery, *My Political Life, Vol 1*, p 178.

8 Buchan, *Memory Hold-the-Door*, pp 101–102.

9 Headlam (ed), *The Milner Papers, Vol II*, p 450.

10 Ibid, p 451.

11 Davenport & Saunders, *South Africa: A Modern History*, p 238.

12 Le May, *British Supremacy in South Africa*, p 158.

13 O'Brien, *Milner*, p 207.

14 Headlam (ed), *The Milner Papers, Vol II*, p 461.

15 Crosby, *Joseph Chamberlain*, p 175.

16 Headlam (ed), *The Milner Papers, Vol II*, p 466.

17 Ibid.

18 Ibid, p 468.

19 Ibid, p 469.

20 Ibid.

21 Ibid, p 470.

22 Thompson, *Forgotten Patriot*, p 227.

23 Davenport & Saunders, *South Africa: A Modern History*, p 240.

24 Ibid.

25 Ibid.

26 Schoeman, *Rekonstruksie*, p 115.

27 Denoon, *A Grand Illusion*, p xiv.

28 'The Natives land Act of 1913', South African History Online, 2021, sahistory.org.za/article/natives-land-act-1913.

29 Ibid.

30 Davenport & Saunders, *South Africa: A Modern History*, p 240.

31 Headlam (ed), *The Milner Papers, Vol II*, p 465.
32 Ibid, p 470.

CHAPTER 23 **Defying the King**

1   O'Brien, *Milner*, p 211.
2   Ibid.
3   Thompson, *Forgotten Patriot*, p.259.
4   Ibid, p 228.
5   Ibid.
6   Crosby, *Joseph Chamberlain*, p 164.
7   Massie, *Dreadnought*, p 324.
8   Ibid.
9   Headlam (ed), *The Milner Papers, Vol II*, p 472.
10 Ibid, p 473.
11 Thompson, *Forgotten Patriot*, p 229.
12 O'Brien, *Milner*, p 212.
13 Headlam (ed), *The Milner Papers, Vol II*, p 475.
14 O'Brien, *Milner*, p 213.
15 Hattersley, *The Edwardians*, p 106.
16 Meintjes, *General Louis Botha*, p 130.
17 Thompson, *Forgotten Patriot*, p 229.
18 Headlam (ed), *The Milner Papers, Vol II*, p 477.
19 Ibid, p 476.
20 O'Brien, *Milner*, p 213.
21 Headlam (ed), *The Milner Papers, Vol II*, p 481.
22 Worsfold, *The Reconstruction of the New Colonies Under Lord Milner, Vol 2*, p 341.
23 Headlam (ed), *The Milner Papers, Vol II*, p 481.
24 Le May, *British Supremacy in South Africa*, p 162.
25 Ibid.
26 Worsfold, *The Reconstruction of the New Colonies Under Lord Milner, Vol 2*, pp 235–236, f1.
27 Meintjes, *General Louis Botha*, p 129.
28 Oakes, D (ed), *Illustrated History of South Africa: The Real Story* (Reader's Digest Association, 1989), p 267.
29 Meintjes, *General Louis Botha*, p 129.
30 Le May, *British Supremacy in South Africa*, p 163.
31 Worsfold, *The Reconstruction of the New Colonies Under Lord Milner, Vol 1*, p 336.
32 Marlowe, *Milner*, p 160.
33 Worsfold, *The Reconstruction of the New Colonies Under Lord Milner, Vol 1*, p 315.
34 Headlam (ed), *The Milner Papers, Vol II*, pp 482–483.
35 Ibid, p 483.
36 Worsfold, *The Reconstruction of the New Colonies Under Lord Milner, Vol 1*, p 349.
37 Headlam (ed), *The Milner Papers, Vol II*, p 484.

CHAPTER 24 **The Chinese**

1   Marlowe, *Milner*, p 164.
2   Headlam (ed), *The Milner Papers, Vol II*, pp 487–488.
3   Oakes (ed), *Illustrated History of South Africa*, p 268.
4   Marlowe, *Milner*, p 165.
5   Headlam (ed), *The Milner Papers, Vol II*, p 477.
6   Gollin, *Proconsul in Politics*, p 65.
7   Ibid, p 64.
8   Ibid.
9   Marlowe, *Milner*, p 163.
10 Headlam (ed), *The Milner Papers, Vol II*, p 487.
11 Gollin, *Proconsul in Politics*, p 65.
12 Thompson, *Forgotten Patriot*, p 231.
13 Headlam (ed), *The Milner Papers, Vol II*, p 484f.
14 Thompson, *Forgotten Patriot*, p 231.
15 Schoeman, K, *Imperiale Somer: Suid-Afrika tussen Oorlog en Unie, 1902–1910* (Protea Boekhuis, 2015), p 27.

16 Headlam (ed), *The Milner Papers*, Vol II, p 505.
17 Ibid, pp 504–505.
18 Marlowe, *Milner*, p 151.
19 Duminy & Guest, *Interfering in Politics*, p 116.
20 Headlam (ed), *The Milner Papers*, Vol II, p 489.
21 Ibid, p 523.
22 Ibid, p 524.
23 Ibid, p 520.
24 Ibid, p 537.
25 Schoeman, *Rekonstruksie*, p 114.
26 Le May, *British Supremacy in South Africa*, p 165.
27 Hancock, WK, *Smuts: The Fields of Force 1919–1950* (Cambridge University Press, 1968), p 195.
28 Communication between the author and Professor Fransjohan Pretorius, October 2021.
29 Davenport & Saunders, *South Africa: A Modern History*, p 250.
30 Headlam (ed), *The Milner Papers*, Vol II, p 531.
31 Communication between the author and Professor Fransjohan Pretorius, October 2021.
32 Davenport, R, & Saunders, C, *South Africa: A Modern History* (Macmillan Press, 2000), p 250.

Chapter 25 **Successes and Failures**

1 Worsfold, *The Reconstruction of the New Colonies Under Lord Milner, Vol 2*, p 1.
2 Marlowe, *Milner*, p 133.
3 Headlam (ed), *The Milner Papers*, Vol II, p.489.
4 Worsfold, *The Reconstruction of the New Colonies Under Lord Milner, Vol 2*, p 2.
5 Davenport & Saunders, *South Africa: A Modern History*, p 237.
6 O'Brien, *Milner*, p 217.
7 Nimocks, *Milner's Young Men*, p 20.
8 Davenport & Saunders, *South Africa: A Modern History*, p 238.
9 Schoeman, *Rekonstruksie*, p 155
10 Schoeman, *Imperiale Somer*, p 39.
11 Headlam (ed), *The Milner Papers*, Vol II, p 367.
12 Schoeman, *Rekonstruksie*, p 143
13 Ibid, p 144.
14 O'Brien, *Milner*, p 218.
15 Denoon, *A Grand Illusion*, p 77.
16 Worsfold, *The Reconstruction of the New Colonies Under Lord Milner, Vol 2*, p 79.
17 Ibid, p 85.
18 O'Brien, *Milner*, p 218.
19 Worsfold, *The Reconstruction of the New Colonies Under Lord Milner, Vol 2*, pp 199–200.
20 Ibid.
21 Ibid.
22 Ibid.

Chapter 26 **Going Home**

1 Headlam (ed), *The Milner Papers*, Vol II, p 537.
2 Ibid, p 539.
3 Ibid.
4 Nimocks, *Milner's Young Men*, p 55.
5 Le May, *British Supremacy in South Africa*, p 174.
6 Ibid, p 171.
7 Schoeman, *Imperiale Somer*, p 33.
8 Le May, *British Supremacy in South Africa*, p 175.
9 Ibid.
10 Le May, *British Supremacy in South Africa*, pp 171–172.
11 Headlam (ed), *The Milner Papers*, Vol II, p 543.
12 Thompson, *A Wider Patriotism*, p 229, note 52.

13 Headlam (ed), *The Milner Papers*, *Vol II*, p 541.
14 Ibid, pp 541–542.
15 Denoon, *A Grand Illusion*, pp 232–233.
16 Headlam (ed), *The Milner Papers*, *Vol II*, p 544.
17 Ibid.
18 Le May, *British Supremacy in South Africa*, p 176.
19 Ibid, p 177.
20 Thompson, *A Wider Patriotism*, p 103.
21 Headlam (ed), *The Milner Papers*, *Vol II*, p 546.
22 Ibid, p 547.
23 Le May, *British Supremacy in South Africa*, pp 175–176.
24 Breckenridge, 'Lord Milner's Registry', p 8.
25 Ibid.
26 Le May, *British Supremacy in South Africa*, p 179.
27 Headlam (ed), *The Milner Papers*, *Vol II*, p 548.
28 Ibid, p 550.
29 Ibid.
30 Marlowe, *Milner*, p 156.
31 Ibid, p 157.
32 Ibid.

Chapter 27 The Kindergarten

1 Nimocks, *Milner's Young Men*, p 44f.
2 Thompson, *A Wider Patriotism*, p 88.
3 Nimocks, *Milner's Young Men*, p 21.
4 Ibid, p 50.
5 Gollin, *Proconsul in Politics*, p 41.
6 Nimocks, *Milner's Young Men*, p 34.
7 Ibid, p 45.
8 Breckenridge, 'Lord Milner's Registry', p 9.
9 Nimocks, *Milner's Young Men*, p 41.
10 Ibid, p 42.
11 Le May, *British Supremacy in South Africa*, p 81.
12 Thakur & Vale, *South Africa, Race and the Making of International Relations*, p 12.
13 Ibid, p 13.
14 Dubow, 'Colonial Nationalism', pp 77–78.
15 Thakur & Vale, *South Africa, Race and the Making of International Relations*, p 74.
16 Ibid, pp 11–12
17 Nimocks, *Milner's Young Men*, p 48.
18 Schoeman, *Rekonstruksie*, p 109.
19 Thompson, *A Wider Patriotism*, p 93.
20 Le May, *British Supremacy in South Africa*, p 180.
21 Ibid, p 181.
22 James, *Churchill and Empire*, p 38.
23 Le May, *British Supremacy in South Africa*, p 181.
24 Dubow, 'Colonial Nationalism', p 58.
25 Thompson, LM, *The Unification of South Africa* (The Clarendon Press, 1960), p 63.
26 Dubow, 'Colonial Nationalism', pp 66–67.
27 Thompson, *The Unification of South Africa 1902–1910*, p 67.
28 Dubow, 'Colonial Nationalism', p 65.
29 Nimocks, *Milner's Young Men*, p 79.
30 Thompson, *The Unification of South Africa*, p 67.
31 Dubow, 'Colonial Nationalism', p 60.
32 Thakur & Vale, p 25.

Chapter 28 A Mixed Reception

1 Gollin, *Proconsul in Politics*, p 44.
2 Marlowe, *Milner*, p 177.
3 O'Brien, *Milner*, p 229.
4 Marlowe, *Milner*, pp 157–158.
5 Gollin, *Proconsul in Politics*, pp 73–74.
6 Ibid, p 77.
7 Ibid.
8 Malherbe, VC, *What They Said: 1795–1910*. History Documents

(Maskew Miller, 1971), p 212.
9   Gollin, *Proconsul in Politics*, p 60.
10 Thompson, *Forgotten Patriot*, p 243.
11 O'Brien, *Milner*, p 230.
12 Thompson, *Forgotten Patriot*, p 243.
13 Marlowe, *Milner*, p 169.
14 Thompson, *Forgotten Patriot*, p 245.
15 Gollin, *Proconsul in Politics*, p 85.
16 Thompson, *Forgotten Patriot*, p 246.
17 Marlowe, *Milner*, p 171.
18 Gollin, *Proconsul in Politics*, p 89.
19 Marlowe, *Milner*, p 171.
20 Ibid, p 172.
21 O'Brien, *Milner*, p 231.
22 Marlowe, *Milner*, p 172.
23 Cecil, *Imperial Marriage*, p 199.
24 Marlowe, *Milner*, p 184
25 Thompson, *A Wider Patriotism*, p 112.
26 Marlowe, *Milner*, pp 183–184.
27 Ibid, p 176.
28 Ibid, p 177.
29 Thompson, *Forgotten Patriot*, p 256.

CHAPTER 29 Freelancing

1   Cecil, *Imperial Marriage*, p 199.
2   Gollin, *Proconsul in Politics*, p 111.
3   Ibid, p 113.
4   Thompson, *A Wider Patriotism*, p 114.
5   Marlowe, *Milner*, p 181.
6   Gollin, *Proconsul in Politics*, p 119.
7   Ibid, p 132.
8   Marlowe, *Milner*, p 185.
9   Ibid, p 186.
10 Thompson, *A Wider Patriotism*, p 116.
11 Marlowe, *Milner*, p 186.
12 Ibid.
13 Thompson, *A Wider Patriotism*, p 117.
14 Ibid.
15 Ibid.
16 Thompson, *Forgotten Patriot*, p 264.
17 Gollin, *Proconsul in Politics*, p 145.
18 O'Brien, *Milner*, pp 236–237.
19 Marlowe, *Milner*, p 187.
20 Ibid, p 189.

21 Thompson, *A Wider Patriotism*, p 131.
22 Thompson, *Forgotten Patriot*, p 269.
23 Cecil, *Imperial Marriage*, p 205.
24 O'Brien, *Milner*, pp 240–241.
25 Gollin, *Proconsul in Politics*, pp 157–158.
26 See Thakur & Vale, *South Africa, Race and the Making of International Relations*, p 12.
27 Marlowe, *Milner*, p 208.
28 Nimocks, *Milner's Young Men*, p 104.
29 Marlowe, *Milner*, p 208.
30 Ibid, p 209.
31 Ibid.
32 Ibid.
33 Ibid, p 179.
34 Ibid, p 210.
35 Gollin, *Proconsul in Politics*, p 166.
36 Schoeman, *Rekonstruksie*, p 117.
37 Marlowe, *Milner*, p 215.
38 Thakur & Vale, *South Africa, Race and the Making of International Relations*, p 11.

CHAPTER 30 Irish Troubles

1   Gollin, *Proconsul in Politics*, p 172.
2   Churchill, W, *Great Contemporaries* (Leo Cooper, 1990), pp 90–91.
3   Marlowe, *Milner*, p 219.
4   Gollin, *Proconsul in Politics*, p 179.
5   Marlowe, *Milner*, p 233.
6   Ibid.
7   Ibid, p 221.
8   Gollin, *Proconsul in Politics*, p 169.
9   Ibid, p 170.
10 Pyrah, GB, *Imperial Policy and South Africa, 1902–10* (The Clarendon Press, 1955), p 14.
11 Thompson, *Forgotten Patriot*, pp 285–286.
12 Marlowe, *Milner*, p 199.
13 Ibid.
14 Thompson, *A Wider Patriotism*, p 146.
15 Marlowe, *Milner*, p 222.

16 Ibid, p 223.
17 Gollin, *Proconsul in Politics*, p 184.
18 Marlowe, *Milner*, p 224.
19 Ibid.
20 Gollin, *Proconsul in Politics*, p 185.
21 Ibid, p 186.
22 Marlowe, *Milner*, p 226.
23 Thompson, *Forgotten Patriot*, p 298.
24 Marlowe, *Milner*, p 227.
25 Thompson, *Forgotten Patriot*, p 299.
26 Gollin, *Proconsul in Politics*, p 198.
27 Ibid, p 191.
28 Ibid, p 194.
29 Ibid, pp 199–200.
30 Massie, *Dreadnought*, p 879.
31 James, *Churchill and Empire*, p 78.
32 Marlowe, *Milner*, p 231.
33 Gollin, *Proconsul in Politics*, p 218.
34 Marlowe, *Milner*, p 231.
35 Hattersley, *The Edwardians*, p 479.
36 Thompson, *Forgotten Patriot*, pp 306–307.
37 Ibid, p 307.

Chapter 31 War

1 James, *Churchill and Empire*, p 89.
2 Gollin, *Proconsul in Politics*, p 240.
3 O'Brien, *Milner*, p 257.
4 Marlowe, *Milner*, p 239.
5 Massie, *Dreadnought*, p xxii.
6 Thompson, *Forgotten Patriot*, p 310.
7 Thompson, *A Wider Patriotism*, p 150.
8 Ibid, p 151.
9 Marlowe, *Milner*, p 240.
10 Wrench, *Alfred Lord Milner*, p 302.
11 Ibid.
12 Gollin, *Proconsul in Politics*, p 227.
13 Ibid, pp 228–229.
14 Ibid, p 248.
15 O'Brien, *Milner*, pp 262–263.
16 Marlowe, *Milner*, p 242.
17 Gollin, *Proconsul in Politics*, p 269.
18 Ibid, pp 277–279.
19 Thompson, *Forgotten Patriot*, p 319.

20 Gollin, *Proconsul in Politics*, p 281.
21 Marlowe, *Milner*, p 246.
22 Gollin, *Proconsul in Politics*, p 347.
23 Wrench, *Alfred Lord Milner*, pp 307–308.
24 Gollin, *Proconsul in Politics*, p 348.
25 Ibid, p 330.
26 Marlowe, *Milner*, p 248.
27 Wrench, *Alfred Lord Milner*, p 302.
28 Thompson, *Forgotten Patriot*, p 320.
29 Ibid.
30 Marlowe, *Milner*, p 249.
31 Gollin, *Proconsul in Politics*, p 349.
32 O'Brien, *Milner*, p 269.
33 Marlowe, *Milner*, p 250.
34 Ibid, p 252.
35 Ibid.
36 Gollin, *Proconsul in Politics*, p 356.
37 Ibid.
38 Gollin, *Proconsul in Politics*, p 364.
39 Ibid

Chapter 32 War Cabinet

1 Thompson, *Forgotten Patriot*, p 331.
2 Marlowe, *Milner*, p 257.
3 Ibid.
4 O'Brien, *Milner*, p 274.
5 Thompson, *Forgotten Patriot*, p 332.
6 Marlowe, *Milner*, p 258.
7 O'Brien, *Milner*, p 273.
8 Thompson, *A Wider Patriotism*, p 160.
9 Louis, *In the Name of God, Go!*, p 66.
10 Thompson, *Forgotten Patriot*, p 337.
11 Thompson, *Forgotten Patriot*, p 427, note 78.
12 Marlowe, *Milner*, p 268.
13 MS Milner, Annual Diary, 1917, dep 88, pp 142 and 157, Milner Papers & Manuscripts, Bodleian Library, Oxford University (hereafter MP).
14 MS Milner, Annual Diary, 1917, pp 360–361, MP.
15 Marlowe, *Milner*, 267–268.
16 Thompson, *A Wider Patriotism*, p 163.

17 Ibid, p 208.
18 Hoare, S, *A Watchmaker Makes His Rounds* (unpublished autobiography, 1959), p 80.
19 Ibid, p 84.
20 Gollin, *Proconsul in Politics*, p 404.
21 Marlowe, *Milner*, pp 263–264.
22 Gollin, *Proconsul in Politics*, pp 404–405.
23 Ibid, p 410.
24 Ibid, pp 411–412.
25 Ibid.
26 Ibid.
27 Marlowe, *Milner*, pp 273–274.
28 MS Milner, Annual Diary, 1917, p 330, MP.
29 Reid, *Five Days from Defeat*, p 201.
30 Marlowe, *Milner*, p 307.
31 James, *Churchill and Empire*, p 120.
32 Ibid, p 122.
33 MS Milner, Annual Diary, 1918, dep 89, p 315, MP.
34 Ibid.
35 Ibid, p 343.
36 Wrench, *Alfred Lord Milner*, p 344.
37 Ibid.
38 Ibid, pp 351-2.

CHAPTER 33 **Colonial Secretary**

1 Marlowe, *Milner*, p 319.
2 Ibid.
3 Gollin, *Proconsul in Politics*, p 579.
4 Thompson, *Forgotten Patriot*, p 356.
5 Ibid, p 355.
6 Ibid, p 356.
7 '1918 United Kingdom general election', Wikipedia.
8 Marlowe, *Milner*, p 321.
9 O'Brien, *Milner*, p 324.
10 Cecil, *Imperial Marriage*, p 287.
11 Gollin, *Proconsul in Politics*, p 584.
12 MS Milner, Annual Diary, 1919, dep 90, p 2, MP.

13 Thompson, *Forgotten Patriot*, p 358.
14 MS Milner, Annual Diary, 1919, dep 90, p 133, MP.
15 Gollin, *Proconsul in Politics*, p 573.
16 Ibid, p 576.
17 Marlowe, *Milner*, p 360.
18 O'Brien, *Milner*, p 335.
19 MS Milner, Annual Diary, 1919, dep 90, p 82. MP
20 Cecil, *Imperial Marriage*, p 292.
21 MS Milner, Annual Diary, 1919, dep 90, p 130, MP.
22 Ibid, pp 137 and 140.
23 Wrench, *Alfred Lord Milner*, p 357.
24 FitzPatrick, *South African Memories*, pp 128–129.
25 Wrench, *Alfred Lord Milner*, pp 357–358.
26 Thompson, *Forgotten Patriot*, p 361.
27 MS Milner, Annual Diary, 1919, dep 90. p 240, MP.
28 Marlowe, *Milner*, p 337.
29 Ibid, p 344.
30 Ibid, p 348.
31 Ibid.
32 Ibid, p 351.
33 MS Milner, Smuts (correspondence with), Eng hist c 691, 61C, MP.
34 Ibid.
35 Gollin, *Proconsul in Politics*, p 584.
36 Ibid, p 596.
37 Thompson, *Forgotten Patriot*, p 368.
38 Gollin, *Proconsul in Politics*, pp 597–598.
39 O'Brien, *Milner*, p 367.

CHAPTER 34 **A Busy Retirement**

1 O'Brien, *Milner*, p 366.
2 Thompson, *Forgotten Patriot*, p 369.
3 O'Brien, *Milner*, p 365.
4 Marlowe, *Milner*, p 338.
5 O'Brien, *Milner*, p 368.
6 Thompson, *Forgotten Patriot*, p 372.
7 Ibid, p 370.

8 Ibid.
9 Cecil, *Imperial Marriage*, p 303.
10 O'Brien, *Milner*, p 370.
11 Ibid.
12 Cecil, *Imperial Marriage*, p 305.
13 Marlowe, *Milner*, p 359.
14 Ibid, pp 359–360.
15 O'Brien, *Milner*, p 374.
16 Marlowe, *Milner*, p 360.
17 Thompson, *Forgotten Patriot*, p 373.
18 Ibid, p 374.
19 O'Brien, *Milner*, p 380.
20 Ibid, p 382.
21 MS Milner, Annual Diary, 1924, dep 95, p 322, MP.
22 Ibid.
23 Ibid, p 323.
24 Ibid, p 327.
25 MS Milner, dep 672, pp 13–14, MP.
26 Headlam (ed), *The Milner Papers, Vol II*, p 534f.
27 MS Milner, dep 672, pp 21–22, MP.
28 MS Milner, Annual Diary, 1924, pp 343–344, MP.
29 Ibid, p 344.
30 MS Milner, dep 672, pp 22–23, MP.
31 MS Milner, Annual Diary, 1924, p 345, MP.
32 MS Milner, dep 672, pp 26-7, MP.
33 MS Milner, Annual Diary, 1924, pp 363–364, MP.
34 MS Milner, dep 103, pp 15–16, MP.
35 O'Brien, *Milner*, pp 383–384.
36 Ibid, p 384.
37 Ibid.
38 MS Milner, dep 103, p 83, MP.
39 Thompson, *A Wider Patriotism*, p 202.
40 MS Milner, dep 103, p 5a, MP.
41 Ibid.
42 Marlowe, *Milner*, p 361.
43 MS Milner, dep 103, p 87, MP.
44 MS Milner, dep 103, pp 85–86, MP.
45 Thompson, *Forgotten Patriot*, p 380.
46 O'Brien, *Milner*, p 385.
47 Wrench, *Alfred Lord Milner*, p 366.
48 Ibid.
49 Thompson, *Forgotten Patriot*, p 384.
50 Ibid, p 381.
51 *Lincolnshire Echo*, 14 May 1925.
52 *The Scotsman*, 15 May 1925.
53 Thompson, *Forgotten Patriot*, p 384; Marlowe, *Milner*, pp 364–365.

CHAPTER 35 Summing Up

1 Greene, G. *The Quiet American*, (Heinemann, 1960), p 61.
2 MacMillan, M. 'Which Past Is Prologue? Heeding the Right Warnings from History', *Foreign Affairs*, Sept/Oct 2020.
3 James, *Churchill and Empire*, p 24.
4 Gollin, *Proconsul in Politics*, p 4.
5 Ibid.
6 Ibid.
7 Thompson, *The Unification of South Africa*, p 58.
8 Smith, *The Origins of the South African War*, p 148.
9 Ibid, pp 414–415.
10 Pakenham, *The Boer War*, p 115.
11 Smith, *The Origins of the South African War*, p 1.
12 Ibid.
13 Gilmour, *The Long Recessional*, p 138.
14 Marlowe, *Milner*, p 99.
15 Buchan, *Memory Hold-the-Door*, Ch. VI, p 6 of 8.
16 Amery, *My Political Life, Vol 1*, p 178.
17 Le May, *British Supremacy in South Africa*, p 212.
18 Ibid, p 30.
19 Ibid, p 177.
20 Ibid, pp 175–176.
21 Ibid.
22 Marlowe, *Milner*, p 175.
23 Taylor, AJP, *From the Boer War to the Cold War: Essays on Twentieth-Century Europe* (Hamish Hamilton, 1995), p 38.

24 Thompson, *Forgotten Patriot*, p 383.
25 O'Brien, *Milner*, p 393.
26 Ibid.
27 Morris, *Farewell the Trumpets*, pp 123–124.
28 Thompson, *The Unification of South Africa*, p 17.

Afterword

1 Cecil, *Imperial Marriage*, p 309.
2 O'Brien, *Milner*, pp 390–391.
3 Gollin, *Proconsul in Politics*, p 606.
4 Ibid.
5 Cecil, *Imperial Marriage*, p 334.
6 Ibid.
7 O'Brien, *Milner*, p 390.
8 Cecil, *Imperial Marriage*, pp 310–311.
9 Ibid.
10 Ibid, p 313.
11 Bush, *Edwardian Ladies and Imperial Power*, p 3.
12 Cecil, *Imperial Marriage*, p 317.
13 Bush, *Edwardian Ladies and Imperial Power*, p 113.
14 Ibid, p 6.
15 Cecil, *Imperial Marriage*, p 315.
16 Bouverie, T, *Appeasing Hitler: Chamberlain, Churchill and the Road to War* (Vintage, 2020), p 149.
17 Ibid, p 69.
18 Cecil, *Imperial Marriage*, p 317.
19 Cecil, *Imperial Marriage*, p 323.
20 Ibid, p 329.
21 Milner, *My Picture Gallery*, p 215.
22 Smuts, JC (jnr), *Jan Christian Smuts* (Cassell, 1952), p 285.
23 MS Milner, 1924, dep 672, pp 22–24, MP.
24 Cecil, *Imperial Marriage*, p 306.
25 Ibid.

Select Bibliography

Books

Allen, C. *Kipling Sahib: India and the Making of Rudyard Kipling.* Abacus, 2008.

Amery, LS (ed). *The Times History of the War in South Africa 1899–1902, Vol 1.* Sampson Low, Marston and Co, 1900.

———. *My Political Life. 2 vols.* Hutchinson, 1953.

Baxter, P. *Gandhi, Smuts and Race in the British Empire: Of Passive and Violent Resistance.* Pen & Sword Books, 2017.

Bossenbroek, MP. *The Boer War.* Jacana, 2015.

Bouverie, T. *Appeasing Hitler: Chamberlain, Churchill, and the Road to War.* Vintage, 2020.

Brendon, P. *The Decline and Fall of the British Empire 1781–1997.* Vintage, 2008.

Brits, E. *Emily Hobhouse: Beloved Traitor.* Tafelberg, 2016.

Buchan, J. *Memory Hold-the-Door.* Read Books Ltd, 2013 (ebook).

Bush, J. *Edwardian Ladies and Imperial Power.* Cassell, 2000.

Cameron, T & Spies, SB (eds). *An Illustrated History of South Africa.* Human & Rousseau, 1988.

Cartwright, AP. *The First South African: The Life and Times of Sir Percy FitzPatrick.* Purnell, 1971.

Cecil, H & M. *Imperial Marriage: An Edwardian War and Peace.* John Murray, 2002.

Churchill, WS. *Great Contemporaries.* Leo Cooper, 1990.

Clarke, P. *Hope and Glory: Britain 1900–2000.* Penguin, 1997.

Colley, R. *World War One.* HarperPress, 2013.

Crafford, FS. *Jan Smuts: A Biography.* Howard Timmins, 1946.

Crankshaw, E. *The Forsaken Idea: A Study of Viscount Milner.* Longmans, Green & Co, 1952.

Crosby, T. *Joseph Chamberlain: A Most Radical Imperialist.* IB Tauris, 2011.

Crwys-Williams, J. *A Country at War, 1939–1945: The Mood of a Nation.* Ashanti, 1992.

Davenport, TRH. *South Africa: A Modern History*. Macmillan, 1991.

——. *The Afrikaner Bond: The History of a South African Political Party*. Oxford University Press, 1966.

Davenport, TRH & Saunders, C. *South Africa: A Modern History*. Macmillan/ St Martin's Press, 2000.

Deedes, WF. *Brief Lives*. Macmillan, 2004.

De Kiewiet, CW. *The Anatomy of South African Misery. The Whidden Lectures 1956*. Oxford University Press, 1956.

——. *A History of South Africa: Social & Economic*. Oxford University Press, 1966.

Denoon, D. *A Grand Illusion: The Failure of Imperial Policy in the Transvaal Colony during the Period of Reconstruction 1900–1905*. Longmans, Green & Co, 1973.

Dubow, S & Jeeves, A (eds). *South Africa's 1940s: Worlds of Possibilities*. Double Storey, 2005.

Duminy, A & Guest, B. *Interfering in Politics: A Biography of Sir Percy FitzPatrick*. Lowry Publishers, 1987.

Egremont, M. *Balfour: A Life of Arthur James Balfour*. Collins, 1980.

Fisher, J. *The Afrikaners*. Cassell, 1969.

FitzPatrick, Sir P. *South African Memories*. Cassell, 1932.

Ferguson, N. *Empire: How Britain Made the Modern World*. Penguin, 2004.

Giliomee, H. *Historian: An Autobiography*. Tafelberg, 2016.

——. *The Afrikaners: Biography of a People*. Tafelberg, 2003.

Giliomee, H & Mbenga, B (eds). *New History of South Africa*. Tafelberg, 2007.

Gilmour, D. *The Long Recessional: The Imperial Life of Rudyard Kipling*. Farrar, Straus and Giroux, 2002.

Gollin, AM. *Proconsul in Politics: A Study of Lord Milner in Opposition and in Power*. Anthony Blond, 1964.

Hancock, WK. *Smuts: The Sanguine Years 1870–1919*. Cambridge University Press, 1968.

——. *The Fields of Force 1919–1950*. Cambridge University Press, 1968.

Hardy, R. *The Poisoned Well: Empire and Its Legacy in the Middle East*. Hurst, 2016.

Hattersley, R. *The Edwardians*. Abacus, 2004.

Headlam, C. (ed). *The Milner Papers, Vol. I: South Africa 1897–1899*. Cassell, 1931.

——. *The Milner Papers, Vol. II: South Africa 1899–1905*. Cassell, 1933.

Heffer, S. *The Age of Decadence: Britain 1880 to 1914*. Random House, 2017.

Heilbroner, R. *The Worldly Philosophers: The Lives, Times, and Ideas of the Great Economic Thinkers*. Simon & Schuster, 1980.

Hoare, S. *A Watchmaker Makes His Rounds*. Unpublished autobiography, 1959.

Hobhouse, E. *Die smarte van die oorlog en wie dit gely het.* Nasionale Pers, 1941.

Holt, E. *The Boer War.* Putnam, 1958.

Human & Rousseau (eds). *They Shaped Our Century: The Most Influential South Africans of the Twentieth Century.* Human & Rousseau, 1999.

Iwan-Muller, EB. *Lord Milner and South Africa.* William Heinemann, 1902

James, L. *Churchill and Empire: Portrait of an Imperialist.* Weidenfeld & Nicolson, 2013.

———. *Empires in the Sun: The Struggle for the Mastery of Africa, 1830–1990.* Jonathan Ball Publishers, 2016.

Jeal, T. *Baden-Powell.* Pimlico, 1991.

Judd, D. *Radical Joe: A Life of Joseph Chamberlain.* Hamilton, 1977.

Judd, D & Surridge, K. *The Boer War: A History,* IB Tauris, 2013.

Keppel-Jones, A. *When Smuts Goes.* Shuter & Shooter, 1949.

Knox, C & Coetzee, C. *Victorian Life at the Cape 1870–1900.* Fernwood Press, 1992.

Kruger, DW. *The Age of the Generals.* Dagbreek, 1958.

Kruger, R. *Good-Bye Dolly Gray: The Story of the Boer War.* Pan Books, 1977.

Le May, GHL. *British Supremacy in South Africa 1899–1907.* The Clarendon Press, 1965.

Lewsen, P. *John X Merriman: Paradoxical South African Statesman.* Yale University Press, 1982.

Lloyd, T. *Empire: The History of the British Empire.* Hambledon and London, 2001.

Louis, WR. *In the Name of God, Go! Leo Amery and the British Empire in the Age of Churchill.* WW Norton, 1992.

Lowry, D (ed). *The South African War Reappraised.* Manchester University Press, 2000.

Malherbe VC. *What They Said: 1795–1910.* History Documents. Maskew Miller, 1971.

Marais, JS. *The Fall of Kruger's Republic.* The Clarendon Press, 1961.

Marlowe, J. *Milner: Apostle of Empire.* Hamish Hamilton, 1976.

Massie, RK. *Dreadnought: Britain, Germany, and the Coming of the Great War.* Jonathan Cape, 1992.

Meredith. M. *Diamonds, Gold and War: The Making of South Africa.* Simon & Schuster, 2007.

———. *Afrikaner Odyssey: The Life and Times of the Reitz Family.* Jonathan Ball Publishers, 2017.

Meintjes, J. *General Louis Botha: A Biography.* Cassell, 1970.

———. *President Paul Kruger: A Biography.* Cassell, 1974.

Michell, Sir L. *The Life of the Rt Hon Cecil John Rhodes, 1853–1902*. Edward Arnold, 1910.

Milner, Lady V. *My Picture Gallery 1886–1901*. John Murray, 1951.

Morris, J. *Pax Britannica: The Climax of an Empire*. Penguin, 1968.

———. *Farewell the Trumpets: An Imperial Retreat*. Penguin, 1979.

Muller, CFJ (ed). *Five Hundred Years: A History of South Africa*. Pretoria Academica, 1969.

Nasson, B. *The War for South Africa*. Tafelberg, 2010.

———. *South Africa at War, 1939–1945*. Jacana Media, 2012.

Nutting, A. *Scramble for Africa: The Great Trek to the Boer War*. Constable, 1994.

Nimocks, W. *Milner's Young Men: The 'Kindergarten' in Edwardian Imperial Affairs*. Hodder & Stoughton, 1970.

Oakes, D (ed). *Illustrated History of South Africa: The Real Story*. Reader's Digest Association, 1989.

O'Brien, TH. *Milner: Viscount Milner of St James's and Cape Town*. Constable, 1979.

Pakenham, T. *The Boer War*. Futura, 1988.

———. *The Scramble for Africa, 1876–1912*. Jonathan Ball Publishers, 1997.

Picard, HWJ. *Lords of Stalplein: Biographical Miniatures of the British Governors of the Cape of Good Hope*. HAUM, 1974.

Pirow, O. *James Barry Munnik Hertzog*. Howard Timmins, no date.

Porter, AN. *Joseph Chamberlain and the Diplomacy of Imperialism 1895–99*. Manchester University Press, 1980.

Pyrah, GB. *Imperial Policy and South Africa, 1902–10*. The Clarendon Press, 1955.

Randall, P. *Little England on the Veld*. Ravan Press, no date.

Reid, W. *Five Days from Defeat: How Britain Nearly Lost the First World War*. Birlinn, 2017.

Reitz, D. *Commando: A Boer Journal of the Boer War*. Faber & Faber, 1975.

Reitz, D & Emslie, T (ed). *Adrift on the Open Veld: The Anglo-Boer War and Its Aftermath, 1899-1943*. Stormberg, 1999.

Roberts, A. *Churchill: Walking with Destiny*. Penguin, 2019.

Roberts, B. *Cecil Rhodes: Flawed Colossus*. WW Norton, 1988.

Rogers, O. *Lawyers in Turmoil: The Johannesburg Conspiracy of 1895*. Stormberg, 2020.

Rose Innes, J. *Autobiography*. Oxford University Press, 1949.

Ross, R, Mager, AK and Nasson, B (eds). *The Cambridge History of South Africa. Vol. 2*. Cambridge University Press, 2016.

Rotberg, R & Shore, M. *The Founder: Cecil Rhodes and the Pursuit of Power*. Oxford University Press, 1988.

Royle, T. *The Kitchener Enigma*. Michael Joseph, 1985.

Samson, A. *Kitchener: The Man Not the Myth*. Helion, 2020.

Schoeman, K. *Imperiale Somer: Suid-Afrika tussen Oorlog en Unie, 1902–1910*. Protea Boekhuis, 2015.

———. *Rekonstruksie: Die Naoorlogsjare in Suid-Afrika, 1902–1905*. Protea Boekhuis, 2021

Shaw, G. *Some Beginnings: The Cape Times (1876–1910)*. Oxford University Press, 1975.

Smith, IR. *The Origins of the South African War, 1899–1902*. Longman, 1996.

Smuts, JC (jnr). *Jan Christian Smuts*. Cassell, 1952.

Sparks, A. *The Mind of South Africa*. Alfred A. Knopf, 1990.

Steyn, JC. *Ons Gaan 'n Taal Maak: Afrikaans sedert Die Patriot-jare*. Kraal Uitgewers, 2014.

Taylor, AJP. *From the Boer War to the Cold War: Essays on Twentieth-Century Europe*. Hamish Hamilton, 1995.

Thakur, V & Vale, P. *South Africa, Race and the Making of International Relations*. Rowman & Littlefield International, 2020.

Thomas, A. *Rhodes: The Race for Africa*. Penguin/BBC Books, 1997.

Thomas, RD. *Two Generals: Buller & Botha in The Boer War*. AuthorHouse, 2012.

Thompson, JL. *Forgotten Patriot: A Life of Alfred, Viscount Milner of St James's and Cape Town, 1854–1925*. Fairleigh Dickinson University Press, 2007.

———. *A Wider Patriotism: Alfred Milner and the British Empire*. Routledge, 2016.

Thompson, LM. *The Unification of South Africa 1902–1910*. The Clarendon Press, 1960.

———. *A History of South Africa*. Radix, 1990.

Trew, P. *The Boer War Generals*. Jonathan Ball Publishers, 1999.

Van den Heever, CM. *General JBM Hertzog*. APB Bookstore, 1946.

Walker, EA. *A History of Southern Africa*. Longmans, Green & Co, 1968.

Warwick P (ed). *The South African War: The Anglo Boer War, 1899–1902*. Longman, 1980.

Weaver, JRH (ed). *The Dictionary of National Biography 1922–30*. Oxford University Press, 1937.

Welsh, F. *A History of South Africa*. HarperCollins, 1998.

Wheatcroft. G. *The Randlords: The Men Who Made South Africa*. Weidenfeld & Nicolson, 1985.

Wilson, AN. *The Victorians*. Arrow Books, 2003.

Wilson, M & Thompson, L (eds). *The Oxford History of South Africa. Vol. II*. The Clarendon Press, 1971.

Worsfold, WB. *Lord Milner's Work in South Africa*. John Murray, 1906.

———. *The Reconstruction of the New Colonies Under Lord Milner. 2 vols.* Kegan Paul, Trench, Trubner & Co, 1913.

Wrench, JE. *Alfred Lord Milner: The Man of No Illusions.* Eyre & Spottiswoode, 1958.

Published papers

Breckenridge, K. 'Lord Milner's Registry: The Origins of South African Exceptionalism'. Seminar paper, University of KwaZulu-Natal, 2004. Available at https://phambo.wiser.org.za/files/seminars/Breckenridge2004.pdf.

Dubow, S. 'Colonial Nationalism, The Milner Kindergarten and the Rise of "South Africanism", 1902–1910'. *History Workshop Journal* 43(1) (1997).

MacMillan, M. 'Which Past Is Prologue? Heeding the Right Warnings from History'. *Foreign Affairs* (September/October 2020).

Marks, S & Trapido, S. 'Lord Milner and the South Africa State'. *History Workshop Journal* 8 (1979).

'Round Table'. *Commonwealth Journal of International Affairs* 30 (1939).

Other sources

Milner Papers & Manuscripts, Bodleian Library, Oxford University

Lady Milner's Papers, Bodleian Library, Oxford University

Templewood Papers, Cambridge University Library

Index

Note: page numbers in italics indicate a photograph.